T0373402

THE I TATTI
RENAISSANCE LIBRARY

James Hankins, General Editor

FICINO

ON DIONYSIUS THE AREOPAGITE

VOLUME I

ITRL 66

MARSILIO FICINO

✦ ✦ ✦

ON DIONYSIUS THE AREOPAGITE

VOLUME I ✦ MYSTICAL THEOLOGY AND THE DIVINE NAMES, PART I

EDITED AND TRANSLATED BY

MICHAEL J. B. ALLEN

THE I TATTI RENAISSANCE LIBRARY
HARVARD UNIVERSITY PRESS
CAMBRIDGE, MASSACHUSETTS
LONDON, ENGLAND
2015

Printed in the United States of America

Series design by Dean Bornstein

Library of Congress Cataloging-in-Publication Data

Ficino, Marsilio, 1433–1499.
[Works. Selections. English]
On Dionysius the Areopagite / Marsilio Ficino;
edited and translated by Michael J. B. Allen.
2 volumes cm. — (The I Tatti Renaissance library ; 66–67)
Translation of Ficino's commentaries on two works ; Latin on the verso and the English translation on the recto; Latin texts was translated from Ancient Greek.
Includes bibliographical references and index.
Contents: volume 1. Mystical theology and the divine names, part 1 (chapters 1–135) — volume 2. The divine names, part 2 (chapters 136–351).
ISBN 978-0-674-05835-4 (vol. 1 : alk. paper)
ISBN 978-0-674-74379-3 (vol. 2 : alk. paper)
1. Pseudo-Dionysius, the Areopagite. De mystica theologia. 2. Pseudo-Dionysius, the Areopagite. De divinis nominibus. 3. Mysticism. 4. Philosophy and religion — History. 5. Neoplatonism. 6. Christianity — Philosophy — History. I. Allen, Michael J. B. II. Pseudo-Dionysius, the Areopagite. De mystica theologia. III. Pseudo-Dionysius, the Areopagite. De mystica theologia. English. IV. Pseudo-Dionysius, the Areopagite. De divinis nominibus. V. Pseudo-Dionysius, the Areopagite. De divinis nominibus. English. VI. Title.
BR65.D66F5313 2015
230′.14092 — dc23 2014037088

Contents

Introduction

Dionysius the Areopagite is a major figure in the history of Neoplatonism. For nigh on a thousand years—from late antiquity to the close of the fifteenth century—he was usually identified with the Dionysius mentioned in Acts 17:34 as one of those who had listened to the "new doctrine" (17:19) St. Paul had preached to the Athenians. This had taken place on the "hill" of Mars (the *Areios/Areos pagos*), the spur jutting out from the western end of the Acropolis and separated from it by a short saddle. Originally the seat of the city's highest court of justice, it had become, in the first century under Roman rule, the seat of a court, or council, focusing on religious matters—and according to tradition, Dionysius sat on that court. The decision by the Apostle to preach there had therefore been a dramatic one. Instead of the "unknown god" inscribed on a city altar, the Apostle to the Gentiles had proclaimed "the God that has made the world and all things therein." This was the God, moreover, who "is not worshipped with men's hands, as though He needed any thing, seeing He giveth to all life and breath" (17:23–25). For "in Him we live and move and have our being," as certain of the Greeks' own poets had already declared (17:28).[1] Paul emphasizes that the Creator has appointed a day "in which He will judge the world in righteousness by that man whom he hath ordained; whereof He hath given assurance unto all men in that He hath raised him from the dead" (17:31). When they heard him speak of the resurrection, some of St. Paul's auditors had mocked him, but others, including Dionysius and a woman named Damaris, had declared that they wanted to hear more of the new teachings before Paul departed for Corinth. This Dionysius, St. Paul's first Athenian convert, is called, appropri-

ately, Dionysius the Areopagite, and the various Eastern Orthodox churches regard him as one of the seventy apostles.

Over a hundred years later, circa 170 CE, another Dionysius, the bishop of Corinth, had referred to the Areopagite as the first bishop of the Church at Athens; and later confusion then identified him with a third Dionysius, who became the legendary St. Denis, the patron saint of France and the bishop of Paris. For hagiography proclaimed that after his conversion, Dionysius the Areopagite had traveled to Jerusalem to attend on Mary in her last days and was struck with amazement at the glory surrounding her. He had stayed there until after her Assumption (or Dormition), before traveling on to Rome and witnessing the martyrdom of St. Paul. Subsequently, he had been sent by St. Clement of Rome to preach in France (ca. 90 CE). Eventually, after converting many, he was accused in the reign of the emperor Domitian, imprisoned with two other saints, and beheaded in 96 CE. In one version his head rolled an especially long way, until it was taken up and buried, along with his body, by a Christian lady, Catula. In another version the decapitated Denis sought to avoid having his remains devoured by wild beasts by trudging two miles with his head under his arm to what is now Montmartre — becoming thereby, like San Miniato of Florence, a *cephalophore*, a head-carrying saint! In 626 CE, his relics and those of two other saints had been collectively deposited in the abbey of St. Denis (the French form of Dionysius). Denis' feast day became October 9 in the Catholic West, and October 3 in the Orthodox East, where he is still celebrated in one commemoration with Dionysius the Areopagite.

More significantly from our viewpoint, in the early sixth century four important treatises and ten letters became linked with a fourth Dionysius, a Christian Neoplatonic theologian, who is now known as the pseudo-Dionysius, or, better, as the pseudo-Areopagite. Some scholars believe he was a Monophysite, others see him as a figure whose thought does not conflict with orthodox,

Chalcedonian Christology. In any case, modern scholarship has demonstrated he was deeply indebted to the thought of Proclus (411–485 CE), the last of the great ancient non-Christian Neoplatonists. This Dionysius' writings were first cited by Severus the Patriarch of Antioch between 518 and 528 CE; and in 532, at a colloquy at Constantinople, the Monophysites appealed to the writings, while attributing them, whether by guile or ignorance it is impossible to determine, to St. Paul's Athenian convert.[2]

This misattribution and attendant misdating had the predictable but profoundly important effect of also misattributing the complexities of later Neoplatonism to St. Paul's Areopagus disciple, and, by association, identifying their origin or at least their inspiration as being St. Paul himself. Linking them with, or cross-referencing them to, certain verses and phrases from St. John's Gospel and Epistles and his book of Revelation, led Christian thinkers to the conclusion that immediately after Christ's death they were already in possession of a divine Platonism that had been perfected in the teachings of Christ and his apostles and rearticulated in the works of Dionysius. On this view, Dionysius' Christian Platonism was again disseminated, though without attribution and in some important respects defectively, in the teachings of the pagan philosopher Plotinus (204/5–270 CE) some two centuries later. Subsequently, it was disseminated, even more defectively, in increasingly scholasticized versions of Plotinus, the work of his successors, and notably of Proclus in the mid- to late fifth century.[3]

From this dramatic perspective, Christ had perfected Plato and his metaphysics. Conversion to Christianity was therefore the culminating act of Platonic philosophers and of humble fisherman on the Sea of Galilee alike. The apostles, the evangelists, and St. Paul had thus perfected the ancient wisdom — and this despite the suspicion that many of their doctrines had remained somehow hidden or encrypted until Plotinus and his successors had gradually

revealed some of them in the third, fourth, and fifth centuries.[4] By the same token the Christian Dionysius, the first bishop of Athens, became the culmination and the column — to use some Ficinian wordplay — of ancient Platonism and of Christian theology alike.

It is true that doubts had been voiced in late antiquity about the attribution of the writings, which, in addition to the *Mystical Theology* and the *Divine Names,* included the *Celestial Hierarchy,* the *Ecclesiastical Hierarchy,* and ten letters, a collection that became known as the *Corpus Dionysiacum* or the *Dionysiaca.* The *Corpus'* authenticity was first defended by John of Scythopolis circa 540, even as several other sixth- and seventh-century Byzantine authors, including Hypatius, bishop of Ephesus in 530–540, questioned the attribution on the twin grounds that earlier ecclesiastical writers had never referred to it (a telling argument) and that the author appeared to have borrowed heavily from the fifth-century Proclus. But Maximus the Confessor and the Lateran Council of 649 settled the question for a millennium by decreeing the apostolic and not the Proclian origin of the *Corpus Dionysiacum* and declaring instead that it was Proclus who had stolen Dionysius' ideas and not the reverse. Henceforth, the prestige of this composite philosopher-theologian-saint and his identification with France's St. Denis, along with the metaphysical and dialectical profundity of the writings attributed to him, made him and his proto-Proclian works central to the philosophy of the Middle Ages.[5] Indeed, a line of gifted interpreters devoted themselves to expounding his theology and to unraveling the many difficulties, circumlocutions, figurations, and obscurities of his prose. He became in short one of the two or three most profound and influential architects of a thousand years of Christian thought and, more important, of Christian mysticism; for his was the way of inner ascent into both darkness and light. In the medieval Latin West,

only Augustine among the Church Fathers had a profounder impact.

Though occasional doubts were also voiced in the Middle Ages, even as Dionysius remained one of the capstones of Christian orthodoxy, the debate about his dates was not energetically reopened until the Renaissance, when Lorenzo Valla (1407–57), in his pathbreaking *Annotations to the New Testament*, raised serious linguistic questions about the dating and thus the genuineness of the *Corpus*. Even so, the majority view prevailed for decades more, and such Quattrocento figures as Ficino and Pico fervently adhered to the traditional notions of Dionysius' Pauline conversion and the first-century provenance and orthodoxy of the awe-inspiring treatises attributed to him.[6]

In the sixteenth century and thereafter, controversy intensified. Attacking the traditional view were not only Protestants — Luther, Scutellius, Dallaeus, and others — but also prominent Catholic theologians, such as Erasmus himself, Beatus Rhenanus, Cajetan, Morinus, Sirmond, Petavius, Le Quien, and Le Nourry. However, the *Corpus* still had its staunch defenders, including such influential churchmen as Cardinal Bellarmine and Baronius.[7] By the nineteenth century a skeptical consensus had emerged that doubted the attribution, even as some, following Franz Hipler, preferred to see Dionysius as a fourth-century theologian, who, because of later misinterpretation of various passages, had been confounded with the Areopagite of the first century.

Finally, in 1895 there appeared, almost simultaneously, the independent findings of two distinguished philologists, Hugo Koch and Joseph Stiglmayr, who demonstrated incontestably that the author of the *De divinis nominibus* 4, sections 19–35, was in fact extracting from Proclus' treatise *De malorum subsistentia*, a treatise known to them and to everyone else at the time only in the Latin translation of Moerbeke, the thirteenth-century Dominican scholar.[8] Points of agreement between the two works could be

documented in the lines of their arguments, in the examples adduced, and in the language deployed. This success in identifying the presence of the *De malorum subsistentia* — a presence already mooted in antiquity as we have seen — prompted a search for parallel passages in other Proclian writings, notably in the *Elements of Theology* (*Institutio theologica*), the *Theologia Platonica*, and the commentaries on Plato's *Parmenides*, *First Alcibiades*, and *Timaeus* (all composed in the later years of the fifth century). Establishing these sources and their contexts enabled other scholars in turn to situate the Dionysian oeuvre in the context of the fifth-century Monophysite controversy.

In this late stage in the history of the *Corpus Dionysiacum*, Dionysius, the Athenian Areopagite of Acts 17:34, was at last clearly distinguished from his various namesakes and most important from the Neoplatonic Pseudo-Areopagite of late antiquity, and from the St. Denis of French hagiography (who lived, it now appears, in the third century). The works themselves were at this point definitively assigned to the Pseudo-Areopagite who flourished in the late fifth or early sixth century and was a Christian follower of Proclus.

Although Christianity eventually lost its first-century grand Platonist, and with it the notion that this disciple of St. Paul had perfected Platonism as a Christian philosophy, in the intervening centuries, the mystical theology that had been derived from the Areopagitian writings, along with the apostolic authority investing them, had become inextricably woven into the texture of medieval Latin and Orthodox spirituality. As a result, Dionysius' reputation, and that of the writings attributed to him, had been effectively secured forever by the distinction and accomplishments of his medieval interpreters. In the Eastern Church, the *Corpus Dionysiacum* came to be regarded indeed as the supreme *summa theologica* by such interpreters as the aforementioned John of Scythop-

olis, St. Maximus the Confessor, Andrew of Crete, and George Pachymeres. In the Western Church, the Greek treatises were translated into Latin in the ninth century by Hilduin (ca. 838) and John Scotus Eriugena (ca. 862), in the twelfth, in part, by John the Saracen (ca. 1165), and in the thirteenth by Robert Grosseteste (ca. 1240).[9] Latin commentators on either all or some of the treatises included such notable figures as Eriugena, Hugh and Thomas of St. Victor, Grosseteste, St. Albert the Great, St. Thomas Aquinas, St. Bonaventure, John Clichtove, and the fourteenth-century mystics Meister Eckhart, John Tauler, Richard Rolle, and others.

In the fifteenth century, beginning in 1431, the treatises were retranslated by Ambrogio Traversari, the vicar general of the Camaldolese Order[10] — a translation that was admired by Pope Nicholas V among others for its clarity and straightforwardness. Then the *Mystical Theology* and the *Divine Names* were retranslated and reinterpreted by Marsilio Ficino (1433–99), who must have been indebted initially to Traversari's versions, as Professor Kristeller has suggested.[11] Later, however, Ficino became convinced that they needed retranslation and commentary *more Platonico*, meaning, presumably, in the light of their Platonic profundities.[12] Or, as he phrases it in an undated letter to a close friend, the Medici doctor and bibliophile Pierleone Leoni da Spoleto, he is going to attempt to translate and comment on the Dionysian texts "using the same sequence or order (*eodem ordine*)" he had used for Plato and Plotinus, interpreting them, that is, "in the light of Platonic reasoning (*Platonica videlicet ratione*)."[13] Since he saw the treatises as the crowning achievement of Platonism and of Christian philosophy alike, he cannot mean by *more platonico* that he had set himself the task of further Platonizing texts that were already profoundly Platonic. To the contrary, he must have supposed that his predecessors had not possessed a full understanding of their metaphysical structures and sublimities — that they were at fault, that is, in

not being truly Platonic interpreters, or in not being sufficiently so. Despite this Proclian-Ficinian achievement, however, the Dionysian texts were translated again, in the sixteenth century by Joachim Perionius and in the seventeenth by Balthasar Cordier and by Pierre Lanssel.[14]

Ironically, of all these translators and exegetes of the treatises in the *Corpus Dionysiacum*, it was Ficino who set greatest store by their putative first-century dating, since it provided him with the justification for his radically Platonic account of the history of philosophy and its intersection with Christian revelation. He never doubted either their authenticity as the work of St. Paul's convert on the Areopagus or their being the key to an understanding of the perfection of the Platonism of the apostles themselves—or rather, the perfection of their pre-Plotinian Plotinianism. In another letter to Pier Leoni, now third in the eleventh book of his *Letters* and dated May 12, 1491, Ficino rhapsodizes, "No form of knowledge is more delightful to me certainly than the Platonic, and of this knowledge, none will ever be more venerable to me than that in Dionysius. I love Plato in Iamblichus, I admire him in Plotinus, but I venerate him in Dionysius."[15]

Again, in chapter 107.3 of his commentary on the *Divine Names*, Ficino declares that Dionysius "always reforms Platonic matters for the better." In the undated letter to Pier Leoni cited above, he designates Dionysius as being "beyond a doubt the most eminent of the Platonists" (*Platonicorum procul dubio summus*).[16] And in his very late and unfinished commentary on St. Paul, *In Epistolas divi Pauli* 15, he refers to Dionysius as writing to none other than St. John the Evangelist himself, alluding, obviously, to the tenth letter in the *Corpus Dionysiacum*, which is addressed to St. John on the island of Patmos.[17]

As *summus Platonicorum*, how is it then, if Dionysius had been converted in the first century, that Ficino and everyone else could find no references to him anywhere in the works of the Neopla-

tonists or, even more important, in those of Augustine, the most authoritative of the Church Fathers? To hazard an answer, let us turn to the problem of the skeptical Platonic academies led by Arcesilas (ca. 316–242 BCE) and Carneades (ca. 214–129 BCE), which, though different, were both inspired by Plato's earlier, essentially eristical, dialogues. For someone like Ficino, who believed in the doctrinal integrity of the Platonic tradition, their espousal of skepticism as a methodology, along with their retreat from doctrinal certainty, would seem to signal an ominous break in that tradition. His guide here was Cicero, who, faced with explaining the emergence and eventually the dominance of skepticism in the later Platonic schools, resorted in the *Academica* 1.12.43–46 and in the *De natura deorum* 1.5.11 to a startling theory that was taken up and amplified by Augustine in Book 3 of his *Contra Academicos*, 17.38–18.40.

Cicero and Augustine argue that Arcesilas had been forced to conceal Plato's doctrines, in order to protect them from the attacks of Zeno of Citium, and to bury them, Augustine says, "as gold that posterity would later discover" (*Contra Academicos* 17.38). Zeno, the founding father of Stoicism, had initially studied in the Academy but subsequently came to espouse "a pernicious materialism" that held that the soul was mortal, that God was a material fire, that all agency was corporeal, and that truth was arrived at through the fantasy and senses and not via the reason. In 17.38–39, Augustine unequivocally assigns both Arcesilas and Carneades the role of disabusing men of these terrible Zenonian errors and adopts the Ciceronian notion that a philosophical break, or divorce (a *discidium*), had separated Zeno from the Academy. Nonetheless, despite their success against Zeno, Arcesilas and Carneades themselves were not blameless: for, when they "pursued ambiguities, they fell away from Plato (*a Platone degeneraverunt*)."[18] The true, the golden Platonism, was now a treasure hidden underground. Though providentially guarded for a long while by sibyls,

priests, prophets, and divinely inspired poets, it was lost to the academic philosophers themselves, even as the hermeneutical art of interpreting Plato's dialogues correctly was also lost to them. Materialism was indeed refuted, but with the aporia and the elenchus, not with the Ideas of Plato's intelligible world.

For Ficino an attendant scenario explains the disappearance of the Dionysian *Corpus* sometime in the third century CE, though the details necessarily differ. In his May 1491 letter to Pier Leoni, he asserts, "I often suspect that the Platonists who came before Plotinus, men such as Ammonius and Numenius, and others perhaps even before them, had perused Dionysius' books before they were hidden away as a consequence of some calamity in the Church no longer familiar to us. Because of their access to these books, the truly Platonic sparks in Dionysius were transmitted to Plotinus and Iamblichus, whence was lit such a raging fire."[19] What sort of calamity can Ficino have imagined or entertained? Did it have anything to do with adherents of an Arian or some other Christological heresy? Or is he invoking the decades of persecution and oppression under the emperors? Exactly when the *Corpus* disappeared remains a mystery for him, moreover, since there is no Zeno to play the critical role of antagonist. Still, the loss must have been after the Pythagorizing Numenius in the second century and Ammonius in the first half of the third had been able to peruse the *Corpus*, in whole or in part, and thus ensure the diffusion of its secrets to Plotinus and his successors. Thence it was used to kindle — to deploy Ficino's own metaphors — the fires of Plotinian thought and thereafter to fan the blaze of post-Plotinian Platonism. Although the Dionysian treatises themselves must have been hidden away, given the absence of any reference to them, their truth continued, says Ficino, to illuminate the Platonic tradition: "Beyond a shadow of a doubt," he writes in chapter 22 of his work of sacerdotal apology, the *De Christiana religione* of 1474, "I myself have found that the principal mysteries in Numenius,

Philo, Plotinus, Iamblichus, and Proclus were in fact received from St. John, St. Paul, Hierotheus, and Dionysius the Areopagite" (Hierotheus being the putative teacher of Dionysius after his conversion). "For everything that the Platonists have to say about the divine mind, the angels, and other theological matters that strike us as admirable they clearly took from them (*ab illis usurpaverunt*)."[20]

Two decades after the *De Christiana religione*, in a letter of February 2, 1495, to Jacopo Rondoni, the bishop of Rimini, Ficino reiterates the ambiguous notion of appropriation or making use of.[21] He writes, "Since the Platonists had access to St. John's Gospel, and some of them to the writings of Dionysius the Areopagite, they gladly made use of (*usurpaverunt*) the Christian formulations of trinitarian dogmas. They also derived the orders of the angels and their names from the Christian formulations, since they could often be reconciled with the words of their Plato, Plato who was after all a follower of Moses."[22] Note that Ficino thinks of the Platonists as being indebted to the Christian truths and as borrowing from them. He is not charging them with committing a theft (*furtum*), though Lefèvre D'Étaples in the sixteenth century, in responding to this same chapter in the *De Christiana religione*, asserts that Ficino was being too soft (*mollior*) on the "adversaries of Christian wisdom" and that he should indeed have charged them with theft (*furati sunt*).[23] But Ficino was obviously up against the immense authority of Augustine, whose *Confessions* and *City of God* had underscored the intermediary role of "certain books of the Platonists," and of the Platonists alone, in returning him to his Christian faith; he had declared, moreover, that Plotinus had understood Plato better than anyone else (*City of God* 9.10). We now know that the books in question were probably translations of portions of the *Enneads* by Marius Victorinus. But is it possible that Ficino still hoped to discover eventually, despite the absence of any proof, that Augustine had indeed had access to the *Corpus Dionysiacum*?

In sum, the misattribution and misdating of that *Corpus* obviously brought with it a radical reconstruction of the history of Platonism, one that was tied to the notion of a calamitous rupture in the transmission of Platonic truth, and with it, to the notion of a golden Platonic trove that first had to be concealed from malevolent interpreters, the materialists and Stoics, but was then recovered in more fortunate times. A special problem for Ficino were the four philosophers who could have profited from this recovery, if not of the *Corpus*, then at least of its premises and methodology, but had failed to do so, or to do so fully, namely, the anti-Christian Porphyry, Celsus, Julian, and Proclus. They should have read the Dionysian treatises with humility and awe, paying homage to them as the pinnacles of the Platonic wisdom they so cherished. Had they done so, they could have been converted to the sublime truths of Christianity instead of being intemperately moved even as *Platonici* to write against believers. If nowadays we are attuned to the derivative nature of the arguments of a Pseudo-Areopagite who is indebted to Proclus, we should constantly bear in mind that Ficino saw the relationship of the two thinkers in complete reverse. The Neoplatonists, and Proclus above all, had derived their latter-day wisdom, whether Christian or not, from the fountainhead of Dionysius' earlier arguments; and, for all their intellectual and Platonic contributions, they had remained deeply indebted to this first-century saint, the luminous architect, not of a pagan *summa*, but of a Christian Platonism learned at the feet of St. Paul and stemming, presumptively, from the secret teachings of Christ Himself.

The notion of a secret wisdom has of course a long history that stretches back to the ancient Pythagoreans and Egyptians and beyond; and it forms the backdrop to Socrates' attacks, in the *Sophist*, the *Philebus*, and elsewhere, on the sophists and on the natural prey of the sophists, namely, contentious, headstrong adolescents. In the case of the Areopagite, however, concealment was rein-

forced by the grounding of Platonic truth in a negative theology, which dominates the two treatises and to which we must now turn.

The brief *De mystica theologia* (*MT*), sometimes known as the *De Trinitate,* and the lengthy *De divinis nominibus* (*DN*) are addressed to a certain Timothy (see for instance *DN* 30.4), even though occasionally they invoke their common master, a mysterious and much venerated Hierotheus, who is described in *DN* 71 as, "the teacher, after Paul, of Dionysius and the one closest in excellence to the apostles," and as the author, *inter alia,* of a treatise entitled *Principles of Theology* that had concluded "with little summaries of marvelous profundity." The *Mystical Theology* and the *Divine Names* present us with complex Neoplatonic accounts of God's utter transcendence and of the necessity of approaching Him by way of the "darkness" of negation. After completing his Plotinus translations and introductions (*argumenta*), and his version of Iamblichus' *De mysteriis,* and while he was still putting the finishing touches to the longer Platonic commentaries he was to publish in 1496, Ficino embarked on a translation of, and a commentary on, the *Mystical Theology.*[24] This was in the autumn of 1490, as we learn from his letter to Bernardo Dovizi.[25] He accomplished this task by the spring of 1491,[26] the year, we recall, of the second edition of Ficino's complete Plato and the year preceding his first Plotinus edition.

Next, Ficino turned to the *Divine Names,*[27] which predictably took him much longer to finish.[28] Even so, he felt able to dedicate it in its unpublished form toward the end of 1492 to the new Medici cardinal, Giovanni, the son of his longtime patron, Lorenzo the Magnificent. In 1494 he had a transcription made for the use of Germanus Ganaiensis (Germain de Ganay),[29] in which he included references to his own *In Parmenidem* and *De sole et lumine,* works completed, or at least edited, only after 1492.[30] Some-

time later, the *editio princeps* of his Dionysius translations and commentaries was published without a date in Florence by Lorenzo Francesco of Venice (Lorenzo d'Alopa). Prefacing it was the dedicatory epistle of 1492 (though this date only pertains to the epistle). Kristeller surmises that the *editio* must have appeared late in 1496 or early in 1497, given the colophon at the end of Ficino's *Commentaria in Platonem* of December 1496. This reads, "But currently being published separately here [in Florence] are Dionysius' *De mystica theologia* and *De divinis nominibus*."[31]

While the relationship of Ficino's Latin translations of the two treatises to those of his predecessors, and notably to those of John Scotus Eriugena and Ambrogio Traversari, awaits exploration, his prefatory remarks emphasize, as we have seen, that he felt the need to supplement earlier versions that had not plumbed, he believed, the depths of Dionysius' Platonic wisdom. One aspect of this is that he immediately recognized, better perhaps than anyone, the crucial role played in the original composition of the treatises by the *Parmenides*, and more particularly by its second part, where Plato explores both positive and negative hypotheses in the course of arguing for the primacy of the One. Nonetheless, it is the *Parmenides* read Neoplatonically, that is, the *Parmenides* as it would later be interpreted elusively in Plotinus' works and with full scholastic rigor in Proclus' *Theologia platonica* and *In Parmenidem*.[32] For the interpretation eventually espoused by Proclus, in general if not in all its details,[33] had always been in Ficino's view the authentic and original one, since Plotinus and then Proclus, or more especially Proclus' master Syrianus and a mysterious Plutarch of Athens, had together rediscovered the keys, Ficino says, to unlocking the profundities of the dialogue as Plato had first intended them. In the process, the later Platonists, culminating with Proclus, had determined that nine was the number of the hypotheses in the dialogue's second part (five positive and four negative) and that embracing this ninefold division was necessarily the first

step for anyone in search of its correct interpretation, an interpretation that had been lost for several academic generations in the succession of skeptical schools under Arcesilas, Carneades, and their disciples.[34]

Most important however, given the Pauline dating for the *Corpus Dionysiacum*, Ficino had to assume that the Areopagite himself had had access somehow to the correct reading of the *Parmenides* and that his *Mystical Theology* and *Divine Names* bore witness to the fact that the dialogue's interpretation, or at least its basic premises, had also been known to first-century Christians, whether or not some one of them had actually commented on it.

In chapter 37.3 of his *Parmenides* Commentary, Dionysius is lauded for interpreting the dialogue as a "theological" text, on the grounds principally that it routinely distinguishes between the absolute One and one being, while affirming that the One is "the principle of being and the creator of one being." Moreover, Ficino sees Dionysius as using "the arguments, the negations and the words of the *Parmenides*" whenever he can,[35] and especially when treating of matters that are "most divine" (*materia divinissima*), "thereby testifying that for him the material in the *Parmenides* is also divine." Similarly, the chapter continues, "Dionysius always places both the Good and the One before essence, using the proofs of Platonists (*ipsis Platonicorum rationibus*)." In 52.1 Ficino asserts that "we often deal with these [ontological] matters in our commentaries on Dionysius (*de his una cum Dionysio Areopagita in commentariis in eum nostris saepe tractamus*)," the present tense suggesting that he was working on the *In Parmenidem* and the Commentary on the *Divine Names* concurrently. In 53.1 he calls Dionysius "the sedulous respecter (*observator*) of Parmenides," on the grounds that "each time he mentions the One . . . he places it above essence . . . and uses the term [the One] to designate the principle of the universe (*universi principium*)." In the following chapter, 54.2, he characterizes negations in the dialogue as signifying in God not a de-

fect of some virtue but an excess, adding, "as we often say in agreement with Dionysius."

Of signal importance are Ficino's twin assumptions: (1) the Areopagite is adopting the Neoplatonic notion that the aged Parmenides himself is teaching profound truths in the dialogue and is not merely someone selected as an interlocutor on literary or dramatic or ironic or whimsical grounds, and (2) Plato is essentially aligning himself with the Eleatic master and his followers even as he is perfecting their wisdom, a wisdom that was itself a perfecting of Pythagorean wisdom and ultimately of its sources in Hermetic and Zoroastrian wisdom. And we should recall that on several occasions Ficino explicitly identifies Parmenides, Melissus, and others as Pythagoreans.

At the finale of his career, Ficino is becoming in effect a Pythagorean-Parmenidean monist and a negative theologian. For without rejecting the Platonic teachings and mysteries of any of Plato's dialogues, or we should add of Plotinus' meditations on them, he is focusing his attention on the *Parmenides* and on the handful of other dialogues open to a Parmenidean interpretation, such as the *Sophist* and *Philebus*. However, the *Parmenides* is being viewed here through a Dionysian lens—that is, as a metaphysical and theological masterpiece, in which the voice of the august figure of Parmenides (as he was envisioned by the Neoplatonists) is now effectively the voice of Plato himself. Of all Plato's chosen interlocutors, Parmenides is the sage with the most gravity, the most authority, an authority that surpassed even that of Socrates. As Ficino himself aged—and we recall he was in his sixties and was to die at sixty-six—he became more susceptible, I would argue, to the supreme achievement of the aged Eleatic and his eponymous dialogue and became more keenly aware perhaps of Plato's debts in composing that dialogue to the Pythagoreans of Magna Graecia, the pre-Platonic sages of his own beloved Italy.

In any event, a deep knowledge of the *Parmenides* and its metaphysical postulates — a knowledge for Ficino that was lacking in the Middle Ages — was required to translate the Areopagitian treatises correctly, let alone to elucidate their inmost mysteries. Ficino must have thought of himself indeed as the rediscoverer of the authentic Platonic meaning of the *Corpus Dionysiacum*, even though he would surely have acknowledged the intellectual and theological authority of at least some of the insights of its medieval interpreters and of their various renderings and interpretations of Dionysius' text. Demonstrably, he had carefully perused, for instance, the authoritative commentary of Thomas Aquinas, even though it was not in itself notably Neoplatonic, or at least consistently so. However, as we have seen from his 1491 letter to Pier Leoni, Ficino's stated endeavor is to interpret Dionysius in the same way (*eodem ordine*) he had already interpreted Plato and Plotinus, that is, from the perspective of someone with a privileged understanding of Platonic reasoning (*Platonica ratione*).[36] The implication, moreover, is that in translating and commenting on Dionysius he will be taking up the supreme challenge of his entire scholarly career, and this is because Plato's Platonism had been perfected in the *Mystical Theology* and the *Divine Names* of the Areopagite, though it had been assuredly perfected again in the *Enneads* of Plotinus, which were indebted, however indirectly, to the two earlier treatises.[37]

An important biblical dimension accompanies Ficino's commitment to interpreting the treatises more Platonically. Dionysius' mystical theology is kataphatic and apophatic, attributive and negatory, and it outlines the ways of ascent through purgation, illumination, and union. In this threefold regard, Ficino reads it in the light of the dramatic account in Exodus of Moses' ascent of Sinai and of his encounter with God in a mystical darkness of unknowing. For Ficino indeed, Moses' experience of God on Mt.

Sinai is the model of all Platonic ascents to a One beyond being, where the images of a triple summit, and of an arduous climb up into dense cloud cover and thence into an electric storm raging above it, serve as the governing metaphors. They predictably remind us of the other paradigmatic mountain event for Christians, the Transfiguration of Jesus on Mt. Tabor, accompanied by Elijah (Elias) and Moses, as described in the synoptic gospels.[38] And the reminder is the more significant in that Moses' face shone when he descended from Sinai in a manner that Christian typologists inevitably saw as prefiguring the transfigurative moment when the Lord's face "did shine as the sun and his raiment was as white as the light."[39] This is presumably the transfigurative condition of any Platonic philosopher in divine ecstasy or trance: that his face will shine as the sun.

Ficino sees in the *Divine Names* the supreme validation of the Neoplatonic metaphysical hierarchy with its emphasis on the experience of union beyond being with a God who is no longer the Creator God, or the God of being, but the invisible, transintelligible God of our unknowing, before whom language and its formulations utterly fail and whom we must worship at last in ineffable silence. Dionysius presents us with a mystical theology, which, in Ficino's interpretation, transcends even Platonic theology. For it points the way beyond philosophy to an indefinable unknowing-knowing that Ficino must have associated, despite their obvious disparities of context and intent, with Socrates' famous apothegm that he only knew that he did not know. In actuality, however, it goes beyond the notion of Socratic ignorance altogether, even if we adduce an Augustinian third level of argument and envisage a Socrates who knows that he does not know that he does not know. Rather, it would seem to return us in a way to the Neoplatonic and yet pre-Socratic notion of a poetic theology embedded in the dicta and enigmas of such philosopher-poet-mythographers as Heraclitus, Empedocles, Orpheus, and the Zo-

roaster of the *Chaldaean Oracles,* a work that was misdated and misattributed by Ficino and others to earliest antiquity.[40]

It is significant that in his proem to the *Mystical Theology,* Ficino describes the Dionysian style not as dialectical but as dithyrambic, as the utterance of a poetic frenzy that resembles a festive incantatory drunkenness.[41] Just as the bacchantes "reel as though they were intoxicated," so, with the Dionysian wine of mystical love, "our inebriated Dionysius runs riot everywhere: he pours forth enigmas, he sings in dithyrambs." This means not only that it is difficult "to penetrate with the understanding the profound meanings" of the Dionysian text but that it is also "equally difficult to penetrate the marvelous texture of his words, and to imitate the Orphic manner as it were of his speaking"; and, Ficino adds, it is especially difficult "to render it into Latin." In other words, just to make some rendering of the Greek, let alone to fathom its arcana and profundities, requires in the translator "an utterly divine frenzy," a Dionysian "reeling," that he must share with the author he is translating.[42] We should recall that after the death of Bessarion in 1472, Ficino was the unrivaled authority in the Latin West on the language of Platonizing discourse and argumentation and the one scholar who could authoritatively deploy what was in effect the full arsenal of Proclian subtleties and distinctions. As a master Hellenist, if he could not at times untangle the meaning of the Greek — even with the interpretative attempts in earlier versions, and notably those of Eriugena and Traversari, to guide him — then what lesser Hellenist could hope to do so?

The Dionysian frenzy, however, is not so much poetic as it is voluntary in the original etymological sense of being tied to the faculty of the *voluntas,* the will. In his prefatory argumentum for the *Mystical Theology,* Ficino writes that the "culmination of the Platonic discipline, that column of Christian theology [that is, Dionysius] — when seeking the divine light, seeks not so much with understanding as with the burning ardor of the will." The

will, purged and illuminated, has supplanted the intellect; and it is the will's strategies and powers, preeminently the power of love and of prayer, that alone can bear the soul aloft toward an ultimate union with the One, the One that it cannot grasp with an understanding — however divinely intuitive — that must now be set aside as inadequate, indeed as an obstacle. Ficino's position on the hallowed medieval debate over the primacy in man[43] of the intellect or the will shifted at various times in his scholarly career, depending it would seem on the text or the context he was interpreting.[44] Nonetheless, his subtle analysis of the will as a faculty that is drawn into and overwhelmed by its unknowable object, in contrast to the intellect that draws the knowable object down into itself, enabled him to identify its workings with that of love, and even at times with the notions of joy (*gaudium*) and supreme intellectual pleasure, the *voluptas*, which Ficino indeed glossed on occasions as *voluntas*.

The Dionysian texts became in Ficino's own estimation, therefore, texts that the interpreter has to love (*diligere*) and to will: to approach with prayer and in a state of overflowing joy. The initial prayer to the Trinity in the *Mystical Theology* serves indeed as the test case precisely because the Trinity itself defies ordinary logic, tri-unity being the kind of "dark conceit" traditionally designated as the subject of highest poetry. While Ficino's own commentary is not itself dithyrambic or rhapsodic, and very much resembles his commentary practice in both his *Platonic Theology* and his Plato and Plotinus commentaries, it is nevertheless poetic in the Ficinian sense that it "plays seriously" with predication (attribution) and negation, with adding and subtracting, with naming and unnaming the names that are and are not God's. Additionally, a number of his commentary chapters are animated by the solemn rhythms, the exhortatory, precatory, trance-inducing cadences that Ficino obviously found appropriate for, perhaps even fundamental

to, his Latinizing of some of Dionysius' obscurer sentences, the convolutions of the Athenian convert's poesy.

As a counterpoint to this serious play, or playful seriousness, governing words and silence is Ficino's continual recourse to images of light and darkness, images that play such a crucial role in Plato's texts. Foremost among them predictably is the allegorical vision of the Cave in the *Republic* and the ascent to the Sun, the latter being identified with the Idea of the Good. Dionysius defines the Trinitarian deity as the One and the Good beyond being, the One who is enveloped in the darkness of dazzling light. Indeed, these two metaphysical absolutes dominate the treatises; but whereas Plato himself had focused on the intellectual ascent to contemplation of the Good, Ficino inherits the role that later Neoplatonic faculty psychology attributed to our own personal unity, to the "flower," or "head," of our mind.[45] This is our highest, our transcendent power or quasipower, in that it alone can return us to God, uniting our oneness with Him as the One in a union that Ficino envisages happening, at least initially, with the suddenness of the spark struck from a flint.

We see the importance here of two passages in Plato's *Seventh Letter* (341CD and 344B), which ancient Neoplatonists had also referred to occasionally, but that Ficino as a Christian came to revere precisely because he could identify the spark, not so much with that of intuitive or angelic knowledge as with the searing incandescence of a love that negates all else. For in these commentaries on Dionysius — the last of his Platonic commentaries, if we leave aside the incomplete commentary on St. Paul's *Epistle to the Romans,* which he was working on when he died — Ficino explores the Areopagite's searching critique of epistemology, even of Platonic epistemology, in order to exhort us to rise above, to set aside, every and any category of thinking. At the same time, he joins Dionysius in warning us against divulging the ineffable mysteries,

however inadvertently, not only to the profane but, more strikingly, to those who are still committed, even piously committed, to an intellect-governed sense of God.[46] For the possibility of such an intellectual comprehension immediately comes up against the mystical notion of the Trinity: of the three Persons in one substance that defies understanding and rational belief.[47] An equally radical critique involves our recourse to language. As we approach the zenith of an ascent to God, words begin to fail us, until we enter at last into the wordless plenitude of divine meaning. Contrariwise, as we descend the ontological scale, and as meaning becomes more and more attenuated, so we have to call upon an embarrassment of more and more verbal riches that speaks to our increasing poverty of understanding and conception.[48] All this is Platonically inspired of course, but it is dominated for Ficino not only by the opening verses of Genesis but also by the equally authoritative account in Exodus of Moses' ascent of Sinai and of his drawing near "unto the thick darkness where God was,"[49] a drawing near, that is, to what a Platonist sees as the metaphysical negations of the divine *Parmenides*. In sum, at the end of his life, Ficino was more intricately engaged than ever in reconciling Scripture with Platonic texts, reconciling Exodus with the *Parmenides*. This was in large part because he had found his most authoritative interpreter in the figure of St. Paul's first Athenian convert.

Perhaps most mysterious of all is Ficino's confrontation with the Proclus-inspired notion, though again it derives from Plato's *Parmenides*, that prime matter is the inverted image of God as the One, insofar as matter alone is the one-without-being (the subhypostatic one), just as God is the One-beyond-being (the suprahypostatic One). The darkness of matter thus reflects, however paradoxically and inversely, the darkness of the Godhead; and just as it defies our intellectual categories at the lowest remove, so does the Godhead defy our intellectual categories at the highest re-

move. We cannot understand matter, and neither it nor we can understand God. For matter's darkness must in some senses be, or be dependent on, the darkness of God, even as the darkness that was spread across the face of the deep — to invoke the phrasing of Genesis 1:2 and in part of Exodus 19:16 — received from the darkness of God the divine command "Let there be light." Thereafter the unfolding and enfolding of light-in-darkness and of darkness-in-light began the process that was and is the enactment of creation itself.[50]

While body and bodies can be understood and subordinated, subject as they are to Aristotelian categorization, matter is unintelligible. As souls, just as we cannot understand God, so we cannot understand matter insofar as it is the extreme witness to God's ineffability, to His ever presence and ever absence both. Hence it is that the notion of matter as a counterpart to the One goes from being a Proclian scholastic subtlety, the necessary consequence of the Proclian method and its chains of reasoning, to being an Areopagitian and ultimately a Mosaic notion — one that acknowledges that the fabled original darkness on the face of the deep is the primal postulate and the primal condition of all Hebraeo-Christian cosmology and its underlying ontology and meontology. Insofar as creation reflects or speaks to its Creator, it speaks to the divinity or quasi divinity of matter itself; for matter too is in the image and likeness of our matter-less God. Indeed, being the first and the last witness to the divine Will, it presents us with the most intractable and yet profound of the mysteries attending the Mosaic recognition that material creation, and not only the intellectual and animate creation, was the product too of God's Will. As "children of the light," we are also the sons and the daughters of its sublime darkness, waiting for the day of the Lord to come, but as a thief in the night (1 Thessalonians 5:2–5).

Again, we must bear in mind, first, that Plato's *Parmenides* had been transformed for Ficino into a Christian text and invested

with the loftiest Neoplatonic wisdom two centuries or more before Plotinus had rediscovered in it the metaphysical postulates we now suppose he generated, and, second, that Ficino's engagement with Plato's dialogue had always focused not so much on its engagement with the Ideas (though he certainly acknowledged their centrality in any Platonic scheme) but rather on its embrace of the One and on the paradoxes attending its affirmation and its negation alike. In these two fundamental respects, he was again indebted to the sublime achievement of the Areopagite and by extension of Hierotheus, St. Paul and St. John, who were his teachers.

The dedicatee of Ficino's two commentaries was Lorenzo the Magnificent's second son, Giovanni de' Medici (1475–1521), who was to become Pope Leo X in 1513. On March 9, 1489, at the pubescent age of thirteen, Giovanni was named a future cardinal with the benefice of Santa Maria in Domnica on Rome's leafy Celian hill, though just two weeks earlier he had been ordained a deacon. He was then sent to study canon law in Pisa for three years until 1492, where on February 1 he received his doctorate. In another ceremony, on March 9 at the Augustinian monastery in Fiesole (the Badia), he received, now in his seventeenth year, his cardinal's red hat. A month later he journeyed to Rome to join the College of Cardinals, and in this same year of 1492 served as legate to the Patrimony of St. Peter and to Florence.[51] In March or April 1489 Ficino had already dedicated to him as "cardinal" his translations of Iamblichus' *De mysteriis*, Proclus' *De sacrificio et magia*, and Porphyry's *De occasionibus sive causis ad intelligibilia ducentibus* (i.e., the *Sententiae*), translations he had finished in 1488.[52] He declares in the 1492 prefatory letter to Giovanni that given Iamblichus' stature as a Platonic "priest"—as the Platonist who had focused on prayer, sacrifices, and theurgy—it was symbolically proper to

dedicate the Areopagite's two priestly masterpieces to the same "High Priest," the dedicatee of the earlier translations.[53]

If the young cardinal, who is addressed here as the "highest" High Priest of the Florentines, ever got round to reading Ficino's Dionysian commentaries (or for that matter the Platonic translations he had sent him in 1489), it would mean that Ficino's Christianized Neoplatonic metaphysics had at last reached a philosopher-potentate-prelate who might have, if not as a cardinal, then as a prospective pontiff, the power to initiate a new Christian-Platonic theology-philosophy. He would thus fulfill Ficino's long cherished goal of inaugurating a new order, a restoration of a golden age of Platonic ruler-thinkers. In the event, it may be doubted whether Giovanni ever read the treatises Ficino had prepared for him, or read them carefully, though he certainly had the intellectual skills and interests to have done so. Even so, the cultured, nepotistic, and expensive life Giovanni embraced was not the austere Dionysian life that Ficino's proem had in mind, however playful the connections adduced there between the rioting twice-born god of inebriation and the most mystically Platonic of all St. Paul's converts.[54]

Nevertheless, Leo X was to be a great pope and patron, and not unworthy of Ficino's dedications or the dedication of another famous scholar, who in 1516 made him the dedicatee of his epoch-making Greek and Latin edition of the New Testament, the *Novum Instrumentum*. Ironically, the honed philological skills that Erasmus was to use to such revolutionary effect in the *Instrumentum* were eventually going to embolden others to redate the *Corpus Dionysiacum* and to question its authorship, if not its orthodoxy. In the process they would also dispel Ficino's fondest historical fantasy: that the first century of the Christian era had seen the triumphant instauration of a Christian Platonism, a Platonism that was even more profound than that elaborated later in the voluminous

works of Plotinus and Proclus and yet marvelously anticipated by Plato himself in his Pythagorean masterworks, above all in the *Parmenides*. At the close of the Quattrocento, however, the effective discrediting of the Dionysian corpus was still decades, even centuries away, despite the criticisms of Valla and others. When Ficino died, in 1499, he would certainly have regarded his commentary on the Areopagite's two speculative metaphysical treatises as the ultimate key for the young Giovanni and his other numerous correspondents to unlocking the deep but dazzling darkness, the *nox quasi dies* of Platonic ontology, where the shadows themselves, in the words of Psalm 139:12, have no shadows: *sicut tenebrae eius, ita et lumen eius*.

I would like to thank Dr. Podolak for his generous comments on some of my readings of *I* and for his kindness in sending me a copy of his critical edition. Would that the stars had ordained our earlier cooperation in engaging these difficult and rarely visited texts.

The translation of Ficino's commentaries, the first in any language, is entirely my own, and I have not consulted any renderings of the *Corpus* itself except, of course, Ficino's. Given the difficulty of the enterprise, I must have erred and strayed like a lost goat, and I would welcome pastoral suggestions for correction or amendment. Obviously, much more work on Ficino's debts and sources remains to be done; I only hope that I have in some measure made these texts more accessible. The first volume contains the *Mystical Theology* and chapters 1 to 135 (i.e., Part 1) of the *Divine Names*, the second volume contains the rest of the *Divine Names*, that is, chapters 136–351 (Part 2). This division into parts has nothing to do with Ficino or the texts involved; it is merely an editorial convenience, to ensure two volumes of roughly equal size. In referring throughout to Dionysius as the Areopagite, and not as the Pseudo-Dionysius or the Pseudo-Areopagite, I have followed Ficino's own usage.

Finally, I am indebted to James Hankins, the editor of the bur-

geoning I Tatti series, with its alluring scabious-blue dust jackets, for his urging me to undertake this arduous climb into thinner air and for his judicious and timely advice, his generosity of spirit, and his wonderful friendship over the passing years.

NOTES

1. Paul is quoting, it is now believed, from Epimenides of Crete's *Cretica*. He then cites line 5 from Aratus' *Phaenomena* (from its opening praise of Zeus), "For we are also his offspring."

2. See Corrigan and Harrington, "Pseudo-Dionysius the Areopagite." (For full references to works cited in short form in this Introduction and in the Notes to the Translation, see Bibliography.)

3. See Allen, *Synoptic Art*, chap. 2.

4. Ibid.

5. In 827 CE the abbey of St. Denis received a manuscript of Dionysius' works in Greek from King Louis the Pious, who had in turn received it as a gift from the Byzantine emperor Michael II. This donation effectively initiated the medieval West's fascination with Dionysus and his theology.

6. See Monfasani, "Pseudo-Dionysius the Areopagite." Apart from Valla, Monfasani points to other fifteenth-century skeptics, such as Pietro Balbi and Theodore of Gaza, and, on the eve of the Reformation, William Grocyn and Erasmus. See also Luscombe, "Denis the Pseudo-Areopagite."

7. Other notable defenders in the early-modern period are Leonardus Lessius, S. J. (1554–1623), Pierre Halloix, S. J. (1571–1656), Balthasar Cordier (1592–1650), and Bernardo Maria de Rubeis (1687–1775).

8. Joseph Stiglmayr, *Das Aufkommen der Pseudo-Dionysischen Schriften und ihr Eindringen in die Christlichen Literatur* (Feldkirch: L. Sausgruber, 1895); Hugo Koch, *Pseudo-Dionysius Areopagita in seinem Beziehungen zum Neuplatonismus und Mysterienwesen* (Mainz: F. Kirchhiem, 1900). See the discussion of Helmut Boese in his edition of Proclus' *Tria Opuscula* (Berlin: De Gruyter, 1960), 172–265. The Greek original of the *De malorum subsisten-*

tia, long considered lost, has now been partially excavated from the treatises written against Proclus by Isaac Sebastocrator; see Kristeller, "Proclus as a Reader of Plato and Plotinus," 199. In *DN* 134.12 Ficino mentions the *De malorum subsistentia* as a text in which Proclus agrees with Dionysius on a particular point; but the reference has all the appearance of being an afterthought. Nothing suggests he had discovered the deep interrelatedness of the two texts. He must have assumed, rather, that Proclus was repeating positions hammered out by his predecessors and preeminently by Dionysius.

9. On the Latin translations of the *Corpus Dionysiacum*, see the *Dionysiaca* edited by Philippe Chevallier. See also Gersh, *From Iamblichus to Eriugena*; and Rorem, *Pseudo-Dionysius. A Commentary on the Texts*, part 4 of which focuses on *DN*, part 5 on *MT*.

10. See the study of Charles L. Stinger, *Humanism and the Church Fathers: Ambrogio Traversari (1386–1439) and Christian Antiquity in the Italian Renaissance* (Albany: State University of New York Press, 1977), now online via the ACLS Humanities E-Book.

11. P. O. Kristeller, *Il pensiero filosofico di Marsilio Ficino* (Florence: Le Lettere, 1988), 109n, draws our attention to Ficino's citing of Traversari's version. See, more fully, Toussaint, "L'influence de Ficin à Paris," at 384–95.

12. *Dionysius Areopagita*, ed. Podolak, x, underscores Ficino's important statement in his *argumentum* to the *DN* that his aim was to emphasize the Platonism of Dionysius, that is, to "pluck" his Platonic "flowers." "Plucking flowers" for taking notes is a recurrent trope.

13. Marsilio Ficino, *Opera Omnia* (Basel: Henricpetri, 1576, with various modern reprints; hereafter, *Op.*), 920.3–921. This is now forty-fifth in book ten of Ficino's *Letters*; it was written probably in March or April 1491.

14. The versions all appear in parallel columns along with the Greek text in Chevallier's massive two-volume *Dionysiaca* edition (see n. 9 above). There are scores, indeed hundreds, of manuscripts awaiting a definitive census. But we do know from the census of the printed editions of both the medieval and the Renaissance translations that they were frequently

printed in the fifteenth through the seventeenth centuries: see ibid. 1:xxii–lxiv.

15. *Op.* 925.2: "Mihi certe nec ulla scientiae forma est gratiosior quam platonica, neque forma haec usquam magis quam in Dionysio veneranda. Amo equidem Platonem in Iamblicho, admiror in Plotino, in Dionsysio veneror." It is not entirely coincidental perhaps that in the letter of September 15, 1489, to the three Pietros summoning them to the defense of his *De vita,* Ficino concludes by noting that just as he had often called Pico Phoebus Apollo, so Pico in turn had often called him Dionysus and Liber. In his last decade, and as the midwife of Renaissance Platonism and its championship of the soul's immortality, it is predictable Ficino would engage even more intently with the hope of being reborn, even as Dionysus had been reborn in the ancient myth from Zeus' thigh. More profoundly, in the 1490s he must have engaged personally with the notion of being reborn as the interpreter of the *Dionysiaca,* reborn as a Christian Dionysus who sought *liber*ation by way of the negative theology underpinning the *libri* and the *liberi,* the books and the children of the Areopagite. It is difficult to assess the seriousness of such etymological and mythopoetic games, though Ficino could turn to the *Cratylus* as his Platonic authority.

16. *Op.* 920.3–921.

17. *Op.* 451: "Dionysius Pauli discipulus scribens ad Ioannem Evangelistam inquit: Animas impiorum in ipso iudicii tempore etiam nullo fugante, procul a divini iudicis cultu pro viribus figuratas."

18. *In Philebum* 1.29 (ed. Allen, 281). For the whole story of Ficino and the history of Platonism, see my *Synoptic Art,* chapter 2, esp. 56–67.

19. *Op.* 925.2. Cf. n. 15 above.

20. *Op.* 25.1.

21. In note 13 of the introduction to her new two-volume edition and translation of Ficino's *Parmenides* commentary in this I Tatti series (2012), Maude Vanhaelen asserts that Ficino's position with regard to Dionysius "remained ambiguous." Though he "never openly repudiated" the authenticity of the *Dionysiaca,* she argues, he oscillated between praise of Dionysius as the "foremost Platonist of all" while recognizing that "he might be

a follower or even a usurper of the Platonists"; and she refers us to chapters 37.3 and 45.1 of the commentary. This contention is misleading: 45.1 merely argues that a pivotal ontological argument "is not foreign (*non alienum*) to the Platonists and is very frequently made use of (*frequentius usurpatum*) by Dionysius," *usurpare* here meaning "to make use of," "to appropriate," or, as in Vanhaelen's correct rendering in her translation, "to take over," not "to usurp" in the sense of "to steal from" (*furari* or *surripere*). Her reference to 37.3 is to a passage merely emphasizing Dionysius' debt to Parmenides [or to the *Parmenides*]: "Utitur [Dionysius] . . . argumentationibus negationibus verbisque Parmenidis saepe quam plurimis in materia divinissima." Again, the operative verb is "to make use of" (*utor*) with no negative connotations. In sum, Ficino never wavered in his belief that all the Neoplatonists, the *Platonici*, came after Dionysius and must have imbibed their wisdom from him, either directly or indirectly.

22. *Op.* 956.2. In this scenario Plato was indebted to Moses via Pythagoras, whom Ambrose in a letter to Irenaeus (no. 28) had characterized as a Jew and as a thinker indebted to Moses and his teachings (Migne, *Patrologia latina*, 16: 1051B): "cum ex populo Judaeorum, ut plerique arbitrantur, genus duxerit, ex ejus disciplina derivavit etiam magisterii praecepta." Cf. the references in Ficino's *Op.* 29–30.

23. Testimonium in Kristeller, *Supplementum*, 2:236, no. 38: "Hec Marsilius et nisi in adversarios christianae sapientiae mollior esse maluisset, plane dixisset: furati sunt." Clearly, Lefèvre realized that Ficino did not want to accuse them of theft, since his whole irenic apologetical program required that they had derived or borrowed wisdom as though they were disciples, true wisdom being unitary. The Platonists borrowed from Dionysius, Dionysius from Plato, Plato from his predecessors, that is, from the Eleatics and Pythagoreans and other ancient theologians, and these in turn from Orpheus, Hermes Trismegistus, and Zoroaster, the source of the tradition.

24. A problem. Kristeller, *Supplementum*, 1:cxv, notes that in the commentary on the *Divine Names* (*Op.* 1036 = chapter 29.7 infra) Ficino declares he has already finished his version of Iamblichus, *anno superiore*. He deduces this to mean "in 1489." But in his entry on the *De mysteriis*

itself, he had argued that the work was finished, or almost so, in 1488 (cxxxii–cxxxiv).

25. *Op.* 913.1. See Kristeller, *Supplementum* 1:cxv–cxvi, citing Dovizi's letter of September or October 1490, and the letter of "about the same time" to Pandolfo Collenuccio (*Op.* 913.2).

26. See the witness of his March-April 1491 letter to Pier Leoni (*Op.* 920.3).

27. At the close of the same letter, he says he is now proceeding with the *Divine Names* (*nomina nunc divina prosequimur*).

28. Kristeller, *Supplementum* 1:cxv–cxvi. On July 20, 1491, he wrote to Martinus Uranius, "I have been working on the divine names for a long time now [*iam pridem*]" (*Op.* 928.2); and on November 24, he wrote to the same Uranius, "I have been delayed in completing the project" (*Op.* 929.3). Again, in the proem to his treatise *De sole* written in the autumn of 1492, he says he still has Dionysius in hand (*Op.* 965).

29. *Op.* 957.2 and 960.2 (the latter dated October 16, 1494); both letters are now in the twelfth, and last, book of Ficino's *Letters*.

30. *Op.* 1056.3 (*De sole et lumine*) and 1119.1 (*In Parmenidem*).

31. Kristeller, *Supplementum* 1:lxviii, cxvi. Note that there are two versions of this dedicatory letter; see Appendix below.

32. See Allen, "Ficino's Theory of the Five Substances and the Neoplatonists' *Parmenides*," now in idem, *Plato's Third Eye: Studies in Marsilio Ficino's Metaphysics and its Sources* (Aldershot, Hampshire: Variorum, 1995), as no. 8. See also Vanhaelen's introduction to her edition of Ficino's *Parmenides* commentary, cited above.

33. See my "The Second Ficino-Pico Controversy: Parmenidean Poetry, Eristic and the One," now in *Plato's Third Eye*, as no. 10, for a study of Ficino's reservations and caveats and his condemnation of the overliteral interpretation of every phrase in Proclus' *Parmenides* Commentary.

34. See my *Synoptic Art*, 56–79, 89–92.

35. Cf. n. 21 above.

36. *Op.* 921.

37. See my *Synoptic Art,* chapter 2, esp. 75–76, 89–end. In emphasizing the lifelong impact of Plotinus on Ficino, I underestimated perhaps that of the Areopagite, particularly in the Florentine's last quinquennial.

38. Matthew 17:1–5; Mark 9:2–7; Luke 9:28–35. The transfiguration was witnessed by Peter, James, and John (though John does not mention it in his gospel). Presumably, Ficino would align the references to three summits in Exodus' account of the ascent of Moses with St. Paul's famous reference in 2 Corinthians 12:2 to his ascent to the third heaven. He must have also had in mind the reference in Revelation 21:10 to John's "rapture in the Spirit" and his vision of "the holy Jerusalem" as taking place from on top of "a great and high mountain." John's authority was enhanced by his being the author of Revelation as well as of the fourth gospel and of three epistles.

39. Exodus 34:29–35; Matthew 17:2–3.

40. We now assign it to two second-century CE forgers or imitators who were subscribing to — or catering to — the Middle Platonic enthusiasms of their age.

41. Cf. Plotinus, *Enneads* 3.5.9, 6.7.35.24ff.: "Better to be drunk in a drunkenness like this than to be more respectably sober." The Platonic source is the drunkenness of Poros in the *Symposium* 203B5.

42. On the concept of "inspired translation," see Hankins, *Plato in the Italian Renaissance,* 1:315–17.

43. But not in the angels, where the intellect and the will are essentially one, where cherubim and seraphim are alike in their adoration of the Lamb.

44. See James Hankins, "Lorenzo de' Medici's *De summo bono* and the Popularization of Ficinian Platonism," in *Humanistica: Per Cesare Vasoli,* ed. Fabrizio Meroi and Elisabetta Scapparone (Florence: Olschki, 2004), 61–69, and idem, "Lorenzo de' Medici as a Student of Ficino: The *De summo bono,* in Hankins, *Humanism and Platonism,* 2:317–50, esp. 335–38.

45. Referred to, for example, in *DN* 15.2 below. Two obvious sources for Ficino are *Chaldaean Oracles,* fr. 1, and Plato's *Phaedrus* 248A3.

46. Plato himself, of course, had pursued anti-intellect arguments in such dialogues as the *Symposium* and *Phaedrus*. For parallel anti-intellect and anti-Porphyrian arguments in Iamblichus, see Gregory Shaw, "Containing Ecstasy: The Strategies of Iamblichean Theurgy," *Dionysius* 21 (2003): 53–88, at 62–64ff.

47. We recall the Augustinian story that held that it was more difficult to understand the doctrine of the Trinity than to imagine a child ladling all of the sea into a puddle.

48. This is a traditional thought-experiment, whereby we systematically strip away the outer layers of meaning to arrive at the kernel. Cf. Ficino, *Platonic Theology* 6.2.16 (ed. Allen-Hankins).

49. Exodus 20:21.

50. See Wolgang Scheuermann-Peilicke, *Licht und Liebe. Lichtmetapher und Metaphysik bei Marsilio Ficino* (Hildesheim: Georg Olms Verlag, 2000).

51. For a full biography, see M. Pellegrini's entry in *Enciclopedia dei papi*, 3 vols. (Rome: Istituto della Enciclopedia Italiana, 2000), 3:42–64.

52. See the two dedicatory proems to Cardinal Giovanni in Ficino's ninth book of letters: *Proemium in Iamblichum* (*Op*. 1:697), and *Proemium in Proculum et Porphyrium* (*Op*. 1:898). For the dating of the completion and dedication of these various translations, see Kristeller, *Supplementum* 1:cxxxii–cxxxv.

53. In a letter to Martin Prenninger (Uranius) dated June 12, 1489, and now also in his ninth book of *Letters*, Ficino praises Plato as the thinker who "had marvelously united the twin ways [of philosopher and of priest] and made them one (*coniunxit in unum*)"; for "everywhere he is equally religious and philosophical." Furthermore, "in harmony with Pythagorean and Socratic principles, he pursues the Mosaic law and anticipates (*auguratur*) the Christian law." For the problematic argument that Ficino's work on Iamblichus is a "twin" to his work on Dionysius, see Podolak, "Le commentaire de Marsile Ficin," 144.

54. See the puns and wordplay in the longer version of the dedicatory letter (Appendix, below).

Index Capitulorum

De Mystica Theologia

Chapter Indices

On Mystical Theology

I Marsilio Ficino, the Florentine, commends himself in supplication to the Reverend Father in Christ, the Lord Cardinal Giovanni de' Medici, 1492.

II Marsilio Ficino the Florentine's proem to Dionysius the Areopagite.

III Marsilio's introductory comment on Dionysius' prayer concerning the Trinity.

IV [Marsilio:] Continuation of his exposition on the Trinity; and that the Good is above essence and unknown because of the superabundance of its light.

V Dionysius: Prayer to the Trinity.

VI Marsilio: The Good is above essence and intellect. It is not attained by understanding. Rather, by similitude of life and by love it is perceived by [our] unity.

VII Dionysius: You must transcend not only sensibles but also intelligibles! And neglecting understanding as it were, and with the love solely of the sole, the first Good, betake yourself to it!

VIII Marsilio: Why divine things must not be divulged to profane men. And who the profane might be. And how the One and the Good is above being.

IX Marsilio: Confirmation that the Good is above essence, life, and understanding. How we enjoy the Good more perfectly than simply by understanding.

XIX Dionysius: Quomodo auferendo omnia que sunt procedamus ad Deum. Et contraria ratione auferamus atque ponamus.

XX Marsilius: De Trinitate et imagine Trinitatis.

XXI Dionysius: De bonitate divina, unitate, trinitate, Iesu appellationibus, figurisque divinis.

XXII Marsilius: De gradibus virium cognoscentium atque rerum cognoscendarum. Et quare sermo de rebus supernis verus brevis esse soleat.

XXIII Dionysius: Sermo de rebus altioribus debet esse brevior.

XXIV Marsilius: Omnia formam aliquam preferentia affirmari de Deo possunt atque negari. Sed affirmatio quidem a superioribus, negatio autem ab inferioribus incohanda.

XXV Dionysius: Affirmatio rerum de Deo contraria via procedit quam negatio.

XXVI Marsilius: Unum est omnium principium, nec est aliquid sensibile vel intelligibile, sed utrisque intervallo quodam infinito prestantius.

XXVII Dionysius: Quod nihil sensibilium est qui sensibilis omnis eminenter est auctor.

XXVIII Marsilius: Quibus gradibus negantur de Deo intelligibilia, scilicet primo que pertinent ad animam, deinde que ad intellectum, tertio que ad ideas, quarto que ad communes Dei appellationes, quinto que ad Trinitatem.

XXIX Dionysius: Quod nullum intelligibilium est qui omnis intelligibilis eminenter est auctor.

De Divinis Nominibus

[Part I, Chapters I–CXXXV]

I Marsilius:

II Dionysius:

III Marsilius: Tantum de divinis asseverandum, quantum divinitus inspirati nobis ostendunt. Item quomodo radius divinus se ipsum nobis accommodat.

IV Dionysius: Tantum de divinis asseverandum quantum inspiratio divina declarat. Item radius divinus pro cuiusque ingenio se infundit.

V Marsilius: Deus nec ab essentia, nec ab intellectu, nec per illam, nec per istum vel comprehendi vel saltem perspici potest.

VI Dionysius: Deus, essentia et intellectu superior, non potest per ullam essentiam vel ab ullo intellectu comprehendi vel saltem propria virtute cerni.

VII Marsilius: Comprehendere Deum nullus intellectus potest; scire quid sit Deus intellectus beatus solus solo lumine supernaturali potest.

VIII Dionysius: Scire quid sit Deus Dei ipsius proprium est, nec ullum divine substantie usquam manifestum vestigium reperitur.

· CHAPTER INDICES ·

On Divine Names

[Part I, Chapters I–CXXXV]

I Marsilio:

II Dionysius:

III Marsilio: We should assert as much about matters divine as men who are divinely inspired reveal them to us. Likewise how the divine ray accommodates itself to us.

IV Dionysius: Only to the extent divine inspiration reveals them to us should we make assertions about things divine. The divine ray pours itself into each person according to the mental capacity of each.

V Marsilio: God is neither from essence nor from intellect, nor can He be understood or even perceived through essence or through intellect.

VI Dionysius: In that He is superior to essence and intellect God cannot be comprehended via any essence or by any intellect, or perceived even by an appropriate power.

VII Marsilio: No intellect can understand God. The blessed intellect alone can know what God is [and] only by a supernatural light.

VIII Dionysius: To know what God is is proper to God Himself. No manifest trace at all of the divine substance is found anywhere.

IX Marsilius: Causa prima et separatissima est et presentissima, atque sicut omnibus impartit bonum, sic multis divinam intelligentiam atque unionem.

X Dionysius: Deus radium intelligentie sue unicuique pro capacitate communicat, intellectusque beati distributo munere contenti vivunt, ac firmiter perfruuntur.

XI Marsilius: Facilius tutiusque divina videmus si mentis aciem ad eloquia sacra convertimus, quam si in ipsum Deum audentius dirigamus.

XII Dionysius: Radii divinitatis fulgentes in sacris eloquiis ad divinam contemplationem facile nos perducunt.

XIII Marsilius: Deus usque adeo potens et intima causa est rebus omnibus bonorum omnium ut ipsemet rebus sit ipsa rerum bona.

XIV Dionysius: Deus omnibus in rebus est omnia rerum bona.

XV Marsilius: Quare Deus multis nominibus appelletur: cur unitas, cur Trinitas, causa, sapientia, pulchritudo, benignitas, ceteraque similiter.

XVI Dionysius: Divina nomina plurimum significant beneficos ex Deo progressus. Deus appellatur unitas, trinitas, causa, sapientia, pulchritudo, benignitas.

XVII Marsilius: Ipsum unum bonumque est superius ente, intellectu, intelligibili; item quare figuris utamur ad divina declaranda. Item de resurrectione et fruitione Dei.

XXVII Marsilio: God not only enacts all things in all things, but is Himself all in all.

XXVIII Dionysius: God enacts all in all, and is Himself all in all. So He is rightly praised if we use the honorable names of all.

XXIX Marsilio: The number of ways in which the divine names are imagined. How matters divine come into our purview.

XXX Dionysius: Divine names are derived not only from God's providence or from the things it provides us, but also from divine visions. But matters divine must not be revealed to the profane.

XXXI Marsilio: What the Deity [is] by way of essence, what by way of participation. In what way goodness is a proper name of God. In the Trinity, what names are common, what are particular.

XXXII Dionysius: What names are common in the Trinity and what particular.

XXXIII Marsilio: The names common to the Trinity sometimes are summarily understood, sometimes are spun out in a discourse. And when they are predicated of one [Person], they are deemed predicated of all [three].

XXXIV Dionysius: Things common to the divine Persons are sometimes summarily comprehended, sometimes attained by going through them one by one.

LXIII Marsilio: The reason why in producing many things God remains one, and in creating beings exists higher than being; and why God is the One itself, and more excellent than any individual one.

LXIV Dionysius: The same.

LXV Marsilio: How by participation in one God the gods are said to be many.

LXVI Dionysius: The same.

LXVII Marsilio: On the name of the Good; on the efficacy of prayer; how God is everywhere.

LXVIII Dionysius: The same.

LXIX Marsilio: The golden or luminous chain hanging from God is the arrangement of things mutually connected to each other but subject to divine providence.

LXX Dionysius: He who prays strives for the changeless God; and in this endeavor he does not move God to himself but rather himself to God.

LXXI Marsilio: An apology for why Hierotheus writes what he has written. Marvelous praise of Hierotheus.

LXXII Dionysius: The same.

LXXIII Marsilio: As it is not the same to see the light in illuminated things and to endure the light itself from the sun, so it is one thing to look upon the divine mysteries, and another to pursue the learning leading up to them.

LXXIV Dionysius: [The same.]

LXXXVII Marsilius: Ab ipso bono intellectus angelici, anime rationales, sensuales et vegetales et corpora perfectionem suam actumque habent.

LXXXVIII Dionysius: Omnia quomodocumque animata vel quomodolibet formata donum ab ipso bono reportaverunt.

LXXXIX Marsilius: Influxus boni usque ad materiam extenditur, ipsumque est essentia et vita intelligentiaque superius.

XC Dionysius: Idem.

XCI Marsilius: Celestia dotes habent mirificas ab ipso bono: efficaciam, temperantiam, firmitatem, pulchritudinem et similia.

XCII Dionysius: Ab ipso bono sunt dotes ordinesque celestes, et moderatio et decus et splendor.

XCIII Marsilius: Lumen est imago boni, sol est celestium dominus et imago Dei.

XCIV Dionysius: Similitudo luminis atque solis ad Deum.

XCV Marsilius: Similitudo rursum solis ad Deum.

XCVI Dionysius: Idem.

XCVII Marsilius: De quinque luminibus. Item quomodo divinum lumen agit in angelos atque animas.

XCVIII Dionysius: Idem.

XCIX Marsilius: Deus est lumen super lumen, illuminat mentes omnes, tum natura tum gratia, atque in unum illuminando conciliat.

C Dionysius: Idem.

CI Marsilius: Ipsum bonum omnia reddit suo lumine pulchra.

CII Dionysius: Idem.

CIII Marsilius: Pulchritudo prima est omnium principium et exemplar et finis, atque est ipsum bonum.

CIV Dionysius: Idem.

CV Marsilius: Idem est primum bonum atque pulchrum. Item a pulchritudine prima sunt rerum essentie, uniones, discretiones, communiones, ordines, proportiones, status, motus.

CVI Dionysius: Idem.

CVII Marsilius: De motu angeli et anime triplici, id est circulari, recto, obliquo.

CVIII Dionysius: Idem.

CIX Marsilius: Ipsum pulchrum bonumque est causa efficiens, exemplaris, finalis, conservatrix omnis status atque motus, et ordinis bonique totius rerum omnium.

CX Dionysius: Idem.

CXI Marsilius: Omnia pro modo suo appetunt ipsum bonum atque pulchrum; quo desiderio agunt quicquid agunt. Item ipsum bonum amore sui omnia facit.

CXII Dionysius: Idem.

C Dionysius: The same.

CI Marsilio: The Good itself renders all things beautiful with its light.

CII Dionysius: The same.

CIII Marsilio: The prime beauty is the beginning, exemplar, and end of all, and is the Good itself.

CIV Dionysius: The same.

CV Marsilio: The prime Good and the beautiful are the same. From prime beauty issue the essences of things, their unions, differentiations, communions, orders, proportions, rests, and motions.

CVI Dionysius: The same.

CVII Marsilio: On the triple motion of the angel and the soul, that is, the circular, the straight, and the oblique.

CVIII Dionysius: The same.

CIX Marsilio: The Beautiful and the Good is the efficient, exemplary, final, and preserving cause of all rest and motion, and of the order and entire good of all things.

CX Dionysius: The same.

CXI Marsilio: All things desire the Good itself and the Beautiful in their own manner, and through this desire they do whatever they do; likewise the Good itself by love of itself creates all.

CXII Dionysius: The same.

CXIII Dionysius: De nomine amoris, et quod intentionem loquentis potius quam verba debemus perpendere.

CXIV Marsilius: Quomodo imaginatio potest aliquid sine sensu, ratio sine imaginatione, intellectus absque ratione, denique habitus animi Deo conformis potest, vacante iam intelligentia, Deo frui.

CXV Dionysius: Verbis utimur propter sensum. Sensus cum sensibilibus superflui sunt, quando intellectus intelligibilia penetravit; superflua et intelligentia, quando animus cum Deo charitate coniungitur.

CXVI Marsilius:

CXVII Dionysius: Nomine amoris utimur in divinis tum quia efficacius illa significat, tum etiam ut vulgarem huius nominis abusum auferamus.

CXVIII Marsilius: Virtus amoris est unire duo in uno quodam tertio, copulare invicem, commiscere ad novum aliquid inde conflandum.

CXIX Dionysius: Idem.

CXX Marsilius: Amor impellit amantem in amatum se transferre. Motionumque et actionum omnium est principium.

CXXI Dionysius: Idem.

CXXII Marsilius: Deus amore facit omnia, adest omnibus ac providet.

ON THE *MYSTICAL THEOLOGY* OF DIONYSIUS THE AREOPAGITE[1]

: I :

Marsilius Ficinus Florentinus
Reverendo[1] *in Christo patri domino*
Ioanni Medici Cardinali
suppliciter se commendat
1492.

Cum et me genius meus semel interpretandis Platonicis destinaverit, et ego magnis Medicibus Platonica ferme omnia dedicaverim, cetera quidem maiorum tuorum fuerint, que vero inter hec in primis ad Theologiam pertinent, et idcirco sacra censentur, ipse sacer antistes iure optimo tibi vendicare videris, itaque Platonicum Iamblichum sacerdotem iampridem ad te misi sacra Egyptiorum mysteria pertractantem. Post hec autem ad Dionysium Areopagitam Platonicum Christianumque Theologum interpretandum tibi me contuli, precipuum Atheniensium antistitem summo Florentinorum antistiti dicaturus. Hunc ergo iam absolutum lege atque vive feliciter.

: II :

Prohemium Marsilii Ficini Florentini[2]
in Dionysium Aeropagitam.

Dionysii[3] dei numen Theologi veteres et Platonici separatarum mentium extasin et excessum esse putant, quando partim amore nativo, partim instigante Deo naturales intelligentie limites

: I :

Marsilio Ficino, the Florentine, commends himself in supplication to the Reverend Father in Christ, the Lord Cardinal Giovanni de' Medici 1492.[2]

My genius has destined me ever to interpret the Platonists, and I have dedicated almost all the Platonic writings to the illustrious Medici. Since this is so, and since the rest of the writings went to your forebears, but you, as the sacred high priest himself, would seem to have the best claim to those among the writings that pertain primarily to theology and are therefore deemed sacred, I therefore sent you some time ago the Platonist, Iamblichus — a priest treating of the sacred mysteries of the Egyptians.[3] Thereafter I set myself to the task of interpreting Dionysius the Areopagite for you, a Platonist and a Christian theologian; and I am going to dedicate this renowned high priest of the Athenians to [you], the supreme high priest of the Florentines. So peruse this interpretation now that it is complete, and live in happiness.

: II :

Marsilio Ficino the Florentine's proem to Dionysius the Areopagite.

The ancient theologians and the Platonists believe that the spirit of the god Dionysus dwells in the ecstasy, the ecstatic departure, of separated minds, when, partly out of inborn love and partly with the god prompting them, they have surpassed the natural

supergresse, in amatum Deum mirabiliter transformantur. Ubi novo quodam nectaris haustu et inestimabili gaudio velut ebrie (ut ita dixerim) debacchantur. Hoc igitur dionysiaco mero Dionysius noster ebrius exultat passim: effundit enigmata, concinit dithyrambos. Itaque quam arduum est profundos illius sensus intelligentia penetrare, tam difficile miras verborum compositiones; et quasi Orphicum dicendi characterem imitari, ac Latinis presertim verbis exprimere. Idem profecto ad id facile consequendum, necessarius omnino nobis divinus est furor. Eadem prorsus oratione[4] Trinitas obsecranda, ut quod Dionysio pie petenti lumen ad penetranda prophetarum apostolorumque mysteria quondam Deus infudit, idem nobis similiter supplicantibus ad illius sensum eloquiumque consequendum et exprimendum feliciter nunc infundat.

: III :

Argumentum Marsilii in orationem Dionysii de Trinitate.

1 Dionysius Areopagita, Platonice discipline culmen et Christiane theologie columen, querens divinum lumen non tam intelligentia perscrutatur quam ardente voluntatis affectu et oratione petit. Quippe cum a Paulo mundi sole didicerit Platone etiam confirmante ipsum universi principium esse intellectu quantumlibet excelso superius, non igitur conatu quodam

limits of understanding, and are wondrously transformed into the beloved god. Then with a new draft of nectar and with unconscionable joy they reel as though they were intoxicated bacchantes. With this Dionysian wine, therefore, our inebriated Dionysius runs riot everywhere: he pours forth enigmas, he sings in dithyrambs.[4] Hence, as taxing as it is to penetrate with the understanding the profound meanings of our Dionysius, so is it equally difficult to penetrate the marvelous texture of his words, and to imitate the Orphic manner as it were of his speaking and especially to render it into Latin. Certainly, to achieve this with ease we must be possessed by an utterly divine frenzy. We must beseech the Trinity in one and the same prayer that, as God once poured into Dionysius the light of piously seeking in order that he might penetrate the mysteries of the prophets and apostles, so God may now pour the same light into us, who likewise ask in supplication that we may grasp Dionysius' meaning and eloquence, and express them felicitously here.

: III :

Marsilio's introductory comment on Dionysius' prayer concerning the Trinity.

Dionysius the Areopagite—that culmination of the Platonic discipline, that column of Christian theology—when seeking the divine light, seeks not so much with understanding as with the burning ardor of the will; and he seeks with prayer. This is because he learned from Paul, the sun of the world, and with Plato confirming it too, that the universe's principle is higher than 1

intelligentie comparari, sed in animum amore prorsus Deo deditum accendi Deum atque ibidem in ardore lucere.

2 Hactenus quam ob causam ab oratione iaciat fundamentum dixisse sufficiat. Que vero orationis sit virtus et quis efficacius oret in presentia pretermittimus. Satis enim diximus in epistola ad Bindacium Recasolanum singulari nobiscum charitate coniunctum. Ad expositionem iam pergamus.

: IV :

[Marsilius:] *Prosecutio expositionis de Trinitate: et quod bonum est super essentiam et propter exuberantiam lucis ignotum.*

1 Res quelibet quo magis bonitate vigent, eo magis sua quadam propagine se communicant. Quapropter ad infinitum bonum propagatio pertinet infinita. Cum vero duo esse infinita non possint, merito infinita bonitas rursusque immensa bonitatis propago natura sunt una, se ipsam videlicet intra se propagans. Tum vero quoniam omnis amor ad bonum necessario fertur, consequens est penes infinitum bonum eiusdemque[5] propaginem infinitam, infinitum quoque amorem spiritumque amatorium ad se ipsum intus existere. Dum vero tres hic[6] quasi naturales proprietates personasque numeramus, interea quoniam quod est infinitum nihil

intellect, however exalted; and that it is not to be procured therefore by any attempt of understanding,[5] but rather that God inflames the rational soul that is entirely given over to Him with love. At that very moment the soul blazes in ardor.

Thus far it is enough to have declared the reason why he lays the foundation with a prayer. But for now let us leave aside the power of prayer and what it means and who may pray the more effectively; for we have said enough in a letter to Bindaccio Ricasoli who is joined to us in singular charity.[6] Let us now proceed to exposition. 2

: IV :

[Marsilio:]
Continuation of his exposition on the Trinity; and that the Good is above essence and unknown because of the superabundance of its light.

All things, the more they abound in goodness, the more they communicate themselves to their particular offspring.[7] Hence infinite propagation pertains to the infinite good. But since two things cannot [both] be infinite, it follows that infinite goodness, and in return the infinite propagation of goodness, are by nature one; goodness, that is, propagates itself within itself. But since all love is necessarily drawn to the good, consequently, in the presence of the infinite good and the infinite propagation of the same good, there exists within an infinite love too, a spirit of love for itself. But here [with the Trinity] while we number three natural properties as it were and persons, yet because what is infinite leaves 1

relinquit extra se sui, nec admittit aliquid alienum, naturam unicam simplicissimamque cogitamus. Perinde ac siquis naturalem solis formam et lucem huic intimam calefactoriamque virtutem unicam solis naturam esse dixerit.

2 Divina Trinitas non est numerus aliquis in quantitatis genere collocatus, nec etiam in substantie genere, nec insuper in essentie ordine computatus. Cum enim appetitui naturali non sufficiat esse, sed affectet insuper bene esse, ideoque entia singula suum quoddam bonum appetant, atque universum ens cupiat universum bonum et ipsum tandem ens primum similiter exoptet primum bonum, merito bonum ipsum, tanquam finis perfectioque entium omnium atque entis, horum omnium est principium. Et idcirco universa essentia primaque superius. Est insuper eminentius deitate quavis et bonitate, per quas videlicet aliquis alicubi Deus sit et aliquid alicubi bonum. Prima enim bonitas, extra omne quomodocunque bonum ac preter omnem compositionem, absoluta penitus simpliciter in se ipsa consistit.

3 Invisibile dicimus tum lumen quam minimum, tum quam maximum; nec enim vel illud prospici vel hoc ab oculis inspici substinerique potest. Sed hoc rite potest superinvisibile nominari. Similiter informis rerum materia, itemque rerum principium sunt ignota, sed materiam ob lucis defectum ignotam dicimus, principium vero ob excessum lucis superignotum.

4 Summus anime ad Deum ascendentis gradus caligo dicitur atque lumen: caligo quidem quatenus animus per negationes quasdam illhuc usque processit, negando videlicet Deum ipsum esse rem hanc aut istam aut illam, vel natura compertam vel a nobis

nothing of itself outside itself and admits nothing foreign, we believe there is just one absolutely simple nature. It is as if someone were to say that the sun's natural form, the light internal to it, and its power to heat constitute together the unique nature of the sun.

The divine Trinity is not some number located in the genus of 2
quantity, nor even in the genus of substance; nor is it reckoned in the order of essence. For since it is not enough for the natural appetite just to be, but it longs besides to possess well-being, and single entities therefore desire their own particular good, and the universal entity desires the universal good, and finally the first entity itself likewise chooses the first good, so it follows that the Good itself, as the end and perfection of all entities and being, is the principle of all these. And so it is higher than the universal and prime essence; and it is more eminent too than any kind of divinity and any goodness, by way of which some person somewhere may be a god and something somewhere may be a good. For the first goodness, outside all particular good whatsoever and beyond all composition, stands as the absolute, the totally simple Goodness in itself.

We call light invisible either when it is the faintest possible or 3
when it is the brightest; for the former light cannot be seen and the latter cannot be received and sustained by the eyes. But the brightest light can rightly be called super-invisible light. Similarly, the formless matter of things and the principle of things are alike unknown; however, we call matter unknown because of the defect of light but the principle super-unknown because of the excess of light.

The highest step for the soul ascending to God is called both 4
darkness and light. The step is called darkness insofar as the rational soul has proceeded thus far through particular negations, that is, by denying that God Himself is this thing or that thing or some other thing, or that God has been found in nature or thought about by us. The step is called light, however, for the

excogitatam; lumen vero qua ratione non aliter de Deo quam ita negando perspicuam consequimur veritatem. Ut tenebre eius, inquit David, ita et lumen eius, et nox tanquam dies illuminabitur.

Deus ipse mentes tunc demum lumine suo penitus implet, quando se ipsas illi quasi iam cecas atque silentes exposuerunt, id est tum singula intelligibilia de Deo negantes, tum etiam intellectualem formam suam actionemque consuetam per divinum amorem mirabiliter trascendentes. Sic igitur animus ita demum vera de Deo loquitur quando non loquitur.

: V :

Dionysius:
Oratio Dionysii ad Trinitatem.

Trinitas essentia, deitate, bonitate superior, divine Christianorum sapientie dux, dirige nos in ipsum superignotum et prefulgens excelsumque mysticorum eloquiorum culmen. Ubi simplicia et absoluta immutabiliaque theologie mysteria latent adoperta prefulgente quadam silentii clam sacra docentis caligine, que quidem ubi maxime videtur obscura, ibi supra modum lucem profert exuberantem. Illic sane quod tangi viderique nullo modo potest splendoribus plusquam pulchris ad exuberantiam implet omnes quasi captos oculis intellectus.

reason that we attain the clearest truth about God in no other way than through negation. As His shadows are, says David, so is His light; and [His] night will be as illuminated as [His] day.[8]

God Himself fills minds utterly with His light only when they have exposed themselves to that [light]. It is as if they were now blinded and struck silent, that is, were denying individual intelligibles of God, and also, through divine love, transcending in a wonderful way their own intellectual form and customary action. Thus the rational soul speaks truths at last about God when it does not speak.

: V :

Dionysius: Prayer to the Trinity.

Trinity higher than essence, deity, and goodness, You who rule over the divine wisdom of Christians, direct us to Him who is beyond knowledge itself, who precedes light, and who is the lofty summit of mystical eloquence. There the simple and absolute and unchangeable mysteries of theology lie hidden in a prefulgent blanket of darkness as it were, a darkness of silence which secretly teaches the sacred truths; and where it seems darkest this darkness there radiates light in abundance beyond measure. For what can in no way be touched or seen fills intellects there in abundance with splendors more than beautiful: it is as though all the intellects have been made captive to their eyes.

: VI :

Marsilius:
Bonum est super essentiam et intellectum, nec attigitur intelligentia, sed per vite similitudinem et amorem percipitur unitate.

1 Quatuor cognitionis species sunt: sensus, imaginatio, ratio, intellectus. Imaginatio non semper indiget ad actionem presentia corporum, qua necessario sensus eget. Verumtamen corporeas quasdam in agendo conditiones sequitur, actionemque mobilem habet atque multiplicem. Ratio non sequitur conditiones particulares corporum, sed iam ad[7] absoluta se confert; mobilis tamen est et necessario multiplex. Intellectus denique motum iam deposuit, dividuam vero multiplicitatem minime, nam et necessitate ordinis eam retinet, et usu declarat sive definiat seu dividat sive componat.

2 Quod igitur principium universi sit super sensum, imaginationem, rationem, nemo aliquando philosophus dubitavit, siquidem incorporeum est penitus et immobile. Esse vero et intellectu intelligibilique superius Platonici una cum Dionysio probant, quippe cum principium quidem sit ipsa simplicitas infinita, intellectus autem agendo per multiplicem et dividuam actionem ad obiectum intelligibile dirigatur necessario multiplex, quod et proportionem quandam cum intelligentia subeat.

: VI :

Marsilio: The Good is above essence and intellect. It is not attained by understanding. Rather, by similitude of life and by love it is perceived by [our] unity.

The cognitive faculties are of four kinds: sensation, imagination, reason, and intellect. In order to act, imagination does not always need the presence of bodies which sensation necessarily needs; yet in acting it does follow certain corporeal conditions: it enacts in mobile and multiple ways. Reason does not follow the particular conditions of bodies, but already betakes itself to absolutes [i.e., things freed from bodies]; yet it is mobile and necessarily multiple. Intellect finally has already put motion aside but not divided multiplicity; for, by the necessity of the [cosmic] order, it retains this multiplicity; and need must declare whether it should define or divide or compound. 1

Therefore, no philosopher will ever doubt that the universe's principle is beyond sensation, imagination, and reason, since the incorporeal is also utterly motionless. But the Platonists, along with Dionysius, prove: (1) that this principle is also higher than both intellect and the intelligible, since it is infinite simplicity itself; but (2) that intellect, in its activity, is directed via multiple and divided action toward an intelligible object that is necessarily multiple, since it is subject to a certain proportion with understanding. 2

3 Proinde cum ipsum intelligibile ipsi enti sit equale vel forte latius atque prestantius, sequitur principium rerum, dum excedit intelligibile, ens item multo magis excedere. Quod autem intelligibile ens exsuperet inde patet quia et que sunt et que non sunt intelligimus, et esse pariter atque non esse, et aliquid ente, et essentia, et ipso esse perfectius. Hinc ergo concludimus principium universi, quod propter inestimabilem simplicitatem eminentiamque ipsum unum cognominamus, excelsius ente putandum, presertim quia ens qua ratione ens est multiplicitatem divisionemque non necessario refugit, sed vel presentem sustinet vel futuram. Ipsum vero unum, et universi principium, talia longe propulsat.

4 Quecunque ab[8] hoc proxime procreantur, intellectus scilicet intellectualesque anime, unitatem hinc quandam quasi paternum characterem sortiuntur. Quo quidem quasi capite vel cardine vel centro suo Deum quandoque tanquam universi centrum possint attingere, quemadmodum Plotinus una cum Dionysio comprobat. Cum igitur nec rationis nec intellectus usu frui Deo possimus, fruituros tamen naturalis ipsa spes et conatus profectusque polliceatur, per unitatem saltem intellectu prestantiorem quandoque fruemur — quando scilicet, posthabitis ceterarum virium actionibus, anime totius attentionem totam in hanc unitatem tanquam ad centrum a circumferentia collegerimus. Hoc divinum illud Arpocraticumque silentium a Mercurio, Pythagora, Socrate, Platone, Plotino, Apollonio celebratum.

· CHAPTER VI ·

Since the intelligible itself is equal to being itself or haply is still 3
more extensive and more eminent, it follows that the principle of things, in exceeding the intelligible, to a much greater degree also exceeds being. That the intelligible exceeds being is obvious from the fact that we may come to know both what are and what are not, and equally being and non-being, and that there is something more perfect than an entity and essence and being itself. Hence we conclude that the universe's principle, since we call it the One itself because of its inestimable simplicity and eminence, must be supposed more eminent than being; and especially because being, by reason of its being, necessarily does not flee from multiplicity and division, but admits what is present or future. But the One, the universe's principle, banishes these and suchlike to a distant exile.

All that the One procreates proximate to itself, namely intel- 4
lects and intellectual souls, are allotted a certain unity from it as a kind of paternal characteristic, by which, as by their head or axis or center, they might be able at some point to attain God as the center of the universe, as Plotinus proves along with Dionysius.[9] Therefore, since we are able to enjoy God using neither reason nor intellect, and yet our natural hope itself, our attempt, and our progress give promise that we will enjoy Him, then at least we will do so through [our] unity which is more eminent than our intellect. But this will happen only when, having set aside the actions of the other powers, we have garnered the undivided attention of the whole soul and brought it into this its unity as from the circumference to the center. This has been celebrated as that divine, that Harpocratian silence by Hermes, Pythagoras, Socrates, Plato, Plotinus, and Apollonius.[10]

5 Efficere vero id potest aliquando solus amor, cuius propria virtus est traductoria pariter et unifica, per quam animum ab inferioribus transferat ad supremum suum, uniatque supremo. Amor videlicet ipsius dumtaxat unius quod est universi principium, qui sane, directus ad unum, animam a multitudine tum aliena, tum sua ad propriam revocat unitatem. Per quam ipsi uni denique copuletur, quando scilicet amorem nunc in multa bona divisum in unum bonum perfecte coniecerit bonorum omnium principium atque finem.

6 Quidnam igitur ad hoc disputationes doctrine, meditationes conferunt? Hec sane tanquam collisiones quedam mutue luminum ipsius primi boni gratia facte, amorem tandem ad ipsum in animo prorsus accendunt. Amor confestim traducit et unit; mox divinum in animo sic accenso superne lumen effulget. Hinc illud Platonis nostri: 'Divinum verbis doceri non potest quemadmodum cetera que discuntur: sed ex diuturna circa rem ipsam consuetudine viteque coniunctione subito tanquam ab igne scintillante accensum in animo lumen se ipsum iam alit.'

7 Hec Dionysius plane confirmat per verba que sequuntur, quibus ea que sunt sive entia nominat substantias incorporeas, que vero non sunt sive non entia, res corporeas atque materiam. Extensionem autem anime appellat amorem ferventem ad Deum in anima pura veritatisque studiosa directum.

Only love, however, can do this at some point—love whose 5
proper virtue is equally to transport and unite, and through which
it transports the rational soul from lower things to its summit,
and then unites it to that summit. In other words, love of the One
itself alone which is the universe's principle, having been directed
to the One, recalls the soul from multiplicity, both alien and its
own, back to its own unity. Through this unity the soul is at last
joined to the One itself, that is, when [its] love—having been divided into many goods in this present world—has been perfectly
reunited to the one Good, the principle and end of all goods.

So what do learning's disputations and meditations contribute 6
to this? Like blows [of a hammer on flint] that together produce
sparks, struck for the sake of the first Good itself, these eventually
kindle love for the Good in the rational soul. By this love it is immediately transported and united; and in the soul thus inflamed,
straightway the divine light blazes down from on high. Hence that
saying of our Plato's: "The divine cannot be taught in words like
the other things we learn. But from daily application to the subject
itself and from communion with it, suddenly, as by a fiery spark,
light, having been ignited in the rational soul, now nourishes itself."[11]

Dionysius plainly confirms all this in the words that follow, 7
where he calls those things which truly exist or are entities incorporeal substances, but those which do not exist or are not entities,
things corporeal and matter. But the soul's reaching out he calls
the fervent love in the soul that is pure and studious of the truth,
the love that is directed toward God.

: VII :

Dionysius:
Transcende non solum sensibilia, sed etiam intelligibilia
et quasi intelligentiam negligens,
solo solius primi boni amore te
confer ad ipsum.

Hec equidem oraverim. Tu vero, amice Timothee, intentissimo circa mystica spectacula studio linque sensus intellectualesque actiones, et sensibilia et intelligibilia omnia, et que sunt et que non sunt. Atque ut ipsi iungaris quod omni essentia et cognitione superius est, te ipsum intende pro viribus quasi cognitione vacantem. Sola enim extensione quadam, tum a te ipso, tum ab omnibus expedita, ad ipsum divine caliginis radium essentia sublimiorem, sublatis omnibus, et absolutus ex omnibus evolabis.

: VIII :

Marsilius:
Quare divina inter profanos divulganda non sint.
Et qui sint profani.
Et quomodo super ens extet[9] *unum atque bonum.*

1 Sicut Plato bis in *Epistolis,* ita Dionysius hic et sepe alibi vetat secretissima theologie mysteria inter profanos effundere, ne, propter iudicii defectum excessumve superbie, vel falsas vanasque opinio-

: VII :

Dionysius:
You must transcend not only sensibles but also intelligibles!
And neglecting understanding as it were,
and with the love solely of the sole, the first Good,
betake yourself to it!

Such will have been my prayer. But you, friend Timothy, in your most intense study of the mystical spectacles, may you abandon the senses and intellectual actions; and may you leave behind sensibles and all intelligibles, and what are and what are not! And in order that you may join yourself to that which is superior to all essence and cognition, you must attend to yourself with all your strength, being empty as it were of cognition! For only with a kind of stretching out, freed both from yourself and from all others, will you wing your way to the ray of the divine darkness, a ray more sublime than essence. With all things abandoned, and being liberated from all, you will soar aloft.

: VIII :

Marsilio:
Why divine things must not be divulged to profane men.
And who the profane might be.
And how the One and the Good is above being.[12]

Like Plato twice in his *Letters*,[13] so often too does Dionysius here 1
and elsewhere forbid the squandering among profane men of the most secret mysteries of theology, lest defect of judgment or excess

nes inde concipiant vel res dignas veneratione derideant. Profanos vero nominat philosophos exceptis Platonicis penes omnes quia nihil altius de Deo cogitaverunt quam quod summus Deus sit mens quedam et essentia prima; nec mirum illud Platonicorum inventum capere potuerunt, ipsum scilicet unum atque bonum esse toto primoque ente intellectuque superius, idque rectius rerum principium nominari. Profanissimos denique iudicat eosdem quos et Plato Epicureos scilicet atque similes, qui nisi quod ipsi pugno stringere possint esse nihil putant. Atque ubi Deum describere compelluntur, ex rebus quibusdam passionibusque corporeis[10] imaginabilibusque componunt.

2 Esse vero unum ipsum atque bonum ente superius una cum Dionysio ceterisque Platonicis et in superioribus significavimus: et ita hic breviter confirmamus. Latius enim hec in *Theologia* nostra et commentariis in Plotinum iam tractavimus.

3 Ratio formalis entis ratioque unius diversa est.[11] Nam enti quidem opponitur non ens, uni vero opponitur multitudo. Quemadmodum igitur multitudo differt a nihilo, ita unum differens est ab ente. De firmitate vero rationis huius agimus in *Parmenide*.[12] Item entis natura[13] multitudinem intus accipere non repugnat, unius vero natura[14] repugnat.

4 Differant[15] igitur inter se dicet quispiam, utrum vero superius? Primo quidem paria[16] esse non possunt, ne forte binarius quidam numerus ex his pariter coniugatis conficiatur. Atque ita[17] super eiusmodi binarium unitas iterum sit querenda. Preterea duo

of pride spur them to conceive of false and vain opinions, or to mock at things worthy rather of veneration. But, with the Platonists being the exception, Dionysius brands as profane almost all those philosophers who have supposed nothing higher about God than that the highest god is a certain mind, a prime essence. Nor have they been able to understand that wonderful discovery of the Platonists, namely that the One and the Good itself is higher than prime being in its totality and higher than intellect, and that it is named more correctly the principle of things. Finally, he regards the same men as Plato regarded as the most profane of all: the Epicureans and suchlike, who, unless they can hold something firmly in their grip, suppose it is nothing. And when they are compelled to describe God, they assemble [Him] from various objects and from corporeal passions and things [merely] imaginable.

That the One and Good itself is superior to being, we signified in the above, along with Dionysius and the rest of the Platonists, and so here we confirm it briefly. For we have treated of it at greater length in our *Theology*[14] and in our commentaries on Plotinus.[15] 2

The rational principle of being and that of the One are different. For non-being is opposed to being, and the many are opposed to the One. Hence, just as the many are different from nothing, so the One is different from being. We treat of the unchanging nature of this rational principle in the *Parmenides*.[16] Likewise, the nature of being does not reject accepting the many into itself, but the nature of the One does reject it. 3

So they differ among themselves, someone will say. But which of them is superior? In the first place they cannot be equal, lest perchance from the two equally conjoined a certain binary number would emerge. Thus we are forced to look again for some unity prior to such a binary. Two particulars, moreover, would 4

quedam forent aeque principia rerum cessaretque communio in rebus et ordo. Non ergo sunt aequalia.

5 Nec rursum ens est superius uno, alioquin ens quidem non foret unius particeps; essetque sic vel multitudo prorsus infinita vel nihilum, unum vero velut inferius particeps ipsius entis evaderet, statimque amissa simplicitate puram similiter perderet unitatem. Est igitur unum ipsum excelsius ente. Quapropter unum quidem simpliciter nominare licet, dicere vero unum esse re vera non licet. Indulgendum tamen est humani sermonis inopie.

6 Preterea non appellamus entia, nisi que formas, habitus, actiones possident. Unum vero dicimus non solum eiusmodi aliquid ut puta visum unum unumque auditum, verum etiam privationes[18] habituum velut unam cecitatem unamque surditatem unumque simpliciter habitum ac privationem pariter unam. Unum igitur ente latius superiusque censendum.

7 Denique participatio unitatis ad privationem materiamque primam usque protenditur. Neque tamen entis hucusque participatio. Nempe cum esse per formam distribuatur, materia prima privatioque quatenus cadit a forma eatenus ab essentia labitur. Neque tamen pariter ab unitate degenerat; nam propter singularem[19] ab aliisque secretam informitatem ferme[20] non minus una materia dicitur, quam res formata dici soleat una, quamvis ob defectum forme materia minime nuncupetur essentia. Cum igitur participatio imperiumque unius amplius sit entis imperio, merito unum excelsius ente conicimus.

8 Similiterque bonum. Nam materia propter potentiam appetitumque ad bonum, et necessitatem eius in universo, appellationem

be equally the universal principles, and [consequently] union and order in things would cease. Hence they are not equal.

Nor again is being superior to the One, otherwise being would not be a participant of the One; and in this event either an utterly infinite many would exist, or there would be nothing; and the One as inferior would emerge as a participant of being itself; and, with its simplicity lost, it would likewise immediately lose its pure unity. Hence the One itself is higher than being; and hence we are allowed to name the One absolutely; but not allowed to say that the One is something as such. Yet we must indulge the inadequacy of human speech. 5

Thus we do not call things "entities" unless they possess forms, dispositions, and acts. But we use "one" to refer not only to enjoying one [act of] seeing, for example, or one of hearing, but also to not enjoying one such, as when we suffer from a blindness or a deafness. We also use "one" to refer to one [bodily] disposition absolutely, and equally so to one loss of it. Hence the One must be judged as more comprehensive than, and higher than being. 6

Finally, participation in unity extends as far even as privation and prime matter. Yet at this furthest point there is no participation in being. Indeed, since being is distributed by way of form, so prime matter or privation, to the extent it falls away from form, also falls away from essence. Yet it does not fall away at the same time from unity. For on account of its singular formlessness (its being set apart from other things), matter is called one matter, no less so almost than a formed thing is usually referred to as one, and even though matter, on account of its not having form, cannot be said to be essence. Therefore, since the empire of the One and participation [in its unity] is more comprehensive than the empire of being, we conjecture, and justly so, that the One is more eminent than being. 7

Similarly with the Good. For matter, on account of its potency and appetite for the Good and the necessity of having it in the 8

boni non, aeque ac munus essentie, amisisse videtur. Bonum summatim atque unum idem penitus esse volumus. Bonum enim sicut unum unione cuncta perficit et conservat, unde quecunque ab unione cadunt a bono similiter et ab essentia delabuntur.

9 Iam vero cum ad principium rerum primum maxime pertineat tum simplicitas et singularitas supereminens, tum virtutis propagatio usque quaque diffusa, merito inde quidem unum, hinc vero nominatur et[21] bonum. Ac revera propter ipsam eminentiam singularem, diffusio quoque universalis adest, atque vicissim ex amplissima largitate singularis agnoscitur eminentia. Que quidem unitas propter propriam sibi summam simplicitatem omnium obtinuit principatum, atque ob providentiam universam beneficum declaravit imperium.

: IX :

Marsilius:
Confirmatio quod bonum sit super essentiam, vitam, intelligentiam. Et quomodo fruamur bono perfectius quam simpliciter intelligendo.

1 Ipsum bonum esse superius ente in superioribus quoque diximus. Simili ratione esse prestantius vita confirmari potest, quoniam vita[22] per se nulli sufficit nisi gratia boni. Non enim vivere simpliciter optant, sed bene vivere; immo et vitam omni bono totaque boni spe destitutam negligunt atque reiciunt.

universe, does not appear to have lost the designation of good in the way it has lost the gift of essence. In sum, we wish the Good and the One to be absolutely the same. For the Good like the One perfects and preserves all things in union; whence all that fall away from union similarly fall away from the Good and from essence.

Now, since what most pertains to the first principle of things is 9
simplicity and super-eminent singularity, and also the propagation of power scattered everywhere, so on the first count it is justly called the One, but on the second, the Good. And in fact on account of its singular eminence, universal diffusion too is present; and from its most ample abundance in turn, its singular eminence is recognized. Indeed, this Unity, on account of the supreme simplicity proper to itself, has obtained the rule over all; and on account of its universal providence, it has declared its empire a beneficent one.

: IX :

Marsilio:
Confirmation that the Good is above essence, life, and understanding. How we enjoy the Good more perfectly than simply by understanding.

In the above we also said the Good itself is superior to being. For 1
a like reason it can be confirmed that it is more eminent than life, because life in itself suffices for naught unless it be for the sake of goodness. For men do not choose simply to live, but to live well; or rather they neglect and reject life that is destitute of every good and of all hope of good.

2 Eadem ratione bonum intelligentie anteponimus. Quisquis enim ad intelligendum nititur et bonum sibi quiddam optat intelligere, et sperat aliquem ex intellectione profectum; immo nec malum sibi quicquam eligit intelligere, sed latere et oblivisci ne cruciet cognoscentem.

3 Accedit ad hec quod pauca quedam naturaliter obtinent intellectum, omnia vero bonum. Item intellectuales anime non semper intelligentiam affectant, semper vero bonum. Rursus statim ab initio naturali quodam instinctu bonum cupiunt, intelligentiam vero et sapientiam tandem consulta quadam electione. Cum igitur bonum et latius sit quam intelligentia et a pluribus sepiusque optetur, appetituque magis naturali queratur, constat bonum esse superius intellectu.

4 Summatim vero neque essentia, neque vita, neque mens se ipsa contenta est, illa enim ad vitam semper annititur, hec ad mentem, mens ad bonum tum intelligendo, tum volendo. Bonum vero, cum in resolvendo sit ultimum, ad aliud non contendit. Solum ergo se ipso contentum est; solum itaque primum.

5 Sed iuvat per hec iterum Platonico more paulo latius evagari. Essentiam, vitam, intellectum inter se differre patet ex eo quod intellectus quidem paucis, vita vero pluribus, essentia denique quam plurimis adest. Cum vero distinctio hec, tanquam maxime formalis et ordinata, nec ex materia nec fortuna contingat, merito ex quadam distinctione procedit essentie, vite, intelligentie prime; distinctione inquam minore quam in rebus, saltem non[23] formali. Illic igitur nec intellectus, nec vita, nec essentia ex se existit.

For the same reason we put the Good before understanding; for whoever strives to understand chooses to understand something that is good for him, and he also hopes for some profit from intellection. Or rather, he elects not to understand something that is bad for himself, but for the bad to be buried and forgotten, lest it harm the knower. 2

Furthermore, few things by nature possess understanding; but all possess the good. Again, intellectual souls do not always desire understanding, but they always desire the good. Again, from the beginning they immediately yearn for the good by a sort of natural instinct, but yearn for understanding and wisdom [only] eventually and after a kind of deliberated choice. Therefore, since the good is more comprehensive than understanding, and chosen by more things, and chosen more often, and sought after by a more natural appetite, it is agreed that it is superior to intellect. 3

In sum, neither essence, nor life, nor mind is content with itself; for the first always strives for life, and life strives for mind, and mind strives for the good both in understanding and in willing. But the good, since it is the ultimate term in this process of resolution, does not contend for anything else. Hence it alone is content with itself; and it alone therefore is the first. 4

It pleases [us] to wander a little further through these matters, however, again in the Platonic manner. That essence, life, and intellect differ among themselves [in this bodily life] is obvious from the fact that intellect is present to a few, life to many more, and essence finally to the most possible. But since the distinction [here], as being in the main both a formal and an ordered one, does not occur because of matter or by chance, it proceeds, and justly so, from the distinction [there] between prime essence, life, and understanding, though it is a distinction [there] that is less [marked] than it is in things [here] and at all events is not a formal one. Accordingly, intellect, life, and essence [there] do not 5

Intellectus enim vitam exigit quodammodo precedentem, vitaque essentiam. Atque essentia per se imperfecta, dum in vitam intellectumque procedendo perficitur proficitque bono, non ex se ipsa fit melior atque optima, sed ipsius boni supereminentis munere. Quod quidem, cum primum esse dedisset, mox vivere atque deinceps intelligere dedit. Hec igitur essentia, vita, mens prima, per intellectualem formam intus superne perfecta, intelligentiam paucioribus quam vitam impartit, ac vitam paucioribus quam[24] essentiam. Ipsum vero bonum et per ipsam tria hec impertit[25] et per se largitur unicuique bonum. Hec Platonice quidem narrata sint utcunque Christianis placet accipienda.

6 Mirabile profecto est boni ipsius imperium, incredibilem namque facilitatem cum immensa potestate coniungit. Cum enim infinitate possit omnia prorsus impellere, vim infert nulli. Omnia vel minima queque quasi persuasione quadam occulta facile ducit; movetque ultro moveri volentia. Cumque nihil res omnes velint suapte natura nisi bonum, nullius imperium magis voluntarium et clementius et suavius est quam boni.

7 Hinc efficitur ut potentiam quidem et sapientiam infinitam possimus odisse, bonitatem vero nequaquam. Cui enim propius[26] naturaliter amor est, inde procul exulat[27] odium. Quonam igitur tandem bonum consecuturi sumus? Non quidem intellectu bonum intellectu superius consequemur, sicut neque intelligibile sensu. Sed eadem ipsa occulta natura tandem attingemus ipsum bonum, intellectu iam vacante, qua naturaliter ab initio, et ante et preter intelligentiam, assidue querebamus et querimus.

exist of themselves. For intellect demands that life should precede it in a way, and life demands that essence should precede it; and essence, imperfect in itself, when it is perfected by proceeding into life and into intellect and profits from the good, is not of itself made better or best, but is made so by the gift of the supereminent Good. And this gift, as soon as it has bestowed being, then bestows living and in turn understanding. So this essence, life, and prime mind—having been supernally perfected internally through [its own] intellectual form—imparts understanding to fewer than it imparts life, and life to fewer than it imparts essence. But the Good itself both by way of the [prime mind] imparts these three gifts and by way of itself bestows the good on each thing.[17] May these matters which have been related in a Platonic manner be accepted in whatever way seems fit to Christians.

Certainly the empire of the Good is wonderful, for it combines 6
incredible ease with measureless power. Since it can impel all things by means of its infinity, it coerces none of them. It easily leads all things, even the smallest, by a sort of secret persuasion; and it moves those wishing to be moved of their own accord. And since all things of their own nature wish for nothing except the good, the empire of none is more voluntary and gentler and sweeter than the empire of the Good.

Hence it is that we have the ability to hate power, for instance, 7
and hate infinite wisdom but not to hate goodness; for love is naturally drawn to what is closer and sends hatred away into distant banishment. With what then are we going eventually to pursue the Good? We will not pursue the Good, which is higher than intellect, with the intellect, just as we will not pursue the intelligible with the senses. But we will eventually pursue the Good, and now that the intellect is void of content, with the very same nature hidden in ourselves with which we were, from the beginning and before and beyond understanding, naturally and continually

Quemadmodum qua levitate ignis petit lune concavum eadem attingit et possidet. Non erit igitur perfecta possessio boni quasi quedam immaginaria consecutio, qualis fieri solet cognitione, sed substantialis, et intima per unitatem anime facta intellectu superiorem prestantioremque essentia.[28] Verum cum preter intelligentiam fruitio tandem perficiatur, merito nec qualis futura sit exprimi nobis ullo modo potest, gustari tamen interim amore et gaudio quodam inextimabili, quo denique non vacante sicut intelligentia sed crescente absolvitur possessio boni. Que quidem sicut amore quesita est assidue, ita tribuitur et amori. Hinc Apostolus Paulus scientiam nostram in patria desinere inquit, charitatem vero nequaquam.

: X :

Dionysius:
Profani sunt qui Deum super essentiam
et intellectum esse non putant;
profanissimi qui Deum ex essentia deteriore
confingunt et imaginatione querunt.

Hec autem cave nequis profanus audiat. Eos autem sic appello, qui occupati duntaxat in his que sunt atque entia nominantur, nihil excelsius entibus (ut ita dixerim) super essentialiter esse putant.

seeking the Good, and with which we are seeking it still. Similarly, fire seeks for the concave of the moon impelled by the same levity with which it attains and possesses it. So perfect possession of the Good will be not a sort of possession by way of images—the kind it customarily is with cognition—but rather a substantial possession, made innermost through the soul's unity, which is higher than intellect and more eminent than essence. In truth, since enjoyment is eventually perfected beyond understanding, we cannot in any manner express what it is going to be like; and justly so. Yet it can be tasted in the meantime in love and in a sort of inestimable joy, a joy eventually which does not empty out like understanding but rather waxes still, until it is brought to completion in the possession of the Good. As possession was sought continually with love, so is it bestowed with love. Hence the Apostle Paul says that in our native land our knowledge ceases, but our love never does.[18]

: X :

Dionysius:
The profane are those who do not believe
that God is above essence and intellect.
The most profane are those who use an inferior essence
to depict God and who seek Him only with their imagination.

Take care that no profane man gets to hear these mysteries; and by profane I mean those who, being preoccupied only with the things which exist [here] and are called entities, think that nothing more excellent than entities exists as it were super-essentially. Rather,

Sed arbitrantur cognitione sibi propria illum apprehendere 'qui[29] tenebras posuit latibulum suum.' Iam vero si hos divina mysteria supereminent, quidnam de illis quispiam dixerit, qui longe profaniores suppremam illam omnium causam ex infimis quoque rebus effingunt nihilque hanc antecellere putant impia simulachra vel imaginamenta variis formis a se conficta?

: XI :

Marsilius: Quomodo fiant affirmationes omnium negationesque de Deo, atque de materia prima.

1 Duo quedam potissima de rerum principio communiter cogitamus: unum quidem quemadmodum omnia inde profluunt semperque dependent; alterum vero quemadmodum ipsum interim est ab omnibus eminentissime segregatum. Prima igitur ratione omnia que divinitus effecta sunt, quatenus inde videntur egredi, de Deo possumus affirmare; quasi non inde venire potuerint, nisi prius illic extiterint. Sic Deum esse affirmabis essentiam, substantiam, vitam, intellectum, animam, naturam, celum, elementa, stellas, item formasque rerum ubique formosas. Sed ratione secunda negare rursum singula de Deo debemus. Quo enim pacto est aliquid eorum que fecit, siquidem est ab eis interim mirabiliter segregatum?

2 Est autem tutior veriorque negatio rerum quam affirmatio circa Deum, quoniam longe plus est quod ipsius Dei separatum est a

they believe that they apprehend God by way of a cognition proper to themselves — God "who has established the shadows as His secret place."[19] If the divine mysteries far surpass these profane men, however, what would anyone say about those others, who, being even more profane, resort to the lowest things in order to imagine that supreme cause of all, and who suppose that this cause is not superior in any way to the impious images and fantasies invented by themselves in various forms?

: XI :

Marsilio: In what way we should affirm and deny all things of God, and on prime matter.

We commonly suppose two most important things about the universal principle: just as all things in the first place flow from it and always depend on it, so secondly it is itself removed meanwhile from all things in its supreme eminence. For the first reason, therefore, all things which have been divinely made, insofar as they seem to issue from God, we can take and affirm about Him: it is as if they could not have come from Him unless they first existed there in Him. Thus we affirm God is essence, substance, life, intellect, soul, nature, the heavens, the elements, the stars, and the comely forms of things everywhere. For the second reason, however, we have in turn to deny singulars of God. For in what way does something partake of the things it has itself made, seeing that in the meantime it is marvelously separated from them? 1

But the negation of things with regard to God is safer and more true than the affirmation of them, because, with God Himself, 2

rebus quam quod rebus est quasi communicatum; hoc enim finitum est omnino, illud autem prorsus immensum. Denique mentiri facilius affirmando possumus quam negando, siquidem affirmatio ad intelligentie nostre limites finire videtur, quod incomparabiliter est immensum.

3 Solet apud nos negatio affirmationi sic opponi ut nequeat simul utraque circa idem esse vera. Ubi enim dixeris, 'Anima vel corpus est substantia,' non licet dicere vicissim non esse substantiam. Divina vero unitas est tam efficax ut contraria etiam inter se in unum in se conciliet. Cumque sit positione et affirmatione qualibet eminentior, merito a privatione quavis positioni opposita mirum in modum separata censetur, presertim quia, cum nullis indigeat, nullis unquam privata putatur. Summatim vero alio sensu affirmamus, alio vero negamus idem circa Deum. Nempe cum dicis, 'Deus est essentia,' Deum intelligis procreare essentiam atque servare. Cum inquis iterum, 'Deus non est essentia,' intelligis Deum non esse hanc ipsam que invenitur vel excogitatur abs te essentie formam.

4 His rationibus Plato noster in *Parmenide* omnia quamvis opposita de ipso uno affirmat pariter atque negat. Poterit quinetiam aliquis[30] circa materiam primam idem ferme facere. Verum quoniam Deus atque materia quasi inter se opposita sunt velut supremum et infimum universi, probabiliter opposito quodam pacto, quecunque inter Deum informemque materiam media cadunt, de utroque possumus affirmare pariter atque negare. Deum igitur dices esse vel habere rem formamque hanc aut illam quoniam facit eam; nec rursus habere quoniam est superior. Materia vero dicetur

that which is separate from things is far more than that which is as it were communicated to them; for the latter is entirely finite, the former utterly beyond measure. Finally, we can speak untruths in affirming more easily than in negating, since affirmation seems confined to the limits of our understanding [whereas] what is measureless is beyond comparison.

With us negation is customarily so opposed to affirmation that 3
affirming and denying something with regard to the same object cannot be simultaneously true. For when you say a soul or body is a substance, you cannot say in turn that it is not a substance. But the divine unity is so effective that within itself it can reconcile even contraries among themselves as one. And since it is far superior to any attribution or affirmation, it is properly deemed, in a wonderful way, separate from any privation opposed to attribution, especially because, since it lacks nothing at all, it is deemed never to be deprived of anything. In sum, in one sense we affirm but in another we deny the very same thing of God. Certainly, when you say, "God is essence," you understand that God procreates and preserves essence. But when you follow this up with, "God is not essence," you mean that God is not a form which has been invented or supposed by you, namely, the form of an essence.

For these reasons, in the *Parmenides* our Plato equally affirms 4
and denies all things, however opposite, of the One itself.[20] Moreover, someone could do almost the same with regard to prime matter. But since God and matter are mutual opposites as it were, being the highest and lowest extremes of the universe, then in all probability, though in an opposite way, we can take anything whatsoever that falls between God and unformed matter and equally affirm and deny it of both. So you will say that God is or has this or that thing or form, since He makes it; and then again that He does not have it because He is superior to it. But you will affirm

rem eandem habere vel esse propterea quod eam patitur; rursumque negabitur quia sit inferior.

: XII :

Dionysius: *Affirmare omnia de Deo decet rursusque negare, sed negatio tutior est et verior quam affirmatio.*

Debemus sane omnes rerum positiones affirmare de Deo, tanquam de omnium causa, vicissimque potiori quadam ratione easdem omnes de Deo negare tanquam cunctis excelsiore. Neque vero putandum est negationes eiusmodi affirmationibus repugnare, sed ipsam universi causam, que omni non solum ablatione sed etiam positione altior est, longe prius privationes omnes exsuperare.

: XIII :

Marsilius: *Quomodo Deus apparet in silentio, et post transitum summitatum, et in caligine.*

1 Mens circa Deum tres (ut videtur) gradus agit: in primo verbis quam plurimis utitur, in secundo paucis, in tertio nullis. Quam plurimis inquam, ubi quotcunque obcurrunt de Deo affirmat pariter atque negat, paribus quidem verbis, sed ratione diversa. Paucis

that matter has or is this same thing because it receives it [passively]; in turn you will deny that matter has this same thing because matter is inferior to it.

: XII :

Dionysius:
It is proper to affirm all things of God and then to deny them, but negation is safer and more true than affirmation.

We ought to affirm of God all that can be posited of things, God being the cause of all; and in turn with even better reason we ought to deny of God all these same attributes, God being more excellent than all things. We must not suppose that such negations are inconsistent with affirmations, however, but that the cause itself of the universe, which is higher not only than all subtraction but also than attribution, far precedes and excels all privations.

: XIII :

Marsilio:
In what way God appears in silence, after the transit of [three] summits, and in darkness.

In contemplating God, it seems mind acts on three levels: in the 1
first it uses as many words as possible, in the second as few, in the third none at all. It uses as many words as possible I say (however many suggest themselves), when it affirms and equally denies of God by calling upon like words but for a different reason. It uses

autem ubi relationibus utitur, referendo videlicet res ad Deum tanquam ad principium, finem, medium conservantem, convertentem, perficientem. Nullis autem, quando nec ulterius res ad Deum refert, neque vicissim; neque negat quicquam; neque dependens a Deo aliquid Deo quodammodo reddit affirmans. Sed ipsum Deum mox affirmatura, sermonem rumpit intimum, siletque protinus, ne affirmando finiens insolenter reportet pro infinito finitum.

2 Tunc igitur si quatenus sermo remittitur eatenus intenditur amor boni, statim (ut diximus) in hoc ipso incendio penes bonum effulget boni lumen spiratque bonum.

3 Oportet vero animam huc accessuram tres saltem (ut ita[31] dixerim) summitates penitus transcendisse, scilicet corpoream, animalem, intellectualem. Summitatem quidem corpoream cogitamus ubi celum fingitur quasi novum, tanto pulchrius hoc celo, quanto celum hoc est terra formosius. Animalem vero ubi in una anima confingitur omnis anima et quelibet exuberans intellectu. Intellectualem denique siquando intellectum excogitamus sic omniformem ut omnes formas omnesque preferat intellectus. Ultra summitates eiusmodi extat ipsum bonum, tanquam ultra sonos verbaque et lumina prius in mente patentia. Habitare vero dicitur in caligine, quoniam, cum primum nihil amplius ex his apparet quasi obrutis iam caligine, apparet bonum—his tanto saltem clarius, quanto meridiana lux profunda nocte fulgentior.

as few words as possible, however, when it uses relationships, that is, the ways things refer to God as to their principle, their end, and their conserving, converting, and perfecting mean. Mind uses no words at all, however, when it no longer refers things to God, or the reverse; and no longer denies anything; and no longer restores to God, in affirmation as it were, anything that depends on Him. Rather, on the point of affirming God Himself, mind cuts off inner articulation and suddenly falls silent, lest, in ending with an affirmation, it might insolently substitute the finite for the infinite.

Therefore, if the more speech is remitted, the more [our] love 2
of the Good is intensified, then immediately (as we said), in this very fire, in the Good's presence, there shines out the light of the Good; and it breathes forth the Good.

But the soul which is about to approach the Good has to have 3
climbed to the top of at least three summits as it were: the corporeal, the animate, and the intellectual. We are thinking of the corporeal summit when we imagine a new sky, so to speak, that is more beautiful than this sky in the same measure that this sky is more beautiful than the earth. We are thinking of the animate summit when in one soul is imagined every soul, any soul that is abounding with intellect. Finally, we are thinking of the intellectual summit whenever we think of the intellect as being so omniform that it displays all forms and all intellects. Beyond such summits exists the Good itself, as if beyond the sounds and words and lights that were evident earlier in the mind.[21] But the Good is said to live in darkness, because, as soon as nothing further appears from these [sounds and words and lights] which are now buried as it were in darkness, then the Good appears. But its radiance eclipses theirs as the noonday light is more dazzling than the depths of the night.

: XIV :

Dionysius:
Sermo de Deo tum plurimus rite, tum paucissimus, tum denique nullus[32] *haberi potest. Deus super essentiam et intelligentiam habitat.*

Hac igitur ratione divinus Bartholomeus ait theologiam esse plurimam atque paucissimam, ipsumque evangelium esse tum latum magnumque tum concisum. Mihi quidem mirifice intellexisse videtur eum qui circa bonam omnium causam versatur, rite posse tum multis verbis uti, tum etiam paucis, tum denique nullis, quippe cum penes eam et verbum et intelligentia cesset. Propterea quod quadam super essentiam ratione omnia supereminet. Solisque illis sublato velamine reveraque[33] fulget quicunque omnia non solum impura sed etiam pura transilierunt, omnemque omnium sanctorum culminum ascensum iam transcenderunt; et cuncta divina lumina et sonos sermonesque celestes deseruerunt, atque eam protinus caliginem subiere ubi ille revera est, ut sacra tradunt eloquia, qui omnibus est excelsior.

: XIV :

Dionysius:
We cannot talk about God, whether we use the most words, or, still better, the fewest, or none at all. God dwells above essence and understanding.

For this reason, therefore, the divine Bartholomew says that theology is the greatest and the least,[22] and that the Gospel itself is both broad and deep and yet concise. To me it seems that he marvelously understood that the person who is concerned with the good and universal cause can duly call upon many words, or few, or eventually none at all, since in the cause's presence word and understanding alike cease. So with a super-essential reason the cause excels all things. With the veil cast aside, it truly shines forth to those alone who have vaulted over all impure and even pure things, and in their ascent have already passed beyond all [three] holy summits, and left behind all the divine lights and sounds and celestial words. And forthwith [he says] they plunge into that darkness where the One truly dwells, the One who is more eminent than all, as the sacred Scriptures tell us.[23]

: XV :

Marsilius:
Quomodo purgetur animus,
per quot gradus ascendat ad Deum.
Quomodo Deus super intellectum et intelligibile habitet—
que sit Platonicorum opinio.

1 Animus, divini montis fastigium ascensurus, in primis cunctis exhortationibus amore solo primi boni est inflammandus. Et quoniam superni caloris officium est ab inferioribus nos purgare, amoris divini flagrantia purgandus est, tum ab affectibus, tum ab imaginationibus singularum[34] rerum corporearum. Tum vero monstrante disciplina, eodemque interim amore duce, traducendus est ad contemplandas formas a corporibus separabiles atque separatas, id est ad intellectuales animas et angelicos intellectus. Sol namque divinus in animis quidem fulget velut in luna, in angelis autem velut in stellis.

2 Utrobique igitur mentis oculus ad solem impotens facilius tanquam familiaria lumina contuetur, quibus conspiciendis, et solem inde divinum auguratur, et aciem ad idem vel intuendum vel quomodocunque percipiendum assuefacit.

3 Hactenus exhortatio quidem purgavit sed disciplina monstravit. Amor autem et emundavit et hucusque perduxit. Amor igitur cum amato tandem feliciter copulabit amantem; in ea videlicet nube, ubi, postquam naturales oculi sub exuberante lumine caligarunt, bonum ipsum benefica gratia illuxit et adspiravit amanti.

: XV :

Marsilio:
How the rational soul is purged.
How many steps the soul needs to ascend to God.
How God dwells above intellect and the intelligible,
this being the view of the Platonists.[24]

The rational soul, which is about to climb to the peak of the divine mountain, must in the first place, as we are everywhere exhorted, be set on fire by love alone of the first Good. And since the office of supernal heat is to purge us of things inferior, the soul by the blazing of divine love must be purged from its appetites for individual corporeal things and its imaginings of them. Then, with learning showing [the way] and guided in the meantime by this same love, the soul must be transported to the contemplation of forms, both those [potentially] separable from bodies and those [actually] separated — to contemplate, in other words, intellectual souls and angelic intellects. For the divine Sun shines in souls as in the moon, but shines in the angels as in the stars. 1

So in both cases the mind's eye, being unable to gaze directly up at the sun, gazes more easily at what are, as it were, familiar lights. In seeing these, it forms conjectures from them about the divine Sun, and it trains its inner apprehension either to look up at this same Sun or to perceive it in some other way. 2

Exhortation has purged [us] thus far, and learning has shown us; but love has purified us and guided us hither. Therefore, love will happily unite the lover at last with the beloved in that cloud,[25] wherein, after the natural eyes have been dimmed because of the dazzling light, the Good itself with beneficent grace has illumined and inspired the lover. 3

4 In hoc autem ascensu actiones ac vires animarum et angelorum in primis obcurrunt, mox vero substantiae: illas sane sub nomine vocum, has autem sub appellatione luminum Moses ipse significat. Annuit etiam purgatis interdum animis intellectuales notiones ob mirabilem efficaciam usque ad purissimos sensus, visum scilicet et auditum, per imaginationem[35] se transferre, quasi sub forma quadam luminum atque vocum.

5 Proinde, ubi Dionysius ait ipsum bonum super summitates intelligibiles locorum suorum incedere, Plotinus et Iamblichus Proclusque dicent intelligibile quidem intellectui velut inde formabili preferendum, immensum vero bonum anteponendum intelligibili proportionem quandam cum intelligentia subeunti.

6 Mitto in presentia distinctionem illam Proculi ubi summa post primum numina vocat intelligibilia, infima vero, sed interim mundo superiora, potius intellectualia nuncupat formanda videlicet a supernis. Sed media utriusque appellationis mixtione cognominat. Missas etiam facio tres illas apud Proculum substantias, triaque sub primo principia: essentiam, vitam, mentem. Probabilius cum Plotino tria hec apud superos ratione quadam inter se differre dicemus potius quam substantia. Sed Plotinus quidem unum hoc sub primo constans ex tribus asserit universi principium, videlicet a primo progenitum. Dionysius autem, quem libentissime sequimur, non unum aliquid eiusmodi tanquam principium sub principio collocat, sed divinas Deo mentes subigit ex his

In this ascent the actions and powers of souls and of angels first suggest themselves, and then their substances; and Moses himself signifies under the name of "voices" angelic substances, and under the name of "lights," soul substances.[26] He indicates that, with the souls having been purged in the meanwhile, intellectual notions transfer themselves, because of their wonderful efficacy, down as far as the purest senses, that is, to the sight and hearing; and that they do so via the imagination and under the form as it were of lights and of voices. 4

Consequently, where Dionysius says that the Good itself "advances above the intelligible summits of its places," Plotinus, Iamblichus, and Proclus will say that the intelligible must be put before the intellect (intellect being formable by the intelligible); and that the measureless Good must be put before the intelligible, as the intelligible is subject [still] to a certain proportion with understanding.[27] 5

For the present, I leave aside Proclus' distinction where he calls the highest spirits after the First [i.e., the One] the intelligibles, but the lowest spirits, although they are superior in the meantime to the world, intellectual instead: they are spirits that must be formed by the supernal [i.e., the highest] spirits. He names those spirits that are intermediate, however, by combining the appellation of each group [i.e., intelligible-intellectual].[28] I shall also leave aside the three substances in Proclus,[29] and the three principles under the First, that is, essence, life and understanding. With Plotinus it is more probable that, in the case of the gods, these latter three differ among themselves in terms of their definition rather than of their substance; yet he asserts that the one which is under the First [One], being constituted from the three principles, is the [one] principle of the universe, since it is born from the First.[30] Dionysius, however, whom we are most eager to follow, locates not one such something as a principle under the Principle, but rather takes the divine intellects, who are divinely constituted from these 6

tribus (essentia, vita, intelligentia) divinitus constitutas; mentesque eiusmodi partim intelligibiles partim intellectuales ideo nuncupat, quoniam inde quidem propter luminis abundantiam capaci cuilibet largissime sese offerunt; hinc autem ob serenissimam perspicaciam lumen quodlibet veritatis ipsius facillime diaphani more suscipiunt.

7 Denique bonum ipsum regionem intelligibilem supereminet, sive regionem eiusmodi platonico more primum ipsum intelligibile nomines, intelligibilium specierum omnium fontem inter se formaliter differentium; sive substantiam quamlibet separatam perspicacem pariter atque lucentem.

: XVI :

Marsilius:
Confirmatio superiorum et quomodo fruamur Deo per modum quendam intellectu prestantiorem.

1 Hoc superceleste celum stellarum suarum id est intelligibilium formarum plenum sol divinus habitat quidem; stelle enim solis lumine lucent, sed mirabiliter supereminet. Celum hoc intellectu videre potes, solem vero non substinet intellectus, qui et in oppositum te deducit; actio enim tum rationis quasi mobilis, tum mentis quasi multiplex et finita[36] ad aliquid mobile, multiplex, finitum,[37] quod principio est oppositum te retorquet. Actio igitur eiusmodi, cum primum intelligibilia per eam consequutus fueris,[38] posthabenda est. Hucusque tantum confert, ulterius impedit,

three—that is, from essence, life, and understanding—and subjects them all to God; and therefore calls such intellects partly intelligible, partly intellectual. This is because on the one hand, on account of the abundance of [their] light, they present themselves most copiously to whosoever is capable of receiving them. On the other hand, on account of [their] most serene clarity, they sustain most easily, and in the manner of something transparent, whatsoever light emanates from the Truth itself.

Finally, the Good itself is more eminent than the intelligible 7
region, whether you call such a region in the Platonic manner the first intelligible itself, which is the fountain of all the intelligible species that differ formally among themselves; or call such a region any substance that is separate, and as transparent as it is shining.

: XVI :

Marsilio:
Confirmation of the above and how we may enjoy God using a more eminent way than the intellect.

The Divine Sun dwells in this supercelestial heaven full of its 1
stars,[31] that is, full of its intelligible forms (for these stars shine with the light of this Sun, but the Sun is marvelously preeminent). You can see this [supercelestial] heaven with the intellect, but the Sun itself the intellect does not sustain; for it leads you away toward what is opposite. For the action both of the reason, which is mobile as it were, and of the mind which is as it were multiple and finite, wrenches you away toward something mobile, multiple, [and] finite, which is opposite to the principle. Such [mental] action, therefore, as soon as you have attained the intelligibles through mind, must be set aside. Up to this point it has

quemadmodum imaginationis usus ad intelligentie principia confert, ulterius obstat.

2 Confirmatur hoc etiam per platonicum illud. 'Sol conspicuus in mundo nobis est imago boni. Sol quidem tam visus generat quam videnda et suscitat ad agendum, cumque oculis videnda coniungit. Similiter ipsum bonum ad intellectus omnes intelligibiliaque se habet.' Hec Plato. Cum igitur intellectus non tam sua quam divina virtute consequatur res intelligendas, consequens est[39] ut nulla penitus facultate sua bonum ipsum assequi possit. Igitur Deo frui non est ad Deum agere, sed potius agi Deo. Non est aliquid per se haurire, sed aliunde prorsus impleri. Non est per intellectum versari circa bonum sed amore transferri atque ipsa unitate nostra intellectu superiore ipsi uni bonoque penitus copulari. Ubi sane animus omnem prorsus actionem affectionemque et ad alia et ad se ipsum iam deposuit. Exuit et formam suam, induit iam divinam, ut etiam Plotinus ait. Iamque sic agit ut Deus sicut aurum ignitum in Apocalypsi celebratum agit ut ignis, et animatum corpus ut anima, atque anima sublimis intellectu formata tanquam intellectus agit. Intellectus igitur reformatus in Deum agit denique tanquam Deus.

helped, but further than this it hinders, just as the use of the imagination helps us to the [various] beginnings of understanding, but subsequently hinders us.

This is also confirmed by way of that Platonic [formulation]: 2
"The sun that is visible in our world is for us the image of the Good. The sun generates both sight and the things to be seen and rouses to action and joins visible things to the eyes. The Good itself operates similarly with regard to all the intellects and the intelligibles."[32] This is what Plato says. Accordingly, since the intellect attains what it needs to understand not so much by its own power as by divine power, consequently it cannot attain the Good itself with any of its own powers at all. So to enjoy God is not to act with regard to God, but rather to be acted upon by God. It is not for us to quaff down anything ourselves; but rather we are filled to the brim from another source. It is not for us to engage with the Good by way of the intellect, but rather to be transported thither by love; and with our unity itself, which is higher than the intellect, to be joined utterly to the One and the Good. And there indeed the rational soul has already laid aside absolutely all action and desire with regard both to others and to itself: it has doffed its own form and already donned its divine form, as Plotinus also says.[33] And now it acts as God, just as the gold "tried in the fire" and celebrated in the Apocalypse acts as the fire;[34] and as the ensouled body acts as the soul; and as the sublime soul formed by the intellect acts as the intellect. Thus the intellect reformed into God acts at last as God does.

: XVII :

Dionysius:
Ascensus ad Deum per purgationem animi atque per transitum intelligibilium specierum. Fruitio Dei per aliquid intellectu prestantius.

1 Iure igitur divinus Moses divinitus admonetur primo quidem ut mundetur ipse, rursumque ut se separet ab immundis. Atque post omnem expiationem buccinarum clangores varios audit, cernitque lumina multa puros atque multiplices radios diffundentia. Post hec a turbis vulgaribus segregatur. Atque cum selectis sacerdotibus ad divinarum ascensionum fastigia sese confert. Ibique non cum ipso quidem Deo commertium habet nec ipsum cernit (non enim est visibilis) sed locum potius ubi stetit.

2 Hoc autem, ut reor, significat divinissima et suprema queque visibilium atque intelligibilium esse rationes quasdam suppositorias significasque[40] eorum que subiecta sunt omnia transcendenti Deo, per que Dei presentia omnem intelligentiam superans demonstratur,[41] super intelligibiles sanctissimorum ipsius locorum summitates incedens, tunc igitur, ipsa quoque visibilia et videntia intelligibiliave[42] dimittens, ipsam ingreditur ignorationis mysticam revera caliginem. Ubi omnes cognitorias perceptiones excutit. Atque in eo qui tactum penitus visumque refugit iam consistit; totusque evadit ipsius qui omnia supereminet. Tunc sane nec sui iuris est, nec est alterius, sed ipsi, qui penitus est incognitus,

: XVII :

Dionysius: The ascent to God by way of the rational soul's purgation and its transit across the intelligible species. Enjoyment of God is via something more eminent than the intellect.

As is meet therefore, the divine Moses is divinely admonished first to cleanse himself and then to separate himself from things unclean. And after all expiation, he hears the mingled brayings of the trumpets; and he sees a multitude of lights sending forth their pure and manifold rays. After this he is separated from the throngs of people and betakes himself with chosen priests to the uppermost slopes of the divine ascents. But there he does not commune directly with God Himself; for he does not see God, God being invisible, but sees instead "the place" where God stood.[35] 1

This place, I believe, signifies that the most divine and highest of visible and intelligible things are the rational principles, those that underlie and stand for all things which are subject to God in His transcendence. Through them Moses proves that God's presence is beyond all understanding, and he advances beyond the intelligible summits of the most sacred places of God. Then, forsaking things visible and those who see them, and abandoning things intelligible, Moses enters into the truly mystical darkness itself of not-knowing. There he casts aside all cognitive perceptions, and stands steadfast now in Him who totally eschews touch and sight. And Moses becomes wholly of Him who exceeds all things. Then indeed he is not subject to his own law or to another's, but is united to God who is utterly unknown, united by the 2

cognitionis omnis vacatione per aliquid cognitione prestantius, est unitus. Ex eo enim quod cognoscit nihil, intelligentiam transcendendo[43] cognoscit.

: XVIII :

Marsilius:
Quomodo auferendo gradatim ascendamus ad Deum tum in homine, tum in mundo toto, tum in sole.

1 Si fecit Deus hominem ad imaginem suam, certe est in homine statua Dei quamvis additamentis abscondita. Primo igitur separa corpus ab anima; secundo ab eadem corporeas passiones; tertio imaginationes a ratione; quarto rationales discursiones ab intellectu; quinto intellectualem multiformitatem ab ipsa anime unitate; sexto ab hac unitate animalem intellectualemque conditionem. In septimo gradu (ut arbitror) conquiesces, invenies enim ipsam simpliciter unitatem, id est[44] Deum, sub tali quadam unitate latentem.

2 Mundum quoque Deus statuam suam fabricatus est sed velaminibus multis opertam. Subtrahe primo materiam, relinque cetera. Iam habes ubique celum cui multi materiam ademerunt. Deme rursum celesti huic mundo dimensionem, serva formas omnes motusque[45] formarum, nactus eris animam universam. Tolle si placet motus formis omnino servatis, universum mox possides intellectum. Sed huic auferto divisos inter se velut in celo formarum radios. Accipe lumen ipsum in se principium radiorum, nec

emptying of all cognition by way of something more eminent than cognition. For the fact that Moses knows nothing, he knows by transcending understanding.

: XVIII :

Marsilio:
How we ascend to God by successive subtractions, first in the case of man, then of the world, and then of the sun.

1 If God made man in His own image, certainly God's statue is in man, although concealed by accretions.[36] First, therefore, separate body from the soul; second, separate bodily passions from this same soul; third, separate the images of the soul's imagination from the reason; fourth, separate the reason's discursive arguments from the intellect; fifth, separate the intellect's multiformity from the soul's unity itself; and sixth, separate the condition even of being soul or being intellect from this unity. You will come to rest (I think) on the seventh step. For you will find the absolute Unity itself, that is, God, lying concealed under [the soul's] particular unity.

2 God has made the world too His statue, but it is enveloped in many veils. First subtract matter and keep what is left. You now have the heavens everywhere from which many have subtracted matter. Next take away dimension from this celestial world [but] save all the forms and the motions of forms; and you will have acquired the universal soul. Take away, if you will, all the motions, leaving only the forms. Straightway you will possess universal intellect. But subtract from this the rays of the forms, divided as the rays are among themselves in heaven; and accept light in itself [as] the principle of the rays but as no [longer] dispersed via the rays

dispersum per radios nec certis radiorum speciebus determinatum, sed absolutissimum et simplicissimum et immensum. Quod et ipsum bonum est omni semper intelligentie voluntatisque conatu quesitum. Hac igitur ratione gradatim auferendo, Deum ipsum primo ex mundo parvo, rursumque ex mundo magno feliciter invenisti.

3 Tertio: forsan invenies similiter ex mundo solari. Cogita colores omnes lucesque rerum: ita ex sole profluere semperque servari ut nihil ferme sint aliud quam solis ipsius lumen sub rebus occultum. Quamobrem si abstuleris[46] a coloribus ubique terrenis terrenam crassamque mixturam, a coloribus vero nubium quandoque fulgentium aqueum terreumque[47] fumum, a lucibus tandem igneis stellaribusque mixturam igneam proprietatemque stellarem, atque, his ita sublatis, lucem pro viribus conservaveris, solem iam habebis.

4 Ubi si molem proprietatemque solis ademeris, luce servata, reportabis ex hoc sole Deum, solis revera solem, certis inde remotis limitibus per immensum regnantem ubique totum. Sic enim beneficum[48] primi boni lumen rebus omnibus inde bonis et pulchris et appetendis est infusum, quemadmodum solis lumen coloratis omnibus atque lucentibus, necnon similibus ferme gradibus distributum. Sed quomodo per gradus rerum quibusve rationibus ascendatur ad Deum in libro *Epistolarum* secundo, et in *Theologia*, ac libro *De raptu Pauli* ad tertium celum latius disputamus.

and no longer limited to certain species of rays, but light in its utterly absolute and simple immensity. This is the Good itself, the goal always of every attempt of the understanding and the will. For this reason, therefore, by gradually subtracting, haply you will find God Himself, first from the little world [of man], then from the great world.

Third, you will similarly find [God] from the world, perchance, 3
of the sun. Think of all things' colors and lights: they radiate out from the sun and are always preserved in such a way that almost nothing exists other than the sun's light itself hidden under things. Wherefore, if you have subtracted from earthly colors everywhere the earthy and gross mixture, and subtracted the watery and earthy vapor from the colors of the clouds whenever they are ablaze, and subtracted finally the fiery mixture and the starry property from the fiery lights and the stars, and if, with all these subtracted, you have preserved as best you can the light itself—you will now have the sun.

And with the sun, if you have taken away its mass and prop- 4
erty, having preserved the light, you will win God [Himself] from this sun, God who is truly the sun's Sun, reigning everywhere through the whole in its immensity, and thence free from all determined limits. For such a beneficent light of the prime Good has thence been infused in all good, beautiful, and desirable things, as the sun's light is diffused in all things that have light and color, and moreover in similar degrees, or almost so. But how one ascends to God through the universal levels, and for what reasons, we have discussed at greater length in our second book of *Letters*,[37] in the [*Platonic*] *Theology*,[38] and in the book on Paul's rapture to the third heaven.[39]

: XIX :

Dionysius: Quomodo auferendo omnia que sunt procedamus ad Deum. Et contraria ratione auferamus atque ponamus.

1 Hanc nos prelucidam caliginem ingredi precamur atque per visus cognitionisque vacationem videre et nosse quod est visione notitiaque superius.

2 Ex hoc ipso videlicet quod nec videamus nec aliquid cognoscamus. Hoc enim est revera videre ac nosse et eum qui essentia eminentior est modo quodam super essentiam, ex[49] omnium videlicet que[50] sunt ablatione laudare. Quemadmodum qui statuam indigenam fabricant auferentes omnia que circum apposita[51] impediunt perspicuum forme latentis intuitum, solaque ablatione pulchritudinem ipsam in se pandentes occultam.

3 Oportet autem ablationes ut arbitror contra ac positiones celebrare. Positiones enim incohantes a primis ac per media ad ultima descendetes adhibebamus.[52] At in auferendo vicissim a postremis ad prima dispositis gradibus ascendentes omnia tollimus, ut submoto velamine ignorationem illam cognoscamus que sub omnibus cognobilibus[53] in entibus omnibus delitescit; illamque caliginem essentia superiorem perspiciamus que ab universo lumine in his que sunt emicante nobis occulitur.

: XIX :

Dionysius: How by subtracting all things that exist we may proceed to God; and how we may subtract for a contrary reason than we may attribute.

We pray to enter this darkness prior to light, and, through the emptying of sight and cognition, to see and to know what is higher than vision and knowledge. 1

And this is because we cannot see or know anything. For truly to see and to know is this: to praise Him who is more eminent than essence and in a way above essence, by subtracting all things which exist. Similarly people who carve an indwelling statue are those who chip away all that surrounds it and all that impedes the clear sight of the hidden form; and who by subtracting alone uncover the hidden beauty itself in themselves. 2

We must celebrate these subtractions I think in a way contrary to that of attributions. For we have attributed things by commencing with the first and descending via intermediaries to the last. But in subtracting we take away in turn all things from the last and ascend by regular steps to the first, so that, when the veil is withdrawn, we may come to know the unknowingness which lies concealed in all entities under all that is knowable; and perceive that darkness which is higher than essence and which is hidden from us by the universal light shining in things existing here. 3

: XX :

Marsilius: De Trinitate et imagine Trinitatis.

Solem una cum Platone diximus esse conspicuam boni ipsius imaginem. Finge igitur ex intima luce que viget in centro solis tria lumina intrinsecus emicare: primum per altitudinem solis effundi, secundum per latitudinem[54] dilatari, tertium profunda[55] penitus occupare. Ex primo secundum, ex secundo cum primo tertium originem ducere. Esse invicem coniuncta pariter et distincta. Similiter in ipso bono tria quedam benefica lumina sic emicare ut extrinsecus non prosiliant, que una cum pululatione permaneant, ac vicissim pululent permanendo. Atque ipsa germinatione inter se distinguantur; rursusque natura sint unum. Possunt vero lumina quodammodo etiam angelos designare eorumque cum[56] Deo et invicem unionem. Reliqua satis patent.

: XX :

Marsilio:
On the Trinity and the image of the Trinity.

Along with Plato, we have said that the sun is the visible image of the Good itself. So imagine three lights beaming inwardly from the inmost light waxing in the center of the sun: the first light is poured forth through the height of the sun, the second extended through its breadth, and the third occupies wholly its depths. Imagine that the second light comes from the first and that the third takes its origin from the second along with the first, and that they are equally conjunct and distinct in turn. Imagine similarly three particular beneficent lights shining in the Good itself, but not in such a way that they shine out externally. For they remain within in the "budding" stage, and they bud in turn in remaining within; and in this germinating they are distinguished among themselves and yet in nature they are one. But the lights are also able in a way [that is, by way of anticipation] to trace out the angels and their union with God and with each other. The remaining issues are sufficiently clear.

: XXI :

Dionysius:
De bonitate divina, unitate, trinitate, Iesu appellationibus, figurisque divinis.

1 In eo libro quem *De Theologicis Institutionibus* inscripsimus, que sint affirmantis theologie precipua diximus:

2 quomodo divina bonaque natura dicitur unica, quomodo ibidem trinitas; que penes hanc ipsam naturam sit ipsa Patris, que Filii notio; quid significet Spiritus Sancti theologia;

3 qua ratione ex incorporeo individuoque bono intima bonitatis lumina pulularunt; permanentque intus non exeuntia nec discedunt a mansione in ipso et in se ipsis et invicem, quippe cum hec ipsa permansio pullulationem perpetuo comitetur;

4 quo item pacto superior essentia Iesus veram possidet humane nature substantiam, et quecunque alia a sacris litteris demonstrata in eo opere celebravimus.[57]

5 Sed in libro *De divinis nominibus,* quomodo bonus appelletur, quomodo ens, vita, sapientia, potestas, ceteraque eiusmodi ad appellationem divinam scilicet intelligibilem pertinentia. In *Theologia* vero per figuras significativa tractavimus que sint a rebus, que sentiuntur appellationes ad divina translate, que forme divine, que figure, membra, instrumenta, que loca divina, que ornamenta, qui furores, que tristitie, indignationes, ebrietates, crapule, iuramenta,

: XXI :

Dionysius:
On divine Goodness, on Unity, on the Trinity, on the appellations of Jesus, and on divine figures or shapes.

In the book we have entitled *On the Principles of Theology* we have 1
talked about what the preeminent features of affirmative theology are:

how, [that is,] the divine and good nature is said to be one, and 2
how it is a trinity at the same time; and how in this very nature dwells the notion of the Father and of the Son; and what the theology of the Holy Spirit signifies;

and why the inner lights of goodness germinate from an incor- 3
poreal and undivided Good and yet stay within and never issue forth or depart from the state of rest in the Good itself and in themselves in turn (since the state of rest perpetually accompanies their germinating);

likewise in what way, being superior to essence, Jesus possesses 4
the true substance of human nature and all else that has been demonstrated by sacred Scripture and that we have celebrated in the aforementioned book.

But in the book *On Divine Names* [we have discussed] in what 5
way God is called good and in what way is called being, life, wisdom, power, and the other terms pertaining to divine, that is, to intelligible naming. But in [our *Symbolic*] *Theology* (proceeding as it does by way of figures) we have discussed: (1) what may derive from things; (2) what are perceived as appellations transferred to the divine; (3) what are forms divine; (4) what are shapes, members, and instruments; (5) what are divine places; and (6) what are divine ornaments, frenzies, sorrows, angers, bouts of inebriation,

execrationes, somni, experrectiones, et quecunque alie significative theologie figurantis Deum formationes sunt sacra ratione conficte.

: XXII :

Marsilius: De gradibus virium cognoscentium atque rerum cognoscendarum. Et quare sermo de rebus supernis verus brevis esse soleat.

1 Sermo de rebus superioribus vere et pro ipsa natura rerum habitus brevior quam sermo de rebus inferioribus, quod et Plato Plotinusque confirmant, esse debet, quod quidem tum ex viribus cognoscentibus, tum etiam ex rebus cognoscendis asseverari potest. Imaginatio una paucioribusque actibus efficit, quotcunque sensus multi actibusque multis efficiunt. Ratio una quadam universali specie sepe complectitur plurima que per imaginationem formis pluribus singulatim percipiuntur. Intellectus immobili quodam subitoque intuitu conspicit que ratio per varium discursum aucupatur. Et quo sublimior intellectus est, propter efficaciam tum nature tum exemplaris forme, eo paucioribus[58] plura cognoscit et efficit. Sicut enim oculus figuram circularem uno quodam semel intuitu iudicat quam cecus tactus sepius attractando perpendit, sic intellectus omnis se habet ad rationem, rursumque ad intellectum inferiorem superior intellectus.

hangovers, oaths, curses, sleeps, awakenings, and whatsoever other formulations symbolic theology can arrive at for figuring God—formulations that have been deduced by sacred reason.

: XXII :

Marsilio:
On the levels of the knowing powers and of things that must be known. And why true speech about supernal things is usually brief.

Talk about higher things in truth and according to the nature itself 1
of the habit of these things has to be briefer than talk about lower things (and Plato and Plotinus confirm this),[40] because it can be asserted at one time from the knowing powers, at another from the things to be known. Imagination brings about with fewer acts whatever the many senses effect with many acts. Reason often embraces with one universal species the host of things that are perceived by way of the imagination in many forms individually. Intellect sees with a motionless and sudden intuition what reason tries to trap by way of its varied discursiveness; and insofar as intellect is more sublime on account of the effectiveness both of its nature and of its exemplary form, it knows and does many things by way of fewer things. For just as the eye judges in one first glance that a shape is circular—a shape which a blind man has to trace out in a longer time with his sense of touch—so is all intellect with regard to reason, and so again is the higher intellect with regard to the lower intellect.

2 De viribus quidem cognoscentibus hactenus. Res[59] quinetiam cognoscende quanto superiores sunt, tanto gradatim numero quidem pauciores, ampliores vero virtute. Utraque igitur ratione sermo legitimus de rebus supernis brevis est, notio vero ampla, que forte si ampla non fuerit, ut minus saltem mentiaris vel repetas, sermo debet esse brevissimus. Tandem in ipso Deo ad modum intellectu superiore non solum discurrens oratio tam interior quam exterior, sed etiam intelligentia cessat. Verum quod deest intelligentie, amore quodam et quasi gustu[60] et tactu unitateque et gratia compensatur. Sed hec latius una cum Plotino in commentariis in eum iam tractavimus.

: XXIII :

Dionysius:
Sermo de rebus altioribus debet esse brevior.

1 Reor autem te deprehendisse extrema verbis esse prolixiora supremis. Oportebat sane theologicas institutiones explicationemque nominum divinorum breviori quam theologiam significativam sermone tractari. Quatenus enim ad sublimiora contendimus, eatenus sermones ipsis intelligibilium conspectibus contrahuntur. Quemadmodum nunc caliginem illam subeuntes, que superat intellectum, non solum in sermonis brevitatem, sed etiam in silentium omnino vacationemque intelligentie protinus incidemus.

Thus far we have discussed the cognitive powers. Even with 2
things that have to be known, furthermore, to the extent they are higher, so are they by gradation fewer in number but more encompassing in power. Therefore, for both these reasons, legitimate talk about supernal things is brief, whereas the notion is encompassing. If perchance the notion were not encompassing, [then] in order for you to speak less falsely at least, or to be less repetitious, speech must be as brief as possible. At length, in God Himself [who is] wholly superior to intellect, not only does [our] discursive argument cease, both interior and exterior, but so too does [our] understanding. But what is missing in [our] understanding is more than offset by a kind of love, and by tasting as it were and touching, and by a unity and grace. But we have already treated of these matters very extensively along with Plotinus in our commentaries on him.[41]

: XXIII :

Dionysius: Talk about higher things has to be very brief.

I think you have discovered that things at the lowest extreme re- 1
quire more prolixity [in discussing them] than those at the highest. To be sure, it was appropriate to treat of theological principles and to explicate the divine names with fewer words than those needed for symbolic theology.[42] For insofar as we aim at the more sublime things, so does everything we say contract in the very sight of the intelligibles, just as, in submitting now to that darkness which reigns over intellect, we will fall straightway not only into brevity of speech, but into silence even, and into the utter emptying of our understanding.

2 Iam vero illic quidem a supremo ad infima descendens oratio, pro quantitate descensus ad latitudinem descensui congruam gradatim extendebatur. Nunc autem ab inferioribus ad sublime sermo conscendens[61] (pro modo ascensus), paulatim evadit[62] angustior. Itaque post omnem ascensum, obmutescet omnino totusque ineffabili coniungetur.

: XXIV :

Marsilius:
Omnia formam aliquam preferentia affirmari de Deo possunt atque negari. Sed affirmatio quidem a superioribus, negatio autem ab inferioribus incohanda.

1 Deus summus super omnem positionem extat quoniam est bonitas infinita. Non potes ergo aliquid tam bonum adhibere Deo, quin melius aliquid reliquum sit ulterius adhibendum. Est etiam super omnem ablationem, quoniam est unitas, eminentia, simplicitas infinita; immo etiam prima ratione omni est ablatione superior. Quamdiu enim licet aliquid admovere Deo tanquam inde profectum, tamdiu idem et removere fas est tanquam hoc ipso quod est inde non sit illud, est autem sub illo semper, et inde quicquid boni repereris vel inveneris.

2 Proinde verisimile est affirmare de Deo quecunque formam, actionem, ordinem habent. Verisimilius autem affirmare de primo

Speech, in descending from the highest eminence toward the lowest things, was by stages there extended, according to the measure of the descent, to a breadth congruent with that descent. But now, in ascending from lower things back toward the highest eminence, little by little speech becomes more restrained and in accord with the mode of the ascent. At the end of the entire ascent, therefore, it will become entirely mute and be joined wholly to the ineffable. 2

: XXIV :

Marsilio: All things presenting some form can be affirmed and denied of God. But affirmation must begin from higher things, and negation from lower.

God on high exists above all attribution because He is infinite goodness. So you cannot add something as a good to God lest something better remains behind that has to be added further. He is also above all subtraction because He is unity, eminence, and infinite simplicity; or rather, He is higher even than the prime rational principle [and] higher than all subtraction. For as long as it is lawful to add something to God as having proceeded from Him, so long is it lawful also to remove the same addition by virtue of the fact that as it is from [the Good] it is not that Good, but is always under it; and from the Good comes whatever particular good you have ascertained or discovered. 1

Therefore probability affirms of God all those things that have form, action, and order. But greater probability affirms of the First 2

perfectiora quam imperfectiora atque vicissim probabilius imperfectissima queque quam perfectiora negare. Si igitur perfectissima primum affirmaveris, nondum affirmasti sequentia. Itaque sermo reliqua gradatim afferens superfluus iudicari non poterit. Sin autem perfectissima primo negaveris, semel cuncta negasti: frustra iam reliqua negaturus. Quamobrem si omnia deinceps media percurrere rite volueris, superiora quidem affirmabis in primis,[63] vicissimque ante alia recte inferiora negabis.

: XXV :

Dionysius:
Affirmatio rerum de Deo contraria via procedit quam[64] negatio.

Fortasse queres: Quare, cum a primo divinas positiones incohare soleamus, vicissim auferre ab extremis incipiamus? Quoniam videlicet, quando ponimus circa illud quod positionem omnem exsuperat suppositoriam affirmationem, oportet ab eo quod est illi cognatius exordiri. Contra vero quando circa illud auferimus quod ablationem omnem excedit, ab his que longius ab eo distant rite incohamus ablationem. Nonne Deus magis est vita et bonitas quam aer atque lapis? Vicissimque potius non crapulatur nec irascitur quam nec dicitur nec intelligitur.

those things that are more perfect rather than more imperfect. And still greater probability in turn denies those things that are most imperfect rather than those that are more perfect. If then you have affirmed of the First the most perfect things, still you have not yet affirmed what follows upon them; so speech cannot be deemed superfluous when it gradually adduces what follows. On the other hand, if you have denied the most perfect things of the First, you have denied everything once and for all, and it will be pointless for speech to set about denying the rest. Wherefore if you then wish to run correctly through all that is intermediate, you will first affirm higher things, and in turn first deny lower things, and rightly so.

: XXV :

Dionysius: Affirmation of things about God proceeds by a contrary route than negation.

Perchance you will ask, since our custom is to begin from the first when making divine attributions, why instead do we begin from the last when making subtractions? The answer is that when we posit a hypothetical affirmation with regard to that which excels all attribution, it behooves us to begin from that which is more nearly related to its preeminence. On the contrary, when we subtract with regard to that which exceeds all subtraction, we should rightly begin from those things which are furthest from it. God is more life surely and goodness than He is air or stone? Alternatively, it is better that He should not be drunk or angry rather than not be spoken about or not understood.

: XXVI :

Marsilius:
Unum est omnium principium,
nec est aliquid sensibile vel intelligibile,
sed utrisque intervallo quodam
infinito prestantius.

1 Duo quae sequuntur capita confirmantia Deum esse causam omnium tam sensibilium quam intelligibilium contra Manicheos adduci possunt, quos et Plotinus confutat, introducentes principia duo, scilicet summum bonum atque summum malum, et illud quidem intelligibilium, hoc autem sensibilium esse principium. Hos etiam nos in *Theologia* et una cum Plotino refellimus, quoniam quod summum fingitur malum nec actionem habet nec essentiam. Nihil enim habet boni. Hec autem expetuntur ut bona.

2 Preterea, cum etiam sensibilia bona, pulchra, ordinata, utilia sint, non a malo sunt principio, sed a bono. Quod Moses confiteri compellit.

3 Denique, nisi utraque ab eodem principio dependerent, communionem inter se nullam habere possent.[65]

4 Ratio vera dictat, quemadmodum proprius quilibet rerum ordo ad proprium reducitur caput unum, sic universalem rerum omnium ordinem ad unum omnium universale caput denique referendum. Si enim quo altior causa est eo latius longiusque suum dilatat imperium, altissima certe causa vim suam actionemque per omnia porrigit. Que cum sit causa causarum prima, proculdubio est maxime causa. Omnium igitur causa est tam conservans ubique

: XXVI :

Marsilio: The One is the principle of all; it is not something sensible or intelligible, but it is more excellent than either by an infinite intervening distance.

1 The two chapters which follow, confirming that God is the cause of all things both sensible and intelligible, can be adduced against the Manicheans whom Plotinus also refuted.[43] The Manicheans introduced two principles, namely the highest good and the highest bad, the former as the principle of things intelligible, the latter of things sensible. Along with Plotinus, we too have rebutted these Manicheans in our *Theology*,[44] because what is imagined as the supreme evil has neither act nor essence; for it has nothing of the good. But act and essence are sought after as goods.

2 Furthermore, since even sensibles are good, beautiful, ordered, and useful, they come not from a bad principle, but from a good one. This Moses forces [us] to acknowledge.[45]

3 Finally, unless both [Manichean principles] were to depend on the same principle, they could have no interaction at all.

4 True reason dictates that just as any proper order of things is restored to the one head that is its own, so the universal order of all things must eventually be referred to the one universal head of all things. For if the higher the cause, the more encompassing and further it extends its sway, then the highest cause certainly extends its power and action through all things. And since it is the first cause of causes, it is certainly the greatest cause. So the cause of all

singula quam efficiens. Reliquas in *Theologia* et Plotino ad idem rationes adducimus.

5 Quamobrem Dionysius noster Deum appellat omnium tam sensibilium quam intelligibilium auctorem. Addit esse causam eminenter. Cetere nanque cause nonnullam habent cum effectibus suis proportionem, quoniam et cause et effectus sub eodem universali rerum principio continentur. Sic igitur sphera ignis cum effectibus calidis proportionem habet, immo et Mars atque Sol confirmantibus id Platonicis. Prima vero causa quod et Plato demonstrat nulla ad opus aliquod proportione; sed absoluta prorsus infinitate facit, alioquin non foret summopere simplex atque prima. Cum igitur causa prima per simplicem eminentiam agat omnia tam sentienda quam intelligenda, merito nihil est eorum, quando nec proportionem quidem ullam habet ad illa.

6 Negaturus autem Dionysius Deo cuncta, ne forte videatur Deum prorsus e medio tollere, proponit in primis ea dumtaxat conditione se negaturum minus bona ut semper intelligatur supra modum meliora daturus. Quando negamus animam esse essentiam corporalem, non negamus simul esse essentiam meliorem scilicet incorpoream. Negamus similiter Deum esse in ordine essentie etiam transcendentis, que in essentiam corpoream et incorpoream potest dividi, et in se existentem et alteri adherentem, et similiter ad omnia derivari singulatimque finiri. Concedimus tamen Deum esse essentiam transcendente simplicius absolutam.

is what equally effects and everywhere preserves single things. We adduce the remaining proofs for the same argument both in our *Theology* and in the Plotinus [commentary].[46]

5 Our Dionysius therefore calls God the author of all things sensible and intelligible alike. He adds that God is a cause in a preeminent way. For the rest of the causes have some proportion with their effects, because causes and effects are contained under the same universal principle of things. Thus the fiery sphere has some proportion with [all] hot effects, or rather Mars and the Sun do, as the Platonists confirm. But the first cause has no proportion at all with any effect, as Plato demonstrates. Rather, it creates absolutely and with absolute infinity, otherwise it would not be utterly simple and first. Thus, since the prime cause through its simple preeminence enacts all things—those to be perceived and understood alike—it is meet that it be none of these, when it has no proportion at all with them.

6 But Dionysius, who is about to deny all things of God and lest he appear perhaps to be doing away with God entirely, proposes first to deny Him the lesser goods; but on this condition only: that it may always be understood that he is about to bestow on God the better goods, and bestow beyond measure. When we deny the soul is a corporeal essence, we do not deny at the same time that it is a better essence, namely an incorporeal essence. Similarly, we deny that God is in the order of essence (even of transcendent essence), essence which can be divided into corporeal and incorporeal essence, and existing in itself and inhering in another, and likewise drawn into all and yet singularly confined. And yet we grant that God is absolute essence in a transcendent and simpler way.

7 Negantes iterum Deum esse vitam que est actus essentie, non prohibemus esse vitam huiusmodi vite causam. Rursus quando negamus Deum esse rationem vel intellectum indagatorem luminis atque boni, non negamus tamen esse intellectum luminis bonique causam intellectibus.

8 Sed quis adeo demens est ut intellectum dicat irrationalem, quia rationis ambagibus non indigeat? Aut rationem appellet cecam, quoniam absque presente oculi minsterio videat? Ita nec Deum amentem[66] suspicari fas est, quoniam, cum sit ipsum lumen bonumque a mente perceptum, mentis usu non indiget.

9 Negat Dionysius in primis Deum esse corpus, deinde nec esse, nec habere conditiones passionesque corporeas, sive in corpore sint, sive circa corpus. Nos ergo vicissim ex eo quod conditiones, defectus, passiones contingentes corpori rerum principio non contingunt, consequenter[67] illud non esse corpus argumentari valemus. In *Theologia* quinetiam nec esse formam corpori adherentem, nec formam rursum huic forme proximam latius declaramus. Ascendit vero Dionysius negando ab inerti corpore ad formam corporis quodammodo efficacem id est accidentalem, ab hac ad efficaciorem substantialem sed nondum vivam, ab hac ad vivam sed irrationalem, que est ita summum sensibilium sicut est intelligibilium ultimum.

Again, in denying that God is life which is an act of essence, we do not prevent Him from being life in the sense of being the cause of such an act. Again, when we deny that God is reason or intellect or the searcher out of light and the good, yet we do not deny that He is intellect in the sense of being the cause in intellects of light and the good. 7

But who is so mindless as to declare that mind is irrational, because it does not need the mazes of reason? Or who calls reason blind because it sees without the present ministry of the eye? So it is forbidden us to hold that God is mindless [merely] because, as the light itself and the good perceived by mind, He does not need the use of mind. 8

Dionysius first denies that God is body, then he says that God is not being and does not have corporeal conditions and emotions, whether they are in body or with regard to body. Thus, from the fact that conditions, defects, and emotions affecting body do not affect the principle of things, we in turn are able to argue in consequence that the principle is not body. In our *Theology*[47] moreover, we declare at greater length that the principle is neither a form inhering in body nor again a form close to this [corporeal] form. But using the method of denial, Dionysius ascends from inactive body to a form of body which is somewhat active—ascends, that is, to accidental form. Then he ascends from this to substantial form which is more active but not yet living; and finally he ascends from this to living but irrational form, which is the highest of things sensible just as it is the lowest of things intelligible. 9

: XXVII :

Dionysius:
Quod nihil sensibilium est qui sensibilis omnis eminenter est auctor.

Causa omnium omnia supereminens nec essentia, nec vita, nec ratione, nec mente capta est. Neque est corpus nec figuram vel speciem, nec qualitatem aut quantitatem, aut molem habet, nec est in loco, neque cernitur. Neque sensibilem tactum habet; nec sentit, nec est sensibilis. Neque perturbationi ordinis experti[68] obnoxia est, a passionibus videlicet materialibus agitata. Rursus, nec est invalida, sensibilibus videlicet subiecta casibus, nec luminis indiga; nec alterationem, vel corruptionem, aut divisionem, aut privationem ullam admittit. Nec aliud quicquam sensibilium aut est aut habet.

: XXVIII :

Marsilius:
Quibus gradibus negantur de Deo intelligibilia, scilicet primo que pertinent ad animam, deinde que ad intellectum, tertio que ad ideas, quarto que ad communes Dei appellationes, quinto que ad Trinitatem.

1 Negaturus de Deo intelligibilia omnia exordium facit ab his que ad genus intelligibile tanquam ultima rediguntur, ab anima scilicet vegetali pergens ad sensualem; ab hac ad imaginantem; hinc ad

: XXVII :

Dionysius:
That He who is preeminently the author of every sensible is not one of the sensibles.

The cause of all, being more eminent than all, is not contained in essence, life, reason, or mind; nor is it body or shape or species or quality or quantity. Nor does it have mass; nor is it in a place; nor is it perceptible. It has no sensible touch; it does not sense; nor is it sensible. Nor is this cause exposed to the perturbation that lacks order, agitated, that is, by material emotions. Again, it is not weakened by sensibles, not made subject, that is, to vicissitudes; nor is it lacking in light; nor does it admit any alteration or corruption or division or privation. Nor is it or has it anything else of the sensible.

: XXVIII :

Marsilio:
By what degrees intelligibles are denied of God: that is, what things pertain first to soul, second to intellect, third to Ideas, fourth to the common names of God, and fifth to the Trinity.

Since he is about to deny all intelligibles of God, [Dionysius] 1
starts with the hierarchy that ends in the genus of the intelligible (the intelligibles being the highest in that hierarchy). From the vegetal soul, that is, he proceeds to the sensual soul; from this to

animam quasi rationalem sagacissimarum scilicet bestiarum; hinc ad rationalem id est humanam; ab ipsa huius ratione ad eiusdem intelligentiam; hinc ad angelicum intellectum.

2 Ab intellectu ad ideas. Sunt enim idee in intellectu quasi celo stelle. Que in intellectu angelico sunt eius supremum, sed in divino quasi sunt ultimum. Inter ideas collocat ideas numerorum, mox vero proportionum numeros comitantium ubi commemorat ordinem. Item ideas dimensionum que resolvuntur in numeros, ubi de magno, parvo, equali loquitur. Preterea qualitatum ideas suis quodammodo dimensionibus indigentium, ubi similitudinem dissimilitudinemque adducit. Tum vero ideas actionum que sequuntur ex qualitatibus, loquens videlicet de motu atque quiete. Accedunt idee formarum substantialium, scilicet elementalium sub potentie nomine; idee rursus celestium sub luminis cognomento. Idee quinetiam animarum corporibus coniunctarum ⟨subá⟩[69] appellatione vite, item separatarum sub essentie cognomento, angelorum quoque eternitate signate. Eternitas autem secum trahit tempus velut imaginem. Demum idea est divine fruitionis sub intelligibili tactu.

3 Hactenus de sublimitate divina negavit et dotes animarum mentiumque et omnes que quomodocunque intelliguntur ideas. Et merito, quoniam eiusmodi quevis idea singulatim definitum quiddam est, ac simul cuncte compositum. Preterea Deus agit omnia pariter et in omnia, idee vero ita inter se distinguntur ut non possint ab una omnes esse, immo et opponuntur, scilicet idea status idee motus, similitudo idealis ideali dissimilitudini. Deus igitur, cum ideas omnes aequaliter proferat, nec aliqua earum est que intelliguntur a nobis, neque etiam cuncte. Sed quis non viderit, si

the imagining soul; hence to the quasi-rational soul of the most sagacious beasts; hence to the rational, the human, soul; hence from the soul's reason itself to the same soul's understanding; and hence to the angelic intellect.

From intellect [he passes] to the Ideas; for Ideas are in intellect 2
as stars in the sky. In the angelic intellect the Ideas are its supreme possession; but in the Divine Intellect they are, as it were, its least. Of the Ideas Dionysius adduces those: (1) of numbers; (2) of the proportions accompanying numbers when he recalls their order; (3) of dimensions which are resolved into numbers when he speaks of the great, the small, and the equal; (4) of qualities which lack in a way their dimensions when he introduces similarity and dissimilarity; (5) of actions which proceed out of qualities when he speaks, that is, of motion and rest; (6) of substantial forms, that is, the Ideas of the elements when he speaks of potency; and (7) of celestials when he speaks of light. Next come the Ideas: (8) of souls joined to bodies under the designation of life; (9) of souls separate [from bodies] under that of essence; and (10) of angels too under that of eternity. But eternity drags time along with it as [its] image. And finally there is the Idea of divine enjoyment under the designation "the intelligible touch."

Thus far, Dionysius has denied, with regard to the divine sub- 3
limity, both the gifts given to souls and minds, and all the Ideas which are in some manner understood. And rightly so, since each such Idea is something defined individually, and all the Ideas together are a composite. Moreover, God enacts all things equally and in all things, but Ideas are so distinguished among themselves that they cannot all derive from one Idea. Indeed, Ideas are even mutually opposed: the Idea of rest is opposed, that is, to the Idea of motion, and ideal similarity is opposed to ideal dissimilarity. So God, since He bestows all the Ideas equally, is not any one of the Ideas which are understood by us, or even all of them. It is obvious indeed that if God Himself were made into the Idea

Deus ipse idea parvitatis fuerit[70] aut motus aut diversitatis, non effecturum magnitudinem et statum et unionem? Quibus autem rationibus talia quaedam de ipso uno Plato in *Parmenide* neget, et prolixum narratu foret et in presentia minime necessarium. De his enim in commentariis in *Parmenidem* disputamus.[71]

4 Negat post hec absolutas quasdam appellationes que communiter Deo digne videntur, ubi ad veritatis appellationem pervenit reliquarumque similium. Tollit tandem e medio notiones humanas de relationibus illis quibus divine persone inter se distinguntur. Notiones enim eiusmodi intelligibiles sunt potius quam divine pro intelligentie nostre captu concepte. Immo et quecunque sublimius a supremis angelis naturaliter concepte sunt Deo inferiores existunt.

5 Docet et cognitionis modum, quoniam est actio intus permanens pro natura cognoscentis effici, ideo nec aliquid entium intellectualiumque cognoscere aliter quam essentiali intellectualique[72] ratione, talesque conceptus intra se formare. Ideo Deum essentia, intellectu intelligibili[73] longe superiorem, eiusmodi notionibus minime circumscribi. Sed verissime[74] tunc intelligi quando iudicatur absolute intelligi nunquam posse. Tum vero Deum inquit omnia que sunt cognoscere, non ea conditione qua sunt, sed pro natura Dei; entia[75] igitur (ut ita dixerim) superenter intelligit, immo et superintelligit multa unice, composita simpliciter, immutabiliter mutabilia, presenti momento preterita pariter et futura velut sibi cuncta presentia.

of smallness or motion or diversity, He would not bring about greatness, rest, and union. In the *Parmenides*[48] Plato will use these arguments to deny such things of the One itself; but it would be too much to say how, and for the present it is not necessary at all. For we argue out these matters in our commentaries on the *Parmenides*.[49]

After this, Dionysius denies certain absolute titles which commonly seem to be worthy of God, when he comes to the title "truth" and to other similar titles. Finally, he does away with human notions about the respects in which the Divine Persons are distinguished among themselves. For such notions are [merely] intelligible rather than divine and are conceived only in the degree to which they can be captured by our [human] understanding. And as to all the notions that the highest angels have naturally conceived, and more sublimely so, they [too] are inferior to God. 4

Dionysius also teaches us that the mode of cognition, because it is an action remaining within, is effective in proportion to the nature of the person knowing; and that therefore the person knows nothing of entities and intellectual beings other than by way of a reason that is [in a way] essential and intellectual; and that he forms such concepts within himself. So God, who is far higher than essence, intellect, and the intelligible, is not circumscribed at all by such notions. He can be understood most truly only when it is adjudged that He can never be understood absolutely. When Dionysius says that God knows all existing things, he means God knows them in proportion to His own nature and not in the condition they exist [here]. So God understands entities superessentially as it were. Or rather, He super-understands the many in a manner that is one: super-understands composites in a simple way, changeable things unchangeably, past and future events alike in the present moment, as if all things were present to Himself. 5

6 Ait deinceps nec figurari quidem et designari Deum per que forsan designari putatur. Nec enim sermonem nos habere de Deo, quia neque nomen ex quo sermo componitur: non inquam nomen, quoniam nec cognitionem, que quidem est ratio prolati nominis, primumque nomen. Sed hec satis in *Parmenide* Plato declarat. Videbitur[76] igitur Deus esse tenebre, id est ipsum omnium obscurissimum, sed quomodo cum clament esse Deum tanquam omnium ubique notissimum? Putabit aliquis vicissim Deum appellari posse lumen, id est omnium notissimum, sed quonam pacto cum omnia finita testificentur ignorari quid sit ipsum quod omnes infinitum proculdubio confitentur? Nec omnino vere de Deo sentiunt homines, qui conceptum humanum superat infinite; nec errant omnino de Deo a quo omne votum et iudicium opusque bonum assidue pendet.

7 Tollit denique Deo et affirmationes et negationes, que tamen aliquando vise sunt divinitati ratione aliqua convenire. Sed revera, quod nusquam attingimus nec ponere possumus nec auferre, sed que sunt post ipsum. Si enim uni ipsi bono bonorum omnium auctori nihil deest boni, quidnam boni huic possumus adhibere? Rursum, si Deus est eminentia simplicissima ab omnibus penitus absoluta, non potes huic auferre quicquam, quia nec assequeris quod semper eminet, neque dividis quod omnium individuorum simplicissimum et absolutissimum iudicatur.

Next Dionysius declares that God is not even figured forth or adumbrated by way of the things He is supposed to be adumbrated by. He says we have no way of talking about God, because [we have] no name [for Him] from which speech might be compounded — no name, I say, because we have no knowledge [of] the rational principle of the revealed name, and the first name.[50] But Plato pronounces on this issue well enough in the *Parmenides*.[51] So it will be apparent that God is darkness, that is, the most hidden of all things. But how so, when men proclaim that, of all things everywhere, God is the most known as it were? Someone will suppose alternatively that God can be called light, the most known, that is, of all things, but how so, when all finite things bear witness that they do not know what it is that all confess is unquestionably infinite? Men do not truly know at all about God, who infinitely surpasses human conception, but neither are they entirely in error about God upon whom every prayer, judgment, and good work unceasingly depend. 6

Finally, Dionysius subtracts from God those affirmations and negations that at some point did indeed seem to accord for a particular reason with His divinity. But in truth that which we cannot attain to anywhere, we cannot add to or subtract from. We can only add to and subtract from what is posterior to God. For if nothing of good is lacking in the One Good itself, the author of all goods, then what can we add of good to this Good? Again, if God is utterly simple, preeminent, and utterly apart from all things, you cannot subtract anything from Him, because you will not have reached what is forever unreachable. Nor are you going to divide what is held to be the most simple and absolute of all undivided things. 7

: XXIX :

Dionysius:
Quod nullum intelligibilium est qui omnis intelligibilis eminenter est auctor.

1 Iterum ascendentes dicimus Deum nec esse[77] animam, nec habere sensum vel phantasiam vel opinionem vel rationem vel intelligentiam, nec esse intellectum, neque intelligentiam, nec dici, nec intelligi.

2 Nec esse numerum, nec ordinem, nec magnitudinem, nec parvitatem, nec aequalitatem, neque similitudinem vel dissimilitudinem, nec stare vel moveri vel quietem agere.

3 Nec habere potentiam, nec esse potentiam, neque lumen, neque vitam, nec essentiam, nec eternitatem aut tempus, nec esse tactum ipsius intelligibilem neque scientiam.

4 Quinetiam[78] nec est veritas, nec regnum, neque sapientia, nec unum,[79] nec unitas, nec bonitas, nec deitas.

5 Nec spiritus est quemadmodum ipsi perpendimus, nec paternitas est eiusmodi, nec ratio filii.

6 Neque aliud quicquam eorum que nobis vel aliis rebus ullis sint[80] cognita. Nec est aliquid eorum que non sunt vel eorum que sunt. Item nec ea que sunt Deum sicut est ipse cognoscunt; nec Deus res pro ipsa rerum conditione cognoscit.

7 Nec ipsius Dei sermo est, neque nomen, neque cognitio, neque tenebre, neque lumen est, neque error, nec veritas.

: XXIX :

Dionysius:
That He who is eminently the author of every intelligible is not one of the intelligibles.

Ascending a second time, we say that God is not soul, nor has He 1
sense or fantasy or opinion or reason or understanding. He is neither intellect nor understanding; nor is He spoken about or understood.

He is not number or [numerical] order or greatness or littleness 2
or equality or likeness or un-likeness; nor does He stay still or move or come to rest.

He has no power; nor is He power or light or life or essence or 3
eternity or time; nor does he intelligibly intuit Himself or have knowledge.

Moreover, He is neither truth nor kingship nor wisdom nor the 4
one nor unity nor goodness nor deity.

Nor is He spirit as we ourselves adjudge it, nor is He the pater- 5
nal principle of such, nor is He the rational principle of a child.

Nor is He any other of those things known to us or to others 6
at all. Nor is He anything of the things which do not exist or anything of those which do. And those which do exist do not know God as He is, nor does God know things in terms of their [fallen] condition.

Of God Himself there is no discourse, no name, no cognition, 7
no darkness, no light, no error, no truth.

8 Nec est ipsius positio prorsus ulla, nec ablatio. Verum nos que post Deum sunt ponentes auferentesve nec ipsum ponimus nec auferimus, quippecum omni positione superior sit singularis illa et omnino perfecta omnium causa; et omni rursum ablatione altior excellentia illius qui ab omnibus est simpliciter absolutus totisque[81] superior.

FINIS

Nor is there any attributing at all of God or any taking away. 8
And with things subsequent to God, when we add or subtract, we are not adding to or subtracting from Him, since as the singular and utterly perfect cause of all He is superior to every addition. And higher than all subtraction in turn is His excellence, He who is simply and absolutely apart from all things, and superior to them all.

THE END

ARGUMENTA MARSILII FICINI FLORENTINI IN DIONYSIUM AREOPAGITAM

DE DIVINIS NOMINIBUS AB EODEM E GRAECA LINGUA IN LATINUM TRANSLATUM

INTRODUCTORY COMMENTS BY MARSILIO FICINO THE FLORENTINE ON DIONYSIUS THE AREOPAGITE

ON *THE DIVINE NAMES,* TRANSLATED BY THE SAME FROM THE GREEK TONGUE INTO THE LATIN

[Part I, Chapters I–CXXXV]

: I :

Marsilius:

1 Cum multi tam Latini quam Greci Dionysii libros longis commentariis explanaverint, non est consilium nunc ad verbum singula commentari, sed ubi potissimum Areopagus Academiam redolet paulo sagacius explorare perque pulcherrimos hortos Dionysii nostri, Platonicorum facile principis, flores passim delibare platonicos. Etsi Dionysium Platonis tanquam pii philosophi sectatorem alicubi declaramus, ipsum tamen non solum ceteris Platonicis propter doctrine Platonice culmen, verum etiam ipsi Platoni propter novum veritatis Christiane lumen anteponendum esse censemus.

2 Instituimus autem non solum sensum eius, summatim ut diximus, Platonica potissimum ratione perstringere, verum etiam Greca in Latinum verba rursus interpretari, ut utrinque pro viribus ipsa secum forma Platonica consentiret; quam recte utrobique referre facile potest nullus: difficilius quidem aliquis, nisi Platonicus; difficillime vero, nisi philosophus.

3 In *Mystica theologia* Platonico simul et Dionysiaco sensu probavimus ipsum universi principium appellatione magis propria ipsum unum bonumque nominandum, idque intellectu et intelligibili quantumlibet excelso superius esse monstravimus. Nullus igitur intellectus per intellectualem actionem id attingit, sed per unionem quandam intelligentia veriorem atque meliorem; eiusmodi autem unio non tam in intellectu fundamentum habet quam in unitate quadam, que quidem est anime intellectualis apex eminentior intellectu.

: I :

Marsilio:

Since many scholars, Latin and Greek alike, have interpreted the books of Dionysius in lengthy commentaries, our present decision is not to comment on single matters in detail, but, where the Areopagite is most redolent of the Academy, to explore a little more eagerly; and [wandering] through the most beautiful gardens of our Dionysius—easily the prince of the Platonists—to gather Platonic blossoms everywhere. Although we speak of Dionysius elsewhere as the follower of the devout philosopher Plato, we are of the opinion nonetheless that he must be situated not only before the rest of the Platonists on account of his being the summit of Platonic doctrine,[1] but also, on account of the new light of the Christian truth, before Plato himself. 1

However, we undertake to touch on his meaning, summarily so to speak, giving in the main a Platonic reason, but also to translate anew the Greek prose into Latin, so that on both counts the Latin might agree as best it can with Platonic form itself. But in each case no one can bring this form rightly to bear easily. If he is not a Platonist, it is very difficult; and if he is not a philosopher, it is with the utmost difficulty. 2

In [commenting on] the *Mystical Theology* we proved, on the basis of both Platonic and at the same time Dionysian reasoning, that the universe's principle should be called by the more appropriate appellation the One itself and the Good. And we showed that this principle is superior to intellect and to any intelligible, however eminent. Therefore no intellect attains the Good by an intellectual act, but through a union that is more true and better than understanding. Such a union has its foundation however not in the intellect so much as in a particular kind of unity which is at the apex of the intellectual soul and is more eminent than intellect. 3

4 Hanc ipsum unum tanquam sui characterem impressit anime; cui simul, et tanquam bonum, naturalem primi boni infudit[1] amorem et assidue suscitat. Anima igitur tunc demum ipso uno bonoque fruitur quando, tum amore eiusmodi instigante, tum etiam trahente Deo, multitudinem omnem exuit ad sensum et rationem et intelligentiam pertinentem; solutaque iam tota surgit in unitatem suam, per quam cum ipso uno rerum principio inextimabilem consequitur unionem.

: II :

Dionysius:

Post *Theologicarum figurationum* librum, beate vir, nunc iam ad divina nomina pro viribus explicanda me conferam. Esto nunc quoque nobis divinorum eloquiorum lex illa prescripta per quam eorum que de Deo dicuntur veritatem asseveremus, non in persuasoriis humane sapientie rationibus, sed in demonstratione potestatis eius quam Sanctus Spiritus in theologis[2] suscitavit, qua quidem ineffabilibus et incognitis ineffabiliter et incognite copulamur[3] per unionem quandam potentia et actione nostra tum rationali tum etiam intellectuali prestantiorem.

The One itself has impressed this unity as its seal or character on the soul. At the same time and as a good it has poured into it a natural love of the prime Good, and continually it awakens this love. So the soul enjoys the One and the Good itself at the very moment when, with such a [natural] love exciting it, and with God attracting it, it doffs all multiplicity pertaining to sense, to reason, and to understanding. Now liberated, it ascends entire into its own unity, and through this unity it attains an inestimable union with the one universal principle. 4

The Book of Dionysius the Areopagite On the Divine Names, translated by Marsilio Ficino.[2]

: II :

Dionysius:

Blessed man, after the book on figurative theology,[3] I must now betake myself to explaining as best I can the divine names. May that prescribed law of divine eloquence be now bestowed upon us too, the law by which we may assert the truth of those things which are spoken of God, "not in the persuasive reasons of human wisdom, but in the demonstration of His power,"[4] the power which the Holy Spirit has aroused in sacred authors. By this power we join with things ineffable and unknown in an ineffable and unknown way, and through a union which is more eminent than our own potency and act, be it rational or even intellectual.

: III :

Marsilius:[4]
Tantum de divinis asseverandum, quantum divinitus inspirati nobis ostendunt. Item quomodo radius divinus se ipsum nobis accommodat.

1 Plato in *Timeo* de rebus divinis credendum, inquit, dei filiis, etiam si nullas afferant rationes; in *Legibus* quoque theologie inventa iubet oraculis confirmari. Dionysius similiter nihil de rebus divinis asseverandum putat nisi quantum divinitus inspirati confirmant.

2 Deum hic, appellatione quadam apud Latinos prodigiosa, superessentialitatem nominat. Essentialitas apud metaphysicos est simplicior quam essentia; Deus igitur non solum simplicissimum est, sed ipsa simplicitas. Si qua huic scientia competit non essentialis illa quidem est dicenda, sed eminentior quam essentia; que rursus ignoratio dicitur, quippe cum nihil alicui note cognitionis habeat, sed est interea ratione, intelligentia, cognitione, essentia melior.

3 Hec igitur dei propria sit. Nobis autem, quamdiu sumus extra patriam, summa cognitio intelligentia est divinam naturam nondum attingens, tantum vero de muneribus divinis viribusque consequens quantum divinus ipse radius per serenas sanctorum mentes transmissus ostenderit; in quibus sane, tanquam in corporibus diaphanis, divinum percipimus solem, quem capere in se ipso non possumus.

4 Quamobrem circa divinorum contemplationem certis quibusdam limitibus cohibiti sumus: primo quidem, quoniam nihil ultra

: III :

Marsilio: We should assert as much about matters divine as men who are divinely inspired reveal them to us. Likewise how the divine ray accommodates itself to us.

In the *Timaeus* Plato says that we must believe in the divine truths told us by the sons of God even if they provide us with no proofs at all.[5] In the *Laws* too he says that the discoveries of theology are confirmed by oracles.[6] Dionysius similarly thinks that we should not assert anything about matters divine except insofar as they are confirmed by those who are divinely inspired. 1

Here he calls God, by way of a sort of strange appellation among the Latins, "super-essentiality." For with the metaphysicians essentiality is simpler than essence. Hence God is not only the most simple, but simplicity itself. Whatever knowledge accords with this must be called, not essential knowledge, but rather knowledge more eminent than essence — knowledge which is called in turn ignorance, since it has nothing of the knowledge known to anyone, but nonetheless is better than reason, understanding, cognition, and essence. 2

So let this be the property of God. For us, however, as long as we are exiled from the fatherland, the highest cognition is an understanding that does not yet attain to the divine nature. But we understand only as much about the divine gifts and powers as the divine ray itself, having been transmitted through the serene minds of the saints, has revealed them to us. In these gifts, as in transparent bodies, we see the divine Sun, which in itself we cannot perceive. 3

Therefore we are circumscribed within certain particular limits in regard to the contemplation of things divine: (1) because we can 4

percipere[5] possumus quam radius offerat; secundo, quia radius ipse in nos sub mensura descendit, non quidem ostensurus nobis naturam ipsam divinam, vel quecumque Deus conspicit in se ipso, vel omnia saltem que penes Deum angeli contuentur, sed pauciora et inferiora quedam, quamvis pretiosissima proculdubio si cum ceteris conferantur; tertio, quoniam radius ille unicuique pro sua dumtaxat capacitate demonstrat iusta quadam ubique pro meritis distributione servata. Ubi certe sol divinus perinde se habet, ac si sol celestis lumen suum singulis passim oculis temperaret: se ergo quasi finitum mentibus finitis offert, infinitatem interea suam occulens in seipso.

5 Denique et unusquisque debet circa divinum radium ita moderari se ipsum ut nec per ignaviam ab illius excellentia decidat in deterius, neque tentet ulterius per superbiam: ibi quidem sanctitas, hic autem temperantia lucet.

: IV :

Dionysius:
Tantum de divinis asseverandum
quantum inspiratio divina declarat.
Item radius divinus
pro cuiusque ingenio se infundit.

1 Nulla igitur ratione audendum est aliquid de occulta deitate, que est superior quam essentia, dicere vel cogitare, preter[6] illa que sacra eloquia divinitus nobis aperuerunt. Ipsi namque quod excelsius est

perceive nothing beyond what the [divine] ray reveals to us; (2) because the ray itself descends into us with less than its full brightness, [since] it is not going to reveal to us the divine nature itself, or all that God contemplates in Himself, or all even that the angels contemplate in God's presence. Rather it shows us things that are less and lower [than the angels see], although they are doubtless most precious if we compare them to all else. And (3) it is because that ray reveals things to each man only according to his capacity, things that are everywhere preserved in a just distribution according to merit. Certainly, the divine Sun in this is analogous to our celestial sun moderating its light everywhere for individual eyes. So to finite minds it offers itself as something as it were finite, while concealing its own infinity in itself.

Finally, every single person should temper himself with regard 5
to the divine ray such that he neither falls short of that ray's excellence through cowardice, nor makes repeated assaults on it through pride.[7] Sanctity should blaze forth [in him] in the first instance but temperance in the second.

: IV :

Dionysius:
Only to the extent divine inspiration reveals them to us should we make assertions about things divine. The divine ray pours itself into each person according to the mental capacity of each.

We should have no reason at all to dare to say or to think anything 1
about the hidden Divinity, which is higher than essence, except for those things the sacred Scriptures divinely reveal to us. For to that

essentia scientiam quoque essentia superiorem, que et ignorantia nominatur sed ratione et intellectu essentiaque prestantior est, debemus adscribere; eatenusque ad excelsa contendere, quatenus precipue divinorum verborum radius se ipsum nobis infundit, dum videlicet ad sublimiores splendores temperantia et sanctitate divinorum veneratrice, cohibiti sumus.

2 Si qua enim sapientissime verissimeque theologie fides habenda est, pro meritis cuiusque proportione revelantur spectanturque divina; ubi sane precipua dei bonitas per iustitiam omnium servatricem ab his, que sub mensuram cadunt, immensitatem ipsam tanquam incomprehensibilem, qua Deum decet[7] providentia, segregat.

: V :

Marsilius: *Deus nec ab essentia, nec ab intellectu, nec per illam, nec per istum vel comprehendi vel saltem perspici potest.*

1 Intelligibilia ita superant sensibilia, item simplicia composita, rursum incorporea similiter corporea sic excedunt, ut superiora illa nec ab his inferioribus neque per hec vel comprehendi vel etiam revera spectari possint.[8]

2 Multo magis principium universi, tum immensitate nature superat essentiam, forma quadam necessario designatam, tum incomparabili simplicitate unitateque penitus absoluta superat mentis formam, ut Plotinus probat, necessario multiformem; longius quoque superat cogitationem non solum multitudine sed etiam

which is higher than essence we ought to ascribe knowledge too which is higher than essence, knowledge which is also called ignorance but is more outstanding than reason or intellect or essence. Indeed, preeminently to the extent the ray of [Scripture's] divine words pours itself into us, we ought to contend for the heights, as long, that is, as we are firmly joined to the splendors on high by temperance, and by sanctity are the worshippers of things divine.

For if any faith is to be accorded the wisest and truest theology, 2
its divine secrets are revealed and seen in proportion according to the merits of each person, wherein God's eminent goodness, the preserver of all through justice, separates immensity itself as incomprehensible—and this befits God's providence—from the things that fall under measure.

: V :

Marsilio:
God is neither from essence nor from intellect, nor can He be understood or even perceived through essence or through intellect.

Intelligibles so excel sensibles, and simple things, composites, and 1
likewise incorporeals so exceed corporeals that the higher cannot be understood through the lower, or even be indeed glimpsed by or through the lower.

Even more so does the universe's principle both by the immen- 2
sity of its nature excel essence (necessarily defined as a sort of form), and by its incomparable simplicity and unity, which is utterly absolute, it excels the form of mind, which, as Plotinus proves, is necessarily multiform.[8] Still more does it also excel rea-

mobilitate dispersam; maxime vero sermonem. Nec igitur ab his, neque per hec, neque per aliud finitum quicquam comprehendi perspicive potest.

3 Est autem Deus unitas non in re quavis unita sedem habens, sed unionis unitatisque ubique causa; essentia quoque et intellectus dici potest tanquam essentie omnis intellectusque causa, non tanquam essentialis quedam intellectualisve forma.

4 Denique cum etiam Peripatetici putent essentiam et esse tanquam communissima a communissimo principio rebus tribui, atque causa communissima potentissimaque causarum sit[9] ab omnibus effectibus expedita, merito primum principium Platonici putant ab essentia et esse solutum. Qua vero ratione intellectus quantumcumque sublimis nunquam primum principium esse possit, sicut neque visus[10] fit quandoque lumen, in *Theologia* nostra planius declaramus.

: VI :

Dionysius:
Deus, essentia et intellectu[11] superior, non potest per ullam essentiam vel ab ullo intellectu comprehendi vel saltem propria virtute cerni.

1 Sicut neque sensibilibus intelligibilia comprehendi spectarive possunt, neque fictis figuratisque simplicia et infigurata, neque per corporum figuras formatis informitas ipsa incorporeorum (refugiens tactum figuraque carens), eadem veritatis ratione ipsa superessentialis infinitas[12] omnes essentias antecellit. Ipsa quoque unitas intellectu[13] superior, omnes supereminet intellectus. Ipsum

soning which is dispersed not only in multiplicity but also in mobility. Most of all it excels speech [i.e., our ability to talk about it]. So it cannot be understood or perceived by or through these means or through anything else finite.

God is unity and yet He does not set up His throne in anything united. Still, He is the cause of union and unity everywhere. And as the cause of all essence and intellect, He can be called essence and intellect, but not as an essential or intellectual form. 3

Finally, since even the Aristotelians think that essence and being, as the most common [attributes], are attributed to things by the principle that is most common, and by the cause that is the most universal and most powerful of causes (being freed from all effects),[9] so the Platonists justly suppose that the first principle is separate from essence and from being.[10] For this reason indeed, intellect, however sublime, can never be the first principle, just as sight can never be light, [as] we clarify further in our *Theology*.[11] 4

: VI :

Dionysius:
In that He is superior to essence and intellect God cannot be comprehended via any essence or by any intellect, or perceived even by an appropriate power.

Just as intelligibles cannot be comprehended or seen by sensibles, or simple and unshaped things by things molded and shaped, or the formlessness itself of incorporeals by things formed in the shapes of bodies (such formlessness flees from touch and is wanting shape), so for the same reason in truth super-essential infinity itself precedes all essences. Unity itself too, being superior to 1

denique unum cogitatione prestantius nullis cogitationibus potest excogitari; atque bonum excelsius omni verbo verbis est ineffabile.

2 Unitas unitatis omnis unifica, superessentialis essentia, intellectus nequaquam intelligibilis, ineloquibile verbum, verbi et intelligentie nominisque vacatio:[14] hec sane iuxta nullum existentium est. Causa quidem omnibus ut sint, ipsa vero non est, tanquam omni essentia superior; et tandem quemadmodum ipsa de se proprie sciteque pronuntiaverit. De hac igitur secretissima deitate que et essentiam antecellit, sicut dictum est, nec loqui nec cogitare quicquam audendum est preter illa que sacra eloquia nobis divine admodum tradiderunt.

: VII :

Marsilius: Comprehendere Deum nullus intellectus potest; scire quid sit Deus intellectus beatus solus solo lumine supernaturali potest.

1 Intellectus lumine naturali potest certis rationibus intelligere primo quidem esse Deum; deinde quid non sit ipse Deus; tertio, quid et quemadmodum efficiat atque regat; quarto, qua conditione res ad Deum omnes sese habeant.

2 Scire vero quid proprie sit ipsa natura dei nec intellectus noster nec angelicus naturali lumine potest; est enim natura illa longo intervallo super essentiam et intelligentiam quantumcumque perfectam. Sed sole beate mentes intelligunt quid sit Deus sub lumine

intellect, towers above all intellects. Finally, the One itself, being more outstanding than reasoning, cannot be considered by any processes of reasoning; and the Good, being more eminent than every word, cannot be expressed in words.

[The One is] the unity unific of all unity, the super-essential essence, the non-intelligible intellect, the inexpressible word, the emptying of word, of understanding, and of name. This unity has no proportion to any existing thing. It is indeed the cause in all that they exist, but it itself does not exist, being superior to all essence. And finally it is as itself that the One will have properly and knowledgeably pronounced upon itself. So concerning this most secret Deity which surpasses essence, one should not venture, as it is said, to utter anything or to think anything except for those truths which the sacred Scriptures have divinely transmitted to us in full. 2

: VII :

Marsilio:
No intellect can understand God. The blessed intellect alone can know what God is [and] only by a supernatural light.

By the natural light and with convincing reasons the intellect is able to understand firstly that God exists, then what God Himself is not, thirdly what and how He effects and rules, and fourthly in what condition all things exist with regard to Him. 1

By a natural light, however, neither our intellect nor the angelic intellect can know what God's nature itself properly is. For that nature is by far and away above essence and understanding, however perfect. But the blessed minds alone understand what God is 2

quodam plusquam naturali; quando Deus ipse se menti coniungit, quasi tanquam formam quam videat et per quam videat.

3 Hinc, Plotinus, animus, inquit, perfecte purgatus prius per unionem divinam Deus efficitur, quam cognoscat quid sit ipse Deus. Sed comprehendere Deum naturamque ipsius sub cunctis rationibus suis apprehendere[15] nullus intellectus nullo lumine valet. Nullum ergo vestigium nobis usquam occurrit eorum qui Deum hac absoluta ratione comprehenderint, quoniam nullis comprehendere licet.

4 Nec rursus eorum quibus palam ipsa divina natura patuerit percipientibus quidem nec interim complectentibus. Nec enim vel ipsi exprimere vel alii capere possunt quod illi contemplati fuerint in excelsis, vel etiam contemplentur. Nam et que Paulus Apostolus cognovit in raptu, non licuit homini loqui, et Plato divina inquit dici docerique non posse, sed in animo pio ad Deum accedente subito tandem divinum[16] ex alto lumen accendi, quod quidem se ipsum intus alat, quasi neget eiusmodi lumen extrinsecus emicare.

: VIII :

Dionysius:
Scire quid sit Deus Dei ipsius proprium est, nec ullum divine substantie usquam manifestum vestigium reperitur.

Quemadmodum enim divinitas in sacris litteris benigne admodum de se ipsa tradidit, eius, quicquid tandem est, scientia contemplatioque omnibus, quecumque sunt, est inaccessa, quippe cum ab

by a kind of light that is more than natural. When God joins Himself to mind, it is almost as if He were a form which the mind may see and may see through it.

Hence, Plotinus says, our rational soul, having been perfectly 3
purged is made God [*or* a god] through union divine before it can know what God Himself is.[12] But to comprehend God and His nature under all His rational principles is impossible for any intellect using any light. So we find no trace anywhere of those who might have comprehended God with absolute reason, since it is permitted to none to comprehend God.

Nor again is any trace left us of those to whom the divine na- 4
ture itself was openly revealed when they perceived it yet did not comprehend it. For neither can they themselves express nor can others understand what they contemplated on high, or may be contemplating still. For what Paul the Apostle knew in a rapture he was not permitted to tell [any] man.[13] And Plato says that matters divine cannot be discussed or taught, but rather that, in the pious soul approaching God, the divine light suddenly and at last is set ablaze from on high, a light which nourishes itself within.[14] It is as though Plato were denying that such a light shines out externally.

: VIII :

Dionysius:
To know what God is is proper to God Himself. No manifest trace at all of the divine substance is found anywhere.

Even as the Divinity in the sacred Scriptures, in its benevolence, has bequeathed us much about itself, yet knowledge and contemplation of that Divinity (whatever it finally is) is inaccessible to

omnibus super essentiali quadam excellentia sit segregata. Iam vero theologos multos invenias divinitatem celebravisse non solum tanquam invisibilem incomprehensibilemque, verum etiam inscrutabilem ininvestigabilemque[17] dixisse, quasi nullum extet vestigium eorum qui ad occultam infinitatem illius accesserint.

: IX :

Marsilius:
Causa prima et separatissima est et presentissima, atque sicut omnibus impartit bonum, sic multis divinam intelligentiam atque unionem.

1 Ad excellentiam cause duo precipua pertinere videntur: primum quidem, ut quo prestantior causa est, eo sit a subditorum conditionibus segregatior; secundum vero, ut pro excellentie sue gradibus vires suas actionesque longius latiusque diffundat. Quamobrem prima omnium causa et separatissima est ab omnibus et interim presentissima. Inde unum, hinc bonum a Platonicis nominatur: inde quidem nihil habet simile cum effectibus atque commune, hinc rursum agit omnia, agit in omnia, conservat assidue, est in omnibus penitus presentissima.

2 Cum ad infinitam illius bonitatem pertineat amplissima virtutum munerumque diffusio, nihil relinquit usquam sue bonitatis expers. Merito igitur et claritatem illam, qua se ipsam cernit, multis impertit, per quam multa Deum contueantur. Sed ipsa cognitio

all things, whatsoever they are, since the Divinity is set apart from all in a sort of super-essential excellence. But you may find now that many theologians have celebrated the Divinity not only as invisible and incomprehensible, but also as inscrutable. They have declared it uninvestigable. It is as if there were no remaining footprint of those who have approached its hidden infinity.

: IX :

Marsilio:
The prime cause is most absent and most present; and just as it imparts good to all, so to many [it imparts] divine understanding and union.

Two features seem to pertain principally to a cause's excellence. 1
The first indeed is that the more outstanding it is as a cause, the more separated it is from the conditions of its subjects. But the second is that in proportion to the levels of its excellence, a cause diffuses its powers and actions further and wider. Hence the prime cause of all is most apart from and yet most present to all things. It is called by the Platonists, on the first count, the One, and on the second, the Good. On the first count, it has nothing similar to or in common with its effects; on the second, to the contrary, it enacts all things, and it acts upon all and constantly preserves and is most present, entirely so, in all.

Since the most ample diffusion of powers and of gifts pertains 2
to the infinite goodness of that [cause], it leaves nothing anywhere deprived of its goodness. In justice therefore it imparts that clarity by which it sees itself to many; and through this clarity many things may gaze up at God. But the knowledge itself of God exists

Dei penes Deum super essentiam extat, in sequentibus vero cognitio Dei non transcendit essentie limites; radium ergo excelsiorem essentia Deus retinet in seipso, essentialem vero communicat; nempe cum primum ex Deo prosilit, essentialis evadit. Per hunc, ut Plato in *Republica* inquit, et species rerum fiunt intelligibiles et mentes evadunt intellective, atque he quidem cum illis harmonice copulantur, ac tandem mentes Deo beate formantur.

3 Distribuit vero lumen Deus suum intellectibus pro sua cuiusque proportione, quemadmodum stelle singule pro natura sua lumen varium a sole suscipiunt. Tum vero[18] beate mentes cum divina voluntate concordes mensura dati muneris contente vivunt, presertim cum ita nature sue fuerit satisfactum, nec affectant ulterius neque decidunt in deterius.

4 Quoniam vero luminis est calefacere, ideo sub hoc intelligentie lumine statim accenduntur amore, congruente videlicet cum ipso lumine, ut nec citra, nec ultra petat. Ipse vero amor est qui, alarum instar, mentes per sublimia sustinet ne ad inferiora labantur.[19] Hinc amorem divinum in *Hymnis* Orpheus alatum canit, et Plato in *Phedro* sublimes animas per amorem divine pulchritudinis pennas inquit recuperare, quibus in celestem patriam denique revolent.

5 Denique amor, sicut et natura, principium motus est atque quietis; itaque si forte mentes dum Deum cognoscunt non mediocriter, interim tamen ament aliud vel mediocriter, statim relicto Deo ad aliud movebuntur.

in God above essence; and yet the knowledge of God in subsequent things does not transcend the limits of essence. Thus God retains in Himself the ray that is more excellent than essence; but the essential ray He communicates [to others]. As soon as it leaps forth from God, it emerges as the essential ray. In the *Republic* Plato says that through this ray the species of things are made intelligible and minds emerge as intellective;[15] and the latter are harmoniously united with the former, and at last minds are blessedly formed by God.

God distributes His light to intellects and according to the proportion of each, just as the individual stars in proportion to their nature sustain a varied light from the sun. But blessed minds in harmony with the divine will live content with the measure of the gift bestowed upon them, especially since it has been made sufficient for their nature such that they neither desire to exceed it, nor do they fall short of it. 3

Since to heat is a property of light, so in this light of understanding minds are instantly set on fire by love, by love in harmony with the light, so that it no longer casts about on one side or another. But love itself, like wings, is what lifts minds aloft through things sublime, so that they no longer turn away toward the depths. Hence Orpheus in his hymns calls divine love "winged."[16] And Plato in the *Phaedrus* says that sublime souls recover their wings through love of divine beauty, and with these wings at last they may fly back to their celestial home.[17] 4

Finally, love, like nature too, is the principle of motion and of rest. Therefore perchance, if minds, while they seek to know God, but not in a measured way, love something else in the meantime even in a measured way, then straightway, having abandoned God, they will be drawn toward that other object. 5

: X :

Dionysius:
Deus radium intelligentie sue
unicuique pro capacitate communicat,
intellectusque beati distributo munere contenti vivunt,
ac firmiter perfruuntur.

Verumtamen summum illud bonum nullum alicubi existentium sui expers esse patitur, sed, cum in seipso stabiliter superessentialem fixerit radium, benigne tamen interea pro cuiusque existentium proportione unicuique fulget; atque ad ipsius contemplationem communionemque et similitudinem, quatenus assequi possint, sacros intellectus extendit. Qui, ut fas est, aciem in ipsum reverenter intendunt, neque ad superiora quam ferat indultus ipsis pro modo suo radius frustra insolenterve[20] contendunt, neque inclinatione quapiam ad deterius vergente ad inferiora labuntur. Sed firmiter indeclinabiliterque ad illucescentem sibi radium aciem intendunt, et amore decentium illustrationum congruo sacra cum reverentia temperate sancteque per sublimia pervolant.

: X :

Dionysius: God communicates the ray of His understanding to every person according to his capacity. Blessed intellects live content with this gift as distributed, and they enjoy it steadfastly.

Yet none of things existing anywhere is destined to receive no part of that highest Good. Though this Good has fixed the superessential ray steadfastly in itself, yet in the meantime, in its benignity and according to the proportion of each existent, it shines out upon each one. And it draws sacred intellects to its contemplation, to communion with it, and to a likeness to it—insofar as they can rise to such states. They reverently focus their attention on it, as is right; and they do not strive pointlessly or insolently toward things higher than the ray bears them aloft, the ray that is granted to them, to each in his own way. Nor do they sink toward lower things weighed down by some inclination veering toward the worse. Rather, steadfastly and unswervingly, they concentrate their gaze upon the ray as it shines in themselves. With a love that accords with this comely and appropriate illumination, and in sacred reverence, they temperately and in holy awe soar aloft through things sublime.

: XI :

Marsilius:
Facilius tutiusque divina videmus si mentis aciem ad eloquia sacra convertimus, quam si[21] *in ipsum Deum audentius dirigamus.*

1 Quod lucet in Deo tanquam solis mundani sole, super essentie et intelligentie limites, non tam perscrutari quam venerari debemus, mentisque oculos, immensam hanc lucem minime sustinentes, hinc ad sacras litteras tanquam ad celos flectere, in quibus nomina sunt cognomentaque divina tradita divinitus, velut stelle oculis nostris accommodate, ex quibus sane stellis nobis emicant proprie Dei vires et appellationes laudesque divine, tanquam solis virtutes in stellis.

2 Ex hoc denique sedulo[22] pioque studio duo quedam potissima reportamus: primum quidem, quod divinos radios hinc haurimus nostro ingenio congruentes; secundum, quod divinum solem radiorum eiusmodi fontem,[23] ut Deo placet, rite laudamus.

3 In nominibus appellationibusque divinis (divinitus[24] videlicet traditis) mirabiles latere virtutes tum ad divina mysteria declaranda, tum ad mirabilia perpetranda Hebrei omnes existimant, et Zoroaster Iamblichusque confirmant.

: XI :

Marsilio:
We see things divine with greater ease and safety if we turn our mind's gaze to the sacred Scriptures rather than directing it more boldly to God Himself.

What shines in God as the Sun of the world's sun, since it is above the limits of essence and understanding, we ought not to examine so much as venerate. Hence we ought to turn the eyes of the mind, which can not bear this immense light, toward the sacred Scriptures, as to the heavens. In the Scriptures the names and divine cognomens are divinely handed down to us, just as the stars are accommodated to our eyes. From these stars indeed the proper powers of God and the appellations and praises that are divine shine in us, as the sun's powers shine in the stars. 1

Finally, from this diligent and pious study [of the Scriptures] we arrive at two important conclusions: first that the divine rays we derive from it are in harmony with our natural intelligence; and second that, as it pleases God, we may rightly praise the divine Sun as the fountain of these rays. 2

The Hebrews all think that the marvelous powers lying concealed in the divine names and appellations (those that have been divinely transmitted) are there both to proclaim the divine mysteries and to perform miracles; and Zoroaster and Iamblichus confirm this.[18] 3

: XII :

Dionysius:
Radii divinitatis fulgentes in sacris eloquiis ad divinam contemplationem facile nos perducunt.

His ergo subditi divinis lancibus, que universos supercelestium ordinum sanctos gubernant exercitus, secretum quidem illud divinitatis intellectu essentiaque excelsius, sanctis intelligentie nihil iam perscrutantis venerationibus, que vero ineffabilia sunt modesto quodam silentio honorantes, ad illos dumtaxat qui in sacris litteris nobis fulgent splendores contendimus. Atque ab eis ad divinos hymnos illuminamur, inde videlicet ultra mundanum modum illuminati atque ad laudationes sacras inde formati: ad hoc ipsum videlicet, ut et divina lumina nobis inde pro modo nostro tradita facile videamus, et beneficum illud principium totius illuminationis rite laudemus quemadmodum et ipsum de se in sacris eloquiis tradidit.

: XIII :

Marsilius:
Deus usque adeo potens et intima causa est rebus omnibus bonorum omnium ut ipsemet rebus sit ipsa rerum bona.

1 Ad rationem cause effectusque pertinet ut hic ab illa pendeat, et quo causa magis causa est effectus etiam magis inde dependeat. Cum igitur causa causarum sit maxime causa, consequens est ut

: XII :

Dionysius: The rays of divinity blazing in the sacred Scriptures lead us with ease toward divine contemplation.

Therefore, being subject to these divine scales [of consideration] which govern the universal, the sacred armies of the supercelestial orders, we strive for that secret of the Divinity which is loftier than intellect and essence. With nothing now of understanding in a seeker's holy acts of veneration, we strive for things which are ineffable, honoring them with an unassuming silence; and we strive only for those splendors which blaze forth in our sacred Scriptures. From them we receive the illumination [to fashion] hymns divine, and we receive it beyond any worldly manner, and thus we are formed for sacred praises. And hence with ease and in our own way we may gaze upon the divine lights bequeathed to us, and rightly praise that beneficent principle of all illumination as it has spoken about itself to us in the sacred Scriptures.

: XIII :

Marsilio: God is so powerful and so much the inmost cause of all goods in all things that in them He Himself is all their goods.

It pertains to the rational principle of the cause and the effect that 1
the latter depends on the former; and the more the cause is the cause, the more too the effect depends upon it. Since therefore the cause of causes is the greatest cause, consequently all things

omnia et omnino inde dependeant. Quamobrem et illa est non solum efficiens omnium causa, sed finalis, nec efficiens tantum, sed conservans, movens, perficiens, iterumque reficiens, et quecumque sunt in opere ab illa omnino dependent. In operibus vero mundanis est essentia, vita, virtus, inclinatio, motus, actio, perseverantia, perfectio. Hec igitur in rebus omnia prima causa facit, servat, perficit, reficit.

2 Proinde causa prima ob immensam potestatem adeo tota totum occupat ut ubique sit omnibus presentissima, tantoque saltem in omnibus interius agat quanto natura interius agat[25] quam ars proculdubio facit. Quoniam igitur tum omnia in rebus narrata a Deo pendent omnino, tum etiam Deus omnibus omnium inest intimus, merito Deus ipse videtur bona hec omnia, que narrata sunt, esse.

3 Speculare imaginem si qua est in speculo: hec autem dependet a vivo ut essentia eius et virtus, et motus, et status sit ipse qui vivit seque ipsum ad speculum speculatur; multo magis Deus ipse est essentia rerum, vita, virtus, actio, perseveratio, perfectio, reformatio, atque in mentibus puritas, illuminatio, perfectio, divinitas.

4 Plato in *Politico, Protagora, Critia,* divinum quiddam inquit vel deiforme quondam animis nostris infusum, idque paulatim multis temporum curriculis aboleri, sed cum primum deletum[26] est, Deum renovare seculum animosque iterum divinitate formare. Id modo Dionysius attigit, qui deinde subdit Deum esse tum eorum qui simplices fiunt simplicitatem, tum eorum qui uniuntur unitatem: sive enim exeundo corporea ad simplicitatem proficiant, resolvi videntur in Deum, qui est ipsa simplicitas; sive posthabita

depend upon it, and wholly so. Wherefore the cause is not only the efficient but the final cause of all; and not the efficient only but the conserving, moving, perfecting, and restoring cause. And all that exist in the work [of the cause] depend entirely on this cause. But in the works of the world there is essence, life, power, inclination, motion, act, perseverance, and perfection. Therefore the prime cause creates all these in things and preserves, perfects, and restores them.

Therefore, on account of its measureless power the prime cause 2
so totally possesses all things that everywhere it is most present in them all. To the extent that nature undoubtedly works more inwardly than art does, to that extent at least [the prime cause] acts more inwardly in all. So because everything we talk about in things entirely depends upon God, and also God is present as the most inward of all in all things, God Himself properly seems to be all these aforementioned goods.

Look at an image, if there is one, in a mirror. This so depends 3
on the living person that its essence, power, motion, and rest is the person himself—the person who is living and looking at himself in the mirror. Much more then is God Himself the essence of things, the life, power, act, steadfastness, perfection, and reformation; and in minds He is their purity, illumination, perfection, and divinity.

In the *Statesman, Protagoras,* and *Critias* Plato says that some- 4
thing divine or deiform was once infused into our souls.[19] This was gradually eroded in the many passages of time. But as soon as it was destroyed, God renewed the age and again invested souls with divinity. Dionysius just touches on this theme, and then adds that God is both the simplicity of those who are made simple and the unity of those who are united. For if, by doffing corporeal things, they progress toward simplicity, they next seem to be melted into God who is simplicity itself. Or if, having set

virium actionumque multitudine ad unum se conferant, rediguntur in Deum, qui est ipsa unitas; sive intellectus tum invicem, tum etiam cum intelligendis uniantur, ita prorsus Deo, qui est ipsa unitas, quasi quodam glutino copulantur; seu tandem cum ipso Deo quasi unum efficiantur, vacant hic iam mentes, divina regnat unitas, unitate divina formate mentes agunt, quod et Plotinus sepe probat Iamblichusque confirmat.

5 Etsi Deus adeo sit rebus intimus, est tamen interea[27] segregatus tanquam principium ratione quadam super essentiam — principium, inquam, super principium, nullam videlicet cum principiis ceteris vel effectibus habens proportionem. Rursus quamvis sit adeo separatus, immensum tamen, quod in se bonum ceu lumen occulit, largissime diffundit in omnia; hinc Orphicum illud Iupiter[28] quam in se ipso lucem occulit edit quandoque foras, ex almo corde operans admiranda.

: XIV :

Dionysius: *Deus omnibus in rebus est omnia rerum bona.*

1 Tradidit autem hec: Deus est causa omnium atque principium essentiaque et vita, tum vero eorum, qui a Deo prolapsi sunt, revocatio atque resurrectio; eorum autem, qui lapsu quodam divinam in se effigiem perdiderunt, renovatio atque reformatio; rursus eorum, qui profana quadam agitatione quatiuntur, confirmatio sacra;

aside the multitude of powers and actions, they turn themselves toward the One, then they are restored to God who is unity itself. Or if intellects are united both with each other and also with things to be understood, then they are directly joined, as with a sort of glue, to God who is unity itself. Or if, finally, they are made one, as it were, with God Himself, then minds are now emptied [of multiplicity] and divine unity reigns: minds then act formed by [this] divine unity. Plotinus often proves this and Iamblichus confirms it.[20]

5 Though God is innermost in things, yet He is in the meantime set apart from them as a principle by a kind of super-essential reason: He is the principle, I say, above principle, that is, He has no proportional relationship at all to the rest of the principles or effects. Again, even though He is separate in this way, yet He diffuses the measureless good which is in Himself (as if it were light He has concealed) into all things at large. Hence that Orphic saying: "Jupiter takes the light which he hides in himself, and at the proper moment radiates it forth, doing wondrous things out of the bounty of his heart."[21]

: XIV :

Dionysius: God in all things is all their goods.

1 Scripture has handed down these truths: [namely] God is the cause and principle of all; He is essence and life. To those who have fallen away from Him, He comes as the summons to resurrection. To those who have lost in a kind of fall the divine likeness in themselves, He is renovation and reformation. To those again who are shaken by a sort of profane turmoil, He is a sacred

permanentium vero tuta securitas; ad eum[29] quoque proficiscentium porrecta manu perductio; illuminatorum fulgor; eorum qui perficiuntur principatus ipse perfectionis, quique in eum assumuntur summa divinitas, eorum quoque qui simplices fiunt ipsa simplicitas, qui in unum conveniunt, similiter unitas.

2 Universi principii ratione quadam super essentiam, principium supra principium; occulti quinetiam, quantum fas est, benefica distributio atque (ut summatim dixerim) viventium vita, existentium essentia, omnis vite essentieque principium atque causa, ob propriam bonitatem omnia ut essent producentem atque conservantem.

: XV :

Marsilius: Quare Deus multis nominibus appelletur: cur unitas, cur Trinitas, causa, sapientia, pulchritudo, benignitas, ceteraque similiter.

1 Nomina, cognomenta, adiectiva que a sacris literis varia tribuuntur Deo non ad hoc inventa sunt, ut ipsam Dei naturam significarent que, cum unica sit et simplex, si nominanda foret, unico foret nomine nominanda. Sed ideo instituta sunt, ut multa variaque bona a divina bonitate largissime profluentia declararent. Si quid vero preter processum ex Deo, aliquid preterea significant

strengthening. To those who remain steadfast, He is abiding security. To those who journey to Him, He is the guidance that stretches out his hand. To those who are illuminated, He is their radiance. To those being perfected, He is the very regimen of perfection. To those who are gathered to Him, He is highest divinity. To those too who are made simple, He is simplicity itself. To those who come together in unity, likewise He is unity.

By reason as it were of being the universal principle above es- 2
sence, He is the principle above principle. Moreover, He is the bounteous distribution of what lies hidden to the extent it is allowed. And in sum, He is the life of things living, the essence of things existing, the principle and cause of all life and essence, by reason of His own goodness which produces and preserves all things that they might exist.

: XV :

Marsilio:
Why God is called by many names. Why He is called unity, trinity, cause, wisdom, beauty, liberality, and the rest likewise.

Names, cognomens, and adjectives which are variously attributed 1
to God by the sacred Scriptures have not been invented for the purpose that they might signify the nature itself of God, which, since it is unique and simple, if it has to be named must be named with a unique name. But they have been instituted so that they might make known the many and various goods that flow forth in richest bounty from the divine goodness. But if in addition to the procession from God, they signify anything in God, they declare

apud Deum, dicunt utique quid non sit Deus. Ubi igitur Deus ipsum unum vel unitas vel monas cognominatur, primo quidem per ista significatur non esse Deos plures sed unicum, item unicum Deum non esse compositum, sed simplicissimum; rursus simplicissimum Deum non esse dividuum, atque ita dicitur, quid non sit Deus.

2 Deinde per eiusmodi appellationes significatur rerum unitas ex divina unitate procedens: singularitas[30] enim et simplicitas individuitasque ubicunque rebus inest, a prima singularitate, simplicitate, individuitate procedit. Sed hoc interest, quod qui in rem aliquam incidit singularem unicamque, hanc habet solam; qui vero unicum Deum habet, iam possidet omnia. Preterea res plurimum simplices compositioni serviture sunt, divina simplicitas compositionibus dominatur. Denique ad individua in rebus velut ad punctum et unitatem devenimus velut ad minima dividendo paulatim vel quomodolibet minuendo; ad individuitatem vero divinam pervenitur velut ad maximum, ubi cum infinita unitate virtus concurrit immensa.

3 Et, ut summatim dicam, quod homo sit unus homo, quod corpus sit unum aliquid et unum aliquid anima, sic ex Deo habent, sicut ex eodem habuerunt ut et simpliciter essent et essent homo, corpus et anima. Partes sane corporis tum humani tum mundani, inter se naturaliter repugnantes, ut in unam formam conciliarentur a prima tandem unitate sortite sunt; per eandem quoque discordes anime vires et affectus et motus dissensione tandem sedata placantur totusque animus sub una intelligentie forma vivit.

4 Sed quis non videat uniones omnium a primo principio dependere? Quatenus enim cuncta sunt ab eodem, et eo quidem

at the least what God is not. So where God is called the One itself or unity or the monad, what is signified by these [names] is firstly that there are not many gods but one God; and likewise that this unique God is not composite but utterly simple; again, that this most simple God is not divisible. And so we declare what God is not.

Next, through these same names is signified the unity of things, 2
a unity proceeding from the divine unity. For singleness, simplicity, and indivisibility wherever it is present in things proceeds from the prime singleness, simplicity, and indivisibility. This is of importance because he who comes across some single unique thing only has this one thing. But if he were to possess God in His uniqueness, he would already possess all things. Moreover, very simple things will serve for a [particular] composition; but divine simplicity rules over every composition. Finally, we arrive at particulars in things as we arrive at a point and at a unity, [that is,] as we arrive at smallest things by dividing little by little or by reducing them in some way. Yet we arrive at divine indivisibility as at the greatest thing, where measureless power is at one with infinite unity.

And to summarize, let me say that the fact a man is one man, a 3
body something one, and a soul something one, this oneness they have from God, just as they have derived from the same God the fact that they simply exist, that they are a man, a body, a soul. The parts of the body, whether the human body or the world's, which are naturally in disagreement with each other, are at length destined by the prime unity to be reconciled to one form. Through this same [form] too the soul's discords, powers, desires, and motions are eventually calmed when dissension has been stilled, and the whole rational soul lives under one form of understanding.

Who cannot see, however, that the unions of all depend on 4
the first principle? For, to the extent all things come from the

simplicissimo individuoque prorsus secumque ipso penitus uniformi, eatenus et invicem conformia sunt confluuntque in idem velut finem, quod et tanquam principium ad se ipsum convertit quecunque produxit, convertendoque in idem, efficit interim ut cuncta inter se sint eadem.

5 Proinde, quemadmodum in *Theologia* nostra probavimus, ad fecunditatem nature pertinet generatio, et interior illa quidem priusquam exterior; et quo excellentior natura est, eo interiorem sibi prolem generat. Prima ergo natura adeo generat intimam, ut unica sit generantis genitique natura, eadem quoque mutui sit amoris. Veritas quidem generationis productionisque postulat ut tres he persone sint existentes, unitas interea infiniti principii facit ut natura sit una; contra in nobis, in quibus una persona in tribus consistit naturis, anima, corpore, spiritu.

6 Quod latine personam dicimus Dionysius dicit *ὑπόστασιν*, quod quidem non debemus substantiam interpretari, sed subpositum, vel subsistens, vel existens, aut subsistentiam vel existentiam. Ita vero conclude: natura communiter prior est et simplicior quam persona; si ergo persona plerunque unitatem suam servat in multitudine naturarum, multo magis convenientiusque natura potest singularem unitatem suam in personarum numero conservare; quod autem et ratione possibile et simul convenientissimum est, ipse in se Deus implet.

7 Divinam Trinitatem ibidem confirmavimus oraculis Chaldeorum; Plato quoque noster scribens ad Hermiam in divinitate patrem nominat atque filium, et mox utrunque singulari numero celebrat. Refert Iamblichus Egyptiorum mysteria, in quibus Deum

same source and from that which is most simple and indivisible and utterly and completely uniform in itself, to that extent they are mutually conforming and flow together into the same channel as to their end. As the principle, this turns all that it has produced back to itself, and, by converting them to the same, it ensures meanwhile that all are the same among themselves.

Therefore, as we have proved in our *Theology*, generation per- 5
tains to nature's fecundity, and interior generation is prior to exterior.[22] And the more excellent the nature is, the more interior the offspring it generates for itself. Hence the very first nature so generates its interior offspring that the nature of what generates and what is generated is one; the nature of [their] mutual love too is the same. The truth of [divine] generation and production demands that the three Persons [of the Trinity] exist, yet the unity of their infinite principle ensures that [their] nature is one. The contrary occurs in us where [our] one person consists of its three natures: soul, body, and spirit.

What we call "person" in Latin, Dionysius calls *hypostasis*. We 6
should not interpret this as [Aristotelian] substance, but as what underlies or is subsisting or existing, or is subsistence or existence. Conclude thus: [a] nature commonly is prior to and simpler than [a] person. Hence, if [our] person for the most part preserves its own unity even amid the plurality of [its three] natures, then much more so, and more appropriately so, can the [divine] Nature preserve its singular unity in the number of [its] Persons. But that which is possible in reason and at the same time is most appropriate, God fulfills in Himself.

In the same *Theology* we have confirmed the divine Trinity 7
in the oracles of the Chaldeans.[23] Our Plato too, writing to Hermias, names the Father and the Son in the Divinity, and in that single number straightway celebrates both.[24] Iamblichus refers to the Egyptians' mysteries in which they introduce God as radiating

inducunt ex se emicantem, suique ipsius patrem filiumque nominant, ubi unam in primo naturam ponunt generantis et geniti. Plotinus ubi de amore divino, item ubi de uno et bono et libertate primi disputat, intimam quandam in divinis generationem ponit, per quam existens aliquid generetur; Deumque asserit ex se ipso prodire.

8 Ex hac igitur fecunditate divina omnis fecunditas emanavit in angelos, in animas, in celestia, in inferiora celo; ex illo quidem generante generantia, ex illo autem genito genita prodierunt; ex producente similiter et producto producentia pariter atque producta. Appellatur etiam Deus causa quoniam omnia essentiam accipiunt a Deo, bonitate videlicet divina ita volente, sicut et Plato in Timeo inquit, non autem necessitate nature. Nominatur sapientia et pulchritudo quoniam harmoniam decoremque rebus inserit — harmoniam, inquam, interiorem, exteriorem vero decorem, per que quidem duo et sunt et bene sunt omnia.

9 Post hec Dionysius eternum[31] Dei filium, inquit, benignitate mirifica humanam sibi naturam assumpsisse nullo interim modo mutatum. Mysterium hoc Platonicus Amelius Evangelium Iohannis commemorans veneratur; Plato quinetiam contra Protagoram disputans non hominem, inquit, esse rerum omnium mensuram, sed Deum, maxime vero si Deus fiat homo. Rationes autem mysterii huius in libro *De Christiana religione* tractavimus.

out from Himself. They name Him the Father and the Son of Himself when they posit in the first [the Father] the one nature of the generator and the generated.[25] Plotinus, when speaking about divine love and likewise about the One and the Good and about the liberty of the First, posits in divine beings a certain inner generation, a generation via which any existing thing is generated; and he asserts that God processes out of Himself.[26]

So all fecundity emanates from this divine fecundity, whether it is in angels, souls, the celestials, or the subcelestials. From that [divine] generating has proceeded [all] things that generate, from that [divine] generated has proceeded [all] things generated. Similarly, from that [divine] producing and produced there has proceeded [all] producing and produced alike. God is also called the cause, because all things accept essence from God, that is, when the divine goodness so wills it, as Plato says in the *Timaeus,* but not by any necessity of His nature.[27] God is called wisdom and beauty, because He sows harmony and comeliness in things, inner harmony, that is, but outer comeliness; and via these two all things exist and are well. 8

Subsequent to these [arguments] Dionysius says that the eternal Son of God out of a wondrous kindness has taken human nature unto Himself, but He is not changed meanwhile in any way. Amelius the Platonist venerates this mystery, recalling John the Evangelist.[28] Plato too, in arguing against Protagoras, says that man is not the measure of all things; rather that God is; but chiefly if God is made man.[29] The reasons of this mystery, however, we have addressed in our book *On the Christian Religion.*[30] 9

: XVI :

Dionysius: Divina nomina plurimum significant beneficos ex Deo[32] *progressus. Deus appellatur unitas, trinitas, causa, sapientia, pulchritudo, benignitas.*

1 Hec tanquam initiati ab eloquiis sacris accepimus. Invenies autem universam (ut ita dixerim) sacram theologorum laudationem ad beneficos summe divinitatis progressus explanandos laudandosque appellationes divinas effingere. Itaque in omni ferme[33] theologica[34] tractatione summam divinitatem sancte celebratam videmus: Ut monadem quidem et unitatem propter simplicitatem unitatemque impartibilitatis ipsius naturam exsuperantis, ex qua tanquam unifica potestate efficimur unum; dividuisque nostris diversitatibus supra mundanum modum conglobatis, in monadem deiformem unionemque Deum imitantem colligimur.

2 Ut trinitatem vero propter superessentialis fecunditatis in suppositis tribus expressionem, ex qua paternitas omnis in celo et in terra existit atque nominator. Preterea ut omnium existentium causam quoniam omnia per bonitatem eius effectricem essentie ut essent acceperunt; tum vero sapientem atque pulchram quia quecunque, ex eorum numero que sunt, nature sue propria servant inviolata, divine omnis harmonie sacrique decoris sunt plena.

3 Precipue vero generi nostro propitiam quoniam in una personarum suarum naturam nostram vere integreque assumpsit revocans ad se sibique applicans humanam humilitatem, ex qua simplex

: XVI :

Dionysius: The divine names signify preeminently the gifts proceeding from God. God is called unity, trinity, cause, wisdom, beauty, and kindness.

As initiates we have accepted these gifts from the sacred Scriptures. But you will find that the universal (if I may call it that) and sacred praise of the theologians is deemed to unfold the gifts proceeding from the highest Divinity and to sing in praise of the divine names. Therefore in almost every theological discussion we see the highest Divinity celebrated in a holy way. [He is celebrated] as a monad and unity on account of the simplicity and unity of His indivisibility which surpasses nature. From this unific power as it were we are made one; and, with our divided diversities gathered together in a supra-mundane way, we are gathered into the godlike monad and the union that imitates God. 1

[God is also celebrated] as a Trinity on account of the expression of His super-essential fecundity in three subjects [i.e., Persons], "from which all paternity exists and is named in the heavens and on earth."[31] Additionally He is celebrated as the cause of all existing things, because, by way of His goodness (which effects essence) all things have been brought into existence. The cause is both wise and beautiful, because all things, if we take the number of existing things that preserve inviolate the properties of their own nature, are full of all divine harmony and sacred beauty. 2

The cause is especially gracious to our human race, because in one of its Persons it has truly and wholly assumed our nature, recalling to itself and applying to itself human humility. From this cause Jesus is both ineffably simple and composite, and He who is 3

Iesus ineffabiliter est compositus, et qui est eternus temporalem sumpsit processionem, atque in intima nature nostre pervenit qui omnem totius nature ordinem super essentie modum eminenter excedit, propria tamen interea immutabilia prorsus et inconfusa conservans.

4 Hec, inquam, tanquam initiati didicimus, et quecunque alia deifica lumina sacris eloquiis hausta secreta divinorum preceptorum nostrorum traditio explanatione nobis perspicua contulit.

: XVII :

Marsilius:
Ipsum unum bonumque est superius ente, intellectu, intelligibili; item quare figuris utamur ad divina declaranda. Item de resurrectione et fruitione Dei.

1 Iam diu lectores admonendi nobis erant vocabula hec, essentia, et ens, et entia philosophis condonanda, ut instrumenta sua cuique artifici concedenda; preterea non posse nos, ubicunque Dionysius οὐσίαν nominat, per substantiam satis interpretari, sed plerunque per essentiam exprimendum, presertim ubi de ipso uno bonoque, ubi de malo, ubi de materia disputat. Philosophi enim non substantiam quidem, que unum predicamentum est, sed essentiam atque ens, quod omnia predicamenta complectitur, in certamen trahunt cum uno atque bono. Peripatetici sane ens, unum, bonum equalia putant, at vero Platonici, inter quos Dionysius noster

eternal took on temporal procession. And He came into our most intimate nature, He who exceeds every order of nature's entirety and who is eminently above the mode of essence. In the meantime, however, He preserved all His own properties as entirely immutable and unconfused.

As initiates we have learned all these things and all the other godlike illuminations which can be derived from sacred Scripture; 4
these too have been handed down to us with a clear explanation in the secret tradition of our divine teachers.

: XVII :

Marsilio:
The One and the Good itself is superior to being, intellect, and the intelligible. Why we use figures [or metaphors] to reveal matters divine. On resurrection and the enjoyment of God.

For a long time now readers have been warning us that these 1
words "essence" and "being" and "entities"—words presented us by the philosophers—must be ceded to each author to use as he will; and besides that, wherever Dionysius uses the noun *ousia* we cannot translate it satisfactorily by "substance." But the majority [say] it should be conveyed by "essence," especially when Dionysius speaks about the One and the Good, about the bad, and about matter. For the philosophers do not bring substance, which is one predicate, into the contest with the One and the Good; but they do bring in essence and being which embraces all [other] predicates. The Aristotelians indeed think that Being, the One, and the Good are equal.[32] But the Platonists, among whom our Dionysius

obtinet principatum, unum bonumque enti extra controversiam anteponunt tanquam amplius, simplicius, prius, sufficientius, ideoque summum Deum unum ac bonum essentia superius libenter appellant.

2 Sed dic age, quando Dionysius materiam informem οὐσίαν inferiorem inquit, interpretaberisne substantia inferiorem? At parum dixeris: nam quatenus est informis, non solum substantiali, sed etiam accidentali est forma deterior. Preterea, ubi malum ait nec esse nec habere οὐσίαν, si substantiam intellexeris ibi negatam, subintelligere poteris malo quantitatem saltem vel qualitatem posse concedi, quod dictu nephas.

3 Proinde Dionysius, una cum Platonicis, quecunque sensibus subiacent entia non vera nominat; substantias vero incorporeas earumque proprietates appellat entia vera et intelligibilia vocitat, quo in genere sunt anime intellectuales et intellectus angelici. Super hec tandem entia vera introducit Deum excelsius ente, intelligibilique superius.

4 Sane quemadmodum unusquisque sensus cum sensibili suo proportionem quandam habet, ita sensus universus cum universo sensibili; item quam proportionem sensus habet ad sensibile, eandem ferme ad intelligibile obtinet intellectus; rursus qua proportione se habet sensus ad intellectum, eadem sensibile ad intelligibile se habere videtur. Quamobrem cum et intellectus et intelligibile proportionem aliquam subeant, merito super utrumque Deus est ab omni proportione penitus absolutus. Est et super substantiam, que sub ente ab accidente dividitur et commertium subit cum accidente; est etiam super essentiam natura sua multiplicabilem in essentias, ipse tamen non ita multiplicandus.

occupies pride of place, put the One and the Good without question before Being in that it is ampler, simpler, prior, and more sufficient. And therefore they willingly call the highest God the One and the Good and superior to essence.

Tell me then, when Dionysius calls unformed matter inferior in *ousia*, shouldn't you interpret this to mean inferior in substance? But you will have said too little. For, to the extent matter is without form, it is worse than not only substantial form but also accidental form. Moreover, if, when he declares that the bad neither is nor has *ousia*, you were to take this to mean that he is denying it substance, you could still be supposing that he is granting the bad [the predicates of] quantity at least or quality. But this is wrong. 2

Along with the Platonists, therefore, Dionysius denominates all things that submit to the senses as not true entities. Rather, he refers to incorporeal substances and their properties as the true entities: he habitually calls them the intelligibles. Intellectual souls are in this class and angelic intellects. Above these true entities, finally, he introduces God as being more excellent than Being and as higher than the intelligible. 3

Indeed, just as every single sense has some proportion with its sensible object, so the universal sense has some proportion with the sensible universe. Similarly, the proportion the sense has with the sensible is almost on par with the proportion the intellect maintains with the intelligible. Again, the proportion that sense has to intellect is the same as that which the sensible seems to have to the intelligible. So, since intellect and the intelligible are subject indeed to some proportion, above them both there has to be God who is utterly free from all proportion. He is also above substance, which under Being is divided from accident, and yet has ties with accident. He is above essence too which by its nature is multipliable into essences; and yet God must not be so multiplied. 4

5 Quoniam vero intellectus noster, propter nimium sensuum sensibiliumque commertium, in eiusmodi vita quodammodo ad intelligibilia pura fit ineptus, ideo prudentes theologi sensibilibus quibusdam (et his quidem honestioribus) intelligibilia vestiunt, ita demum intellectui nostro magis accommodate qui lumen intelligibile ita temperatum tam facile cernit quam oculi lumen quodlibet in corporibus videt quodammodo solidis[35] alioquin minime discernendum.

6 Deum quoque excelsius ente et quovis intelligibili mirabiliter eminentius entibus intelligibilibusque ad angelos et animas pertinentibus induere solent. Sic intellectui temperandum sicut sol ipse, qui alioqui tollerari non potest, rara sepius nebula oculis temperatur ita lumen figuramque solis tuto cernentibus.

7 His itaque rationibus Plato noster animam intellectumque per lineas, circulos, musicos numeros, currus, alas, similiaque describit, et Deum in sole figurat; Isaias quoque Dominum videt in solio excelso sedentem et seraphinos fingit alatos, ut Ezechielem in presentia ceterosque dimittam.

8 Et, ut summatim dicam, sicut in genere sensibilium puriora tanquam velamina quedam rebus intelligendis apponunt, scilicet puncta, lineas, figuras, unitatem, numeros, lumina, per punctum quidem et unitatem significantes naturam indivisibilem, per lumen vero intelligentie certitudinem, sic que summa sunt in ipso intelligibilium ordine Deo adhibent, ut essentiam, vitam, intelligentiam, veritatem, sapientiam, intelligibile lumen; verum, sicut illa intelligibilibus deteriora sunt, ita hec inferiora Deo.

· CHAPTER XVII ·

Since our intellect, on account of its excessive dealings with the 5
senses and with sensibles, has been rendered by such a life unsuit-
able in a way for the pure intelligibles, far-seeing theologians
clothe the intelligibles in particular sensibles, and these the more
honorable. In this way the intelligibles are more adapted at last to
our intellect, which sees the intelligible light, thus tempered, as
easily as the light of the eyes sees something in bodies that are in
a way solid, something that is otherwise indiscernible.

That God also exists more excellently than Being, and more 6
eminently—wondrously so—than any intelligible, the theologians
are accustomed to assume from the intelligible entities, [i.e.,]
those which pertain to angels and souls. Thus God must be "tempered" for the intellect [to contemplate Him], just as the sun,
whose blaze cannot otherwise be endured by our eyes, is often
tempered for them by a thin cloud; in this way the sun's light and
shape is safely seen by those gazing up at it.

For these reasons, therefore, our Plato describes the soul and 7
intellect by way of lines, circles, musical numbers, chariots, wings,
and suchlike;[33] and he figures God in [the image of] the sun.[34]
Isaiah too sees the Lord sitting on a throne on high; and he imagines the seraphim as winged.[35] But for the present I will set aside
Ezekiel and the rest of the prophets.[36]

To sum up, let me say that just as they adduce purer images in 8
the class of sensibles [to use as] particular veils in order for us to
understand concepts—images like points, lines, shapes, unity,
numbers, lights—signifying through the point and unity the indivisible nature, but through light the certitude of understanding—
so what are highest in the order itself of intelligibles they attribute
to God, for instance, essence, life, understanding, truth, wisdom,
and intelligible light. But just as sensibles are lower than intelligibles, so are intelligibles inferior to God.

9 Resurrectionem corporum humanorum divina potestate futuram Plato in libro *De regno* describit, quam olim Zoroaster asseruit; itaque legimus in Magorum carminibus, quod omnes usurpavere Platonici, animam nostram preter terrenum corpus habere celeste, quicum quasi curru quodam reversura sit in celum; item animas Deo deditas terrenum quoque corpus terre tandem non relicturas, sed una cum celesti suo corpore id quoque corpus celo reddituras illuminandum; quibus in verbis et resurrectio corporum et beatorum splendor asseritur.

10 Profecto, quemadmodum sol in vere terre visceribus condita semina suscitat et pleraque pulcherrimis floribus ornat, ita splendidissimum Christi corpus, statutis temporibus, coniectis usquequaque radiis, hominum corpora suscitabit multaque preterea splendoribus exornabit. Hinc illud Pauli: 'conformabis corpus humilitatis nostre configuratum corpori claritatis sue.'

11 Quando igitur ita filii resurrectionis erimus, id est, ex eo qui primus iam resurrexit in similitudinem eius renati fuerimus, celoque donati terno[36] Christi lumine perfruemur: per visum quidem visibili corporis Christi luce, per intellectum vero iam ab omni contagione corporea liberum intelligibili lumine ex intellectuali, videlicet Christi anima in nostram intelligentiam emicante. Sed per unitatem illam anime, quam Plato in *Phedro* mentis caput appellat, intellectu prestantius, consequemur unionem quandam intelligentia meliorem cum unitate bonitateque divina, que quidem infinito intervallo superat intellectum, sed coniectis in

In the book *On Rule* [i.e., the *Statesman*], Plato describes the future resurrection of human bodies by divine power, which Zoroaster had earlier maintained.[37] So we read in the verses of the Magi, which all the Platonists have co-opted, that our soul has a celestial body over and beyond this earthly one, in which it will return to heaven as in a sort of chariot.[38] Likewise we read that souls dedicated to God will not leave the earthly body behind on earth at the end, but along with its celestial body they will return that earthly body too to heaven to be filled with light.[39] In these words are affirmed both the resurrection of bodies and the splendor of the blessed. 9

Certainly, just as the sun in the spring awakens the seeds preserved in the womb of the earth and adorns most of them with most beautiful flowers, so Christ's most splendid body, at the appointed time, will awaken the bodies of men with its far-flung rays everywhere; and adorn many of them besides with splendors. Hence that saying of Paul: "He shall change our lowly body that it may be fashioned like unto His glorious body."[40] 10

Accordingly, when we become "sons of the resurrection,"[41] that is, reborn from Him who already was the first to rise, and having been reborn in His likeness and granted the third heaven,[42] we shall enjoy the light of Christ. Through our sight we will enjoy the visible light of Christ's body. But through our intellect, freed now from all corporeal contagion, we will enjoy the intelligible light radiating from His intellectual [light]—enjoy, that is, the soul of Christ shining forth in our understanding. But through that unity of the soul, which in the *Phaedrus* Plato calls the mind's head[43] and which is more outstanding than intellect, we will attain a sort of union that is better than understanding, a union with the unity and goodness divine, which surpasses the intellect by an infinite interval. Having darted His rays into our unity, rays higher than the intelligible order, [God] will 11

unitatem nostram radiis intelligibili sorte superioribus uniet sibi mentem, que ita formata Deo[37] per Deum ipsum Deum protinus percipit formatorem.

: XVIII :

Dionysius: Divina rite docentur per signa. Item qualis gloria celestis futura sit.

1 Nunc quidem in his erudimur pro nostri ingenii facultate, cui sane indulgens benignitas sanctarum litterarum sacerdotaliumque traditionum, per sacra velamina intelligibilia quidem sensibilibus, que vero essentiam superant rebus que habent essentiam obtegit; formasque et figuras his que formam figuramque refugiunt rite circundat, excelsam denique infigurabilemque simplicitatem signorum dividuorum varietate multiplicat et effingit.

2 At quando incorruptibiles immortalesque facti erimus sortemque Christo similem beatamque adepti semper, ut scriptum est, cum domino erimus, visibili quidem divinoque ipsius spectaculo per castissimam speculationem iam impleti, lucidissimis tunc nos circumfulgente luminibus, quemadmodum discipulos suos[38] in divinissima illa transfiguratione sua.

3 Intelligibilis autem illuminationis eius intellectu a perturbatione materiaque separato participes;[39] unionis vero intellectu superioris

unite [our] mind to Himself. Thus the mind, being formed by God through God Himself, will straightway perceive God [as] the creator of form.[44]

: XVIII :

Dionysius: Divine matters are rightly taught via signs. What the celestial glory will be like.

In this life we are instructed in these [divine] matters through the power of our native intelligence: the kindness of sacred Scripture and of the priestly tradition indulges it in this. Using sacred veils it conceals intelligibles in sensibles, and what surpasses essence it conceals in things which have essence. It turns to forms and shapes to enclose those things which rightly shy away from form and shape. Finally, it takes the surpassing and unfigurable simplicity, and in multiplying it imagines it in a variety of divided signs. 1

But when we are made incorruptible and immortal and have attained the blessed condition that resembles Christ's, as it is written "we will always be with the Lord,"[45] then we will be filled by way of purest contemplation with the visible and divine spectacle of Christ, a spectacle that will then blaze around us with lights of intensest clarity, just as it blazed around His disciples at His most divine Transfiguration.[46] 2

We will participate in the intelligible illumination of Him but will do so in an intellect separated from perturbation and matter. And we will be in possession of a union higher than intellect, a 3

prefulgentium radiorum incognitis beatisque iactibus compotes erimus, in diviniore videlicet supercelestium mentium imitatione. Erimus enim, ut divinorum eloquiorum veritas ait, equales angelis filiique Dei, quandoquidem resurrectionis filii futuri simus.

: XIX :

Marsilius:
Quare circa divina imaginibus et comparationibus uti deceat, et quomodo Deus essentiam cognitionemque[40] *antecellat.*

1 In hoc vite statu anima quidem corpore vestita est, ratio vero imaginatione, mens denique ratione. Tum vero imaginatio, qua utimur vivimusque quam plurimum, intelligentie notiones assidue sensibilium imaginibus induit, quocirca nec iniuria cognitioni nostre non tam nuda quam vestita quedam accommodata videntur. Induunt igitur sapientes merito, sicut diximus, sensibilibus quidem intelligibilia, his vero divina.

2 Hac Plato providentia iubet hominem sub tenebroso specu nutritum ad intuendam meridianam lucem non subito compellendum, sed monstrandum huic solem primo quidem ad lucerne lumen in aqua, deinde in luna sub nocte serena, demum in ipsa aeris serenitate diurna; similibus quoque gradibus rude vult ingenium ad contemplandam perduci divinitatem.

3 Linee undique contingentes centrum non longitudine quidem sua signum illud tangunt magnitudinis expers, sed suo queque signo signum; quod quidem etsi non est longum neque plura,

union of refulgent rays hurled blessedly upon us from the unknown; that is, we will be [sharing] in the even more divine imitation of the supercelestial minds. For we will be, as the truth of the divine Scriptures says, "equal to the angels" and be "sons of God, being the children of the resurrection."[47]

: XIX :

Marsilio:
Why with matters divine we must use images and comparisons; and how God precedes essence and cognition.

In this state of life, soul is clothed with body, reason with imagination, and mind finally with reason. But here more than ever the imagination, which we use and by which we live as much as possible, constantly clothes the notions of understanding with the images of sensibles. Therefore, not unjustly, certain topics seem proper to our cognition, not as naked, but as clothed. Hence wise men, as we have said, duly clothe intelligibles with sensibles, and divine matters with intelligibles. 1

By way of this providence, Plato says that a man nurtured within a shadowy cave should not suddenly be forced to look at the noonday light. Rather, the sun should be presented to him firstly in the light of a lantern on water, then in the moon on a quiet night, finally in the diurnal serenity itself of the air.[48] By similar steps too he wants our rude natural intelligence to be led to the contemplation of divinity. 2

Lines that everywhere reach to the center do not touch with their length that central point which lacks magnitude. Rather, it is with their point that all touch that [central] point which indeed, although it is neither long nor many, yet embraces the 3

plurimarum tamen longarumque linearum terminos, id est puncta, eodem sui puncto complectitur. Iam vero cum linee cuncte earumque termini ab eo profluant, merito in se eminenter anticipat[41] omnes; eadem ratione sphere minores multe sphera quadam ampliore comprehense, centris queque suis attingunt sphere continentis centrum mirabiliter in se et circulos omnes et centra complectens.

4 His ferme comparationibus Plotinus magnus utitur, ostensurus qua ratione quam plurime simul mentes in unum ipsum universi principium figant[42] intuitus, ipsumque in se comprehendat et intellectus omnes et summa queque intellectualium actionum. Idem hic ante Plotinum Dionysius attigisse videtur, probans preterea intellectus, ubi Deum attingunt, intellectuales actiones posthabere quasi multiplices (ideo divine oppositas unitati) atque per unitatem potius amoremque attingere, quod et Plotinus sepe comprobat.

5 Quemadmodum vita ante se essentiam postulat, nisi enim sit non vivit, ita cognitio vitam, nempe non cognoscit, nisi prius vivat. Omnis ergo cognitio in essentia viva fundamentum habet, et ideo circa essentias atque entia tanquam fines dirigit actionem. Hinc aiunt naturalem quidem philosphiam circa ens iam quale mobileque versari, mathematicam vero circa ens iam quantum, metaphysicam denique ipsum simpliciter ens spectare; quod tametsi nondum substantia est vel accidens nec dum quantum vel quale vel mobile, potest tamen per hec omnia quandoque finiri: ideo nec est simpliciter infinitum.

6 Sed (ut summatim dicam) cum cognitio quidem et essentia sit posterior et desinat in essentias velut fines, merito Deus essentiam supereminens, cognitionem[43] etiam antecellit, nec igitur attingi cognitione potest. Essentiam vero bono posteriorem esse testantur,

ends of many long lines, that is, their points, with its same point. Now since all the lines and their ends radiate from that [central point], it duly anticipates them all eminently in itself. For the same reason, many minor spheres are embraced by a greater sphere and all touch with their centers the center of the containing sphere which in itself marvelously embraces all the circles and centers.

The great Plotinus generally uses these comparisons when he is 4
about to show why minds, however many, may fasten their intuitive glances together upon the one principle itself of the universe; and why this principle comprehends in itself all intellects and the summits themselves of intellectual actions.[49] Again, Dionysius seems to have touched on this before Plotinus,[50] when he proves, moreover, that intellects, in attaining God, set aside intellectual actions as being multiple and thus opposite to the divine unity: they succeed instead through unity and love. Plotinus frequently proves this.[51]

Just as life demands essence prior to itself—for unless it exists 5
it does not live—so cognition demands life; for unless it first lives, it does not know. Therefore all cognition has its foundation in living essence; and thus it directs [its] action with regard to essences and entities as to its ends. Hence they say that natural philosophy treats being in terms of what kind it is already, and how mobile; while mathematical philosophy looks to being as already quantified; and metaphysical philosophy finally looks to simple being in itself. Such being, though it is not yet substance or accident, nor yet quantified or qualified or mobile, can nevertheless be determined on occasion by way of all these predicates. Hence this being is not absolutely infinite.

However, to summarize, since cognition is both subsequent to 6
essence and yet terminates in essences as its ends, it is fitting that God, who dwells above essence, be superior to cognition too, and so cannot be attained by cognition. But they testify that essence is posterior to the Good, given that all essences do not stay at rest in

essentie quelibet in se ipsis minime quiescentes, sed annitentes semper ad actionem—ad actionem videlicet circa bonum: unaquemque suum, qua quidem ratione ipsa simpliciter primaque essentia agere iam convincitur ad ipsum simpliciter primumque bonum.

: XX :

Dionysius:
Signis congrue utimur ad divina, ipse vero Deus essentiam cognitionemque antecedit.

Nunc autem pro ingenii viribus congrue ad divina signis utimur; rursumque ex his ad simplicem unitamque intelligibilium spectaculorum veritatem modo quodam proportionis assurgimus; atque post omnem nostram divinorum intelligentiam, sistentes intellectuales actiones nostras, ad sublimiorem essentia[44] radium, quantum fas est, contendimus. In quo quidem termini omnes omnium cognitionum plusquam ineffabiliter preexistunt, quem nec intelligere nec eloqui licet, neque quomodocunque aliter speculari, propterea quod est ab omnibus segregatus et eminenter ignotus. Iam vero essentialium omnium cognitionum atque virium superessentiali[45] virtute fines simul omnes anticipavit, atque incomprehensibili potestate supercelestibus quoque mentibus altior extat. Si enim cognitiones omnes tum entium sunt, tum etiam in entia desinunt, qui omni essentia superior est consequenter est ab omni cognitione semotus.

themselves, but always strive for action—action, that is, with regard to the good. Each single essence strives for its own good, for the very [same] reason indeed that the absolutely prime essence itself is already proven to act for the absolutely prime Good itself.

: XX :

Dionysius:
We properly use signs to signify matters divine, but God Himself precedes essence and cognition.

On earth we use appropriate symbols (those our wits are best capable of devising) for things divine. Again we rise upward by way of proportion from these symbols to the simple and united truth of the intelligible spectacles. And after all our understanding of things divine, we cease our intellectual actions, and, insofar as it is permissible, we strive toward the ray higher than essence. In this ray preexist, in a manner more than ineffable, all the ends of all cognition. We are not permitted to understand, or to speak about, or to otherwise observe this ray in any way, because it is apart from all things and is eminently unknown. But by super-essential power it has already simultaneously anticipated all the ends of all essential cognitions and powers. And with incomprehensible power it exists far above supercelestial minds too. For, if all cognitions are of entities and remain still in being, the ray which is higher than all essence is consequently far beyond all cognition.

: XXI :

Marsilius:
Deus amplectitur, complectitur, anticipat omnia. Mysterium divinum nec anime[46] nec angeli per intelligentiam assequuntur, sed per unionem intelligentia meliorem.

1 Deus omnia amplectitur, complectitur, anticipat: amplectitur quidem per excellentiam potestatis, velut extrinsecus circumfusus. Complectitur autem una quadam penes se natura unice colligens singula quantumlibet[47] inter se diversa. Anticipat denique, quoniam et antequam sint possidet ipse et gradu longe prestantiore quam sint.

2 Deum neque scientia neque tactu percipere possumus: id autem est neque conclusione quadam antecedentibus principiis consequente, neque subito quodam intellectus intuitu. Ipsum bonum ob infinitatem suam intellectu finito assequi non valemus; rursus unitatem eius propter incomparabilem simplicitatem intelligentia semper multiplici non attingimus. Tres insuper illas (ut ita dixerim) existentias in unitate simplicissima subsistentes vestigiis nullis investigare licet, presertim quoniam quilibet trium illic existentium eque Deus est atque bonus, totusque Deus totumque bonum.

3 Angeli quinetiam naturali intelligentie lumine mysteria eiusmodi non attingunt, sed divinitus infuso supernaturali quodam lumine in angelicam unitatem intellectu prestantiorem coniunguntur Deo, unione quadam intelligentiam superante; per quam

: XXI :

Marsilio:
God encircles, embraces, and anticipates all things. Neither souls nor angels attain the divine mystery through understanding, but rather through the union which is better than understanding.

God encircles, embraces, and anticipates all things. He encircles by 1
way of the excellence of His power, as having surrounded things externally. He embraces them when He collects and unites in [His] one nature as it were all single things in His possession, however diverse among themselves. Lastly He anticipates all because He Himself possesses them before they exist and possesses them in a far more eminent degree than they exist.

We can perceive God neither by knowledge nor by touch, that 2
is, neither by some conclusion consequent on antecedent principles, nor by some sudden intuition of the intellect. We cannot attain the Good itself with the finite intellect on account of the Good's infinity; nor again do we attain the Good's unity with an understanding that is always multiple because of the Good's incomparable simplicity. And as for the three existences so to speak which subsist in [God's] utterly simple unity, no one can lawfully search for any of [their] traces at all, especially because each of the three [Persons] existing there is equally God, is the good and entire God, is the totally Good.

Moreover, the angels do not attain such mysteries by the natu- 3
ral light of understanding, but they are joined to God by a supernatural light that is divinely infused into their angelic unity, a unity more eminent than intellect; and joined in a union superior to understanding. Through this union they enjoy God and

utique unionem fruentes Deo hec mysteria, etsi non omnino comprehendunt, certissimis tamen rationibus consequuntur; angelos dico non omnes, sed beatos: hi namque soli inter angelos supernaturali lumine digni sunt habiti.

4 Anime quoque in patria iam beate, et sique preterea quasi separate viventes in corpore extra corpus aliquando divinitus rapiuntur, facte iam angelice, eodem ad tempus cum angelis munere potiuntur; similium dumtaxat animorum officium est divina nobis nomina rite tradere.

5 Quoniam vero nomina hec non rite pandunt nisi coniuncte Deo, coniuncte vero non sunt nisi seiuncte prius non solum a corpore fuerint, verum etiam a propriis intelligentie actionibus, rursus ab omnibus tum que sunt, tum etiam que intelliguntur esse, idcirco prima eiusmodi nomina tam ablationem rerum a Deo quam separationem Dei ipsius a rebus significaverunt.

6 Uniones quibus beati vel angeli vel animi Deo iunguntur appellat vel *ἐπιβολάς* vel *παραδοχάς*: primum quidem significat iactus, ictus, aspectus, intuitus; secundum vero perceptiones, acceptiones, susceptiones. Disiunctio hec originem ducit a diversis opinionibus circa visum:[48] Platonici enim putant visum foras emittere radios, Peripatetici vero contra[49] imagines a re videnda suscipere. Beati vero nec iaciunt suos in Deum radios nec Deum ipsum accipiunt, sed ab ipso Deo lumen hauriunt, quo statim hausto non Deus quidem beato coniungitur, sed beatus Deo: non enim beatus Deum accipit, sed beatum sibi Deus assumit.

although they do not entirely comprehend these mysteries, yet they pursue them with reasons that are most certain. I do not say all the angels, but the blessed ones. For they alone among the angels are held worthy of the supernatural light.

And souls too, those already blessed in their homeland, and 4
those moreover living separately as it were in the body who are at some point divinely enraptured outside the body and already made angelic — these souls, at the right time, take possession of the same gift as the angels. Of suchlike souls alone is it the office to transmit to us the divine names correctly.

Since they do not reveal these names correctly unless they have 5
been united with God — but they are not united unless they have first been separated not only from the body but also from their own actions of understanding, and again separated from all things which exist and which are understood to exist — accordingly such prime names have signified both the taking away of things from God and the separation of God Himself from things.

The unions by which the blessed, whether angels or souls, are 6
joined to God, Dionysius calls *epibolas* or *paradochas*. The first signifies throws, strikes, or glances at, or intuitions of. The second signifies perceptions, acceptances, or receptions. This distinction takes its origin from diverse opinions with regard to sight. For the Platonists think that the sight throws out rays;[52] but the Peripatetics to the contrary think that it receives images from the object to be seen.[53] But the blessed neither hurl their rays at God nor do they receive God Himself. Rather, they derive light from God Himself, and once they have derived it, God is not joined to the blessed person but the blessed person to God. For the blessed person does not take God in; rather God takes up the blessed person into Himself.

7 Forme quidem materiales, id est cum materia quanta usquequaque dividue, ab ipsa materia suscipiuntur atque sustinentur; individue vero forme et a materia separabiles materiam ipse suscipiunt atque regunt. Similiter accipi quidem rerum formas ab anima licet dicere, Deum vero nequaquam, sed animam ab ipso Deo vicissim.

: XXII :

Dionysius:
Soli sancti, per divinam inspirationem facti iam angelici, ita per unionem cognoscunt Deum ut recte possint divina nomina constituere.

1 At vero si ipsa omnium causa est omni sermone cognitioneque prestantior atque intellectu universaliter essentiaque superior, quippe cum amplectatur, complectatur, anticipet omnia, ipsaque a nullis usquam comprehendi possit; rursus si neque sensus ipsius est ullus, nec imaginatio, nec opinio, nec nomen, nec sermo, nec tactus, nec scientia, quonam pacto divina nomina pertractabimus, quippe cum ostenderimus deitatem excelsiorem essentia consequenter nec vocabulum nec nomen habere?

2 Ceterum, quemadmodum diximus ubi divinas ὑποτυπώσεις (id est figurationes vel institutiones) exponebamus, quid sit ipsum unum atque bonum essentia superius et ignotum—quid, inquam, sit in ipsa unitate Trinitas et in Trinitate quilibet eque Deus, eque bonus, nec dici nec intelligi potest.

Material forms, those divided everywhere in quantified matter, are received and sustained by matter itself, whereas undivided forms and those separable from matter themselves sustain matter and rule over it. Similarly, we can say that the forms of things, but not God by any means, are received by the soul, whereas the soul is received by God Himself. 7

: XXII :

Dionysius:
The saints alone, having already been made angelic by divine inspiration, come to know God through union such that they are able rightly to determine the divine names.

But if the cause itself of all is more eminent than all speech and cognition, and is universally superior to intellect and essence, since it encircles, embraces, and anticipates all things and cannot itself be comprehended at all anywhere; and again if there is neither any sense perception of it, nor imagination, nor opinion, nor name, nor speech, nor contact, nor knowledge, then how shall we treat of the divine names when we have shown that the Deity is more excellent than essence and thus has no designation or name? 1

Moreover, as we said when we were expounding the divine *hupotuposeis* (that is, figurations or principles), the reason why the One itself and the Good is higher than essence and is unknown, and why, I repeat, in the Unity itself is the Trinity, and why in the Trinity each [Person] may be equally God and equally good—all this cannot be spoken about or understood. 2

3 Ipse quinetiam sanctarum virtutum convenientes angelis uniones, sive eas iactus dicere oportet sive perceptiones circa bonitatem plusquam ignotam atque prefulgentem, ineffabiles sunt nobisque incognite: solis angelis illis insunt qui supra[50] cognitionis angelice modum his digni habiti sunt.

4 His utique unionibus intellectus quoque conformes Deo, angelos imitantes, quantum fas est uniti, cum per totius intellectualis actionis vacationem eiusmodi unio mentium Deo raptarum ad ipsum lumen excelsum confecta sit, consequenter lumen ipsum propria admodum ratione per ablationem omnium celebrant, ad hoc ipsum vere mirabiliterque illuminati ex beatissima ad idem unione, quod videlicet rerum quidem omnium causa est, ipsum vero nihil est ex omnibus, utpote quod ab omnibus entibus sit supra modum essentie segregatum.

: XXIII :

Marsilius:

Deus dupliciter considerari potest: tum a rebus longissime segregatus, tum omnibus maxime se communicans. Item ipsum bonum est accommodatissimum Deo nomen.

1 Alibi diximus duo ad primum rerum principium potissima pertinere: primum quidem excellentiam cuncta immenso spatio supereminentem; secundum vero bonitatem per omnia se ipsam creando, conservando, movendo, perficiendo, largissime diffundentem.

Moreover, those unions of sacred powers that befit the angels—whether we must call them attempts at, or perceptions of, a goodness more than unknown and more than dazzling—are ineffable and unknown to us. They are present only in those angels, who, over and beyond the manner of angelic cognition, are deemed worthy of them. 3

In these unions, intellects too, in conforming to God and imitating the angels, are united insofar as it is allowed, since such a union is achieved through the emptying of all intellectual action—a union of minds enraptured by God to the supreme light itself. Subsequently, they celebrate the light, and wholly for the proper reason, by way of subtracting all [attributes]. For this they have been truly and marvelously illuminated as a result of their most blessed union with the same [light]—the light which is the cause of all things, but is not itself from all, inasmuch as, being above the mode of essence, it is separated from all entities. 4

: XXIII :

Marsilio:

God can be considered in two ways: as completely separated from things and as imparting Himself in the highest degree to all things. Again the Good Itself is the name most fitting for God.

Elsewhere we said that two things most pertain to the first principle of things: first, an excellence that surpasses all by a measureless interval; second, a goodness diffusing itself through all things in abundance by way of creating, conserving, moving, and 1

In prima quidem contemplatione nullum Deo nomen accommodamus rerum prorsus ullarum, sive sint sive esse possint atque fingi; in secunda vero attribuere quodammodo Deo bonorum ab eo procedentium nomina possumus, qua ratione omnium in Deo vigor efficax exemplarque proculdubio viget.

2 Negat Dionysius de Deo quecumque formali aliqua ratione pertinent ad proprietates rerum naturalium animarumque et mentium, vel etiam entis illius universi in quo Platonici essentiam, vitam, intellectum collocant, item motum, statum, identitatem, diversitatem tanquam genera rerum, rursus infinitatem atque terminum, veluti prima omnium elementa. Utitur quinetiam prima Platonis epistola, dicente: 'circa regem omnium cuncta sunt, ipsius gratia omnia, ipse causa est bonorum omnium:' primum ex his tribus omnia dicit ex Deo pendere, secundum declarat illic tanquam a causa finali; tertium, velut ab efficiente, omnia dependere.

3 Preterea probat ipsum bonum esse accomodatissimum primo rerum principio nomen: primo, quoniam ad ipsum bonum amplissima diffusio pertinet, eademque pariter pertinet ad principium; deinde quia bonum rationem cause finalis habet quandoquidem, tanquam finem, omnia bonum appetunt: finis autem est causa causarum (causas enim ceteras movet); tertio, quoniam omnia principium suum appetunt, ut ibi[51] vel inde perficiantur; nihil[52] vero aliud expetunt preter bonum.

4 Bonum igitur omnium est principium quemadmodum est et finis. Non appetunt omnia intellectum nec omnia vitam, et que saltem affectant essentiam, non simpliciter eam optant, sed gratia boni, videlicet ut etiam bene sint et bono quodam essendo fruantur. Quamobrem nec intellectus, nec vita, nec essentia ita Deo

perfecting. In the first mode of contemplation we apply no name whatsoever to God: whether of things that exist or that could exist or could be imagined. In the second, we can in some manner attribute to God the names of the goods proceeding from Him for the reason that in Him waxes all of their creative energy and certainly He is their model.

Dionysius denies of God all that pertains with any formal reason to the properties of natural things, of souls, and of minds, and even of that universal being in which the Platonists locate essence, life, and intellect, and likewise motion, rest, sameness, and difference as the classes of things, and infinity and the limit as the prime elements of all.[54] He uses Plato's *First Letter,* furthermore, which says that "Around the king of all are all: all things are for his sake: he is the cause of all good things."[55] The first of these three propositions says that all things depend upon God; the second declares that all depend there as on the final cause; the third, that all depend on God as on the efficient [cause]. 2

Moreover, Dionysius proves that the Good itself is the name most befitting the first principle of things: first because the amplest diffusion pertains to the Good itself and the same equally pertains to the [first] principle; next because the Good has the rational principle of the final cause, since all things desire the Good as their end, but the end is the cause of causes (for it moves the rest of the causes); and third because all things desire their own principle so that at some point they might be. But nothing looks for anything beyond the Good. 3

So the Good is the principle of all, just as it is the end. But all things do not desire intellect, nor do all things desire life, and those that desire essence do not choose it simply for itself but for the sake of some good, that is, that they may also be well and enjoy a certain well-being. Wherefore neither intellect, nor life, nor essence is as befitting God as goodness is. But remember 4

conveniunt sicut bonum. Memento vero quatenus singula proprium bonum cupiunt, eatenus quodammodo ipsum quoque simpliciter bonum desiderare. Ab[53] hoc enim tum ab initio, tum perpetuo habent singula, ut bona appetendaque sint.

Que de bono ex mente Dionysii diximus a Plotino et Proculo post Dionysium sunt maxime confirmata.

: XXIV :

Dionysius:
Deum tum ex nullis nominare licet, tum etiam ex omnibus celebrare, siquidem ipsum bonum suo modo appetunt omnia, tanquam inde create.[54]

1 Ipsum igitur deitatis excelse superessentiale, ipsa scilicet superbonitatis superessentia, quicquid denique sit, neque ut rationem vel potestatem, neque ut intellectum aut vitam vel essentiam laudare fas est nulli ex his qui veritatis omni veritate superioris sunt amatores; sed ut excellentissime segregatam ab omni habitu, vel motu, vita, imaginatione, opinione, nomine, sermone, cogitatione,[55] intelligentia, essentia, statu, firmatione, unione, termino, infinitate et universaliter ab omnibus que in ordine entium collocantur.

2 Verum quoniam tanquam subsistentia bonitatis ipso suo esse entium omnium causa est, haud ab re excelse deitatis providentiam bonorum principium ex omnibus inde creatis laudare decet, quandoquidem circa ipsam omnia atque eius gratia, ipsaque est ante omnia et in ipsa cuncta consistunt, atque eo ipso quod ex[56] ipsa universa producta sunt atque subsistunt.

that however much single things long for their own good, to that extent they also desire in a way the Good itself absolutely. For from this Good, from the beginning and forever, single things derive the fact that they may be both good and desirable.

The points we have raised about the Good from the viewpoint 5
of Dionysius are in large part confirmed after Dionysius by Plotinus and Proclus.[56]

: XXIV :

Dionysius: We are allowed both to name God from nothing and to celebrate Him from everything, since all things desire the Good itself in their own way as being created from it.

Among those who are lovers of the Truth which is higher than 1
every truth, nobody is permitted, therefore, to take the super-essential self of highest Deity—that is, the super-essence of super-goodness, or whatever it is finally—and praise it as reason or power or as intellect or life or essence. But [we can] praise it as separated in its supreme excellence from all habit, motion, life, imagination, opinion, name, speech, cogitation, understanding, essence, rest, stability, union, limit, infinity, and universally from all things which are located in the order of existents.

But because, as that which underlies all goodness, it is the cause 2
of all entities by its own being, it is not unbefitting to praise the providence of the highest Deity, the principle of good things, by using all the things created from it, seeing: (1) that all things are "around" [or "with regard to"] this providence and are "for its sake";[57] (2) that it is before all; (3) that all things consist of it; and (4) that all things are produced and subsist from it.

3 Idcirco hanc appetunt omnia: intellectualia quidem rationaliaque scienter, inferiora vero his sensuali conditione, sequentia rursus per vitalem[57] motum aut per aptitudinem quandam essentialem et in quodam habitu consistentem.

: XXV :

Marsilius: *Qua ratione negari omnia de Deo ac pariter affirmari possint.*

1 Mysteria Dionysii sententia illa Mercurii ter maximi confirmantur: Deus, inquit, nihil est omnium, Deus est omnia; Deus nomen nullum habet, Deus habet omne nomen. Ita ferme res omnes in Deo sunt pariter atque non sunt, sicut domus in architecto, forme membrorum in vegetali seminariaque natura, igneus in sole calor, in unitate numeri, longitudo linee in puncto, unde Pythagorica ratione producitur, linee in centro circuli, radii omnes in centro solis, in lumine vero colores.[58]

2 Res sane nulla preter Deum ea forma, qua vel est vel fingitur, est in Deo finita, videlicet in Deo penitus infinito; res item omnes, tanquam a Deo non casu sed ratione in formam suam edite, in Deo presunt gradu quidem certo, sed infinite prestantiore quam in se ipsis. Merito igitur Parmenides Pythagoricus, apud Platonem, omnia de ipso uno rerum principio negat pariter et affirmat.

3 Nomina vero affirmative de Deo dicta non significant ipsam Dei naturam, ficta videlicet ab intelligentia naturam illam penitus

Therefore all things desire this providence: intellectual and rational things by way of knowledge; but things lower than these by way of a sensual condition; and the rest that follow by way of vital motion, or through a certain essential aptitude that consists of a certain habit. 3

: XXV :

Marsilio:
Why all things can be denied and affirmed of God equally.

The mystery of Dionysius is confirmed by the judgment of thrice-great Mercury. God, he says, is not of all; God is all. God has no name; God has every name.[58] Thus almost all things are and equally are not in God, just as a house is in an architect, as the forms of limbs are in the vegetal and seminary nature, as fiery heat is in the sun, as numbers are in the number one, as the length of a line is in the point (whence it is produced according to the Pythagorean reasoning),[59] as lines are in a circle's center, as all the rays are in the sun's center, and as colors are in light. 1

Excepting God, no thing at all is in God in the finite form in which it exists [here] or is imagined [here] — is in God, that is, who is utterly infinite. On the other hand, all things, as having issued into their form from God, not by chance but by reason, are present in God in a certain degree, but in a degree that is infinitely more outstanding than they are in themselves. So in Plato Parmenides the Pythagorean equally denies and affirms — and deservedly so — all things of the One itself, the principle of things.[60] 2

But names pronounced affirmatively of God do not signify God's nature itself — names imagined, in other words, by the understanding that is totally ignorant of that nature. But they do 3

ignorante, sed significant actum quendam qui ad Deum quidem comparatus productio ad res autem processio dici potest. Iam vero quando Deus nominatur vita, significat et actum Dei vivificum et vitam in res quandam actione eiusmodi procedentem; similiter essentia, et intellectus, et bonitas et cognomenta ceteraque affirmant.

: XXVI :

Dionysius: Qua ratione Deo nullum convenit nomen, rursusque conveniunt omnia nomina.

1 Hoc igitur intelligentes theologi divinitatem partim tanquam nomine carentem, partim ex omni nomine celebrant: ut carentem quidem nomine, quando supremam divinitatem aiunt in una quadam secretarum occultumque aliquid significantium visionum apparentem increpasse[59] eum, qui interrogaverat: 'Quod est nomen tuum?' ac veluti eum ab omni divine appellationis cognitione deterrentem, dixisse: 'Quidnam meum nomen interrogas?' Atqui et 'hoc est mirabile.' An vero nonne est istud revera mirabile nomen, quod est super omne nomen, quod est[60] innominabile, quod quidem omne nomen exuperat quodcunque nominatur, vel in hoc seculo vel in futuro?

2 Vicissim quoque tanquam plurimis nominibus preditum laudant, ubi Deum rursus dicentem inducunt: 'Ego sum qui sum,' 'vita,' 'lumen,' 'Deus,' 'veritas,' et quando divina sapientia prediti ipsam omnium causam varia denominatione ex creatis omnibus

signify a certain act, which when compared indeed to God can be called [His] production, but when compared to things, [their] procession. When God is called life, life signifies both God's life-giving act and the particular life proceeding into things from such an act. And the like goes for essence, intellect, and goodness, and for the rest of the names affirmed [of God].

: XXVI :

Dionysius:
Why no name is appropriate for God. And yet all names are appropriate.

In their understanding of this matter, theologians celebrate the divinity as in part without a name and in part [knowable] from every name. As without a name, when they speak of the highest Divinity, who, when He had appeared in one of those mystical visions signifying something secret, had rebuked him [Jacob] who had asked, "What is your name?"[61] As if to frighten him away from all knowledge of a divine name, [the Divinity] had replied, "Why do you ask my name?"[62] and declared, "The name is wonderful."[63] But isn't this name truly wonderful in that it is above every name and is not nameable; and in that "it excels every name howsoever it is named, whether in this world or in the world to come."[64] 1

Alternatively the theologians also praise God as endowed with many names, when they introduce God as saying again: "I am who I am,"[65] and when they adduce the names "Life," "Light," "God," and "Truth"[66] ; and when those endowed with divine wisdom proclaim the universal cause itself using various designations culled 2

predicant ut bonum, ut pulchrum, ut sapientem, amabilem, Deum Deorum, Dominum Dominorum, sanctum sanctorum, ut eternum, ut existentem, ut causam seculorum, ut auctorem vite, sapientiam, intellectum, rationem, cognitorem, ut thesauros totius cognitionis omnes anticipantem, ut potentiam, potentem, regem regum, antiquum dierum, insenescibilem, immutabilem, salutem, iustitiam, sanctificationem, redemptionem, magnitudine omnia excedentem, in aura tenui.

3 Iam vero et in mentibus esse Deum dicunt, et in animis et in corporibus, et in celo et in terra, atque simul in eodem eundem, in mundo, circa mundum, super mundum, supercelestem, superessentialem, solem, stellam, ignem, aquam, spiritum, roris nubem, ipsum lapidem, atque petram, omnia que sunt, nullum eorum que sunt.

: XXVII :

Marsilius: Deus non solum omnia in omnibus agit, sed etiam ipse est in omnibus omnia.

1 Plato in *Epistolis* inquit omnia a Deo regente pendere, tanquam ab efficiente pariter atque fine. Preterea in quarto *Legum* idem confirmat his verbis: 'Deus, ut prisci tradunt, principium et finem et media omnium comprehendens[61] recta via peragit, et secundum naturam omnia circuit'; in *Timeo* atque *Parmenide* omnia deducit ab uno.

from the host of created things. For example, they use the designations "good," "beautiful," "wise," "meet to be loved," "God of gods," "Lord of lords," and "Holy of holies"; as "eternal," "existent," "the cause of the ages, the author of life," "wisdom," "intellect," "reason"; as "He who knows"; as "He who anticipates all the treasures of all knowledge"; as "power," "the powerful," "the King of kings," "the ancient of days," "He who can never age," "the immutable," "salvation," "justice," "sanctification," "redemption," "in greatness exceeding all things," and [yet as being] "in the lightest breeze."[67]

And indeed they say that God is in minds, in souls, and in bodies, and in heaven and on earth, and at the same time that He is the same in the same; that He is in the world, and round the world, and above the world; that He is the supercelestial, the super-essential, the sun, the star, fire, water, spirit, the canopy of dew, stone itself, and rock, all things which exist, and none which exists. 3

: XXVII :

Marsilio:
God not only enacts all things in all things, but is Himself all in all.

In his *Letters* Plato says that all things depend on God as king, as on the efficient and the final cause equally.[68] Moreover, in the fourth book of his *Laws* he confirms the same idea with these words, "God, as the ancients declare, comprehending the beginning, end, and middle of all things, pursues the right path and naturally encircles all."[69] In the *Timaeus* and *Parmenides* he derives all things from the One.[70] 1

2 Quamobrem Plotinus et Iamblichus et Proculus omnesque extra controversiam Platonici, quamvis res, virtutes, eventus differentes in causas quoque differentes proxime referant, omnes tamen et effectus et causas in primam redigunt causam causarum, unde cause omnes habent et ut sint, et cause sint, et sua queque naturaliter agant, et certo quodam ordine moveantur. Idcirco mediarum causarum effectus a causis suis proficiscuntur, in omnibus causis agente prima, ideoque et a prima sunt omnes.

3 Tam vero efficaciter agit in causis agentibus effectibusque procedentibus causa prima, cuius virtute actuque omnia faciunt atque fiunt, ut mirifice dotes omnes in rebus quibuscunque reperte non solum a causa prima sint, verum etiam excellenter considerate causa ipsa sint prima; immo prima causa sit omnes eiusmodi dotes, quemadmodum anima in oculo quidem est visus, in auribus autem est auditus, in ceterisque membris et ceteri sensus atque vires.

4 Tradunt astrologi per aspectum quendam lune ad solem vires summatim congregatas stellarum omnium hauriri, quoniam videlicet vires omnium et existant a sole et in sole consistant per lumen usquequaque diffusum singulis virtutes singulas conferente. Itaque non solum quidquid stelle faciunt sol quoque facit, sed etiam virtutes in stellis differentes. Ipse sol existit: in Saturno quidem solis lumen est ipsa saturnia firmitas, in Iove virtus alma, in Marte motus efficax, in Venere gratia, in Mercurio agilitas et industria, in luna vividus humor, in ceterisque similiter est et cetera.

Therefore Plotinus, Iamblichus, and Proclus and all the Platonists without controversy, though they go on to attribute differing effects, powers, and events to differing causes also, yet they return all the effects and causes to the first cause of causes. From it all the causes derive the fact that they exist, that they are causes, that they naturally enact their own effects, and that they are moved in a certain order. So the effects of the middle causes proceed from their own causes, with the prime cause nonetheless acting in all the causes. And thus all are from the first cause. 2

The first cause acts so efficiently in the agent causes and the unfolding effects — by its power and activity all things make and are made — that marvelously all the gifts found in everything whatsoever are not only from this first cause, but also, when considered in their excellence, they are the first cause itself. Or rather, the first cause is all such gifts, just as the [irrational] soul in the eye is sight, but in the ears is hearing, and in the rest of the members is the other senses and powers. 3

The astronomers tell us that from a certain aspect of the Moon in relation to the Sun are derived the powers summarily congregated of all the stars. This is because the powers of all [the stars] come from the Sun and through the light diffused everywhere depend on the Sun, a light which confers individual powers on individual things. Thus not only does the Sun do whatever the stars do, it also makes the differing powers in the stars. The Sun itself exists. But in Saturn the Sun's light is saturnian steadfastness itself; in Jupiter it is the nourishing power; in Mars, effective motion; in Venus, grace; in Mercury, agility and industry; in the Moon lively wetness; and in the rest [of the stars] it is similarly the remaining [attributes]. 4

5 Quid ergo mirum, si Deus sit nominibus omnium appellandus, cum ipse Deus in essentia sit ipsum essentie firmamentum; in vita vero sit ipse ad universalem motum vigor intimus; in intellectu perspicacia pariter atque claritas, in omnibus denique summitas uniuscuiusque boni?

6 Huc denique tendunt que Dionysius de universali Dei actione et regno et providentia disputat. Ita vero universale et absolutum est Dei regnum ut non solum omnia in omnibus agat, sed ipse quoque excellenter sit in omnibus omnia; agit quidem regitque cuncta absque inclinatione habitudineque ad subdita; est quoque omnia sine mixtione ad alia, sine detrimento sui.

7 Habet insuper in se omnia simpliciter ac prorsus indefinite—simpliciter, inquam, atque unice quoniam que in rebus forme sunt multe in Deo forma sunt una, sicut lux, calor, siccitas, levitas, in igne quidem qualitates multe sunt, sed in celo una sunt qualitas, lumen unum. Diximus insuper indefinite quoniam vita, sapientia, iustitia, cetereque virtutes que in anima atque mente inter se formaliter distincte sunt speciebusque propriis definite, in Deo sunt una virtus absoluta prorsus, ipse Deus immensus, quemadmodum innumerabiles radii inter se discreti e solis globo prosiliunt in conum passim determinati, sed in ipso sole sunt lux unica solis, nondum discreta conis, sed orbem sibi retinens naturalem.

Why is it wonderful then if God is meet to be called by the names of all, since God Himself in essence is the foundation itself of essence, but in life is the inner force itself for universal motion; and in intellect is perspicacity and clarity equally; finally in all things is the acme of every single good? 5

To conclude, the arguments which Dionysius adduces concerning the universal action, rule, and providence of God all bear upon this. But God's rule is so universal and absolute that not only does He enact all things in all, but also is Himself, by way of excellence, all things in all. He enacts and rules all without turning toward, or being disposed toward, things subordinate; and He is all things, without being mingled in all things, and He is so without detriment to Himself. 6

Moreover, He has all in Himself simply and absolutely without limit—simply I say and uniquely, because what are many forms in things are one form in God, just as light, heat, dryness, and levity are several qualities in fire, but in heaven are one quality, are one light. We said without limit too, because life, wisdom, justice, and the other virtues which are in the soul and mind are formally distinguished among themselves and defined in their proper species. But in God they are one totally absolute power, God Himself without measure. Similarly, numberless rays, distinguished among themselves, leap forth from the solar orb and are structured everywhere into a cone [of light]. But in the Sun itself they are the unique light of the Sun, a light not yet divided into cones, but retaining for itself its natural orb. 7

: XXVIII :

Dionysius:
Deus omnia in omnibus agit atque ipse est in omnibus omnia, ideo ex honestis omnium nominibus rite laudatur.

1 Hac igitur ratione ipsam omnium causam super omnia existentem, tum privatio nominum, tum etiam rerum omnium nomina decent, ut universorum exacta ratione sit regnum atque circa ipsam omnia sint, et ex ipsa tanquam causa, tanquam principio, tanquam fine dependeant, ipsaque, ut scriptum est, omnia sit in omnibus.

2 Sic igitur vere laudatur tanquam omnibus subsistentiam exhibens, incohans, perficiens, continens, custodia omnium atque sedes et ad se ipsam cuncta convertens. Sed agit hec omnia unite, absolute, eminenter: iam vero neque complexionis aut vite aut perfectionis dumtaxat causa est, ut ab hac sola vel alia providentia bonitas illa que est super omne nomen proprie nominetur, immo vero simpliciter omnia et incircumscripte[62] in se ipsa complectitur, perfectissimis videlicet ipsius unius omniumque cause providentie beneficiis, quamobrem ex rebus omnibus congrua ratione laudatur atque nominatur.

: XXVIII :

Dionysius:
God enacts all in all, and is Himself all in all. So He is rightly praised if we use the honorable names of all.

So for this reason both the taking away of the names and the tak- 1
ing up of the names of all things are proper for the cause of all, which exists itself above all, so that it is, for this precise reason, the sovereign of all. And all things are around this cause, and all depend upon it as the cause, as the principle, and as the end,[71] so that, as it is written, God "may be all in all."[72]

Thus it is truly praised as giving existence to all; as beginning, 2
perfecting, and containing; as the guardian and seat of all; and as converting all things to itself. But it enacts all these by way of union, absolutely and eminently. It is not only the cause of union, life, and perfection, insofar as by this or some other providential [gift] it may be properly named the goodness which is above every name. Rather, it embraces all things in itself in a simple manner and without circumscription, that is, with the most perfect benefits of the providence of the One itself, of the cause of all. Hence, and for good reason, all things are used to praise and to name it.

: XXIX :

Marsilius:
Quot modis fingantur divina nomina, et quomodo divina in visum veniant.

1 Divina nomina fingi solent vel per negationes, de quibus in *Mystica theologia* tractatur, vel per affirmationes, atque id quidem duplici ratione: aut enim secundum intelligibiles ex Deo processiones formantur, de quibus hic agitur, aut secundum sensibilium rerum similitudines adducuntur, quod sane *De symbolica theologia* liber explicat.

2 Liber vero presens, per processiones intelligibiles nomina fingens, ex tribus principiis ea ducit: aut enim universalem Dei providentiam beneficentiamque significant per omnia procedentem ut unum, bonum, essentia; aut providentiam quasi particularem, ut vita, veritas, intellectus; particularem quoque magis ut iustitia, temperantia, fortitudo; aut forte non tam ipsam Dei providentiam proferunt quam res providentia gubernatas, ut quando Deus nominatur sol, ignis, homo.

3 Denique quod vetat divina temere divulgari, confirmatur auctoritate Platonis in *Epistolis* prohibentis inter divinorum imperitos efferri divina: ait enim nulla rudibus magis ridicula videri quam divina, nulla sapientibus admirabiliora quam divina putari.

: XXIX :

Marsilio:
The number of ways in which the divine names are imagined. How matters divine come into our purview.

The divine names are customarily imagined either by way of negations (we have treated of this in the *Mystical Theology*), or by way of affirmations; and this for a dual reason. Either affirmations are formed according to the intelligible processions from God (we are treating of them here), or they are adduced according to the likenesses of sensible things (which indeed the book *On Symbolic Theology* unfolds).[73] 1

But the present book, in imagining the names by way of intelligible processions, deduces them from three principles. For either they signify the universal providence and beneficence of God proceeding through all things, as in the case of the one, the good, and essence. Or they signify a particular providence as it were, as with life, truth, and intellect; or even more particularly as with justice, temperance, and courage. Or perchance they present us not so much with God's providence itself as with things governed by that providence, as when God is called the sun, fire, and man. 2

Finally, that he [Dionysius] forbids us rashly from divulging the divine mysteries is confirmed by the authority of Plato in his *Letters*: he forbids us to speak of matters divine in the presence of those ignorant of such matters. For he asserts that to the unlearned nothing seems more ridiculous than matters divine, but to the wise nothing is thought more admirable than such matters.[74] 3

4 Ceterum quod de divinorum visis seu visionibus adducit in medium, quonam modo putabimus exponendum? Numquid divina, que plus quam intelligibilia sunt, condensato quotidie aere circumfundi atque ita externis oculis sub variis seipsa figuris offerre; an potius intelligibile inde lumen intellectui nostro uberius se infundens, ex intellectu protinus in imaginationem nostram exuberare, ibique, variis vestitum figuris ac iam imaginabile factum, in visum quoque ipsum intrinsecus exundare, atque hic efficacius apparere veriusque videri,quam si per inferiora media extrinsecus incidisset?

5 Hac utique ratione divinorum plurimum visa fieri Platonici putant, idemque presentia Dionysii verba sonare videntur ubi eos quibus hec apparent et tunc illuminatos dicit et prophetas nominat preceptoresque sacrorum.

6 Ratio quidem Platonica forte dictaret visa per Deum summum angelosque sublimes effecta secunda hac fieri ratione; facta vero per inferiores angelos sepius ratione prima, presertim quando hominibus non admodum excellentibus offeruntur. Nos autem ita denique sentiemus, ut theologorum cetus maxime comprobaverit.

7 Si varia diversorum numinum visa desideras intelligere, lege Iamblichi librum, quem anno superiore sumus interpretati, de his latissime disputantem.

For the rest, how shall we suppose that what Dionysius adduces about the appearances or visions of the divine should be explained? Should we say that divine visions, which are more than intelligible, are surrounded by the air which is condensed every day [into clouds], and thus present themselves to external eyes in various shapes? Or should we say rather that the intelligible light from these visions, pouring itself more abundantly into our intellect, overflows straightway from our intellect into our imagination; and that clothed in various shapes and now made imaginable, it flows inwardly also into the sight; and that it appears more effectually here and seems more true than if it had fallen upon the sight externally by way of some more lowly means? 4

This is the reason, so the Platonists suppose, why the majority 5
of divine visions become visible. The present words of Dionysius seem to speak to the same notion, when he talks about people to whom these visions appear and who are then illuminated. He calls them prophets and teachers of matters sacred.

Platonic reason perchance has argued that the visions effected 6
by way of God on high, and by way of the sublime angels, occur for this second reason [i.e., inwardly], but that those effected via the lower angels more often occur for the first reason [i.e., via the condensing of air], especially when they are presented to men who are not totally pure. But to conclude, we will espouse whatever view an assembly of theologians would most approve.

If you desire to understand the way different spirits variously 7
appear, read Iamblichus' book,[75] which we translated in the past year, and which discusses this topic at considerable length.

: XXX :

Dionysius:
Divina nomina ducuntur non solum a providentia Dei rebusve provisis, sed etiam a visionibus divinis; sed divina non sunt patefacienda profanis.

1 Neque vero hec tantum divina nomina theologi celebrant que a providentiis universalibus particularibusve, aut ab his que providentia divina reguntur originem ducunt, sed etiam a divinis quibusdam interdum visis, quibus preceptores sacrorum vel prophete in sacris edibus aut alibi illuminati sunt. Ex aliis et aliis causis atque viribus, nominare solent bonitatem omni nomine omnique luce prorsus excelsiorem.

2 Iam vero formas illi figurasque humanas vel ignis vel electri circumponunt, ipsiusque oculos auresque et crines, facies, manus, scapulas, alas, brachia, humeros, pedes laudant, coronas quinetiam, sedes, pocula, pateras, et alia quedam id genus mystica circa Deum fingunt, de quibus in *Significativa theologia* pro ingenii facultate dicemus.

3 Nunc autem quecunque ad presens opus pertinent ex libris theologicis colligentes, atque his que dicta sunt tanquam regula quadam utentes, ad quam aciem dirigamus, ad explicanda intelligibilia Dei nomina iam pergamus. Iam vero, quod nobis in universa theologia lex sacra sancit, intentissima in Deum mente divinitus effulgentia (ut proprie dixerim) spectacula speculemur; atqui et aures expiatas sacrorum Dei nominum explanationibus

: XXX :

Dionysius: Divine names are derived not only from God's providence or from the things it provides us, but also from divine visions. But matters divine must not be revealed to the profane.

1 But the divine names the theologians celebrate are not only those that take their origin from the workings of universal or particular providence, or from things which are ruled by divine providence, but also from certain divine revelations witnessed occasionally—revelations by which teachers of things sacred or prophets in sacred edifices or elsewhere are illuminated. From various and sundry causes and powers they are accustomed to naming the Goodness that is more excellent by far than every name and than every light.

2 Indeed, they surround Him with human forms and shapes, or the shapes of fire or of amber.[76] And they praise His eyes, ears, and locks of hair, and His face, hands, shoulders, wings, lower arms, upper arms, and feet. And they imagine God with crowns, thrones, drinks, drinking vessels, and other mystical symbols of that kind. We will discuss these in the *Symbolic Theology* as best we can intuit them.

3 For the present, by collecting whatever pertains to the work in hand from books of theology and using the aforementioned as a model, let us direct our attention to that model; and let us proceed to unfold the intelligible names of God. But because the sacred law ratifies it for us in universal theology, let us gaze, with our mind most intent upon God, at the effulgent spectacles from on high (to put it properly). Let us lend our purified ears to the explanations of the sacred names of God as we begin to approach

adhibeamus, sancta sanctis ex traditione divina dumtaxat insinuantes, eaque a risu illusioneque profanorum interim vindicantes, immo vero illos ipsos, si qui omnino sunt tales, ab hoc errore divinis repugnante pro viribus liberantes.[63]

4 Te quidem ista conservare oportet, optime Timothee, iuxta sacratissimam sanctionem, neque inter profanos eloqui aut efferre divina. Mihi autem prestet Deus rite, ut divina decet, laudare benefica et multiplicia nomina deitatis appellatione nomineque carentis, nec ori meo verbum auferat veritatis.

: XXXI :

Marsilius:

Que deitas per essentiam, que per participationem, quomodo bonitas sit proprium Dei nomen. In Trinitate que communia sint, que propria.

1 Thearchia[64] usitatissima apud Dionysium appellatio Dei, interpretatu durissima, significant deitatem primam deitatis divinitatisque uniuscuiusque principium. Opinantur enim Platonici Deum primum intellectibus omnibus tam humanis quam angelicis impressisse proprium quendam sui characterem, tanquam proxime a se creatis, quam alibi appellavimus unitatem atque etiam bonitatem; que quidem unitas in naturis intellectualibus sociam superat multitudinem, in naturis vero deterioribus sepius a cognata multitudine superatur.

things sacred to the saints [and] from the divine tradition alone. Meanwhile let us protect them from the scorn and mockery of men profane, or rather, as best we can, let us free such men, if they exist, from the error of rejecting things divine.

Excellent Timothy, it behooves you to preserve these matters 4
according to this most holy decree and not to introduce them in the presence of the profane, or broadcast things divine. But God has given me the task rightly to praise (as befits divine matters) the beneficent and manifold names of the Deity, the Deity who is without appellation and name. May the word of truth not be snatched from my mouth.

: XXXI :

Marsilio:

What the Deity [is] by way of essence, what by way of participation. In what way goodness is a proper name of God. In the Trinity, what names are common, what are particular.

Thearchy, the most usual name of God in Dionysius and the most 1
hard to interpret, signifies the first Deity of deity and the principle of every single divinity. For the Platonists are of the opinion that the first God has impressed on all intellects, human and angelic alike, a particular and proper "character" [or seal] of Himself, intellects being what He has created closest to Himself. We have everywhere denominated this character "unity" and also "goodness." In intellectual natures this unity rules over its companion multitude; but in worse natures it is overruled too often by its multitudinous kin.

2 Intellectus igitur ob naturalem excellentemque unitatem divini dicuntur, et quatenus in eam collecti per eam fruuntur et[65] Deo, dii quandoque cognominantur. Hac igitur ratione Deus ipse, alioquin simpliciter proferendus, dicitur et primus Deorum Deus et divinitatis deitatisque universe principium.

3 Ipsa per se bonitas, cum significet summam tum sufficientiam, tum etiam amplitudinem, pre ceteris exprimit principii primi naturam, presertim quia proprietas illius est omnia facere. Boni quoque ipsius est efficere omnia, siquidem eiusdem est cuncta perficere. Intellectus autem qua ratione simpliciter intellectus existit, non est sibi ipsi sufficiens, sed est quasi quidam oculus institutus et adspirans ad intelligibile lumen. Neque hoc ipsum lumen est primus ipse Deus; subit enim quandam, ut diximus alibi, cum intellectu proportionem. Multo minus essentia atque vita sibimet sufficiunt, quandoquidem intellectus, qui perfectior est,[66] non satis sibi ipse facit.

4 Denique si verum est, quod plerique Peripatetici putant, ipsum videlicet ens qua ratione ens esse intellectus obiectum intellectui adequatum, nimirum nec ens, nec essentia esse potest principium universi, quippe cum intellectus hoc inferior ens universum undique circumlustret et penetret et distinguat et componat atque definiat, tanquam rem proportione quadam intellectui coniugatam.

5 Omnia communiter nomina a sapientibus attributa Deo, propterea quod perfectionem simpliciter excellentiamque significent, singulis Trinitatis divine personis eque conveniunt, ut bonitas ipsa, immensa potestas, causa omnium prima atque similia.

On account of their natural, excelling unity, intellects are therefore called divine. And insofar as, collected into that unity, they thereby enjoy God also, they are at times called gods. For this reason, therefore, God Himself, who should otherwise be expressed [only] in terms of simplicity, is called both the first God of gods and the principle of universal divinity and deity. 2

Goodness of itself, since it signifies alike the highest sufficiency and amplitude, expresses before all else the nature of the first principle, especially because the property of that principle is to make [or cause] all things. It is the property of the Good itself also to effect all, since it is the property of the same to perfect all.[77] But intellect by reason that it simply exists as intellect, is not sufficient for itself: it is, as it were, an eye made for, and made to aspire to, the intelligible light. Nor is this very light the first God Himself; for it is subject (as we said elsewhere) to having a certain proportion with intellect. Much less do essence and life suffice for themselves, given that intellect, which is more perfect [than they are], is not enough for itself. 3

Finally, if what most of the Peripatetics think is true, namely that being itself, *qua* being, is an object of intellect that is adequate to intellect, certainly neither being nor essence can be the principle of the universe, given that intellect takes this lower universal being and illuminates it on every side, and penetrates, distinguishes, composes, and defines it as something joined to the intellect in a certain proportion. 4

All the names the wise commonly attribute to God, because they signify perfection simply and excellence, accord equally with the separate Persons of the divine Trinity: for example, goodness itself, measureless power, the first cause of all, and the like. 5

Nam et eiusmodi nomina ad celebrandam divinam naturam institute sunt, et natura divina tota in singulis personis est penitus una.

6 Que vero proprietatem persone significant personis ceteris non conveniunt, ut Pater, Filius, Spiritus; item generare, generari, procedere; proprium quoque Filii est humanam sibi naturam assumere.

7 Genitor quo potentior est eo similiorem sibi prolem generat; potestas igitur infinita infinite consimilem; similitudo vero, ad equalitatem adolescens, gradatim in ipsam identitatem postremo resolvitur. Una est igitur nature in Patre et Filio singularitas, tanta dumtaxat distinctione servata, quanta est omnino inter genitorem ac genitum necessaria, id autem est, ut hoc quidem sit ab illo, neque vicissim.

8 Similis quoque distinctio est inter Patrem una cum Filio producentem Spiritumque productum atque procedentem; que quidem distinctio priorem alium alio sola forsan designat origine, quia videlicet hic ab illo, neque contra. Neque propterea prior est alius alio vel tempore vel natura: non tempore, quoniam et hic et ille pariter est eternus; non natura, quoniam ita natura singularis est una, quemadmodum in nobis. Natura in Patre Filioque specialis est eadem, que quidem in nobis, ac multo magis in igne vel lumine, ad identitatem summam videtur anniti quam ab evo possidet in divinis.

For such names have been instituted to celebrate the divine nature; and the divine nature is utterly one and entire in the individual Persons [of the Trinity].

But those that signify a property of [just one] Person are not 6
appropriate for the other [two] Persons, for example [the designations] Father, Son, and Spirit; and similarly to generate, to be generated, and to proceed. Also a property of the Son is to assume human nature for Himself.

A father, the more power he has, the more he generates an off- 7
spring like himself. Thus infinite power [generates] what is infinitely like itself. But likeness, in waxing to equality, by degrees finally matures into identity itself. So in the Father and the Son there is one singleness of nature: only as much distinction is preserved as is entirely necessary between being the generator and being the generated. This is in order that the generated may come from Him who generates and not the reverse.

A like distinction pertains between the Father producing along 8
with the Son, and the Spirit that is produced and that proceeds [from them]. This distinction designates perhaps the fact that one Person is prior to the other in origin alone, inasmuch as the one comes from the other and not the contrary. So one Person is not prior to the other in time or in nature: not in time, because both the one and the other Person is equally eternal; and not in nature, because their single nature is one as it is with us. The special nature in the Father and the Son is the same just as it is in us and even more so in fire or light. For in the latter it seems to strive toward the highest identity it possesses from eternity in things divine.

: XXXII :

Dionysius:
Que in Trinitate communia sint, que propria.

1 Ipsa per se bonitas a sacris litteris[67] celebratur tanquam definiens atque exprimens totam deitatis supreme substantiam, quicquid tandem existit. Quid enim aliud ex sacra theologia discere licet, quando supernum[68] ipsum Deum ait exponendo dixisse: 'Quid me interrogas de bono? Nullus bonus nisi solus Deus.'

2 Hoc igitur et alibi a nobis discussum est atque demonstratum, omnes semper denominationes Deo dignas non divisim per partes, sed in tota, perfecta, integra, plena deitate a sanctis eloquiis celebrari, ipsasque omnes individue, absolute, preter omnem discriminis observantiam, integra videlicet ratione, universe integritati perfecte totiusque deitatis attribui.

3 Iam vero, quemadmodum in *Theologicis institutionibus* admonuimus, nisi quis hoc de tota deitate dictum confiteatur, scindere audet temeritate nefanda unitatem ipsam superunitam, dicendum igitur de tota deitate hoc accipi oportere. Nempe Verbum quoque ipsum natura bonum, 'Ego, inquit, bonus sum,' atque aliquis ex prophetis divinitus occupatis canit, 'Spiritum bonum.' Huc tendit et illud: 'Ego sum qui sum': nisi de tota dictum deitate consentiant, sed per unam dumtaxat partem circumscribere annitantur, quodammodo illud accipient: 'Haec[69] ait qui est, qui erat, qui venturus est, qui est omnipotens'? Item illud, 'Tu autem idem ipse es,' necnon et illud: 'Spiritus veritatis, qui est, qui a patre procedit.'

: XXXII :

Dionysius:
What names are common in the Trinity and what particular.

Goodness itself per se is celebrated by sacred Scripture as defining and expressing the whole substance of the highest Deity (whatever at last it is). For what else is one permitted to learn from sacred theology when it has declared, in talking about God Himself on high, "Why do you ask me about the good: there is no good at all except God alone."[78] 1

We have therefore discussed and demonstrated this elsewhere: namely that all names worthy of God are not divisible always through His parts but are celebrated by sacred Scripture in the whole, perfect, integral, and full Deity; and that all these names without division, absolutely, and beyond all observance of distinction—in other words, with entire reason—are attributed to the universal integrity of the perfect and entire Deity. 2

Now as in the *Principles of Theology* we have warned that, unless someone accepts this dictum as concerning the whole Deity, he is daring with impious temerity to divide the super-united unity itself. So it must be said that we have to interpret this dictum as concerning the whole Deity. The Word itself too, good by nature, declares, "I am good."[79] And from among the prophets who are divinely inspired there is one who sings, "The spirit is good."[80] That verse too pertains: "I am who I am."[81] Unless they agree that this is said of the whole Deity and strive instead to limit it by way of one part only, in what way will they interpret the verse which declares, "Such is He who is, who was, who will be, who is almighty"[82] or similarly interpret the [verse]: "But you [are] the same"[83] or the verse, "The Spirit of truth who is, who proceeds from the Father"?[84] 3

4 Atqui nisi totam deitatem esse vitam dicant atque vivificam, quonam modo verum est verbum sacrum quod ait: 'Quemadmodum Pater suscitat mortuos, et vivificat, sic et Filius, quos vult, vivificat,' et illud: 'Spiritus est qui vivificat'? Iam vero quod tota deitas habeat omnium dominatum perspicue patet; nempe de fecunda Patris deitate, vel deitate Filii, non facile narratu est (ut arbitror) quam multis theologie locis predicetur 'Dominus' de Filio pariter atque Patre; 'Spiritus quinetiam Dominus est.'

5 Ipsum quoque pulchrum atque sapiens in tota deitate laudatur; lumen preterea potestasque deifica similiter atque causa; cuncta summatim, que totius deitatis supreme sunt, sacre littere in universam deitatem referunt celebrandam.

: XXXIII :

Marsilius:

Nomina Trinitati communia quandoque summatim comprehenduntur, quandoque discursione quadam enarrantur, ac dum de uno predicantur de omnibus predicata censentur.

1 Paulus, scribens ad Colosenses,[70] Filium inquit Dei esse Patris quidem imaginem, mundi vero exemplar, in quo sint omnia genita; item per ipsum tanquam efficientem causam omnia facta fuisse; rursus in ipsum vel ad ipsum referri omnia ut ad finem; denique in eo cuncta consistere, velut in causa conservante. Dum vero de Filio loquens, ipsum esse omnium causam inquit exemplarem, efficientem, finalem, conservantem, quatuor hec munera non solum Filii, sed etiam Patris Sanctique spiritus esse censet.

Unless they were to say that it is the whole Deity who is life and life-giving, in what way is the sacred Word true that declares, "As the Father raises and brings life to the dead, so does the Son bring life to those He wills"?[85] And the verse "It is the spirit that gives life"?[86] But it is transparently obvious that the whole Deity has dominion over all. With regard to the Father's paternal deity or the deity of the Son it is not easy to tell, I think, in how many places in theology "Lord" is predicated of the Son and of the Father equally. "The Spirit moreover is Lord."[87] 4

The beautiful itself too and the wise is praised in the whole Deity; and light and deific power and the cause similarly—all, in short, are of the whole, the supreme Deity, and the sacred Scriptures refer to them to celebrate the universal Deity. 5

: XXXIII :

Marsilio:
The names common to the Trinity sometimes are summarily understood, sometimes are spun out in a discourse. And when they are predicated of one [Person], they are deemed predicated of all [three].

Paul, in writing to the Colossians says the Son of God is the image of the Father, but the model of the world; in Him are begotten all things.[88] Likewise, all things have been made through Him as the efficient cause. Again, all things are referred to Him or toward Him as to their end. Finally, all things depend on Him as on their conserving cause. But when, in speaking of the Son, Paul says He is the cause of all, the exemplary, efficient, final, and conserving cause,[89] he supposes that these four gifts are not only the Son's but also the Father's and the Holy Spirit's. 1

2 David quoque ubi ait Spiritum creare omnia, intelligi vult Patrem quoque et Filium una cum Spiritu procreare; quam sane communionem declarat Evangelium, ubi Filius inquit Patri: 'Tua omnia mea sunt,' atque vicissim. Denique Spiritui quoque dantur quecunque Patri Filioque traduntur; sed aliquando munera hec, eiusmodi discursione et quasi distinctione quadam, gradatim divinis personis attribuuntur (ut diximus), interdum vero summatim, ut quando dicitur: 'omnia sunt ex Deo.'

: XXXIV :

Dionysius: Divinis personis communia aliquando summatim comprehenduntur, aliquando attinguntur articulatim.

1 Que personis divinis communia sunt littere sacre aliquando summatim comprehendunt, velut quando dicitur: 'Omnia sunt ex Deo,' aliquando discursione et quasi distinctione quadam, ut quando dixerit quispiam: 'Omnia per ipsum, atque in ipsum create sunt, et in eo cuncta consistunt'; rursus illud: 'Emittes spiritum tuum et creabuntur.' Atque, ut summatim dicatur, Verbum ipsum supreme divinum inquit: 'Ego et Pater unum sumus,' et 'Omnia que habet Pater, mea sunt,' et quando sic Patrem alloquitur: 'Mea omnia tua sunt, atque tua sunt et mea.' Preterea quecumque Patris sunt atque Filii, Spiritui quoque supreme divino communicabiliter

David also, when he says that the Spirit creates all things,[90] 2
means it to be understood that the Father and the Son also create along with the Holy Spirit. The Gospel declares this is a mutual union when the Son says to the Father "all that are yours are mine and the reverse."[91] Finally, all things whatsoever that are granted to the Spirit are granted to the Father and the Son. But sometimes, in such an extended consideration or distinction-making as it were, these gifts are attributed to the divine Persons by degrees (as we said). Now and then, however, they are attributed in a summary manner as when Paul says "all things are from God."[92]

: XXXIV :

Dionysius:
Things common to the divine Persons are sometimes summarily comprehended, sometimes attained by going through them one by one.

Things common to the divine Persons the sacred Scriptures at 1
times comprehend in a summary fashion, as when they say, "all things come from God";[93] but at other times discursively and with a certain distinguishing as it were, as when someone said, "All things are created through Him and in Him,"[94] and "all things subsist in Him."[95] And again, "You will send forth your Spirit and they will be created."[96] And in sum the supremely divine Word itself says, "I and the Father are one";[97] and "All that my Father has are mine";[98] and, in speaking of the Father, "All that are mine are yours and what are yours are also mine."[99] Moreover, all that are the Father's and the Son's the Scriptures attribute, in a sharing and unitive manner, also to the supremely divine Spirit: [enacting]

uniteque attribuunt:[71] deificas operationes, venerationem, fontanam[72] indeficientemque causam, optimorum munerum distributionem.

2 Iam vero neminem arbitror ex his qui in divinis eloquiis recta immutabilique intelligentia sunt educati huic sententie contradicturum, quod videlicet quecunque Deo digna censentur toti Divinitati insunt ratione divinitatis absolutissima.

3 Cum igitur hec in presentia quidem breviter atque ex parte, alibi vero sufficienter sacrorum eloquiorum testimonio ostenderimus atque distinxerimus, deinceps
quamcumque divinam denominationem integram explicare tentemus, hanc ad totam divinitatem pertinere putandum.

: XXXV :

Marsilius:

Eloquia divinitus inspirata sunt totius theologie principia,
in qua mysteria multa humanam superant rationem:
illis ergo principiis adquiescendum.
Si quis illa negaverit non est
cum illo de theologia loquendum.

deific operations [i.e., miracles], [inspiring] veneration, [serving as] the fountain-like and indefectible cause, and distributing the best of gifts.

I think that of those who are educated in the divine Scriptures, 2
those with a correct and firm-set understanding of them, none will contend against the opinion that all things deemed worthy of God are present in the whole Divinity, the rational principle of Divinity being wholly absolute.

Since, therefore, we have revealed and distinguished [the divine 3
names] — for the present briefly and partially, but elsewhere more sufficiently and with the testimony of the sacred Scriptures — we will next attempt to unfold every integral divine denomination, supposing that it pertains to the whole Divinity.

: XXXV :

Marsilio:

The divinely inspired Scriptures are the principles of the whole of theology wherein the many mysteries overwhelm human reason. So we must acquiesce in these mysteries. One should never speak about theology with any one who denies the mysteries.

: XXXVI :

Dionysius:[73]
⟨Idem.⟩

1 Si quis autem obiecerit confusionem nos hac ratione contra distinctionem divinitati convenientem introducere, nos hunc arbitramur se vera dicere nunquam persuasurum. Si enim is est, qui omnino sacris litteris resistat, a philosophia quoque nostra procul admodum aberit; atqui nisi cure illi sit divina sanctorum eloquiorum sapientia, quonam pacto nobis cure erit ad theologicam scientiam hunc adducere?

2 Sin autem sacrorum eloquiorum veritatem quasi signum spectat, hac et nos regula luceque freti ad rationem nostram pro viribus contra obiecta reddendam indeclinabili sententia iam pergemus, principio dicentes theologiam alia quidem unite, alia vero discrete nobis tradere. Quare neque unita dividere fas est, neque discreta confundere, sed ipsam sequendo quantum vires suppetunt ad divinos splendores conferre nos expedit.

3 Iam vero nos illinc[74] divinas explicationes suscipientes tanquam regulam quandam veritatis pulcherrimam, que ibi posita sunt in nobis ipsis conservare studemus, nec addentes quicquam nec minuentes, nec etiam permutantes, in servandis divinis eloquiis nos interim conservati, atque ab ipsis ad conservandos eorum observatores corroborati.

: XXXVI :

Dionysius:
[The same.]

However, if someone were to object that we are introducing confusion in order to introduce something contrary to the distinction that befits divinity, we believe that this person will never persuade himself to speak the truth. But if there is someone who utterly rejects the sacred Scriptures, he will be far removed too from our philosophy. Unless he cares about the divine wisdom of the sacred Scriptures, why should we care about leading him toward theological knowledge? 1

But if he does look to the truth of the sacred Scriptures as to a sign, we too will now proceed, relying on this guide and on light, to call upon our reason as best we can to counter the objections of unyielding opinion. We will say at the onset that theology transmits some things to us in a unitary way, other things in a divided way. So it is not permissible to divide things united, or to join things divided. But in pursuing theology, insofar as our powers may serve us, it helps us to betake ourselves to the splendors divine. 2

In receiving the divine unfoldings from theology, however, as the most beautiful model of truth, we study to preserve in ourselves the truths deposited there, without adding or subtracting or even changing anything. In preserving the divine Scriptures, we ourselves are meanwhile preserved; and by those Scriptures we are emboldened to preserve the observers of them. 3

: XXXVII :

Marsilius: Que sint in divinitate communia, que propria.

1 Alia in divinitate communia sunt, alia propria. Duo vero sunt communium genera: aut enim excellentes quedam negationes sunt, ut super bonum, super essentiam[75] atque similia, aut progressus ex Deo benefici, ut bonum,[76] essentia, ceteraque similia.

2 Duo quoque sunt genera propriorum: aut enim persone ipse divine sunt personarumque proprietates, aut humanitatis assumptio a Verbo divino tantum facta. Etsi quod est Patris proprium, id est generare, non sit commune Filio, cui est proprium generari, non tamen propterea Filius gradum tenet inferiorem, quia nec tempore nec natura posterior est quam Pater, nec minus divinitatis habet: tota enim est utrobique eadem[77] divinitas, hoc tantum differens quod hic existit inde, neque vicissim.

: XXXVII :

Marsilio:
The names that are common to the Divinity and those that are particular.

Some names in the Divinity are in common, others are particular. 1
But of those in common the classes are two. For either they are negations that betoken [a transcendent] excellence, such as the super-good, the super-essence and the like; or they are beneficent progressions from God, such as the good, essence, and the like.

There are also two classes of particular properties. For either 2
the Persons themselves are divine and the properties of the Persons [are divine], or the assumption of [our] humanity is made by the divine Word alone. Although that which is the property of the Father, that is, to generate, is not common to the Son, to whom it is proper to be generated, nonetheless it is not because the Son occupies a lower rank. For neither in time nor in nature is He later than the Father, nor does He have less of divinity. For the same whole divinity is common to both Persons, differing only in the fact that the Son exists from the Father, not the reverse.

: XXXVIII :

Dionysius:
Que sint in divinitate communia,
que propria.

1 Communia quidem toti divinitati sunt, quemadmodum in *Theologicis institutionibus* latius ex sacris litteris demonstravimus, ipsum quod dicitur[78] super bonum, super deitatem, super essentiam, super vitam, super sapientiam, et quecunque in excellente quadam negatione consistunt, quorum in ordine sunt etiam que ad expressionem cause pertinent, scilicet bonum, pulchrum, ens, vivificum, sapiens, et quecunque nomina ex beneficis ipsius donis bonorum omnium cause tribuuntur.

2 Discreta vero in Divinitate sunt superessentiale Patris nomen resque ipsa proprie Patri, itemque Filii Spiritusque sancti, quippe cum nulla in iis conversio aut omnino communitas inducatur. Discreta preterea est perfecta immutabilisque Iesu substantia cum nostra natura communicans et quecunque substantialia mysteria sunt ad ipsam Iesu substantiam humanitatemque benignissimam pertinentia.

: XXXVIII :

Dionysius: Those names that are common to the Divinity, and those that are particular.

Certain shared names are attributed to the Divinity as a whole, as we have shown more fully in the *Principles of Theology* using the sacred Scriptures: [namely] that God is called super-good, super-deity, super-essence, super-life, super-wisdom, and all those titles that consist of a negation bespeaking [a transcendent] excellence. In the same order are those too which pertain to the express unfolding of the cause, that is, the good, the beautiful, being, what bestows life, the wise, and all the names that spring from the beneficent gifts of God and are attributed to the cause of all goods. 1

But in the Divinity the super-essential name of the Father and what is properly the Father's is not shared; and likewise the name of the Son and of the Holy Spirit, since there is no converting these names and they are not held in common at all. Distinguished too is the perfect and immutable substance of Jesus who shares our nature, and all the substantial mysteries pertaining to the substance of Jesus and His most benign humanity. 2

: XXXIX :

Marsilius:
De unitate et discretione divina.

1 Unitatem appellamus in Deo ipsam divine infinitatis singularitatem nulli foris communicabilem, discretionem vero dicimus processionem rerum ex Deo manantium. Nisi enim processio fiat, nec Deus habebit a quo distinguatur, nec ulla rerum erit inter se distinctio, cuncta siquidem in Deo sunt unum. Res ipse procedentes conservant interim mutuam unionem, nam in uno quodam conveniunt cum sint ab uno.

2 Item penes divinam unitatem, qualem modo diximus, personarum consideramus distinctionem; rursus in hac distinctione communionem, tum quia dotes omnes per excellentiam Deo tribute sic in una quavis persona sunt, sicut in alia, tum quia persona quelibet est in aliis coniuncta[79] simul atque distincta, quemadmodum lumina luminibus insunt.

: XL :

Dionysius:
De unitate et discretione divina.

1 Opere pretium vero est (ut arbitror) ut planius resumentes perfectum divine unionis distinctionisque modum exponamus, quo sermo nobis omnis sit conspicuous varietatem[80] quidem omnem

: XXXIX :

Marsilio:
On divine unity and differentiation.

Unity in God we call the singleness itself of the divine infinity which cannot be imparted to anything external. But division we call the procession of things emanating from God; for, unless there were procession, nothing would be distinguishable in God, nor would there be any distinction of things among themselves, since all in God are one. Things proceeding [from Him] preserve meanwhile their mutual union; for they agree in being one, since they come from the One. 1

Likewise, within the divine unity we ponder (in the manner we have just noted) the distinction of [its] Persons, and in this distinction again, their communion. This is because all the gifts attributed to God by way of excellence are in one Person as in another, and also because each Person is joined to the other two and yet at the same time is distinct. Similarly one light is present in [various] lights. 2

: XL :

Dionysius:
On divine unity and differentiation.

It is important, I think, that we expound the perfect mode of divine union and differentiation by resuming [the argument] more clearly, so that all our discourse may be transparent to all, shun- 1

obscuritatemque devitans, distincte vero et manifeste et ordinate pro viribus propria digerens.

2 Theologice traditionis nostre preceptores appellant, ut alibi dixi, unitates quidem divinas excellentes quasdam ipsius plusquam ineffabilis et supra modum, incognite singularitatis stabilitatisve firmitates secretas penitus, nusquam vero prodeuntes. Discretiones autem vocant beneficas supreme divinitatis progressiones atque expressiones.

3 Iam vero eloquiorum sacrorum observatores tradunt unionis modo dicte propria quedam, rursumque discretionis proprias quasdam uniones atque discretiones. Velut in unione divina, sive natura illa essentiam superante, commune quidem est unice principalique Trinitati existentia essentiam superans, deitas divinitate superior, bonitas bonitate prestantior, item identitas ipsa totius proprietatis omnia superantis, omnia superans, unitas quoque principio eminentior; preterea ineffabile vicissimque multis vocibus predicabile, ignoratio quinetiam ac vicissim per omnia intelligibile, omnium positio omniumve negatio, excellentia quoque omnem positionem ablationemque excedens.

4 Personarum preterea ratione principii dominantium, si dicere ita licet, mansio in se invicem atque sedes, integre supra modum unita nullaque ex parte confusa, quemadmodum lumina lampadum, ut sensibilibus propriisque utamur exemplis, in domo una cum sint et tota in totis mutuo sunt et sincera interim exactaque a se invicem discretione propria secernuntur, discretione quidem coniuncta et vicissim unione inter se discreta.

ning all variation and obscurity, and arranging properties distinctly, manifestly, and in order as best we can.

The teachers of our theological tradition call divine unities, as I 2
said elsewhere, those particular excellences of God who is more than ineffable and above modality — those utterly secret, unchanging excellences of His unknown singleness or unchangingness that nowhere issue forth. But the teachers call divisions the beneficent progressions and expressions of the highest Divinity.

Students of the sacred Scriptures tell us, however, that certain 3
properties are by way of the said union, and again that certain properties (unions and differentiations alike) are by way of differentiation. For instance, in the divine union or the nature superior to essence, what is common uniquely and principally to the Trinity is as follows: existence excelling essence; deity higher than divinity; goodness far surpassing goodness; the identity itself of the whole property excelling all and ruling over all; unity more eminent than each principle; what is ineffable and yet proclaimable by many voices; what is not known of itself but what is knowable in turn through all; the positing of all and yet the denial of all; the excellence, finally, that exceeds every attribution and subtraction.

Moreover, by reason of the principle of their being Almighty — 4
if it is permissible to speak thus — the Persons are perpetually enthroned and wholly united in themselves above all modality, in no part confused. Similarly, with the lights of lamps — to use sensible and apt examples — when they are in one house, the lights in all the lamps are one light in common, and yet, if we are careful and precise, we may distinguish them from each other. In distinction they are joined, and in union they are divided among themselves.

: XLI :

Marsilius: De unione et discretione luminum atque divinorum.

1 Si in aula lucernis tribus illustri deambules, tres umbre resultant; preterea si ingentem tabulam lucernis illis opponas,[81] cuius in medio sit foramen, lucerne tres per foramen illud tria lumina e transverso trahiciunt in oppositum. Unde coniicimus emicantia lumina in aere invicem non confundi, sed quanvis sint coniuncta[82] loco, pura tamen sunt suamque proprietatem servant inter se discretam. Spiritalis enim eorum natura facit ut non commisceantur invicem in novam communemque formam sicut solent corporee qualitates. Quanquam astrologi putant e[83] multis radiis vim novam aliquam procreari, radiis tamen interim non commixtis.

2 Quamobrem unumquodque lumen discerni potest ab alio, nec alieni quicquam secum ferens nec relinquens sui, atque, ut Plotinus ait, principium suum passim et assidue comitans. Profecto pluribus lucernis adductis splendor inde fit ingentior, unaquaque subducta fit minor; unaqueque enim lumen suum et affert veniens et aufert inde discedens.

3 Si lumina ob incorpoream proprietatem in corpore tamen existentia[84] munus id consequuntur, ut et unita invicem et simul discreta inter se mirabiliter esse possint, multo magis id habent que magis sunt a corporibus separata, ut anime ipsius[85] virtutes atque scientie; magis etiam ipse inter se substantie animarum; magis

: XLI :

Marsilio: On the union and differentiation of lights and of the Persons divine.

If you walk in a hall illuminated by three lamps, three shadows will follow you. Moreover, if you set up a huge plank opposite those lamps in the middle of which there is a hole, then through that hole the three lamps will cast their three lights sideways on a surface opposite. From this we deduce that the emanating lights are not muddled together in the air. Though they are joined in a place, yet they remain pure and preserve their own property and keep it separate in itself; for their spiritual nature ensures that they are not mingled together in a new and shared form, as corporeal qualities are. Though the astrologers think that some new force is procreated from many [focused] rays, still, the rays are not commingled. 1

Wherefore every single light can be distinguished from another, without bearing in itself anything of the others, or leaving anything of its own behind; and, as Plotinus says, it constantly accompanies its own principle everywhere.[100] Certainly, when many lamps are assembled together, the splendor from them becomes brighter; and when each one is subtracted, it becomes dimmer. For each lamp comes bearing its own light, and, when it is removed, it takes its light away. 2

If lights, on account of their bodiless property while still existing in a body, have the gift of being able, marvelously, to be united together and at the same time to be distinguished among themselves, then it is even more true of those things which are still more separated from bodies, for example, the soul's virtues and knowledge. And it is still more true of the substances of souls 3

insuper invicem intellectus angelici; maxime omnium Trinitatis divine persone, cuius quidem tam unitatis quam discretionis participatione quadam singula deinceps pro modo suo gradatim unionem discretionemque[86] reportant.

: XLII :

Dionysius: *De unione discretioneque luminum.*

1 Quando in eadem aula lampades accense sunt plures, videmus omnium lumina ad unum aliquid coniuncta lumen unumque splendorem individuum preferentia, neque posset (ut arbitror) aliquis lampadis huius lumen ab aliis ex aere cuncta lumina continente secernere, et alterum absque altero cernere, quippe cum tota in totis sine mixtione sint inserta. Iam vero si quis lampadem unam e medio tollat, lumen quoque proprium eius totum abeuntem lampadem comitabitur, nec quicquam aliorum luminum secum trahens, neque ex suo ceteris aliquid linquens. Erat enim (ut diximus) illic totorum ad tota exacta quidem unio nec ullo modo commixta nec ulla ex parte confusa. Id quidem ita se habet, quamvis lumen sit in corpore aereo[87] atque ex igne materiali dependeat.

2 Unionem igitur illam essentia superiorem transcendere dicimus non uniones tantum que fiunt in corpore, sed eas etiam que in animis ipsis conficiuntur, immo et illas que efficiuntur in mentibus; quas quidem tota illa divina et supercelestia lumina per tota, ratione plus quam mundana, sincere admodum possident,

among themselves; and still more again of angelic intellects. And it will be most of all true of the divine Persons of the Trinity, from participation as it were in whose unity and differentiation individuals thereafter derive by degrees, and each in his own way, both union and differentiation.

: XLII :

Dionysius: On the union and differentiation of lights.

When many lamps in the same hall are ablaze, we see the lights of all joined into one light and presenting one undivided splendor. No one (I think) would be able to separate out from the air containing all the lights the light of this lamp from among others, and perceive one light without another, since all the lights are present in the whole light without being commingled. But if some one removes one lamp from the midst, then its own light too, the whole of it, will depart with the departing lamp: the lamp does not take away with it anything of the other lights, nor does it leave behind any of its own light for the rest. In this case, as I said, a precise union pertains of wholes with respect to wholes, a union neither commingled in any way, nor in any part confused. Thus the lamp possesses this light itself, even though the light is in an aery body and depends on material fire. 1

Hence we maintain that the union higher than essence transcends not only the unions which are in the body but those which are effected in souls themselves, nay, those too which are effected in minds. These are the unions which the whole, divine, and supercelestial lights possess throughout their totality, and for a reason more than mundane; and they wholly possess them by 2

participatione quadam unitatis illius omnibus eminentis et unicuique pro cuiusque modo se ipsam impertientis.

: XLIII :

Marsilius:
Discretio divinarum personarum duplex.

Geminam in Trinitate consideramus discretionem, tum quia existentia Patris alia est atque Filii et existentia Filii Patrisque alia est atque Spiritus, tum etiam quoniam actus Patri proprius (quod est generare) non convenit Filio, neque actus Filio proprius (id est nasci) Patri competit, similiterque procedere ad Spiritum solum pertinet; ideo nec Pater est Filius, neque Filius est Pater neque Spiritus simili ratione.

: XLIV :

Dionysius:
Idem.

Est autem discretio apud supremam theologiam, non solum quam modo dicebam, quia videlicet iuxta ipsam unitatem divina quelibet subsistentia puram et impermixtam suam sibi servat proprietatem, sed etiam quoniam divina illic generatio invicem non convertitur. Nempe superessentialis deitatis fons solus est Pater, neque Pater est Filius, neque Filius est Pater; sacri igitur hymni sua

participating in that unity which is higher than all things, and which imparts itself to every single thing according to the mode of each.

: XLIII :

Marsilio:
The twofold differentiation of the divine Persons.

Let us consider a twin differentiation in the Trinity both because the Father's existence is other than that of the Son and the Son's and Father's existence is other than that of the Spirit, but also because the act proper to the Father which is to generate is not fitting for the Son, nor is the act proper to the Son which is to be born fitting for the Father. Similarly, "to proceed" pertains only to the Spirit. Thus the Father is not the Son, nor the Son the Father, nor, for a like reason, is the Spirit.

: XLIV :

Dionysius:
The same.[101]

In highest theology there is a differentiation not only in the way I have talked about, namely, that immediately next to unity itself each divine existence [i.e., Person] preserves for itself its own property pure and unmixed; but also in the way that divine generation there is not interchangeable. The super-essential fountain of deity is the Father alone: the Father is not the Son nor is the

unicuique divinarum personarum pie planeque conservant. He quidem secundum ineffabilem unitatem atque existentiam uniones et discretiones existunt.

: XLV :

Marsilius: De discretione et unione divina in creaturarum processione.

1 In processione rerum ex Deo consideratur discretio simul et unio: discretio quidem, quia Deus videtur se ipsum (id est similitudinem suam) in plures imagines derivare, sicut et sol lucem suam in radios quam plurimos et vultus unus circa speculum effigiem suam in multas imagines.

2 Unionem quoque interim cogitamus, tum quia nec unitas ipsa divina vel multiplicatur intus, vel dividitur foris, vel admiscetur, tum etiam quia bonorum progressio cunctorum eque fit a Filio atque Spiritu sicut a Patre. Profluunt autem ex Deo bona quam plurima, precipua vero tria, scilicet essentia, vita, intelligentia, quemadmodum a sole lumen, calor, ordo formarum.

3 Preterea sicut a puncto circuli medio linee circum quam plurime producuntur, ipso interim in longitudinem non producto ab aliisque distincto, linee vero inde et suum quodque punctum possident et individuitatem in latum profundumque suam; rursum sicut multe impressiones ex uno eodemque sigillo non multiplicato, non diviso, non omnino coniuncto, ita ferme rerum processio

Son the Father. Thus sacred hymns reverently and openly preserve for each of the divine Persons the attributes which are His own. These unions and divisions [in the Persons] exist in accord with [God's] ineffable unity and existence.

: XLV :

Marsilio: On divine differentiation and union in the procession of creatures.

In the procession of things from God, differentiation must be considered along with union: differentiation because God seems to distribute Himself, that is, His likeness, into many images, just as the sun disperses its light into a multitude of rays, and one face close to a mirror renders its likeness into many images. 1

At the same time, we think of union too, both because the divine unity itself is neither multiplied within nor divided without nor mingled; and because the progression of all good things is brought about by the Son and the Spirit as well as by the Father. As many goods as possible flow forth from God, but chiefly these three: essence, life, and understanding, just as from the sun comes light, heat, and the order of the forms. 2

Take the analogy, moreover, of the lines that in their abundance radiate out from the midpoint of a circle. Even as the point is not extended in length and is distinct from the other points, the lines radiating from it each possess their own point and indivisibility in breadth and depth. Again, take the analogy of many impressions from one and the same seal where the seal itself is neither multiplied nor divided from [the impression] nor entirely joined to it. So, or almost so, is the procession of things coming from God. Yet 3

fit ex Deo, divina tamen simplicitas absque proportione segregatior est a rebus inde fluentibus quam centrum atque sigillum; divina quoque potestas est rebus presentior quam alterutrum.

: XLVI :

Dionysius:
Idem.

1 Si autem divina quoque discretio est beneficus unitatis divine progressus se ipsam plusquam unite, bonitate sua propagantis atque multiplicantis unite, quidem sunt in discretione divina traditiones ipse donorum a rebus penitus absolute, sive essentia, sive vita, seu sapientia inde procedat, ceteraque cause omnium bonitatis munera, iuxta que ex participationibus atque participantibus celebrantur, que participantur interim nequaquam participata.

2 Id sane commune unitumque est et unum toti penitus deitati ipsam videlicet omnem totamque ab unoquoque participante sumi atque a nullo interim ulla ex parte percipi, quemadmodum circuli centrum ab omnibus circumfusis rectis in circulo lineis, atque veluti sigilli figuramenta plurima principalis figure participia sunt, ubi et in singulis figurationibus idem totumque sigillum est et in nullo ulla ex parte rursus existit.

the divine simplicity, in bearing no proportion to the procession of these things, is more aloof from what proceeds from it than the circle's center and the seal are set apart from their lines and impressions. The divine power too is more present in things than either the center or the seal is present.

: XLVI :

Dionysius:
The same.

But if divine differentiation too is the beneficent progression of divine unity more than united to itself, unity propagating and multiplying itself in its goodness, then united in this divine differentiation is the gift-giving which is entirely apart from things, whether it is essence that proceeds or life or wisdom, or the rest of the gifts of the goodness which is the universal cause. Below these are the things celebrated as coming from participations and participatings—the things which participate but are never themselves participated. 1

That which is common to the whole Deity and is united and one is assumed by every single one of us participating in it to be the Deity entire and whole: no one perceives it to be just from some part. Similarly, the circle's center is participated by all the straight radii radiating in a circle around it; and the many imprints of a seal are the participants of its principal shape, where the same entire seal is in the individual imprints, and not, to the contrary, just existing partially in any one of them. 2

3 Supereminet autem hec incommunicabile illud deitatis omnium auctoris, propterea quod neque tactus illius est ullus nec alia quevis ad participantia permixta communio.

: XLVII :

Marsilius: Differentes sub eadem idea resultantur imagines ob differentiam subiectorum.

1 Sigillum manu potenti ductum imaginem suam eandem, universam, exactam, quantum in se est, subiecto cuique tribuit. Multe vero fiunt sigilli eiusdem imagines, quia multe materie sunt, perfectionis quoque gradibus differentes evadunt, quoniam materie admoventur gradibus diversis affecte.

2 Similiter ferme se habent divini exemplaris idee quelibet ad subiectas sibi materias vel naturas: materie vero vel nature non solum per medias causas ad divinum exemplar varie disponuntur, sed et ipsa providentia Dei ad prescriptum finem medias ubique causas agitante, que et ita naturas ab initio varias procreavit.

But that incommunicable divinity of the Deity, the author of all, excels these [analogies], because there is no touching upon it at all, and no other sharing of it that would mix it with things participating in it. 3

: XLVII :

Marsilio: Different images emerge, though under the same idea, because of the difference of subjects.

The seal controlled by a steady hand impresses the same image, all of it exactly insofar it can, into each material subject to it. But many images of the same seal occur because the materials are many. They emerge differing in degrees of perfection too, because the materials are changed and affected in different degrees. 1

All the ideas of a divine exemplar similarly relate, or almost so, to the materials or natures that are their substrates. But materials or natures are variously disposed for the divine exemplar not only by way of intermediate causes, but also by way of God's providence itself, in that it is moving the intermediate causes everywhere to the prescribed end, and has thus created the various natures from the beginning. 2

: XLVIII :

Dionysius:
Idem.

Obiiciet forte quispiam sigillum nec idem nec totum in totis formationibus esse. Sed sigillum non est in causa: illud namque se totum idemque imprimit unicuique; differentia vero participantium dissimiles unius totiusque et eiusdem exemplaris primi reddit[88] effigies. Si enim subiecta sint mollia formatuque facilia et lenia figurisque vacua, neque resistentia duraque, neque fluxa rursus neque inconstantia, figuram certe puram et expressam permansuramque reportabunt. Siquid vero ex his (que diximus) preparamentis defuerit, defectus eiusmodi erit in causa ut et figura minime congruat exemplari et obscura contingat atque ut cetera quoque accidant quotcumque participationis ineptitudine fiunt.

: XLIX :

Marsilius:
De discretione rursus et unione divina circa Christum.

1 Duas in presentia circa Deum discretiones consideramus: primam, quod nec Pater nec Spiritus sed Filius naturam assumpsit humanam—naturam dico,[89] non personam; sed in ipsa divine unione

: XLVIII :

Dionysius:
The same.

Perhaps someone will object that the seal is not the same seal, or is not entire, in all that it imprints. The seal is not responsible, however, since the seal imprints itself as the same whole in each imprint. But the difference in the materials receiving the imprint produces dissimilar copies of the one, entire, and identical prime model. If the subject materials are soft, easily formed, malleable, void of shapes, not resistant or hard, and not on the other hand fluid or inconstant, they will certainly render the imprint clean, clear, and durable. But if any matter lacks the preparatory features we have just described, it will be responsible for the said defect, and the resulting imprint will not accord at all with its model and it will emerge as indistinct. The same will also happen to all the other materials unfitted to participate [in the seal].

: XLIX :

Marsilio:
On differentiation again and on divine union with regard to Christ.

Let us for the present consider two differentiations with regard to 1
God: first that neither the Father nor the Spirit but the Son assumed human nature—nature I say not person, though one in

persone. Secundam, quod actiones passionesque Christi prorsus humane ut concipi, nasci, esurire, commedere, dormire, dolere, quodammodo quidem attribui Filio possunt, videlicet humanam induto naturam; Patri vero Spirituique nullo modo possunt.

2 Sed geminam vicissim unionem excogitamus: primam quod Pater, Filius, Spiritus voluntate eadem penitus consenserunt, Filium videlicet hominem effici; secundam, quod divine omnes in Christo operationes eque sunt toti Trinitati communes.

3 Notabis interea eternum Dei Verbum assumpsisse corpus humanum, non ex celo, ut opinatus est Celestinus atque Valerianus,[90] sed ex nobis; item totam naturam nostram non subtracta anima vel intellectu, quod Arrius Apollinarisque suspicantur; denique naturam veram, non imaginariam, qualem Manichei somniaverunt. Tres enim hos errores ipsa Dionysii verba proculdubio confutant.

: L :

Dionysius: Idem.

1 In ipsa quidem operatione divina erga nos benefica munus hoc discretum est, quod videlicet supersubstantiale Dei Verbum secundum nos et ex nobis integram atque veram adsumpsit naturam; item, quod gessit et pertulit quodcunque divinitatis ipsius facte iam humane propria sunt atque precipua. In his enim Pater et Spiritus nullam habuere communionem, nisi forte quis dixerit in

union itself with [His] divine Person. Second, that the actions and passions of Christ, being entirely human—being conceived, for example, or being born, thirsting, eating, sleeping, grieving—can be attributed in a way to the Son having assumed human nature. But they cannot in any way be attributed to the Father and the Spirit.

Alternatively, however, let us consider their twofold union: first that the Father, Son, and Spirit are in utter accord and possess the 2
same will, namely, that the Son be made man; and second that all the divine operations in Christ are equally those of the whole Trinity.

You will note meanwhile that God's eternal Word assumed the 3
human body, a body derived not from heaven as Celestinus and Valerianus[102] supposed, but from us; next, that He assumed our whole nature, not our nature with the soul or intellect subtracted, as Arius[103] and Apollinaris surmised;[104] and finally that He assumed a true not an imaginary nature as the Manicheans dreamed.[105] For Dionysius' very words confute these three errors beyond the shadow of a doubt.

: L :

Dionysius: The same.

In the divine operation which is a blessing to us, the following 1
gift has been distinguished: namely that the super-substantial Word of God has assumed an entire and true nature that accords with us and that comes from us; likewise that it has put on and perfected all that is proper and special to divinity now made human. For the Father and Spirit played no part in this at all, unless

benefica clementique voluntate circa assumptionem eiusmodi consensisse, rursumque convenisse simul in omni operatione divina ineffabili penitus et excelsa, humanam naturam exsuperante, quam gessit Dei Verbum, secundum quidem nos factum homo, sed divinitate penitus immutabile.

2 Hac igitur et nos ratione unire et discernere divina disserendo studemus, quemadmodum ipsa divina coniuncta sunt atque discreta.

: LI :

Marsilius:
Duabus viis ad Deum accedimus, ratione et[91] *veneratione.*

1 Ad divina duabus precipue viis accedimus: aut enim ratione aut[92] veneratione movemur: ratione quidem ad cognoscendum esse Deum ex ordine mundi, esse potentissimum ex motu totius rerumque effectu, esse optimum ex usu rerum et commoditate mirabilis. Eadem quoque via principium universi ex participationibus suis cognominamus Deum quia deos efficiat vel divinos, essentiam, vitam, sapientiam, bonitatem, quia esse rebus tribuat, vitamque et sapientiam, sive ordinem et benefica dona.

2 Hucusque humana ratio lumine naturali procedit; ad[93] ipsam vero naturam Dei in se ipsa manentem et mysteria Trinitatis atque similia veneratione potius preparamur. Veneratio ad Deum

perchance someone were to assert that, in their merciful and beneficent will, they consented to [His] assuming [our nature] in this way, while agreeing that His assumption was in harmony at the same time with every divine, totally ineffable, and lofty operation far surpassing our human nature, a human nature which God's Word bore for us indeed, having been made man, but bore with utterly immutable divinity.

So this is the reason we study to both unite and divide in dis- 2
cussing matters divine, just as divine things themselves are both conjoined and differentiated.

: LI :

Marsilio:
We come to God by two paths: by reason and by worship.

We come to matters divine principally by two paths. We are 1
moved either by reason or by worship. We are moved by reason to learn from the world's order that God exists; to learn from the motion of the whole and the effecting of things that He is all powerful; and to learn from their use and their marvelous fitness that He is the best. By the same path [of reason] let us also call God the universal principle by virtue of what participates in Him, because He makes gods or divine beings. And let us call Him essence, life, wisdom, and goodness, because He gives being, life, wisdom (or order), and the gifts of His beneficence to things.

Thus far human reason proceeds by a natural light, but to ap- 2
proach God's nature itself (a nature remaining in itself), and for the mysteries of the Trinity and the like, let us prepare ourselves instead by way of worship. Worship flies to God on twin wings,

geminis pervolat alis, fide videlicet et amore, quibus denique Deo coniungimur unione quadam intelligentiam superante.

3 Qui tandem ita Deo fruitur agnoscit protinus non esse Deum vel penes Deum simile vel tale aliquid quale prius excogitaverat, quando principium rerum ex participantibus participationibus donis cognominabat. Huic Platonicum illud in epistola ad Dionysium simile: 'Animus noster affectat qualia divina sint intelligere, aspiciens in ea que sibi cognata sunt, quorum nihil sufficienter se habet. Nam in ipso rege omnium, et penes ipsum nihil est eiusmodi, quod autem post ipsum est, animus dicit': hec Plato.

4 Cognata quidem animo sunt substantia incorporea, viva, vivifica, sensualis, rationalis, intellectualis, intelligibilis, sapiens. Nam ipsa anima vel hec ipsa est, vel horum particeps atque compos; quatenus vero in se ipsam suaque respicit, per hec Deum iudicat atque nominat, eatenus quoque fallitur. Transiturus vero animus quandoque est hec omnia, tum demum non amplius mentiturus.

: LII :

Dionysius: Idem.

1 Sed harum unionum atque discretionum rationes Deo dignas, quascunque in divinis eloquiis invenimus, in *Theologicis institutionibus* propria seorsum de singulis distinguentes pro viribus exposuimus:

on faith and on love, and we are thereby joined to God at last in a union surpassing understanding.

For he who finally enjoys God knows straightway that nothing 3
is like God or being in God's presence, and that God is not as he had first thought of Him when he named Him the principle of things from those things participating in His gifts and from the participations themselves. That Platonic saying in the letter to Dionysius affirms much the same: "Our rational soul desires to understand divine matters, whatever they may be, by gazing at those things which are akin to itself, none of which is sufficient. For nothing of this kind exists in the universal king or in his presence. But the rational soul can speak [only] to what comes after the king."[106] This is Plato.

Cognate to the rational soul is incorporeal substance, living, 4
life-giving, knowing by way of the sense, the reason, the intellect, the intelligible itself. For the soul either is these, or is a participant of these, or is compounded from them. To the degree it looks back to itself and to these as its own, and judges and denominates God through them, to this extent it is also deceived. The rational soul, however, that sets out at some point to transcend all these will in the end no longer deceive itself.

: LII :

Dionysius: The same.

But the reasons for these unions and differentiations proper to 1
God, the ones we have found in sacred Scripture, we have expounded as far as we can in our *Principles of Theology*, separately and individually distinguishing their properties. Some we unfold

alia quidem vera ratione evolventes et explicantes atque ita sacrum tranquillumque intellectum ad perspicua sacrorum eloquiorum spectacula perducentes; aliis autem, tanquam mysticis, ex traditione divina super intellectualem actionem intendentes.

2 Divina enim omnia, etiam que nobis patuerunt, solis participationibus cognoscuntur; hoc ipsum vero, qualia in se ipsis existant secundum proprium principium atque sedem, super intelligentiam extat omnemque essentiam et notitiam supereminet;[94] veluti si superessentiale illud atque secretum appellamus[95] Deum aut vitam aut essentiam, vel[96] lumen vel rationem atque verbum, nihil intelligimus aliud quam aliquas in nos ex eo profluentes participationes atque virtutes que videlicet divinum[97] aliquid faciant, vel essentiam, aut vitam, aut sapientiam largiantur;

3 Ipsi vero secrete nature per quandam omnium intellectualium actionum vacationem penitus absolutam appropinquamus, nullam iam aspicientes deificentiam aut vitam aut essentiam que omnino similis sit ipsi omnium cause cuncta prorsus per omnem excellentiam superanti.

: LIII :

Marsilius:
De Trinitate et donis Trinitatis in naturis intellectualibus.

1 Ex fecunda solis natura nascitur ipsa lux intima solis, equalis generanti nature et a centro[98] ad superficiem solis usque producta; a superficie rursus eadem equalitate reflectit undique se ad centrum

and explicate using our true reason, thus bringing a sacred and tranquil intellect to bear on the pellucid visions of the sacred Scriptures; but for others, being mystical, we look to the divine tradition for an action that is super-intellectual.

For all divine matters, even those which have been revealed to us, are known by participations alone. But the [mystical] kind—like the kinds which exist in themselves according to their own principle and on their own throne—exists above understanding and excels all essence and any rational conception. It is as if we were to name this super-essential and secret kind "God" or "life" or "essence" or "light" or "reason" or "word," and yet understand by it nothing other than that they are some of the participations and powers issuing from Him, namely those which render something divine or bestow essence or life or wisdom. 2

But we ourselves approach this secret nature via a certain utter and complete emptying of all intellectual actions, not looking now at any deification or life or essence which might be similar at all to the universal cause itself, the cause which surpasses all things utterly and by way of every excellence. 3

: LIII :

Marsilio: On the Trinity and the gifts of the Trinity in intellectual natures.

From the sun's generative nature is born the sun's inmost light itself which is equal to that generating nature: the light is produced from the center out to the sun's surface. From the surface, and again with the same equality, the heat-causing splendor 1

splendor ipse calefactorius ex natura luceque profectus. Eodem ferme modo in divinis ex Patre Filius Spiritusque existunt, tametsi modus ille intelligentiam nostram superat supra modum.

2 Verum qualiscumque modus ille sit, intelligentia saltem hucusque progreditur ut excogitet, quemadmodum a sole omnia diaphana (id est luci pervia) evadunt momento lucentia penitus ideoque solaria, sic ex Deo intellectuales substantias puritate diaphanas, suscepto protinus fulgore divino, divinas et quasi deos evadere. Atque fulgoris huius fecunditate intellectus ubique superiores lumen in sequentes effundere, cuius infusione illi quidem hos quasi regenerent, hi vero illinc quodammodo renascantur, ferme quemadmodum luna ex sole illuminante renascitur.

3 Hac igitur ratione divini Patris Filiique munera per generationem et nativitatem in sequentes perveniunt intellectus; pervenit quoque munus Sancti spiritus dum ille suum cunctis inspirat amorem. Unde per amatorium affectum intellectus tum superiores generant, tum inferiores inde nascuntur, quatenus hi semper ab illis convertuntur, purgantur, illuminantur, perficiuntur.[99]

4 Denique sicut materia corporalis per potentiam formabilem ad actum forme paratur, unde generatio sequitur, ita substantie spiritales per amatorium affectum, qui Sanctum spiritum representat,[100] superioribus intellectibus exponuntur atque expositi renascuntur. Ratio tamen ipsa generationis, nativitatis, spirationis, Divinitati propria; sequentia hec, quamvis quoquomodo similia, infinito prorsus superat intervallo.

turns itself everywhere back toward the center, having proceeded from both the nature and the light. In the same way almost, in the divine [Trinity], the Son and the Spirit exist from the Father, although the manner in which they do so utterly excels our understanding.

But whatever that manner is, our understanding at least progresses to the point that it recognizes that, just as all transparent things (things pervious, that is, to light) issue from the sun for a moment utterly ablaze and therefore sun-like, so intellectual substances, transparent in their purity and having straightway received the divine brightness, issue from God as divine, as gods almost. And our understanding recognizes that, from the abundance of this brightness, these higher intellects everywhere pour the light forth upon those who follow; and by the infusion of this light the higher may regenerate in a way the lower. The latter are in a way reborn from it, almost as the moon is reborn from the sun illuminating it. 2

For this reason the gifts of the divine Father and Son descend via generation and nativity to the intellects succeeding them. The gift of the Holy Spirit also reaches them when it breathes its love into all. Whence the higher intellects generate through amatory desire, and from it the lower intellects are generated insofar as they are always converted, purged, illumined, and perfected by the higher intellects. 3

Finally, just as corporeal matter is prepared through its formable potency for the act of its form, and generation ensues, so spiritual substances, through the amatory desire which represents the Holy Spirit, are brought forth from the higher intellects and are thus born again. Nonetheless, the rational principle itself of generation, birth, and inspiration is proper to the Divinity. It surpasses all that follow it, however similar they may be, by an utterly infinite interval. 4

: LIV :

Dionysius: Idem.

1 Accepimus insuper a sanctis eloquiis Patrem quidem esse fontanam (ut ita dixerim) deitatem, Filium vero Spiritumque fecunde deitatis, si modo ita licet loqui, germina divinitus pullulantia et quasi flores et supersubstantialia lumina.

2 Sed qua ratione hec sint, nec loqui nec intelligere possumus; hactenus vero nostra omnis intellectualis actio se extendit, ut videlicet excogitet omnem patris ipsius ac filii rationem ab ipsa ratione Patris Filiique prima omnibus eminente et nobis et virtutibus supercelestibus esse tributam. Ex qua quidem intellectus divinam imaginem preferentes et dii et deorum filii et deorum patres fiunt atque nominantur, dum videlicet id patris filiique munus spiritaliter ubique peragitur, id est incorporea, immateriali, intelligibili[101] ratione. Ipso interim divino Spiritu quicquid intelligibile, immateriale, divinum fingitur excellentissime superante, similiterque Patre atque Filio ab omni divino patris filiique officio eminenter exceptis.

: LIV :

Dionysius: The same.

We have also learned from the sacred Scriptures that the Father is the fountain Deity as it were, but the Son and Spirit are the seeds of this Deity in its bounty (if we are permitted to speak in this way) divinely sprouting with flowers as it were, and with supersubstantial lights. 1

The reason for this, however, we cannot declare or understand. 2
In truth, all our intellectual action extends itself only so far as it may conceive that the rational principle entire of father and son comes from the prime rational principle, eminent over all, of Father and Son—which principle has been granted to us and to the supercelestial powers. From it are born intellects bearing the divine image; and they are called both gods and sons of gods and fathers of gods, so long, that is, as that gift of being father and son is enacted everywhere spiritually, that is, by way of incorporeal, immaterial, and intelligible reason. Meanwhile something intelligible, immaterial, and divine is only imagined in the divine Spirit, surpassing as it is in excellence. And the like goes for the Father and the Son, who are eminently apart from every office [albeit] divine of father and son.

: LV :

Marsilius: Causa superat effectum, nec est in effectu ad superiorem causam perfecta similitudo.

1 Causa tanto saltem excedit effectum, quanto movere et agere superat moveri atque pati. Hac utique ratione causa quelibet, quomodocunque efficiens, prestantior est effectu, presertim quoniam causa quidem effectum profert, hic autem neque se ipsum neque[102] illam proferre potest.

2 Potissimum vero cause ille operibus suis prestantiores sunt que non eadem specie comprehenduntur, sicut ignis generans cum igne genito, sed ad genus quiddam[103] superius attinent, quemadmodum Sol atque Mars ad ignem se habere videntur. Iam vero eiusmodi causa simpliciter gignit effectum, ceu Sol cum Marte simpliciter generat ignem. Hic autem ignis, quando alium generat ignem, non generat ipsum simpliciter ignem (alioquin et ipsum et precedentem ignem progeneraret), sed hunc ignem hic atque nunc et in tali materia gignit, immo producit et quasi propagat iam existentem.

3 Quando igitur efficientes causas operibus anteponimus negamusque opera perfectam ad causas similitudinem obtinere, de causis specie differentibus ab effectu verba facimus. Quamobrem neque sol necessario similiter calet propterea quod ignem generet ita calidum, neque rursus calor ipse similiter calet, quamvis causa sit formalis qua caleat ignis; neque iterum calefit ignis, licet causa

: LV :

Marsilio: The cause is superior to the effect. In the effect there is no perfect likeness to its superior cause.

The cause exceeds the effect at least to the extent that moving and acting surpass being moved and being acted upon. For this reason any cause, howsoever efficient, is more outstanding than its effect, especially because the cause produces the effect, but the effect cannot produce either itself or the cause. 1

The causes which are more outstanding, supremely so, than their effects are not those that are included in the same species, as [for instance] the fire which ignites with the fire ignited, but are those that pertain to some higher genus, as seems to be the case with the Sun and Mars and fire. But such a cause produces its effect simply,[107] just as the Sun and Mars generate fire simply. But generated fire when it generates another fire is not simply generating fire itself, otherwise it would be generating itself and [all] fire before it. But it generates the fire that is here and now and in a material of some sort. Or rather it produces, and propagates as it were, an already existing fire. 2

So when we put efficient causes prior to their works and deny that the works attain a perfect likeness to their causes, we are talking about causes differing in species from the effect. So the Sun likewise is not necessarily hot because it generates fire that is hot. Nor again is heat similarly hot though it is the formal cause 3

sit efficiens qua calefiat lignum, neque vivificatur vita, quando corpus ipsa vivificat, neque etiam vivit ea videlicet participatione vite qua per ipsam vivit corpus. Verum si vita dicatur vivere, hoc ipsum in ea vivere est ipsam vitam actu suo prorsus existere vel naturalem sibi actum in se ipsa secum penitus edere.

: LVI :

Dionysius:
Idem.

Neque enim est effectibus ad causas similitudo perfecta, sed habent quidem effectus quas preferre possunt imagines causarum. Ipse vero cause segregate ab effectibus in se superius extant, ipsa videlicet sua ratione principii. Atque, ut exemplis nostris utamur, voluptates et dolores efficere quidem dicuntur ut oblectemur[104] atque doleamus, ipsa vero neque letantur neque merent. Atque et ignis,[105] cum calefaciat utraque, neque uri tamen neque calefieri dici solet. Tum vero si quis dixerit ipsam vitam vivere vel lumen ipsum illuminari, meo quidem iudicio non recte loquetur, nisi forte alia quadam conditione hec acceperit: quoniam videlicet que pertinent ad effectus, ratione quadam essentiali atque exuberante, in causis preexistunt.

that fire becomes hot. Nor again is fire similarly made hot, although it is the efficient cause that makes wood hot. Nor is life itself alive when it vivifies the body. Nor is it even alive by participating in the life with which it enlivens body via itself. But if we say life lives, this living in life is life itself existing utterly by its own act or initiating wholly in itself the act natural to itself.

: LVI :

Dionysius:
The same.

For in effects there is no perfect likeness to causes. But the effects have the images which they can display of the causes. But the causes themselves (segregated from the effects) exist in a superior way in themselves, namely in their own principle's reason. And—to use examples familiar to us—pleasures and sorrows are said to cause us to rejoice and to grieve; but they themselves are not joyful nor do they grieve. Fire certainly, though it heats other things, is nonetheless not customarily said to be burning or be made hot itself. But if someone were to say that life itself lives, or that light itself is illuminated, then in my judgment he would not be speaking correctly, unless perhaps he were to take these [statements] in a different sense. This is because everything that pertains to effects preexists by way of an essential and overflowing rational principle in their causes.

: LVII :

Marsilius:
De conceptione Christi et assumptione humanitatis atque miraculis.

1 Tria circa Christum omnem intelligentiam superant, vel angelicam: conceptio, assumptio, prodigium. In conceptione quidem impossibile intellectu est quomodo Spiritus sanctus virgineum fovens uterum, vel quasi tactu quodam ceu gallina, vel quasi aspectu ceu struthus[106] ovum,[107] sanguinem non qualencumque, sed ex toto purissimum, undique traxerit in matricem, qui fomento Spiritus statim coaluerit in infantem non paulatim, sed momento perfectum, id est penitus figuratum; quo quidem momento intellectualis anima se infuderit eodemque divini Verbi persona naturam sibi hanc assumpserit in unitate persone.

2 In assumptione rursus intellectus nullus intelligit qualis unio divini Verbi cum humana natura facta fuerit. Non enim confectum est unum aliquid tertium ex hoc et illa, sicut ex forma simul atque materia, quemadmodum animam cum corpore coire in unam speciem Peripatetici putant. An forte sicut ex anima rationali atque nostro corpore per animam irrationalem iam vivente[108] quodammodo fieri unum dicitur a Platonicis? Anima tamen rationali interim separabili necnon quodammodo separata et quasi quo modo

: LVII :

Marsilio:
On Christ's conception and His assuming our humanity, and on His miracles.

Three things about Christ excel all understanding, even angelic understanding: [His] conception, His becoming man, and His miracle-working. In His conception it is impossible for the intellect [to understand] how the Holy Spirit quickens the womb of a virgin. Whether it is by a sort of touching like the hen, or by glancing at the egg like the ostrich,[108] the Spirit will have everywhere conveyed blood, not any kind of blood but blood at its very purest, into the womb. With this "fomentation" the Spirit will have united at once with the babe who is perfected in a moment, not gradually; that is, is perfectly shaped. In this moment the intellectual soul will have infused itself. At the same [moment] the Person of the divine Word will have assumed this [human] nature for Himself in the unity of His person. 1

Again, in His assuming [our nature] no intellect understands what kind of union of the divine Word with human nature was effected. For no one third something was compounded from the Word and from our nature as from form and matter in the way the Aristotelians believe soul is joined with body into one species.[109] Or is it perhaps as if one thing were fashioned in a way from the rational soul and from our body (living as it already does through the irrational soul), as the Platonists maintain?[110] Is the rational soul nevertheless separable meanwhile, and even in some 2

Averrois cogitativum in nobis animal intellectui subigit separato? Non penitus ita, sed aliter.

3 Numquid sicut intellectus lingue manibusque se coniungit, ita Deus homini? Nec ita prorsus, sed modo quodam apud Deum cognito, ubi et copula quidem arctissima sit, et interim divinitas per humanitatem subiunctam nihilo permutata.

4 Quo etiam pacto miracula Christus effecerit, perfecte nullus intelligit; solum autem hoc intelligimus, ex admirandis operibus adesse Deum. Hinc Amelius Platonicus: 'divinum inquit Verbum, humanam induisse naturam, atque in hac ipsa nature divine a celsitudinem ostendisse.' Iam vero, quando Christus aque superficiem siccis pedibus pertransivit, numquid aque potentiam indidit resistendi, ne pedes immergerentur? An forte pedibus sustulit interea pondus? An potius animalem virtutem rectricem membrorum multiplicavit in pedibus? An denique respiratione vehementi aerem quam plurimum hausisse[109] dicetur, cuius levitate corpus et sustineretur atque pervolaret?

5 Hisne similibusque rationibus Christianorum miraculorum modos et quasi rationes quasdam investigabimus? Nequaquam: sicut enim supra vires nature, ita super rationes intelligentie facta censentur.

way separated, and in the manner of Averroes is the cogitative animal in us subject to a separated intellect?[111] It is absolutely not like this, but otherwise.[112]

But is God joined to man in the manner the intellect attaches itself to tongue and to hands? Absolutely not in this way. Rather it is in a manner known to God, where, [though] the bond [to humanity] is the tightest, yet the Divinity changes not at all through the humanity subjoined to it. 3

How Christ effected miracles too no one understands perfectly. We understand from these marvelous works only the fact that God was present. Hence the Platonist Amelius says that "the divine Word donned human nature and that in this human nature He exhibited the loftiness of [His] divine nature."[113] But when Christ passed over the surface of the water with dry feet, did he take on the water's power of buoying him up so that His feet were not immersed? Or did He perchance lift the weight Himself meanwhile from His feet? Or rather did He take the animal power [i.e., the irrational soul's power] which ruled over his [other] members and multiply it in His feet? Or finally shall we say that he inhaled as much air as possible by breathing deeply; and by the lightness of the air say that His body was buoyed up and that He flew over the water? 4

Using these or similar reasons, shall we investigate the modalities of Christ's miracles and their particular reasons as it were? Not at all. For just as these deeds are adjudged to be above the powers of nature, so are they adjudged to be above the reasons propounded by [our] understanding. 5

: LVIII :

Dionysius:
Idem.

Preterea, quod inter omnia theologie mysteria apparet evidentissimum, quod videlicet Iesus formatus est in natura nostra divinitus, ineffabile prorsus est omni sermoni omnique ignotum intelligentie, ipsi quoque antiquissimorum angelorum primo. Iam vero quod essentiam virilem assumpserit accepimus in mysteriis, ignoramus autem quo pacto ex virgineis sanguinibus lege quadam non naturali formatus fuerit, et quomodo siccis pedibus corporale pondus materieque gravitatem habentibus liquidam instabilemque substantiam perambulaverit aliaque perfecerit quotcumque supernaturalem Iesu[110] naturam rationemque declarant.

: LIX :

Marsilius:
Quot modis divina cognosci possint.[111]

1 Tribus modis divina percipimus: aut enim actione, aut passione, aut motu quodam quasi mixto. Actione quidem precipue, quando non ab aliis eruditi,[112] sed rationis proprie discursionibus sub naturali lumine hec inventa consequimur; passione vero, cum divinitus afflati percipimus; mixto denique motu (id est partim patiendo,

: LVIII :

Dionysius: The same.

Moreover, the fact that among all the mysteries of theology the most evident appears to be that Jesus was formed divinely in our nature, is utterly beyond all explanation and unknown to all understanding, even to the first of the most illustrious angels. That Jesus assumed a manly essence, we have accepted from the mysteries. But we do not know how He was formed from virginal blood by a certain law not natural; and how He walked with dry feet, given His corporeal weight and the heaviness of matter, over the flood's ever-changing substance. These and the other numerous miracles that He performed declare the supernatural nature and rational principle of Jesus.

: LIX :

Marsilio: In how many ways divine matters can be known.

We perceive matters divine in three ways; either actively, or in a passive way, or in a motion that is as it were mixed. We perceive actively mainly when we come to these discoveries ourselves, not when we have been informed by others, but by using the discursiveness proper to our reason and in the light of nature. We perceive in passivity when we perceive we are divinely inspired. Finally, we perceive with a mixed motion, that is, partly by being 1

partim agendo) ubi docente alio aut verbis aut litteris erudimur. Tunc enim quatenus aliunde movemur, quodammodo patimur, quatenus autem proprium ipsi iudicium examenque adhibemus, videmur et agere.

2 Ceterum et aliena disciplina et inventio propria divinorum ad hoc velut ad signum dumtaxat dirigenda est, ut Deo assidue nos pulsanti penitus exponamur. Id autem solo in eum amore perficimus. Hoc enim dumtaxat et ad Deum dirigimus omnia, et Deo subicimur clam pulsanti, atque illo inspirante et quasi movente agenteque, subito commovemur atque compatimur spirituque replemur.

3 Affectio vero eiusmodi passio nuncupatur, tum quoniam amatoria est (amor autem transferens in amatum amantem inde pati compellit), tum quia, vacantibus tunc propriis rationis intelligentieque actionibus, divina luce formamur patimurque formati.

4 Ad hanc utique lucem amore solum ferventissimo preparamur. Sicut enim opacas sepe materias invias luci calor ingens purgat, extenuat, pervias luci prebet, sic amatorius in Deum fervor a corporeis perturbationibus nebulisque purgans animum quasi serenum reddit lucique divine paratum, cum qua et unionem arctiorem intelligentia et fidem humana[113] scientia certiorem denique consequamur.[114]

5 Ad hunc utique statum, ut et[115] Plato ait, neque doctrina pervenimus nec propria quavis inventione, neque vicissim hunc exprimere possumus ceterosve docere. Amare vero bonum ipsum non

acted upon and partly by acting, when we are taught by a teacher or by words or by letters. For at that point, to the extent we are being moved from another direction, we are in a way being acted upon, but to the extent we bring our own judgment and scrutiny to bear, we seem to be acting too.

Moreover, both external teaching and our own discovery of 2
matters divine must be directed as to a sign only to this goal: namely that we should be utterly open to God who is continually inspiring us. But we perfect this in the love of Him alone. For this only we direct all things to God, and we submit to God who is secretly inspiring us. With Him inspiring and moving us as it were and acting upon us, suddenly we are moved by, and submit to, and are filled with the Spirit.

But such an affective state is called passion or passivity, (1) be- 3
cause it is an amatory feeling (but love, in transferring the lover into the beloved, compels the lover to become passive), and (2) because, now that our own proper actions are empty of reason and understanding, we are formed by the divine light, formed, that is, passively.

Let us prepare for this light only with the most fervent love. For 4
just as a fierce heat often purges or attenuates opaque materials, those impervious to light, and makes them pervious to light, so our amatory fervor for God, in purging the rational soul as it were from the perturbations and storm clouds of the body, makes it, so to speak, serene again and prepared for the divine light. With this light we finally attain both a union closer than understanding and a faith more certain than human knowledge.

We arrive at this state, as Plato too says, neither by way of doc- 5
trine, nor by way of our own finding out, nor in turn can we express this state or teach [it] to others.[114] But to love the Good

tam persuadendi sumus quam docendi: hoc enim instigante natura assidue in singulis bonis amandis consequenter amamus. Sed distractum in varia bona colligere debemus amorem atque in ipsum dumtaxat intendere, quo bona sunt omnia et nobis amanda.

: LX :

Dionysius: Idem.

Hec autem et nos alibi satis tractavimus et inclitus preceptor noster in *Theologicis Elementis* supra nature modum mirabiliter celebravit que ipse vel a theologis sanctis accepit, vel artificiosa litterarum sacrarum indagatione perspexit, frequenti circa illas exercitatione studioque diuturno, aut etiam diviniore quadam inspiratione percepit, non solum discens[116] divina, sed patiens, atque ex quadam ad illa compassione, si modo ita loqui licet, ad indocibilem secretamque eorum unionem ac fidem denique consummatus. Sed ut plurimas beatasque contemplationes excellentis ipsius intelligentie paucissimis afferamus, hec de Iesu in *Theologicis Elementis* summatim collectis inquit.

itself we must be not so much persuaded as taught. For with nature constantly prompting us, in loving individual goods we must as a consequence love the Good itself. We must garner up this love that has been misdirected toward various goods and focus it only on the Good itself, whereby all things are good and worthy to be loved by us.

: LX :

Dionysius:
The same.

We have sufficiently treated these matters elsewhere and our distinguished preceptor has marvelously and preternaturally celebrated them in his *Principles of Theology*. Either he himself accepted them from the holy theologians. Or he perceived them by a subtle exploration of the sacred Scriptures by constantly reading them and studying them daily. Or he intuited them in a more divine inspiration, not only learning about divine things but receiving them. And from being passive with regard to them, if one can say this, he finally achieved an incommunicable and secret union with them: that is, he achieved faith. But in order that we might have the many blessed contemplations of his excellent understanding assembled in just a few words, he says that the mysteries concerning Jesus are in his summary compilation, the *Principles of Theology*.

: LXI :

Marsilius: Expositio Hierothei de divinitate Christi.

1 Si Arriani similesque heretici legissent hec et similia Hierothei Dionysiique verba et equo animo perpendissent, ausi certe nunquam fuissent (ut opinor) divinitatem in Christo creatam ponere vel secundam, quanquam et in Paulo Apostolo et Iohanne Evangelista idem nec negligenter nec ambitiose legentibus patere potuerat.

2 Ad primum sane Deum, tanquam maxime causam atque communissimam, pertinet non hec aut illa dumtaxat, sed omnia facere, omnibus omnia dare, in omnibus omnia operari. Cum igitur divinitas ipsa cum Christo communicans in unione persone prorsus ita se habeat, certe prima est Christo communicata divinitas: ita vero se habere extra controversiam Hierothei et Dionysii dicta declarant.

3 Si omnia preter Deum ex partibus quibusdam viribusque suis composita sunt, certe Deus omnia faciendo ubique conficit et componit. Componit autem in singulis conficiendis multas uniuscuiusque partes in unam formam in ipso toto perfectam, per quam auctorem suum, qui est ipsa unitas, pro viribus imitentur.

4 Non possunt autem multa conflari prorsus in unum nisi proportionibus connectantur harmonicis, quod quidem Pythagoras et Plato senserunt ac Hierotheus Dionysiusque consentiunt.[117] Et nos in ultimo *Legum* atque *Timeo* proportiones harmonicas exposuimus, ad eiusmodi copulam conferentes.

: LXI :

Marsilio: Hierotheus' Exposition of Christ's Divinity.

If the Arians and similar heretics had read these and the like words of Hierotheus and Dionysius, and if they had weighed them patiently, they would certainly have never dared (I opine) to make the divinity in Christ created or secondary—although the same view would possibly have been evident to careful and sincere readers of St. Paul and John the Evangelist.[115] 1

To the first God, as to the greatest and most universal cause, neither doing this alone pertains, nor doing that alone, but doing all, giving all to all, operating all in all. So since the divinity imparting itself to Christ in the union of His Person is thus so utterly [divine], certainly it is the first divinity which is imparted to Christ. The dicta of Hierotheus and Dionysius declare beyond all controversy that this is so. 2

If all things with the exception of God are compounded from their particular parts and powers, then God, in making all things, certainly makes and compounds them universally. But in making single things, He compounds the many parts of each single thing and makes one form perfect in all of itself. Through this form the parts imitate their author, who is unity itself, to the best of their powers. 3

But many things cannot be conflated into one completely, unless they are connected in harmonic proportions; this Pythagoras and Plato perceived, and Hierotheus and Dionysius agree upon it here. And in [commenting on] the last book of the *Laws*[116] and on the *Timaeus*,[117] we have expounded on the harmonic proportions that govern this connection. 4

5 Nominatur autem hic preter partes singulas tum totum, tum etiam totalitas (ut ita dixerim) vel universitas. Totum quidem, ubi distincte loquimur, est partes ipse simul cuncte, nec preterea quicquam; totalitas autem est res quedam formaque nova ex cunctis rite conspirantibus postremo resultans. Rite vero conspirant, si et pars alia cum alia consonet, et cuncte sint penitus cum forma conficienda concordes; alioquin nec simul permanet, nec[118] conficitur nova forma vel conservatur.

6 Deus interim neque partes nec ulla partium est, nec totum, nec universitas, alioquin aliunde penderet; verumtamen alia quadam ratione est hec omnia, quoniam quidquid boni his inest habet et ille. Habet quidem non eodem modo quo illa, ideo nec proprie videtur habere; possidet autem eminentius atque prius — eminentius, inquam, id est gradu quodam admodum[119] altiore; prius quoque, id est antequam illa, tempore pariter atque natura.

7 Cognomenta Dei, que hic affirmando negandoque afferuntur, in septem capita colligi possunt: totum, sive (ut ita dixerim) totalitatem,[120] perfectionem, speciem, essentiam, mensuram, plenitudinem, exuberantiam. In ipsa quidem (ut ita loquar) totalitate perfectio partium tota consistit; perfectio vero forma quedam est; forma rursus[121] vel per formam existit essentia; essentia prima est mensura sequentium; mensura non sepius repetita, sed semel plena vel plenitude; plenitudo non adequata rebus, sed prorsus exuberans.

8 Deus, ad imperfecta vel informia comparatus, perfectio dicitur atque forma quoniam forme omnis et perfectionis est auctor; comparatus vero ad perfecta formosaque, nec perfectio quedam est nec forma, quoniam non eadem proprietate qua illa, sed longe diversa

But over and beyond the single parts, the whole is named here, 5
and also totality so to speak or universality. The whole, when we make the proper distinctions, is the parts themselves collectively, and not anything more. But totality is something else: it is a new form resulting from all [the parts] in correct accord at last. But the parts accord correctly if one part agrees with another and if all are utterly concordant with the form to be attained. Otherwise they can never stay together, nor can a new form be attained or preserved.

Yet God is neither the parts, nor any one of the parts, nor the 6
whole, nor [even] totality, otherwise He would depend on something else. Yet for a different reason He is all these things, because whatever of good is present in them, He too possesses it. He does not have the good in the same way they do (and thus He appears to have it improperly); rather, He possesses it more eminently and prior: more eminently, that is, in a more eminent degree; and prior, meaning before they do in time and equally in nature.

God's names, which are adduced here by way of both affirma- 7
tion and denial, can be collected under seven heads: as a whole (or as totality as I have just said), as perfection, species, essence, measure, plenitude, and overflowing abundance. In totality itself so to speak, perfection exists as the whole of the parts. But perfection is a certain form [or species]. Again by form or through form essence exists. Essence is the prime measure of what follows. Measure is not repeated forever but at some point reaches plenitude. Finally, plenitude is no longer just adequately matched to things but overflows in superabundance.

When compared to imperfect or unformed things, God is 8
called perfection and form, because He is the author of all form and perfection. But when compared to perfected and fully formed things, He is not a particular perfection or form, because He does not possess these in the same manner as they do, but in a manner

ac infinito spatio celsiore, adeo ut super formam perfectionemque dici debeat potius quam forma vel perfectio, vel alicubi reperta[122] vel a nobis excogitata.

9 Proinde quemadmodum tempus est mensura fluentium, sic evum mensura est existentium — mensura, inquam, existentibus adequata, quemadmodum tempus fluentibus est equale. Deus igitur si ad fluentia referatur est evum, sin referatur ad existentia est super evum: ipsum namque bonum unumque toto ente superius entibus non equatur.

10 Varii rerum ordines ad principia varia, velut propria proxime reducuntur; eiusmodi vero principia, multa quidem et definita, ad principium unum rediguntur immensum,[123] quod quidem est principium super unumquodque principium. Disponit principiorum numerum, subigit suum cuique ordinem, metitur rerum ordines sub principiis, metitur principia sub se ipso. Eatenus unumquodque sub ipso principium est, quatenus accipit id munus[124] ab illo; et quo illi propinquius est atque similius, eo[125] magis et principium iudicatur.

11 Naturale dicimus quod motum aliquem vel mutationem quamlibet habet vel habere potest. Intellectum igitur mobili ratione superiorem solemus supernaturale aliquid appellare, essentiale tamen; unitatem vero ipsam, quam Plato in *Phedro* mentis caput appellat, superessentiale aliquid nominamus. Utroque Deus ipse superior extat, unde supernaturale et superessentiale vocatur. Sed munus hoc et illud ratione quadam supernaturali atque superessentiali possidere censetur.

12 Essentia quelibet creata, vel rationalis vel angelica, unitatem quidem illam habet que superessentiale quiddam est, sed id possidens in essentia, merito id essentiali tenet proprietate. Habet et intellectum supernaturale munus, sed naturali quadam conditione,

that is far different and infinitely higher. The reality is such that He ought to be described as being above form and above perfection rather than being form or perfection, whether we discover it somewhere or excogitate it ourselves.

Therefore, just as time is the measure of things flowing, so eternity is the measure of things existing: the measure, I say, which can fittingly measure existing things, just as time can fittingly measure things in flux.[118] When compared, therefore, to things in flux, God is eternity; but when compared to things [eternally] existing, God is above eternity. For the Good and the One is superior to all being and cannot be compared to entities at all. 9

Various orders of things are brought back to various principles as to the principles that are most their own. But such principles—many and defined—are in turn led back to the one immeasurable principle, which indeed is the principle above any single principle. It arranges the host of [lesser] principles; it imposes its order on each one; it measures the orders of things under the principles; and it measures the principles under itself. Every single principle is under it to the extent that it accepts the gift [of order] from it. And the closer and more similar it is to that [ultimate principle], the more it too is adjudged to be a principle. 10

We call something natural that has or can have some motion or some change. So the intellect which is higher than the mobile, discursive reason we usually call something super-natural, yet essential. But the unity itself, which Plato calls the mind's head in the *Phaedrus*,[119] we call something super-essential. God Himself is superior to both, whence He is called both super-natural and super-essential. He is adjudged to possess this or that gift with a super-natural and a super-essential reason. 11

However, every created essence, whether rational or angelic, has that unity which is something super-essential. But in possessing that unity essentially, it has to possess it with an essential property. It also has the intellect as a super-natural gift but in a natural 12

quoniam id habet in essentia vel potentia quoquomodo mutabili. Solus itaque Deus munus tantum supernaturali et superessentiali possidet ratione, cetera vero nequaquam, quemadmodum serenus aer et habet lucem et hanc quidem habet lucide, aer vero nubilus non lucide lucem habet.

13 Denique si anima rationalis coniuncta corpori, corpore aucto, diminuto, usto, secto, non augetur ipsa similiter, non minuitur, non uritur, non secatur, multo minus divinitas in Christo, utcunque libuit humanitati coniuncta, similiter humanitate patiente compatitur. Preterea, sicut anima corpori copulata munera quedam tribuit corpori non corporea, itaque multo magis Deus homini se coniungens dona largitur homini non humana.

: LXII :

Dionysius: Hierothei verbis loquitur.[126] *Mirabilia Hierothei dicta de divinitate et operibus eius et excellentia Christi.*

1 Iesu divinitas, que omnium causa est et implet omnia ac partes consonas universitati conservat, neque pars neque totum est, rursusque et pars est et totum, utpote que partem omnem et omne totum in se ipsa comprehenderit et eminenter habeat atque prehabeat; perfecta quidem est in rebus imperfectis, utpote perfectionis princeps; in rebus vero perfectis imperfecta, quippe cum perfectionem excellentia origineque precedat.

condition, because it has it in what is somehow an essence or power that is changeable. Therefore God alone possesses such an immense gift with a reason that is super-natural and super-essential. The rest do not at all. Similarly, the cloudless air has light and has it indeed transparently. But cloudy air does not have light transparently.

Finally, if, when the body is increased, diminished, burned, or cut, the rational soul joined to the body is not similarly increased itself or lessened or burned or cut, much less so is the divinity in Christ, however much it pleased Him to be joined to humanity and similarly to suffer with suffering humanity. Moreover, just as the soul joined to the body gives particular non-corporeal gifts to the body, much more so does God, in joining Himself to man, give gifts to man that are not human gifts. 13

: LXII :

Dionysius:
He speaks with the words of Hierotheus. The marvelous sayings of Hierotheus about the divinity and works and excellence of Christ.

Jesus' divinity, which is the cause of all things and fills all and preserves the parts in accord with the universe, is neither a part nor the whole; and yet it is a part and it is the whole inasmuch as it comprehends in itself every part and the entire whole; and it possesses them or prepossesses them in an eminent way. It is perfect in imperfect things as the prince of perfection; and in perfect things it is non-perfect in the sense that it precedes perfection both in excellence and in origin. 1

2 Preterea in rebus carentibus specie species est specifica, tanquam principium speciei, in speciebus autem specie carens, ut speciem superans; essentia quinetiam totis procul a contagione essentiis insidens, atque super essentiam extans, ab omni essentia penitus absoluta; universa principia ordinesque determinans, et super omne principium ordinemque locata. Mensura entium est et evum atque super evum et ante evum. Plena quidem in rebus egenis, in plenis autem exuberans; ineffabilis, non pronuntiabilis, super intellectum, super vitam, super essentiam; supernaturale munus supernaturaliter habet, superessentiale superessentiali etiam[127] ratione.

3 Quamobrem quando usque ad naturam ob summam benignitatem venit vereque substantiam nostre carnis accepit, summusque ille Deus vir est appellatus (propitia vero sint que in presentia intellectum sermonemque superantia laudantur a nobis), tunc quoque in his supernaturale et superessentiale munus emicuit, non solum quia immutabiliter et inconfuse nobis communicavit[128] nihil in exuberante sua plenitudine ab ineffabili exinanitione perpessus, sed etiam quia, quod novitatum omnium est maxime novum, in naturalibus nostris supernaturalis erat, in his que nostre sunt essentie super essentiam, omnia nostra ex nobis et super[129] nos possidens excellenter.

4 Sed de his satis; ad ipsum sermonis nostri signum iam pergamus, communia coniunctaque divine discretionis nomina pro viribus tractaturi.

Moreover, in things lacking species His divinity is [their] specific species, being the principle of species. But among species themselves it lacks species in that it surpasses all species. Furthermore, it is the essence residing in all essences and far removed from contamination; and yet it exists above essence and is absolutely divorced from all essence. It determines the universal principles and orders and yet is located above all principle and order. It is the measure of beings and is eternity; and yet it is above eternity and before eternity. It is full in things wanting, but overflowing in things full. It is ineffable, unpronounceable, above intellect, above life, and above essence. His divinity has the super-natural gift super-naturally, [and] the super-essential [gift] for a super-essential reason as well. 2

Therefore, when Jesus descended out of the goodness of His will as far as nature and truly accepted the substance of our flesh, and when as the highest God He was called man—may those [mysteries] which we are praising now be gracious to us, surpassing as they do intellect and speech—then in these events too shone forth His super-natural and super-essential gift. It did so not only because He shared with us in an unchanging way and without confusion—Jesus in His overflowing plenitude having suffered nothing from any kind of ineffable emptying—but also because—and this is the greatest novelty of all novelties—He was super-natural amid our natural conditions. In those things which are our essences, He remained above essence, possessing in His excellence everything that is ours, that comes from us, and yet is above us. 3

But enough of these matters. Let us now proceed to the very goal of our discourse: to treat as best we can both of the names that [the Persons of the Trinity] share in common and of the names that are linked to [their] divine differentiation. 4

: LXIII :

Marsilius:
Qua ratione Deus producendo multa permaneat unus, atque extet ente superior entia procreando, sitque unum ipsum uno quolibet excellentius.

1 Sequentis disputationis institutum est divina nomina recensere que quidem significant beneficas quasdam ex ipso Deo processions, in quibus sane processionibus videtur unitas ipsa divina multiplicari, quemadmodum lux intima solis in radios quam plurimos inde micantes, aut vultus unus in quam plurimas illinc imagines quomodolibet resultantes. Atque ita ferme Deus, sicut lux et vultus, in varia bonorum diffusione permanet unus.

2 Distribuit autem munera Deus unite pariter atque unice: unite quidem quia universa omnium distributio, eodem actu penitus singulari, ad Filium pertinet ut ad Patrem pertinet, et ad Spiritum ut ad illos; unice vero, quoniam et[130] nulla Deo varietas inde contingit et procedentia, licet varia, unum tamen sunt quatenus ab eodem ad idemque pendentia conveniunt et in uno.

3 Dicitur autem Deus ens (ut ita dixerim) superenter, quia videlicet entia procreat; dicitur et entia superenter excedere, quoniam non[131] in summo gradu entium collocatur, reliqua in secundo vel tertio; alioquin partim cum ceteris conveniret quidem, partim vero differret, foretque ita compositus, presertim si una sit entis ipsius

: LXIII :

Marsilio:

The reason why in producing many things God remains one, and in creating beings exists higher than being; and why God is the One itself, more excellent than any individual one.

The arrangement of the following discussion is to review the divine names which signify indeed particular beneficent progressions from God Himself, in which processions the divine unity itself appears to be multiplied. Similarly, the sun's inner light is seen shining in the orb of rays radiating from it; or one face is seen in the multitude of images leaping from it in various ways. And thus God is almost like the light and the face: He remains one in the varying diffusion of [His] goods. 1

God distributes His gifts in a united way and equally in a unique way: in a united way in the sense that the universal distribution of all His gifts in the same completely singular act pertains equally to the Son as to the Father and it pertains also to the Spirit as to them; but in a unique way in the sense that no variety befalls God because of His giving; and things proceeding [from Him], although various, are yet one to the extent that, depending on the same and for the same, they are in one accord. 2

But God is called being in a super-being way (so to speak), because He creates beings. He is also said to surpass beings in a super-being way, since He is not located in the highest degree of such beings with the remainder situated in the second and third degrees. Otherwise He would partly accord with the rest, but partly differ from them, and hence would be compound. This is especially so if there is one univocal reason of being itself, the 3

univoca ratio entibus quibuscunque communis, quod illustres metaphysici nonnulli una cum Platonico Plethone senserunt.

4 Deus itaque et extra et supra totam entium latitudinem excellenter existit, presertim quia ratio formalis entis, etsi indeterminata est secundum omnes entium species, determinabilis tamen est ad omnes. Deus autem non solum indeterminatus, sed etiam indeterminabilis esse debet. Cum igitur Deus ens universum entiaque[132] singula ab ipso procedentia mirum in modum superet, inestimabiliter segregatus, consequens est ut nec in processione rerum a suo statu digrediatur, nec in derivatione inde fluentium deinceps ipse minus sit plenus, nec in multitudine illinc per processionem derivationemque imaginum propagata minus ipse sit unus.

5 Denique cum Deus sit ipsa simpliciter unitas a certo quolibet uno penitus absoluta, merito nec est una quevis entium species neque unum ens, neque vita una, nec intellectus unus, nec una quedam pars alterius totius, neque unum aliquod totum, sed horum omnium principium atque finis.

: LXIV :

Dionysius: Idem.

1 Ut autem perspicue de omnibus que sequuntur ante definiamus, discretionem divinam, ut dictum est, appellamus beneficas deitatis processiones. Cum enim omnibus que sunt, dum eminet,

reason common to all beings whatsoever. Several illustrious metaphysicians along with the Platonist Pletho agree on this.[120]

Therefore, God exists both outside and above the entire range of entities in a manner that excels them, especially because the formal rational principle of an entity, though it may be [as yet] undetermined with regard to all the species of entities, nonetheless is determinable for them. But God is not only undetermined, He has to be undeterminable too. Thus, since God excels universal being in a marvelous way and excels all single entities proceeding from it, and is separated from them in a measureless degree, consequently He does not depart from His own state in the procession of things, nor, in the derivation of things flowing out of Him successively, is He Himself less full; nor in the multitude propagated from Him, via the procession and derivation of images, is He less one. 4

Finally, since God is unity itself absolutely, unity that is utterly free from any one particular thing, He is rightly neither any one species of existing beings, nor one being, nor one life, nor one intellect, nor any one part of another whole, nor some one whole. But He is the beginning and end of all these. 5

: LXIV :

Dionysius: The same.

In order for us to set limits clearly beforehand for all the statements which follow, let us take the divine differentiation (as it is referred to) and call it the beneficent processions of the Deity. Since to all things that exist it gives (though remaining above 1

bonorum cunctorum consortia largiatur, unite quidem discernitur, amplificatur autem unice, ac dum multiplicatur non discedit ab uno.

2 Puta quoniam Deus ens est (ut ita dixerim) superenter, largitur autem esse his que sunt omnibus et omnes producit essentias, unum illud ens multiplicari dicitur dum entia ex se multa producit. Manet ille nihilominus in multiplicatione unus et in processione unitus, et in discretione[133] plenus, propterea quod ab omnibus entibus superenter sit absolutus, et unico actu producat omnia, atque indiminuta profusione indeficientia[134] ipsius munera[135] largiatur.

3 Atqui cum sit unum omnique parti et toti et uni et multitudini participationem unius impertiat, unum permanet eodem pacto, superessentiali videlicet ratione. Nec pars est multitudinis alicuius, nec aliquod ex partibus totum; sicque nec unum est, nec unius[136] particeps, neque habet unum, longeque ab his existit super unum illud quod entibus inest, multitudo quinetiam impartibilis, inexplebilis, superplena, omne unum multitudinemque producens et perficiens atque continens.

: LXV :

Marsilius: Quomodo Dei unius participatione dii multi dicantur.

1 Sol, ut putat Plato noster, visibilis imago Dei proprietatem suam multis tum celestibus tum terrenis impartit, unde solaria fiunt atque nominantur, quod quidem in libro *De vita* tertio

them) their participation in all good things, it is differentiated in a united manner, but multiplied in a unique manner; and even as it is multiplied, it does not descend from the One.

For example, because God is being above being (so to speak), 2
but grants being to all those who exist, and because He produces all essences, that one being is said to be multiplied when it produces many entities from itself. Nonetheless, God remains one in multiplication, united in procession, and undiminished in differentiation, on account of the fact that He is being above being and is utterly free from all beings; and He produces all things by his unique act, and gives in undiminished profusion the never failing gifts of Himself.

Since He is one and imparts participation in His oneness to 3
every part and whole, to [every] one and many, He remains one, and one in the same way, that is, for a super-essential reason. He is not a part of any many, nor is He some whole from parts, and thus He is not one thing or a participant of one thing; nor does He have one thing. But far removed from these, He exists above the one that is present in entities; nay, He is even indivisible multitude, not fillable [yet] super-full, producing, perfecting, and containing every one and every many.

: LXV :

Marsilio: How by participation in one God the gods are said to be many.

The sun, so our Plato thinks,[121] is the visible image of God and 1
imparts its property to many both celestial and earthly, whence they become and are called solarian. We spoke of this in the third

declaravimus.[137] Similiter Deus angelis animisque divinam impartit proprietatem, ob quam multi sub uno apud Platonem dii cognominantur. Maxime vero ad Deum pertinet ut omnibus provideat ab omnibus segregatus; ob segregatam quidem singularitatem unum ipsum cognominatur; ob universalem vero providentiam appellatur et bonum.

2 Angeli igitur ferme omnes animique plerique munus id ab ipso Deo nacti, quo ferme similiter ab inferioribus segregati inferioribus interea late provideant, dii merito nominantur, dii videlicet participatione primi Dei, qui solus sit Deus per essentiam atque summus. Cum enim alii spiritus aliis diviniores sint nonnullique divinissimi, merito ad unicam atque summam denique deitatem referendi censentur.

3 Que quidem per imagines suas in multis quasi participata, dum ita discerni videtur, nihilominus permanet una semper ac penitus individua, sicut neque facies evadit multiplex ex imaginum inde resultantium multitudine.

4 Platonici in rebus quidem divinis multitudinem ab unitate motumque a statu superari putant, ideoque indissolubiles permanere; cetera vero, in quibus unitas statusque a multitudine motuve superantur, posse quandoque dissolvi. Excedit quoque apud Deum unitas multitudinem quoniam videlicet unica natura Dei inextimabiliter superat imaginum inde fluentium multitudinem, nec inde fit multiplex.

5 Denique omnia cognomenta Deo propter excellentiam attributa, quemadmodum alibi diximus, unicuique Trinitatis divine persone pari dignitate conveniunt.

book of *On Life*.[122] Similarly, God imparts [His] divine property to angels and to souls, and on account of this property many gods are named under the One [god] in Plato.[123] But what most pertains to God is that He provides for all while being apart from all; and on account of this separated singleness, He is called the One itself, but on account of [His] universal providence He is also called the Good.

Accordingly, it is proper that almost all the angels and the ma- 2
jority of souls, having acquired that gift from God Himself—whereby, in almost the same way, they are separated from inferiors, even as they widely provide for inferiors—are named gods, gods by participation, that is, in the prime God who alone is God on high by way of essence. For, since some spirits are more divine than others and several spirits are completely divine, they must at last be considered, and rightly so, as related to the unique and highest Deity.

This Deity has been participated as it were through its images 3
in many things; and while it seems thus to be divided, yet it remains always one and utterly undivided, just as a face escapes being multiple from the multitude of mirror images resulting from it.

The Platonists think that in divine things multitude is excelled 4
by unity, and movement by rest; and thus they remain indissoluble. But other things, those wherein unity and rest are surpassed by multitude or motion, are vulnerable at some point to dissolution. Unity exceeds multitude also in God, because God's unique nature, in a measureless way, surpasses the multitude of images flowing from Himself. Nor is He thence made multiple.

Finally, all the names attributed to God on account of [His] 5
excellence, as we said elsewhere, with equal dignity are proper to each divine Person of the Trinity.

: LXVI :

Dionysius:
Idem.

1 Preterea ex deifico Dei actu, quo unusquisque pro facultate sua deiformis evadit, dii plures efficiuntur. Qua quidem in re videtur et dicitur Deus ipse unus discerni quodammodo atque multiplicari; est autem nihilominus Deus ipse divinitatis princeps et divinitate qualibet essentiaque sublimior, Deus unus in distributis inde diis non distributus, sed unitus ipse sibi nec permixtus multis, nec in multiplicatis multiplicatus.

2 Id sane mirabiliter contemplatus communis ille noster preceptorisque nostri dux, qui ad divinam illuminationem nos provexit, divinis abundans et mundi lumen, hec in sanctis litteris suis[138] divinitus afflatus ait: 'Siquidem sunt qui dicuntur dii vel in celo vel in terra, quemadmodum profecto sunt dii multi et domini multi, unus tamen nobis est Deus Pater ex quo omnia, et nos ad ipsum, et unus Dominus Iesus Christus per quem omnia, et nos per ipsum.' In rebus nempe divinis uniones excedunt discretiones atque ducunt, nihiloque minus divina secum sunt unita post discretionem participem unitatis et ab ipso uno minime discedentem.

3 Has itaque nos communes unitasque totius deitatis distinctiones, sive beneficas ex Deo processiones, ex divinis cognomentis declarantibus eas in sanctis litteris pro viribus celebrare conabimur, quando videlicet hoc, ut alibi predictum est, prius

: LXVI :

Dionysius:
The same.

From God's deific action, moreover, whereby each single [soul] according to its ability emerges godlike, many gods are made. And in this it appears, and is so declared, that the one God Himself is divided in a way and multiplied. Nonetheless, God Himself is the lord over divinity and is more sublime than any divinity and essence. He is the one God and is not distributed in the gods that come from Him. He is united to Himself, and He is neither mingled in the many nor multiplied in what are multiplied. 1

Having marvelously contemplated this, [St. Paul], our leader in common and the leader of our teacher, he who has borne us toward divine illumination and who overflows in matters divine and is "the light of the world"[124] and divinely inspired, says the following in his sacred Epistles: "If indeed there are those who are called gods either in heaven or on earth (as there are certainly many gods and many lords), yet there is one God for us, the Father, from whom come all things, and we [return] to Him; and there is one lord Jesus Christ through whom are all things, and we through Him."[125] In things divine, unions exceed and preside over differentiations, yet such divine things are no less divine or less united to Him after [a] differentiation which participates in unity and does not depart at all from the One itself. 2

So we will try as best we can to celebrate these distinctions which either are common to and united to the whole Godhead, or are benefic processions from God, by referring to the divine names which declare these distinctions in sacred Scripture. But this can only happen when, as we said earlier elsewhere, we have first 3

definierimus: omnem beneficam appellationem Dei de quacunque divinarum personarum dicatur absque ulla distinctionis observatione in tota simul accipi deitate.

: LXVII :

Marsilius: De appellatione boni, efficacia orationis; quomodo Deus ubique.

1 In sequentibus libri capitibus ordine quodam quasi Platonico primo quidem tractabit de bono, secundo de ente atque ideis, tertio de vita, quarto de intelligentia, deinceps vero de quibusdam ad hanc ordine consequentibus.

2 Inter omnia Dei nomina precipuum est ipsum bonum: omnia enim nomina que processiones[139] et munera Dei significant in hoc uno nomine tripliciter comprehenduntur: primo, quia hec omnia dona[140] tanquam varia bona uno communique continentur bono; secundo, quoniam Deus exuberanti nature voluntatisque bonitate cuncta largitur velut efficiens; tertio, quoniam ad suam bonitatem communicandam et representandam, tanquam finis, omnia refert.

3 Due videntur potissime ad bonum vie: inquisitio disputans, oratio supplicans; illa quidem ad cognoscendum bonum contendit, hec autem ducit ad consequendum et consecutione perfectissime cognoscendum.

4 Tria vero sunt ad orationis efficaciam summopere necessaria: primum quidem perturbationes sensuum cohibere que ad corporea longissime a divinitate distantia nos detorquent; secundum expellere, tanquam nebulas, fallacias et machinamenta

defined the situation thus: Every benefic name of God concerning each of the divine Persons must be said to be accepted as applying to the whole Godhead simultaneously, without there being any observance at all of distinction.

: LXVII :

Marsilio: On the name of the Good; on the efficacy of prayer; how God is everywhere.

In the following chapters of the book, in a certain Platonic order as it were, Dionysius will treat first of the Good, second of being and the Ideas, third of life, fourth of understanding, and then of certain other things consequent in order upon this understanding. 1

Among all God's names preeminent is the Good itself; for all names which signify the processions and gifts of God are comprehended triply in this one name. First, because all these gifts as various goods are contained in the one common good. Second, because God gives all from the overflowing goodness of His nature and His will as the efficient [cause]. Third, because in order to share and reproduce His own goodness all relate to Him as the final [cause]. 2

The best approaches to the Good seem to be two: the way of inquiry and argument, and the way of prayer and supplication. The former strives to know the Good, the latter is our guide to attaining it, and in its attainment, to knowing it perfectly. 3

Three things are especially necessary for the effectiveness of prayer. The first is to restrain the perturbations of our senses which drag us down toward corporeal things far distant from divinity. The second is to expel the fallacies and machinations of the 4

imaginationis ab intellectu; tertium universum voluntatis affectum, in diversa nunc bona distractum, in primum bonum tota prorsus amoris intentione convertere. Ita enim fervor obsecrantis animum coniungit Deo sicut sulphureus calor copulat lignum flame. Huc tendit Zoroastricum illud: 'Si mentem igneam ad opus pietatis intenderis, caducum quoque corpus inde servabis.'

5 Quatuor proinde rerum gradus considera: res sane dividua certis loci limitibus circumscribitur; res individua quidem sed virtute finita, etsi non[141] continetur loco, finitum tamen spectat locum; hec itaque si virtutem habet rebus quibusdam equalem, eas ipsas facile presentia lustrat; si rebus cunctis equalem, facile totum habitat; quod autem immensam possidet potestatem, non tam dicendum est rebus cunctis inesse, quam adesse pariter et preesse.

: LXVIII :

Dionysius:
Idem.

1 Principio, si placet, perfectissimam omnesque divinas processiones exprimentem appellationem boni consideremus, invocantes videlicet Trinitatem bonorum principium atque superbonam, optimas quasque suas providentias explicantem.

2 Oportet enim nos votis in primis ad ipsam tanquam bonorum originem provehi atque ita ad illam propius accedentes in hoc ipso gradu optima queque dona penes ipsam sita perdiscere. Illa enim

imagination, like clouds, from the intellect. The third is to convert the universal desire of the will, distracted now toward different goods, back toward the prime Good by focusing all our love upon it. For fervor joins the rational soul of the person praying to God, just as the heat of sulfur unites the log to the flame. That Zoroastrian maxim speaks to this: "If you have focused your fiery mind on the work of piety, you will then save the fallen body too."[126]

Consider then four universal levels: (1) a thing divided is cir- 5
cumscribed by the fixed limits of place; (2) a thing undivided but
finite in power, even though it is not circumscribed by place, still
looks to finite place; (3) this [undivided] thing, therefore, if it has
power equal only to particular things alone, easily encircles them
with its presence; but (4) if it has power equal to all things, it easily dwells in the whole. But what possesses measureless power
must be said, not so much to dwell in all things, as to be present
in them and at the same time to be preeminent.

: LXVIII :

Dionysius:
The same.

In the beginning, if we agree, let us consider the Good as the most 1
perfect name, the name expressing all the divine processions, as we
invoke the Trinity, the principle of good things, itself super-good,
unfolding the best, [that is,] each of its providential gifts.

For in the first place we must be conveyed by prayers to the 2
Trinity as the origin itself of good things; and, in approaching it
closer, at this first level we must learn through and through about
all the best gifts, those situated in its presence. For the Trinity is

omnibus adest, non tamen omnia illi adsunt; quando vero illam castissimis precibus et intellectu tranquillo affectuque ad divinam unionem apto precamur, tunc nos etiam illi adsumus. Iam vero illa nec est in loco, ut propterea absit ab ullo aut ab aliis se ad alia transferat; immo etiam dicere hanc in rebus omnibus esse longe deficit ab ipsa infinitate, que et excedit et complectitur omnia. Quamobrem nos ipsos ad divinorum salutariumque radiorum sublimiorem intuitum orationibus[142] elevamus.

: LXIX :

Marsilius:
Catena aurea vel luminosa a Deo dependens est dispositio rerum sibi invicem connexarum divine providentie subdita.

1 Finge catenam variis contextam luminibus, quasi anulis per totum celum diffusam et ad terram usque porrectam, qualem Plato in decimo *De republica* fingit, qualem rursus apud Homerum Iupiter Deos convocans per celum proiicit promittitque sursum se tracturum quicquid catenam apprehenderit, se vero trahi non posse deorsum.

2 Catena vero hec est ordo seriesque rerum divine providentie parens — series, inquam, luminum partim quidem invisibilium, partim etiam visibilium; occulta quidem lumina sunt intellectus angelici animalesque; manifesta vero sunt celestia lumina. Est autem communio quedam et connexio mutua, tum in ipsis intellectibus, tum etiam in celestibus, tum denique celestibus ad intellectus

present to all, yet not all things are present to it. But when we pray with the chastest prayers, with tranquil intellect, and with desire eager for divine union, then we are also present to it. But the Trinity is not in one place in the sense that it is absent from another place or that it transfers itself from one place to another. Rather, even to say this Trinity is in all things is to fall far short of that infinity which both exceeds and embraces all things. Hence by prayers we must elevate ourselves to gaze more sublimely at those divine and salutary rays.

: LXIX :

Marsilio:
The golden or luminous chain hanging from God is the arrangement of things mutually connected to each other but subject to divine providence.

Imagine a chain linked with various lights as rings stretching across the whole sky and reaching down to earth. Such a chain Plato imagines in the tenth book of the *Republic*.[127] Again in Homer, Jupiter, when he assembles the gods, casts such a chain down through the heavens, and promises that he will himself draw up whatever clutches hold of the chain.[128] But he himself cannot be dragged down. 1

This chain is in truth the order and series of things obeying divine providence: the series, I say, of lights partly invisible and also partly visible. The hidden lights are angelic intellects and animate beings, the manifest lights are the celestial lights [of the stars]. But a certain communion, a mutual connection, exists both among the intellects themselves and among the celestials, and finally among the celestials with regard to the intellects and vice 2

atque vicissim. Universus sane contextus eiusmodi catena dici potest, sed ibi quidem intellectualis et aurea atque providentie; hic autem naturalis et argentea atque fatalis. Series vero fatalis ordini providentie subest, per quem anime pie solvi a fato quandoque possunt, ut Platonicis placet et Magis atque astronomis Hebreorum.

3 Ex verbis denique Dionysii colligitur divinam providentiam usque ad minima se prorsus intendere, atque dum ipsa immutabilis est, ordine mutabilia ducere locumque relinquere arbitrio animarum atque votis, quod sane Plotinus sepe confirmat.

4 Catenam quidem fatalem per infimos eius anulos Magi prensant ut gradatim trahantur ad celestia bona; catene autem intellectualis gradus propinquiores attrectant metaphysici contemplatores, ut paulatim perveniant ad intelligibile lumen. Sed quenam catena est quam adorator debet apprehendere a Deo summo facile quod optat impetraturus? Catena profecto hec est divina lex et naturaliter insita mentibus et modis ubique variis promulgata, dictans primo quidem unum summumque Deum esse, deinde hunc esse bonorum omnium auctorem, tertio ab omnibus in primis amandum.

5 Iamblichus Platonicus votum longo intervallo sacrificiis anteponit probatque hec ab illo totam vim accipere, nihilque adoratione vehementius animam cum divinitate coniungere, nec mutari orationibus Deum, sed animum intrinsecus permutari atque ad dona divinitus capienda parari. Plato in *Epistolis* inquit omnibus in rebus principium a Deo faciendum esse,[143] et dicendi et cogitandi; in *Timeo* potissimum a Deo inchoandum inquit ubi agitur de divinis et opificio Dei.

versa. Such a linked universe can be called a chain. Up there it is intellectual and golden and it is the chain of providence; but down here it is natural and silver and it is the chain of fate. But the fatal series is subject to the order of providence via which pious souls are able at some point to be released from fate as the Platonists agree,[129] as do the Magi and the astrologers of the Hebrews.[130]

Finally, from the words of Dionysius we gather that the divine providence extends itself down as far even as the smallest things; and while it is unchanging itself, it leads changing things in due order, and leaves room for souls' free choice and for their prayers; which indeed Plotinus often confirms.[131] 3

The Magi clutch at the fatal chain by way of its lowest rings so that they may be lifted up by degrees toward the celestial goods. But the degrees of the intellectual chain closer [to God] attract the contemplators of metaphysics, with the result that little by little they arrive at the intelligible light. But what is the chain that the worshipper must grasp that he may easily obtain his choices from God on high? Certainly this is the divine law naturally sown in minds and promulgated in various ways everywhere. This law states repeatedly, first, that there is one God on high; then, that He is the author of all goods; and third, that He must be loved preeminently by all.[132] 4

Iamblichus the Platonist puts prayer far above sacrifices: he acknowledges that sacrifices receive all their power from prayer; that nothing more vehemently unites the soul with divinity than adoration; and that God is not changed by prayers. Rather, by prayers the rational soul itself is inwardly changed, and made ready to accept gifts from above.[133] In his *Letters* Plato says that in all things we must make our beginning from God, both in speaking and in thinking.[134] In the *Timaeus*, where he deals with matters divine and with the craftsmanship of God, he says we must begin before all else from God.[135] 5

: LXX :

Dionysius:
Qui adorat innititur immobili Deo
per quem nixum non Deum ad se
sed se ipsum movet ad Deum.

1 Veluti si catena quedam multis contexta luminibus a summo celo suspensa usque ad infima protendatur, nosque hanc manibus semper alternis in anteriora porrectis apprehendamus, trahere quidem ipsam ad nos videbimur. Re autem vera non deducemus eam ad[144] nos, supra videlicet infraque presentem, sed ipsi potius ad excelsiores radiorum varie lucentium splendores feliciter provehemur.

2 Aut forte quemadmodum si ingressi navim funes ex petra quadam ad nos extentos teneamus, quippe quorum nitamur auxilio non petram quidem ad nos sed nos potius navimque revera provehemus[145] ad petram; quemadmodum vicissim si quis stans in navi maritimum percutiat saxum, in illud quidem tanquam immobile permanens nihil efficiet, sed seipsum potius arcebit a saxo, et quantum vehementius contendet impellere, tanto illinc longius repelletur.

3 Quamobrem ante omnem actum, precipue theologicum, ab oratione nobis exordiendum, non quidem ut potestatem illam ubique presentem et nusquam addictam ad nos quandoque trahamus, verum ut divinis commemorationibus invocationibusque nos ipsos illi dedamus et unione iungamus.

: LXX :

Dionysius: He who prays strives for the changeless God; and in this endeavor he does not move God to himself but rather himself to God.

It is as if a chain studded with many lights and suspended from the highest heaven were to extend down to the lowest things, and we, having grasped this by alternately moving our hands one always in front of the other, would appear to be drawing the chain toward ourselves. But in reality we would not be drawing it toward us, since it extends above and below us: rather we would be drawing up ourselves, happily so, toward the higher splendors of the [heavenly] rays shining in their variousness. 1

Or perchance it is as if, having entered a boat, we were to grasp hold of ropes stretched out from a rock to us: with their help we will bring not the rock to us but ourselves and the boat in fact toward the rock. Again, it is as if someone standing in the boat were to push away from the rock on shore. He will not be doing anything to the rock in its immovability; rather he will be keeping himself at a distance from the rock. And the more vigorously he strives to push at the rock, the further he will be pushed back away from it. 2

Therefore, before every action, and especially an action involving God, we must begin with a prayer, not that at any time we may draw to ourselves the power that is present everywhere though constrained nowhere, but that we may give ourselves over to it in divine remembrances and prayers, and that we may join it in union. 3

: LXXI :

Marsilius:
Apologia cur scribit que scripserat Hierotheus.
Mira Hierothei laus.

Plato in *Protagora* scribit antiquorum doctrinam nihil aliud fuisse quam breviloquium quiddam, idque esse viri absolute sapientis, paucis videlicet multa complecti. Hac ratione Hippocrates composuit Aphorismos, Pythagoras quoque Symbola, et Proverbia Salomon. Quo enim altior intellectus est in angelis, eo formis paucioribus plura comprehendit et agit. Hierotheus igitur post Paulum Dionysii doctor et apostolis excellentia proximus, theologiam summulis mira profunditate conclusit,[146] scripsitque expiatissimis mentibus atque doctissimis. Dionysius autem et Hierothei[147] iussu et Timothei rogatu universales illas summulas Hierothei in notiones singulas derivavit.

: LXXII :

Dionysius:
Idem.

1 Purgatione forsan nobis opus est. Cum enim inclitus preceptor noster Hierotheus *Theologica elementa* mirabiliter profecto collegerit, mirabitur[148] forte aliquis cur nos, quasi minus illa sufficiant, et alibi et hic theologica conscripserimus. Iam vero si ille omnia

: LXXI :

Marsilio:
An apology for why Hierotheus writes what he has written. Marvelous praise of Hierotheus.

In the *Protagoras* Plato writes that the ancients' doctrine was [contained in] nothing other than this aphorism — that of a superlatively wise man — to the effect that in a few things many things are included.[136] For this reason Hippocrates composed his *Aphorisms,* Pythagoras his *Symbols,* and Solomon his *Proverbs.* For the higher the intellect is in angels, the more it comprehends and acts with fewer forms. Therefore Hierotheus, the teacher, after Paul, of Dionysius and the one closest in excellence to the apostles, concluded [his] *Theology*[137] with little summaries of marvelous profundity; and he wrote for minds that are most purified and most learned. But at the command of Hierotheus, and the request of Timothy, Dionysius condensed those universal summaries of Hierotheus into individual notions.

: LXXII :

Dionysius:
The same.

Perhaps we need a justification [here]. For since our famous teacher Hierotheus has certainly assembled the *Principles of Theology* in a marvelous way, perhaps someone will wonder why here and elsewhere we have written [on] matters theological as if those *Principles* [of his] were not enough. Had he wished, however, to set 1

theologica ordine deinceps disposito digerere voluisset particularibusque explicationibus unumquodque totius theologie caput disposuisset, nunquam nos in tantum furoris vel ruditatis incidissemus, ut vel perspicacius vel divinius quam ille theologica penetrare posse mysteria confideremus, aut eadem bis dicendo superflua frustra tractare vellemus; atque ita preceptorem amicumque nostrum iniuria auderemus afficere, et preclarissimam intelligentiam expositionemque illius, a quo post divinum Paulum instituti sumus, nobis usurpare non dubitaremus.

2 Ceterum ille, divina venerabiliter exponens, summas profecto quasdam perspicacia compendiosa refertas nobis exposuit in uno videlicet plurima complectentes; precipiens videlicet nobis ceterisque[149] rudium[150] animorum magistris explicare pro viribus atque distinguere, sermone nobis congruo, lucentia intus compendiosaque mysteria a virtute illius apprime intellectuali manantia.

3 Preterea et ipse ad idem sepe nos exhortatus es, librumque ipsum, ut supra modum excellens quiddam, remisisti. Quamobrem nos quoque ipsum, velut perfectorum seniliumque animorum magistrum, his dumtaxat assignamus qui intelligentia ceteros antecellunt, tanquam secunda quedam eloquia sacra apostolicam auctoritatem proxime consequentia. Nos autem his qui nobis propinquiores sunt, pro ingenii nostri proportione, divina trademus; si enim cibus solidus perfectorum est, hoc certe et alios pascere quante perfectionis extimandum esse censemus?

out every theological issue in a successively disposed order, and had he arranged every single principle of the whole of theology with particular explications, then we would never have succumbed to such madness or ignorance as to presume that we could penetrate theological matters more insightfully or divinely than he; or wish to treat the same matters twice and in vain by voicing superfluities. This would be daring to inflict injustices on our teacher and friend, and not hesitating to usurp for ourselves the preeminence of understanding and exposition of that very man who, after the divine Paul, has taught us [most].

That man, moreover, in venerably expounding matters divine 2
and in presenting to us—and with compendious perspicacity—sundry packed statements, that is, statements that included many things in one, taught us and the other masters of uncultivated souls to unfold and distinguish as best we can (and in language suited to ourselves) the illuminating and compendious mysteries that dwelt in him, those emanating from his special intellectual power.

Moreover, you yourself [Timothy] have often exhorted us to 3
the same, and you have returned the book itself as something of special excellence. Wherefore we too should only assign it, as the guide of perfect and aged souls, to those men who surpass the rest in understanding—as being as it were sacred writings following close upon the apostolic authority [of Paul] and second [only] to his. To those men who are closer to ourselves we will transmit matters divine according to the proportion of our acuity. For if solid food is for perfect men,[138] certainly for this food to feed others, how much perfection in them do we deem is necessary?

: LXXIII :

Marsilius:
Sicut non est idem lumen hoc in rebus illuminatis aspicere
atque lucem ipsam in sole suspicere,
sic aliud est divina mysteria introspicere,
aliud disciplinam ad illam conferentem prosequi.

Illud quidem Hierotheum[151] effecisse Dionysius ait, hoc autem se profiteri non negat.

: LXXIV :

Dionysius:
⟨Idem.⟩

Recte igitur id quoque nobis est dictum, contemplationem quidem intelligibilia eloquia prorsus inspicientem compendiosamque eorum doctrinam consummate virtutis existere, scientiam vero sermonum ad id conducentium atque eiusmodi disciplinam inferioris meriti preceptoribus discipulisque congruere. Enim vero diligentissime id observavimus, ut que divinus ille preceptor plane nobis expressit nunquam attingeremus, ne forte repeteremus eadem ad id exponendum quod in verborum divinorum explanatione fuisset ab eo propositum.

: LXXIII :

Marsilio:
As it is not the same to see the light in illuminated things and to endure the light itself from the sun, so it is one thing to look upon the divine mysteries, and another to pursue the learning leading up to them.

Dionysius says that Hierotheus did the former, but he does not deny that he professed the latter too.

: LXXIV :

Dionysius:
[The same.]

Thus we have also been told correctly that while the contemplation that focuses on discussing the intelligibles, and on the doctrine embracing them, is of the highest virtue, knowledge of the [preliminary] teachings leading up to that goal, along with the attendant learning, is proper to teachers and disciples of lower merit. For we have observed most diligently that what our divine teacher clearly expressed to us we would never attain, unless perforce we were to seek out the same [methods] for expounding what had been proposed by him in explanation of the words divine.

: LXXV :

Marsilius:
Salutatio Marie virginis, mira Petri et Hierothei laus, modestia Dionysii singularis.

Quantum multi sensu valent afficiunturque ad corporea et quando corporis oblectamenta commemorant, eadem quodammodo patiuntur; tantum Hierotheus pollebat intelligentia et afficiebatur ad incorporea, laudansque divina patiebatur eadem; simile quiddam narrat Porphyrius de Plotino.

: LXXVI :

Dionysius:
⟨Idem.⟩

1 Convenimus quandoque apud pontifices nostros Deo plenos, ut nosti, nos simul et ipse multique sancti fratres nostri visuri corpus illud quod vite principem Deum suscepit; ubi aderant et Iacobus frater Domini et Petrus excelsum et antiquissimum theologorum culmen.

2 Illic ergo post contuitum placuit ut pontifices omnes pro viribus quisque suis infinite potentem debilitatis[152] divine bonitatem laudarent. Hierotheus autem alios omnes ibi doctores sacros, ut nosti,

: LXXV :

Marsilio:
The visit to the Virgin Mary.[139] *The wonderful praise of Peter and Hierotheus. The singular modesty of Dionysius.*

To the extent many men are dominated by sensation and are drawn to corporeals, and in their recollection of the allurements of the body, experience in a way the same allurements, so [by contrast] Hierotheus waxed mighty in understanding and was drawn toward incorporeals, and in praising things divine he experienced the same. Porphyry says something similar about Plotinus.[140]

: LXXVI :

Dionysius:
[The same.]

We assembled at one point with our [fellow] priests who were filled with God, as you know, we and Hierotheus and our many saintly brothers, to see the body [of Mary] the bearer of God, the prince of life. Present there were James, the Lord's brother, and Peter, the most eminent and eldest of the [apostolic?] theologians[141] and their crown. 1

After viewing the body, it pleased all the priests there, each with his own powers, to praise the infinitely powerful goodness of divine weakness [in accepting incarnation]. But Hierotheus excelled all the other sacred doctors there, as you know, the doctors who 2

post ipsos theologos superavit, totus excedens, totus extra se positus, eorum que laudabat communionem patiens. Quamobrem ab omnibus qui audiebant eum atque videbant, sive cognoscerent ipsum seu non cognoscerent, occupatus Deo divinusque laudator est iudicatus.

3 Sed quidnam illa tibi referam que illic sunt theologica ratione tractata? Iam vero nisi mei oblitus sum, memini me partes quasdam divinarum illarum laudationum abs te sepius accepisse: adeo studuisti divina diligentissime prosequi.

: LXXVII :

Marsilius: *Mira in Dionysio et reverentia erga Hierotheum preceptorem, et modestia erga omnes.*

1 Sicut sensui amor est ingenitus ad caduca, sic intellectui ad eterna. Igitur eterna pro facultate sua et querere debet et quandoque invenire potest, potest et eternitate frui.

2 Venerati sunt Pythagoram Pythagorici et Plato Socratem, multo magis Dionysius Hierotheum.

came after the theologians. He was wholly transported, wholly situated outside himself; and he experienced communion with the very objects of his praise. Wherefore he was adjudged by all who heard and saw him, whether they recognized him or did not know him, to be a man possessed by God and a divine singer of lauds.

But why am I referring you [Timothy] to those matters which were treated there by way of theological reason? Unless I have forgotten myself, I [now] recall that it was from you that I most often received sundry parts of those praises divine, you who have studied indeed with the greatest diligence to pursue matters divine. 3

: LXXVII :

Marsilio:
The wonderful reverence in Dionysius for Hierotheus, his teacher, and his wonderful modesty toward all.

Just as love for fallen things is innate to sense, so love for eternal things is innate to intellect. Therefore intellect has to seek eternal things according to its ability; and, at some point, it is able to find them and to enjoy eternity. 1

The Pythagoreans venerated Pythagoras, and Plato venerated Socrates; even more so does Dionysius venerate Hierotheus. 2

: LXXVIII :

Dionysius:
⟨Idem.⟩

1 Verum que illic mystice tractata sunt missa in presentia faciamus, quippe cum nec multis exprimi possint et tibi nota sint. Quotiens autem oporteret nostra multis communia facere, et quam multos possemus in sanctam disciplinam nostram introducere, erat profecto mirandum quam longe Hierotheus sanctorum doctorum plurimos antecelleret, et diuturna docendi sedulitate, et puritate mentis, et exacta diligentia demonstrandi, ac ceteris omnibus quecunque ad sacra eloquia pertinent.

2 Itaque nos nunquam adversus solem tam ingentem fingere auderemus obtutus. Sic enim nobis conscii sumus nec ignoramus nos nec intelligibilia quidem ipsa divinorum satis intelligere posse, vel ineffabilia divine cognitionis mysteria verbis exprimere; et profecto longe divinorum virorum scientia veritatem theologicam spectante inferiores sumus.

3 Huc profecto reverentia summa nos adduxit, ut nec audire nec loqui de divina philosophia quicquam auderemus, nisi id prorsus insedisset animo, non oportere divinarum rerum cognitionem, quatenus assequi licet nos negligere. Id autem nobis persuaserunt non solum naturalia mentium desideria amatorio quodam affectu contemplationem rerum sublimium, quantam capere possunt, desiderantia, sed ipsa quoque optima legum institutio divinarum, que supra nos sunt inquirere vetans, quippe cum et nostra merita superent et comprehendi non possint; que vero preter id quod

: LXXVIII :

Dionysius:
[The same.]

The matters that have been treated there mystically, let us dismiss for the present, since they cannot be told to the many, and they are known to you. But whenever it was fitting to make known the [beliefs] we shared to the multitude, and to introduce as many people as we could to our sacred discipline, it was certainly wonderful how far Hierotheus excelled the host of sacred doctors in his daily assiduity in teaching, in his mind's purity, and in the precise care he took in demonstration and [in observing] all the remaining aspects whatsoever that pertain to sacred discourse. 1

So we should never dare to imagine our having gazed at such an immense sun. For we are conscious in ourselves and are not unaware of the fact that we can neither know sufficiently the intelligible truths of matters divine, nor express in words the ineffable mysteries of divine cognition. And certainly we are inferior by far to the knowledge of divine men, the knowledge which looks to theological truth. 2

Thus far he has led us with the highest reverence, with the result that we would not have dared to hear or to speak anything about divine philosophy unless he had planted deep in our soul the fact that we should not neglect knowledge of things divine insofar as it is permitted us to attain it. Not only have the natural desires of minds—moved by a certain amatory desire to take up contemplation insofar as they can of things sublime—persuaded us to do this; but so too has the very institution, in its absolute goodness, of the divine laws. This forbids us to inquire into those sublimities which are above us, since they excel our merits and cannot be comprehended. Yet it reminds us that, quite apart from 3

naturaliter appetuntur notitie quoque nostre concessa sunt studiose perdiscere ceterisque benigne tradere admonens.

4 His igitur et nos persuasi nec labore nec ignavia perterremur quominus divina pro facultate nobis concessa queramus. Immo vero eos etiam qui humano ingenio superiora contemplari non possunt absque auxilio deserendos minime iudicantes descendimus ad scribendum, novi quidem nihil audentes inferre, sed minutioribus quibusdam et per singula dispositis inquisitionibus discernentes et explicantes ea que ab illo vere Hierotheo (id est sacro quodam deo) perspicacia compendiosa sunt tradita.

: LXXIX :

Marsilius:
In solo Deo idem est esse simpliciter atque bene esse. Item Deus hoc ipso quod natura facit, simul intelligentia facit et voluntate.

1 In omni re post primum aliud quidem est essentia, aliud vero bonitas, aliud esse simpliciter, aliud autem bene esse: alioquin in ipso primo puroque essendi momento penitus conquiescerent nec ad aliud aliquid niterentur intrinsecus vel extrinsecus adquirendum. Sed in quolibet revera est aliquid quasi adhuc informe imperfectumque ad formam absolutam natura contendens, que quidem sua

our naturally desiring them, divine matters have also been given to our understanding to learn diligently by heart, and to pass on generously to others.

Persuaded by these [arguments] we should not be made fearful, 4
therefore, by the difficulty of seeking matters divine according to the ability conceded us, or made fearful out of cowardice. Rather, in deciding not to abandon those who cannot, without some help, contemplate higher matters with mere human subtlety, we will descend to writing. We will not venture to introduce anything novel, but distinguish and unfold particular details and answer individual questions about the mysteries transmitted to us with abundant clarity by Hierotheus himself—that is, by a kind of holy god

: LXXIX :

Marsilio: In God alone, simply being and well-being are the same. Again, by virtue of the fact that God creates by way of His nature, He creates with His understanding and His will together.

In everything after the first, essence is one thing but goodness an- 1
other; and simply being is one thing, well-being, another. Otherwise things would come to rest completely in the first and pure moment of being, and not strive toward acquiring something more internally or externally. But it is true in anything whatsoever that there is something as yet unformed as it were and imperfect, striving by nature toward absolute form which is called each thing's

cuiusque bonitas appellatur, qua iam comparata rursus movetur ad finem aliquem ut ad bonum.

2 In primo vero rerum principio ipsa simplex existentia prima est ipsa bonitas absoluta. Sicut et sol per essentiam luminosus et ignis per essentiam calidus, preter hoc ipsum eiusmodi esse, non indiget alio quopiam adminiculo ad agendum sed eiusmodi esse suo illuminat atque calefacit; sic ipsum bonum, cuius natura est absolutissima bonitas, preter hanc non eget deliberatione quadam et electione cuius adminiculo benefaciat. Sed ipsa sua existentia (que est bonitas) benefacit, id est bona omnia procreat et perficit procreata.

3 Est autem idem penes Deum velle atque intelligere quod et esse: dum[153] igitur essendo facit, intelligendo pariter efficit atque volendo. Id noster Plato confirmat, qui mundi huius opificem natura sua mundum fecisse putans, intelligentia tamen et voluntate usum in opificio fuisse fatetur.

4 In sexto *De republica* solem inquit esse boni ipsius imaginem filiumque visibilem, unde sequitur ipsum bonum esse imaginis huius exemplar. Deum igitur esse solem primum atque verum, nostrum vero hunc secundum imaginariumque solem esse putandum. De sole quidem tam divino quam corporeo librum scripsit Platonicus Iulianus, preceptorem Iamblichum imitatus; qui sane ubi distincte loquuntur, soles saltem tres inducunt: divinum et angelicum et celestem.

5 Sed de sole in sequentibus; nunc autem gradus quatuor agendi considera: humana ratio agit consilio ac sequente consilium electione; ars quoque similiter quamdiu est imperfecta; consummata vero ars ad faciendum electione non indiget, sed ita facit habitu sicut natura virtute; naturale agens naturali virtute, id est bonitate

own goodness. When it has already achieved this, it is moved again to some [other] end as to the good.

But in the first principle of things simple existence is itself the 2
prime and absolute goodness itself. Just as the sun, in its essence luminous, and fire, in its essence hot, do not need any other aid to act beyond this their being—and [each] illuminates and heats by way of this being—so the Good itself, whose nature is absolute goodness, does not need beyond this goodness any deliberation or choice by whose aid it might impart blessings. Rather, by its very existence, which is goodness, it imparts blessings. That is, it procreates all goods, and perfects what it has created.

But willing and understanding in God are the same as being. 3
Hence when God creates by being, He makes equally by understanding and by willing.[142] Our Plato confirms this. In supposing this world's artificer had made the world by his nature, he acknowledges that in the workmanship he had used understanding and willing.[143]

In the sixth book of the *Republic*, Plato says the sun is the image 4
and visible son of the Good itself.[144] Whence it follows that the Good is the exemplar of this its image. Therefore God is the first Sun, the true Sun. But our sun must be thought of as the second sun, the image-like sun. Julian the Platonist wrote a book about the divine and the corporeal sun alike, having imitated his teacher Iamblichus. But in drawing a finer distinction, they introduce at least three suns: the divine, the angelic, and the celestial.[145]

But [more] about the sun in what follows. For the present con- 5
sider four [ascending] degrees of acting: Human reason acts by deliberation and subsequent to deliberation by choosing. Art too, as long as it is imperfect, does the same; but perfect art does not need to choose to make: it makes by [ingrained] habit, just as nature makes by [its inner] power. A natural agent acts by its natural

facit, non essentia pura; Deus denique, tanquam ipsum bonum, ipsa sua existentia pura, id est bonitate facit, siquidem participatione boni cetera faciunt quicquid agunt.

: LXXX :

Dionysius:
Sicut sol, ita bonum natura sua radios suos per cuncta diffundit.

1 Age igitur ad ipsam appellationem boni explicandam iam pergamus, quam theologi deitati plusquam divine ex omnibus excellenter attribuunt, ipsam[154] divinitatis principem, ut arbitror, existentiam bonitatem appellantes, quippe cum eo ipso quod est bonum, utpote quod substantiale bonum est, bonitatem in omnia que sunt diffundat.

2 Nam quemadmodum sol hic nobis conspicuus nec cogitatione nec electione, sed eo ipso quod est illuminat omnia que pro modo suo participationem lucis admittunt, sic et ipsum bonum, non aliter solem superans quam exemplar primum exilem excellenter antecellit imaginem. Ipsa sua existentia per ea que sunt omnia pro sua cuiusque capacitate bonitatis sue radios abunde diffundit.

power, that is, out of its goodness, not by its pure essence. Finally, God as the Good itself creates by His own pure existence, that is, by His goodness, while other things do whatever they do by participation in that Good.

: LXXX :

Dionysius: Like the sun, the Good by its nature diffuses its rays through all.

Well then, let us now proceed to explaining the name itself of the 1
good. Out of all names theologians attribute this name surpassingly to the more-than-divine Deity, calling this Deity the prince of divinity (as I think), existence, [and] goodness, since by the very fact it is good, and inasmuch as it is substantial [or essential] good, it diffuses goodness into all existing things.

For just as this sun is conspicuous to us not by way of thinking 2
or choosing, but because it illuminates all things which admit the participation of light, each in its own way, so the Good itself, like the sun, but more than it (being the prime exemplar), surpasses in its excellence the sun's paltry image. By its existence it abundantly diffuses the rays of its goodness through all existing things, according to the capacity of each.

: LXXXI :

Marsilius:
Ipsum bonum, sicut et sol, per septem gradus suum diffundit lumen; item quid stelle a sole, quid angeli a Deo reportent.

1 Sol per septem rerum gradus lumen usquequaque diffundit: per stellas fixas, per planetas sex eodem semper tenore fulgentes, per lunam lumine variam, per ignem, per aerem, per[155] aquam atque per terram. Similiter sol ille solis, summus Deus, ipsum bonum per septem gradus beneficos radios ubique distribuit: per angelos, per animas ratione preditas, per animas sensu viventes, per animas vegetales, per celestia corpora, per corpora elementaria que ex materia constant perque materiam.

2 Lumina quidem a sole distributa stellis visibilia sunt atque visualia—visibilia, inquam, quia clara et ingentia sunt; visualia vero quia viva sensuque pollentia. Preterea quoniam unumquodque stellarium luminum absque impedimento manat a sole naturales in se virtutes omnes mirabiliter complectente, merito et uniuscuiusque stelle fixe lumen virtutes illinc et in se omnes amplectitur et ad sequentia traiicit. Denique, virtute solis procul ab impedimento stellis ubique presente, stelle naturam virtutemque solarem, ut ab initio semel, ita semper habent.

3 Eadem ratione beneficum lumen ab ipso bono procedens statim in primo summoque participationis sue gradu procreat, tanquam scintillas, substantias penitus a corpore separatas essentia, virtute,

: LXXXI :

Marsilio:
The Good itself like the sun diffuses its light through seven levels. Also, what the stars take from the sun and the angels from God.

The sun everywhere diffuses its light through the seven levels of 1
the world: through the fixed stars; through the six planets shining always in their same steady course; through the moon varied as it is in light; and through fire, air, water, and earth. Likewise, that Sun of the sun, the highest God, the Good itself, distributes its benefic rays everywhere through seven levels: through the angels; through the souls endowed with reason; through the souls living by sense; through vegetal souls; through celestial bodies; through elementary bodies which are made from matter; and through matter [itself].

The lights distributed by the sun to the stars are visible and 2
visual: visible because they are clear and very bright; but visual because they are alive and have power over the sense. Moreover, because every single one of the starry lights without hindrance emanates from the sun, which marvelously embraces all the natural powers in itself, so too the light of every fixed star thence duly embraces all the virtues from the sun in itself and transfers them to subsequents. Finally, through the sun's power, which, completely unhindered, is everywhere present to the stars, a star's nature and its sun-derived power are always such as they once were at the beginning.

For the same reason, the benefic light proceeding from the 3
Good itself immediately creates, in the first and highest level of its participation, substances, like sparks, utterly separated from body

actione preditas sempiterna; que quidem illinc cum intelligibiles, tum etiam intellectuales cognominantur, sive supremi angeli, ut Iamblicho et Proculo placet, nominentur intelligibiles, sequentes autem intellectuales, quoniam isti illuminantur ab illis; sive unusquisque angelus, more Plotini, et intelligibilis et intellectualis pariter appelletur.

4 Ipsum profecto intelligibile qua ratione intelligibile eminentius est[156] et prius quam intellectuale; hoc enim[157] participatione quadam illius intelligit. Ideo boni ipsius lumen[158] infusum angelo in summa illic plenitudine sua intelligibile nuncupatur; in gradu vero sui sequente, quasi perspicuitate statim comitante, lucem intellectuale potius appellatur; verum sibimet et intelligibile et intellectuale censetur. Hec autem est Plotini magni sententia, eandem esse arbitror Dionysii.

5 Peripatetici sane, hac in re a Platonicis minime discrepantes, formam quidem materialem nec intellectualem ullo modo nec actu intelligibilem esse putant, sed potentia quatenus per efficacem agentis intelligentie radium quodammodo absolvitur a materia. Formam vero immaterialem statim intellectualem intelligibilemque evadere, quod et Dionysius hic attigisse videtur.

6 Angelos enim appellat intelligibiles eo ipso quod sunt a materia segregati, eadem quoque ratione intellectuales, intelligentes quinetiam non modo quodam mundano quo videlicet rerum imagines per sensus a corporibus mutuentur, sed modo quodam prestantiore, quo scilicet entium, id est rerum verarum. Rationes ipsas essentiales ab ipso bono sub eius splendore reportent et in sequentes subinde transfundant.

and endowed with essence, power, and sempiternal action. These substances are called both intelligible and intellectual, whether it is because the highest angels, as Iamblichus and Proclus agree, are called intelligible, while those following them are called intellectual (because the latter are illuminated by the former);[146] or because every single angel, in the manner of Plotinus, is called equally intelligible and intellectual.[147]

The intelligible itself, in that it is intelligible, is more eminent than and prior to the intellectual. For the latter understands by participating as it were the former. Therefore the light of the Good infused into the angel, yonder in its highest plenitude, is called the intelligible light. But on the level following it, as in the clarity immediately accompanying it, the light is called intellectual, though in itself it is deemed to be both intelligible and intellectual. But this is the view of great Plotinus and I think the same is Dionysius' view. 4

The Aristotelians, in this matter not dissenting much from the Platonists, think that the material form is neither intellectual in any way nor actually intelligible, but is so [only] potentially, to the extent that, through the effective ray of the agent understanding, this material form may in some manner be freed from matter. But as immaterial form it immediately becomes intellectual and intelligible. And this view Dionysius seems to have touched upon here. 5

For he calls the angels intelligible in that they are divorced from matter; for the same reason too they are intellectual. Moreover, angels understand, not in a mundane way—in the way we borrow things' images from bodies through the senses—but in a more eminent way, the way of [immaterial] entities, that is, of true things. They take the essential rational principles from the Good where they are subject to its splendor, and straightway transfer them to things subsequent. 6

7 Quamobrem angeli divini luminis participatione totum habent; illinc enim, tanquam a causa efficiente, substantiam vivam intelligibilem, intellectualem, et hanc quidem eternam, nacti sunt. Rursus, velut a causa exemplari, rationibus rerum omnium inde formati. Denique, tanquam a causa finali, sortiti sunt ut amore illuc assidue convertantur, conversi confirmentur ibidem, in eodemque perpetue consistentes divinique iam facti, boni ipsius instar, bona in sequentes abunde traducant.

: LXXXII :

Dionysius:
Quomodo angeli habent ab ipso bono ut sint et vivant et intelligibiles intellectualesque sint atque in eodem firmiter perseverent.

1 Per ipsos bonitatis divine radios subsistunt omnes intelligibiles intellectualesque essentie et virtutes et actiones; per eosdem sunt vitamque indeficientem et indiminutam habent, ab omni videlicet corruptione et morte ac materia generationeque segregate et instabili fluxaque et alias aliter agitata transmutatione semote. Iam vero tanquam incorporee immaterialesque substantie munus id nacte sunt, ut intelligibiles essent, atque insuper, tanquam intellectus, supra mundanam conditionem intelligunt.

2 Rationes quinetiam rerum ipsarum illustratione divina tanquam peculiares reportaverunt, rursumque ad illa que sibi cognata

Wherefore the angels in the participation of this divine light have the whole light. From it, as from the efficient cause, they acquire living, intelligible, and intellectual substance, and this is eternal. Again, as from the exemplary cause, they are informed with the rational principles of all things. Finally, as from the final cause, they have been destined: (1) to be converted to it continually by love; (2) in that conversion, to be confirmed in that very place; and (3) standing perpetually firm in that same place and rendered now divine, like the Good itself, to transfer good things in abundance down to those who follow. 7

: LXXXII :

Dionysius:
How the angels derive from the Good itself the fact that they exist and live and are intelligible and intellectual and abide steadfastly in the same.

All intelligible and intellectual essences and powers and actions abide through the very rays of divine goodness. By the same they exist and have life without deficiency or diminution. The [angelic] substances are apart, that is, from all corruption and death and matter and generation, and are removed from unstable, flowing, and agitated transmutation of all kinds. But as incorporeal and immaterial substances, they acquire the gift of being intelligible; and as intellects moreover, they understand the supra-mundane condition. 1

Moreover, the angels have taken the rational principles of things themselves and by divine illumination have made them their own; and in turn they transfer their gifts to things that are related to 2

sunt sua dona traiciunt. Ab ipsa quoque bonitate perseverantiam habent et firmitatem, atque inde continentur custodiunturque; domiciliumque illinc habent pabulumque bonorum; atqui, bonitatem ipsam amantes, ut et sint beneque sint inde sibi vendicant, atque ad illam pro viribus conformate bonitatis speciem perferunt atque, ut divina lex dictat, sequentibus donorum[159] ex ipso bono provenientium consortium exhibent.

: LXXXIII :

Marsilius: Quemadmodum stelle et invicem et ad solem, sic angeli se habent invicem et ad Deum.

1 Stelle omnes habent a sole tum naturam scilicet stellarem, tum etiam ordinem scilicet et invicem et ad solem; illinc enim et mutuam inter se communionem habent, in eodem scilicet solis lumine et distinctionem illam qua varie stelle sub variis solis radiis varias sunt nacte virtutes. Habent ut alia vicissim sit in alia: sic in Saturno Iupiter et in Iove Saturnus; unaqueque enim stella non nihil aliarum in se possidet. Illinc insuper habent ut stella superior in inferiorem radios abunde proiciat et ab inferiore vicissim in superiorem radii reflectantur, et que inter se cognate sunt et quodammodo pares, coniectis mutuo radiis, virtutes invicem mutuentur et mutuent; conservat interim unaqueque proprietatem sub sole suam.

them. They also have persistence and steadfastness from goodness itself: thence they are contained and guarded, and watched over, and thence they have their home and the sustenance of good things. Indeed, by loving goodness itself, they lay claim for themselves the fact that they exist and exist well. And in harmony with that goodness to the extent of their powers, they bear the species itself of goodness; and as the divine law dictates, they reveal to those who follow the aggregate of goods deriving from the Good itself.

: LXXXIII :

Marsilio: As the stars relate to themselves and to the sun, so do the angels relate to each other and to God.

All the stars derive from the sun both their stellar nature and also an orderly relationship to each other and to the sun. For from the sun they derive mutual communion among themselves: they are in the same light, that is, of the sun; and [yet] they have that distinction whereby various stars under the sun's various rays come by various powers. They derive in turn the fact that some are in others: thus Jupiter is in Saturn and Saturn in Jove; for every single star possesses in itself something of the others. Moreover, they derive from the sun the fact that a higher star abundantly projects its rays onto a lower star; and rays in turn are reflected from a lower star back to a higher. And the stars which are related to each other and are in a way equal (their rays intersecting each other) borrow and share powers together. Yet each star preserves its own property under the sun. 1

2 Superiores quinetiam quodammodo purgant inferiores et illuminant atque perficiunt: purgant quidem dum a defectu luminis arcent; illuminant quoque dum proprio insuper lumine complent; perficiunt denique quatenus sui quoque muneris largiuntur effectum. Cuncte insuper stelle in eundem solem quasi spectandum et venerandum radios velut oculos affectusque coniciunt. Lucem denique solis, que in ipso superat aciem oculorum, ipse oculis in se contemperant conspicuamque facile reddunt.

3 Si que dicta sunt singula ad angelos Deumque referes, cognosces eadem comparatione angelos ad Deum atque invicem se habere.

: LXXXIV :

Dionysius: *Ordines in angelis sunt ab ipso bono.*

1 Inde illis adsunt mundo superiores ordines, uniones susceptionesque mutue, inconfuse quoque distinctiones, virtutes etiam inferiora revocantes ad superiora; superiorum quinetiam ad inferiora providentia multiplex; propriarum cuiusque virium conservatio; immutabiles preterea in se ipsas revolutiones; item identitates summitatesque circa boni ipsius amorem et quotcumque alia dicta sunt a nobis in libro *De proprietatibus et ordinibus angelorum.*

2 Denique quecunque celestis hierarchie propria sunt, ipse scilicet purgationes angelice, illustrationes quoque supermundane et perfectionis[160] consummationes[161] angelice, id sane totum ex ipsa omnium causa et principali bonitate procedit; unde et illis boni

Indeed, the higher stars in a way purge the lower, and illuminate and perfect them. They purge them when they keep them away from the absence of light. They illuminate them when they fill them besides with their own light. Finally, they perfect them to the extent they also bestow upon them the effect of each one's gift. Moreover, all the stars fling their rays like eyes and desires toward the same sun as if to see and to venerate it. Finally, the stars themselves take the sun's light, the sun which in itself excels the capacity of eyes, and in themselves adapt it to the eyes, and render the light easily seen. 2

If you take the individual points that have been raised and refer them to the angels and to God, you will learn by the same comparison how the angels relate to God and in turn to each other. 3

: LXXXIV :

Dionysius: The orders among the angels are from the Good itself.

Hence the superior orders are present to those in the world along with their mutual unions and acceptances, and their unconfused distinctions, and the powers recalling inferiors to superiors, and the manifold providence of superiors to inferiors, and the conservation of the powers proper to each, and the unchanging revolutions in themselves, and the identities and sublimities with regard to the love of the Good itself, and the many other things we talked about in the book *On the Properties and Orders of the Angels*.[148] 1

Finally, all that are proper to the celestial hierarchy—the angelic purgations themselves, the super-mundane illuminations, and the angelic consummations of perfection—all proceed from the universal cause itself and from the principal goodness. Whence the 2

indoles est indulta munusque tributum quo occultam illam in se ipsa bonitatem ipse in se patefacerent angelique existerent, tanquam divinum silentium nuntiantes, et quasi conspicua quedam lumina tanquam e vestibulo bonum ipsum in adytis latens sequentibus declarantia.

: LXXXV :

Marsilius:
Anime rationales a bonitate divina sex precipue dotes habent.

1 Anime rationales bonitatis divine munere dona sex precipue possident:

2 Quod sint intellectuales, id est lumine divini solis ita referte ut absoluta, simplicia, incorporea, eterna querant, inveniant, comprehendant. Angeli quidem intellectus, anime vero intellectuales esse dicuntur, quoniam angelus totum id quod est intellectus et purus et totus existit, anima vero et ex quadam sui parte intellectum et partem habet intelligentie.

3 Item quod vitam essentialem habeant, id est ab essentia sua prorsus inseparabilem; non enim potest earum vita resolvi in essentiam non ultra viventem, nec ipsum earum vivere actus est compositi necessario, sed proprius est actus essentie; propterea et immortales sunt, quemadmodum in *Theologia* nostra probamus.

innate excellence of the Good is conferred upon them: they are given the gift whereby they might reveal in themselves the goodness which is hidden in itself, and the angels might exist as heralds of the divine silence and as particular and conspicuous lights proclaiming to things subsequent, as from the vestibule, the Good itself which is hidden in the sanctuaries within.

: LXXXV :

Marsilio:
Rational souls have six principal gifts from divine goodness.

1 Rational souls have six principal gifts bestowed on them by divine goodness:

2 [First] that they may be intellectual, that is, so filled with the light of the divine Sun that they may seek and find and understand things absolute, simple, incorporeal, and eternal. Angels are called intellects, but souls are called intellectual. This is because the angel is that whole which is intellect and which exists as pure and total intellect, whereas the soul is an intellect only from a part of itself and has merely a portion of understanding.

3 Next, that rational souls may have essential life — in other words, a life that is utterly inseparable from their essence; for the life of souls cannot be released to an essence that is no longer living. And necessarily their being alive is not the act of a compound, but is the act proper to [their] essence. Therefore souls are immortal as we proved in our *Theology*.[149]

4 Preterea quod ipsa essentia virtuteque ad angelos se extendant. Cum enim in actione, id est affectu intelligentiaque eternorum, atque divinorum veneratione cum angelis ipsis conveniant, nimirum cum eisdem virtute quoque et essentia congruunt sempiterna.

5 Necnon quod intellectuales ex Deo revelationes quales angeli pro viribus nanciscantur.[162]

6 Rursum quod duces angelos habeant ad divina, quatenus et angeli communiter omnes animas omnes illustrant et unaqueque anima ad certum angelum precipue pertinet ut rectorem.

7 Denique quod eiusdem divini muneris, id est gratie beatitudinisque divine, cuius et angeli, compotes esse possint, sua tamen proportione servata. Iamblichus Platonicus probat animas non solum per angelos, sed etiam per se nonnunquam ad gradum equalem angelis, Deo videlicet ductas, ascendere posse.

: LXXXVI :

Dionysius:
Idem.

Post sacros illos sanctosque intellectus anime omniaque animarum bona per ipsam consistunt bonitatem plusquam bonam: inde virtutem intellectualem habent, inde essentialem vitam et immortalem, inde quod ipsa essentia potentiaque ad angelicas vitas adspirant, inde quod per angelos, tanquam bonos duces, revocantur ad

Next, that rational souls may extend themselves in essence and power to the angels. Since in action, that is, in the desire for and understanding of eternals, and in the veneration of things divine, these souls agree with the angels themselves, it is certain that sempiternal things also accord in power and essence with these same [souls]. 4

Next, that they may receive as best they can the [same] intellectual revelations from God that the angels obtain. 5

Next, that rational souls may have guiding angels to lead them toward the divine inasmuch as all angels commonly illuminate all the souls, and also every single soul has an assigned angel as its principal guide. 6

Finally, that they be able to share the same divine gift as the angels, that is, grace and divine happiness, yet with their proportion preserved. Iamblichus the Platonist proves that souls can sometimes ascend by way not only of the angels but also of themselves to a level equal to the angels, drawn aloft there, that is, by God.[150] 7

: LXXXVI :

Dionysius: The same.

Coming after those sacred and holy intellects [i.e., the angels] are souls, and all the goods of souls existing through Goodness itself, through the Goodness that is more than good. Thence they have intellectual power; thence they have essential and immortal life; thence they aspire in essence and power itself to angelic lives; thence they are recalled by way of the angels (as good leaders) to

ipsam bonorum omnium principium[163] bonitatem, splendorumque inde micantium pro modo suo compotes evadunt atque doni ipsius ad boni speciem pertinentis pro viribus participes fiunt; illinc denique quotcumque alia in his que scripsimus *De anima* numeravimus.

: LXXXVII :

Marsilius:

Ab ipso bono intellectus angelici, anime rationales, sensuales et vegetales et corpora perfectionem suam actumque habent.

1 Sicut omnia corpora virtute solis habent, ut non solum inertem molem sortita sint, sed preterea formam, figuram, colorem, vim, motum habeant, sic res omnes ipsius boni munere preter potentiam formabilem formale aliquid nacte sunt: supreme quidem intellectum, secunde rationem, tertie imaginationem, quarte sensum, quinte vitam, sexte essentialem virtutem et qualitatem atque habitum.

2 Angeli sunt quidem boniformes,[164] sed intellectus veri; anime rationales intellectuales quidem sunt, sed anime vere; irrationales autem non sunt anime vere, sed animationes quedam; vegetales sunt vestigia vite; forme sequentes sunt umbre vite.

Goodness itself as the principle of all goods; and thence they emerge according to their capacity in possession of radiant splendors and become participants, as best they can, of the very gift pertaining to the species itself of the Good. Thence, finally, emerge all the other things, however many, that we have written about and enumerated in *On the Soul*.[151]

: LXXXVII :

Marsilio:
From the Good itself angelic intellects, rational souls, sensual and vegetal souls and bodies all have their perfection and act.

Just as all bodies derive from the sun's power not only that they have been allotted inert mass but that they also have form, shape, color, strength, and motion besides, so all things by way of the gift of the Good itself have acquired, beyond the formable power, what is formal [in act]: firstly intellect, secondly reason, thirdly imagination, fourthly sense, fifthly life, and sixthly essential virtue, quality, and habit. 1

Angels are like the Good but are true intellects. Rational souls are intellectual but are true souls. Irrational souls, however, are not true souls but animations of a sort. Vegetal souls are mere footprints of life; and the forms following them are life's shadows. 2

: LXXXVIII :

Dionysius:
Omnia quomodocumque animata vel quomodolibet formata donum ab ipso bono reportaverunt.

1 Preterea, si de animabus animalibusve irrationabilibus hic loqui licet que vel aerem dividunt, vel per terram gradiuntur, vel serpunt humi, vel in aquis vitam sortita sunt aut in aqua vicissim atque terra, vel sub terram insita pressaque luto vivunt, et simpliciter quecunque sensualem animam aut vitam habent. Hec, inquam, omnia insuper per ipsum bonum consecuta sunt ut animarentur et viverent.

2 Plante item omnes vitam nutritivam motricemque ab ipso bono sortite sunt, et quecunque essentia anime viteque expers est per ipsum bonum est atque per idem essentialem habitum reportavit.[165]

: LXXXIX :

Marsilius:
Influxus boni usque ad materiam extenditur, ipsumque est essentia et vita intelligentiaque superius.

1 Quemadmodum esse hoc et istud et illud per hanc formam et istam habetur atque[166] illam, sic ipsum simpliciter esse per ipsam simpliciter formam necessario datur. In ipso igitur simpliciter vel quomodolibet ente est aliquid loco forme et aliquid huic

: LXXXVIII :

Dionysius:
All things, howsoever animated or formed in some way, have derived this gift from the Good itself.

Moreover, if we can speak here about souls or about irrational animals—those which divide the air or walk the earth or crawl in the soil or are allotted life in the water or live in turn in the water and on land or live under the earth (embedded and impressed in the mud)—in brief whatever they are, they have a sensual soul or life. But through the Good itself all these things have derived the fact that they were brought into life and have lived. 1

Likewise all plants have been allotted their nutritive and growing life from the Good itself. And every essence that is deprived of soul and life exists through the Good itself, and has derived its essential habit through the same. 2

: LXXXIX :

Marsilio:
The overflowing of the Good extends as far as matter; and it is superior to essence, life, and understanding.

Just as this being or that or another is because of this form or that or another, so being in its simplicity is necessarily given through form itself in its simplicity. So in simple being, or in any being, there is something by way of form; and what submits to this form 1

quodammodo formabile subest; principium vero rerum primum eiusmodi esse non potest: est igitur tota entis latitudine et ratione superius.

2 Materia vero vicissim universa entis amplitudine rationeque inferior iudicatur quoniam nihil in ipsa formale cogitari potest, sed velut speculum (ut Plotinus ait) esse hoc imaginale vel illud ab obiectis mutuari videtur, mox amissurum, sic ab entibus formisque materia.

3 Usque ad hanc tamen[167] ipsius boni procedit influxus: hec enim bonum appetit (utpote que boni ipsius est effectus) cum appetendo formam convertatur ad illud sitque mundo valde bono penitus necessaria. Cum igitur influxus boni longius quam entis progrediatur, consequens est bonum esse superius et potentius ente, presertim cum ens non aliunde quam a bono potentiam habeat et virtutem, atque habeat ab eodem ut sit causa. Non enim cum primum aliquid est aut quomodolibet est, hoc ipso generat atque efficit, sed quando bene se habet atque propter ipsum bonum est in natura et virtute perfectum. Ipsum itaque bonum est prima maximeque causa, quando per illud ens quodlibet et ipsum simpliciter ens habet ut sit causa.

4 Sed quis negat bonum esse primam et maxime causam, cum omnia bonum appetant tanquam finem, finis autem causas omnes ubique moveat tanquam causa causarum? Iam vero si bonum atque ens tanquam duo quedam sublimia cogitatione secernas, bonum certe restabit ut finis; ens autem non supererit tanquam finis; non enim appetitur esse simpliciter, sed bene esse; neque sufficit ulli esse nisi cum ipso esse sit bonum. Erit igitur non ut finalis

is in a way formable. But the first principle of things cannot be such. Therefore, it is superior to the whole span of being and of reason.

But matter is adjudged in turn inferior both to the universal breadth of being and to reason, because nothing can be considered formal in matter. But just as a mirror (as Plotinus says) seems to borrow from objects this or that imaginary being—a being soon to be lost[152]—so does matter borrow from entities and forms. 2

Yet the overflowing of the Good itself proceeds as far as this matter. For matter desires good inasmuch as it is the effect of the Good, since by desiring form it will be converted to the [Good]; and matter is utterly necessary to a completely good world. Since therefore the influence of the Good proceeds far beyond that of being, consequently the Good is superior to being and more powerful than being, especially since being has power and virtue from no other source than from the Good. And from the same Good, being has the power to be a cause. For as soon as it is something, or exists in any way, this being in itself does not generate and produce; it only does so when it has well being. And it is on account of the Good itself that it is perfect in nature and power [i.e., has well-being]. Thus the Good itself is the first and greatest cause, since through it any individual being whatsoever and being itself in its simplicity may exist as a cause. 3

But who denies that the Good is the first and greatest cause, since all things desire good as their end; but the end moves all causes everywhere as the cause of causes? Now if in a process of thought you were to divide goodness from being as two different sublimities, goodness will certainly remain as the end [cause]. Being however will not remain as the end; for simply existing is not what is desired but well-being. Nor does being suffice for anything, unless, along with being itself, there is goodness. So being would function, not as the final cause which is the 4

causa, que quidem summa est, sed ut effectus boni, quippe cum referatur ad bonum, etsi quam habeat rationem cause, erit tanquam efficiens aut formalis,[168] et id quidem virtute boni. Due vero he cause, cm moveantur a fine, nimirum et ducuntur a bono.

5 Summus Deus et materia infima similitudinem quandam inter se habere videntur quatenus utrunque est informe. Sed rursus dissimilia sunt, quoniam Deus est superior omni forma omnemque facit; materia vero forma qualibet est inferior omnesque patitur.

6 Platonici, sicut diximus alibi, entia nominant res sub Deo formales et sempiternas. Deum vero super entia cogitant, res substantia mobiles entia non vera;. Materia[169] denique non ens, sed hec formis a Deo venturis naturali quodam instinctu videtur exposita, Deumque dupliciter emulari: tum ex hoc quod formas inde subit, tum quia naturaliter est informis. Informis quoque Deus, sed et hoc iterum ratione diversa.

7 Qua denique ratione Dionysius Deum cogitat essentie et vite intelligentieque expertem, eadem post illum cogitat et Plotinus, id est eminentius aliquid essentia et vita intelligentiaque habentem, atque hec omnia facientem.

: XC :

Dionysius: Idem.

Si autem ipsum bonum est super omnia que sunt, ut certe est, nimirum ipsum quod illic est informe format omnia; et in ipso solo, quod dicitur expers essentie et vite et intelligentie, est

highest cause, but as an effect of the Good, since it is related to the Good—although the causal structure it may have will be like an efficient or formal cause, and that would certainly be by virtue of the Good. But these two causes, since they are moved by an end, are certainly drawn there by the Good.

Highest God and lowest matter seem to share a certain likeness insofar as each is without form. Yet they are [utterly] unlike because God is higher than every form and creates every form; but matter is lower than every form and is subject to all forms. 5

The Platonists, as we said elsewhere,[153] call formal and sempiternal things under God entities: they think of God as above entities, and they think of things mobile in substance as not true entities. Finally, matter is not an entity, but seems to be open by a certain natural instinct to forms coming from God; and it seems to emulate God in two respects: because it submits to forms from Him, and because it is naturally without form. God too is without form but again this is for a different reason. 6

Finally, the reason that Dionysius thinks God is without essence, life, and understanding is the same reason that prompted Plotinus after him: namely that God has something more eminent than essence, life, and understanding, and that He is the maker of these.[154] 7

: XC :

Dionysius: The same.

But if the Good itself is above all things which exist, as it certainly is, then that which is there without form forms all things, and in Him alone what is said not to participate in essence, life, and

excessus essentie et eminentissima vita excellentissimaque sapientia; et quotcumque in ipso bono modo quodam informium nominator, ad potestatem pertinent sublimiorem formis formas excellenter efficientem. Denique, si dictu fas est, ipsum quoque non ens appetit ipsum bonum omnibus que sunt excelsius, contenditque quodammodo ipsum quoque in bono esse essentia prorsus superiore per negationem quandam omnia inde tollentem.

: XCI :

Marsilius: Celestia dotes habent mirificas ab ipso bono: efficaciam, temperantiam, firmitatem, pulchritudinem et similia.

1 Celum quia valde particeps est principii rerum (quod est ipsum bonum) ideo evidenter habet multa ad bonum peculiariter pertinentia. Quapropter celum est principium corporeorum omnium atque finis: generat enim hec tanquam principium et conservat; rursus definit unicuique tempus atque locum et ad imitationem sui pro viribus omnia revocat; substantiamque ipsum ex bono possidet immutabilem dispositaque sunt in eo prima mediaque et ultima pro voluntate boni.

2 Preterea sicut bonum 'attingit a fine usque ad finem fortiter[170] et disponit omnia suaviter,' ita celum, quanvis magnitudinis potestatisque excessu motuque rapidissimo pulsans et penetrans universa mox videatur violenter omnia concussurum, se ipsum tamen omnium commoditati prorsus accommodat ac sine strepitu violentiaque dispensat.

understanding is the excess of essence, is the most eminent life, is the most excellent wisdom. And whenever we talk of things being formless in a way in the Good, we mean they pertain to a power higher than forms, a power that in its excellence produces forms. Finally, if it is lawful to say so, even non-being itself desires the Good that is loftier than all things which exist; and it strives in a way to be in the Good that is higher than essence, absolutely so, by way of a kind of negation that strips all things away from it.

: XCI :

Marsilio: The celestials have marvelous gifts from the Good itself, effectiveness, temperance, steadfastness, beauty, and the like.

Because it participates very much in the principle of things which is the Good, heaven evidently has many things peculiarly pertaining to the Good. So heaven is the principle and end of all corporeal things; for as the principle it generates and preserves them. Again, for each thing it establishes the time and place, and it recalls all things to imitate it as best they can. And heaven possesses its immutable substance from the Good, and in it are arranged the first, middle, and last things, as the Good wills. 1

Moreover, just as heaven "resolutely holds to the Good from end to end and delightfully disposes all things,"[155] so, although it seems — given the vast bulk of [its] magnitude and power and [its] most rapid motion — to be about to strike and penetrate all things everywhere and violently to shake them all, yet it wholly accommodates itself to the advantage of all and dispenses without uproar and violence. 2

3 Quodve mirum est, sphere celestes, corporum omnium tenuissime et ut ita dixerim liquidissime, motu quam celerrimo se invicem absque ulla collisione et dissipatione contingunt, rectore videlicet celi sic bonitate sua celestia invicem temperante. Hinc Orpheus, in *Hymno Nature*, naturam inquit circuitum agere providenter et incedere sine strepitu. Dicuntur vero celestia liquida quia, tanquam a terra separatissima, duritiam terrenam nullam habent; dici etiam quodammodo solida possunt quoniam virtute mirabili conservant substantie sue, figure, mensure perpetuam firmitatem.

4 Cur autem motus tam vehementes contactu frequenti combustionem ibi nullam inferunt, cum motus naturaliter auctor sit caloris? Quoniam videlicet ipsum bonum extrema spherarum globorumque labia ubi mutuo se contingunt aquea (ut ita dixerim) virtute perfundit,[171] quod quidem Hebreorum Astrologi non negabunt. Que sane virtutes humifice forte apud Mosem[172] et Davidem sunt aque celestes.

5 Denique, Pythagorica quidem ratione concinere celestia possunt melodiamque conficere terrenis auribus non perceptam, strepere vero non possunt: sic apud Orpheum Apollo supercelestis in lyra celesti fides feliciter tonosque mundanorum iucunditati contemperat.

6 Proinde stelle firmamenti ex ipsa boni dispositione habent ut ordine certo in imagines pulcherrimas disposite sint, et in sua sede firme soloque radiorum iactu, velut intuitu quodam atque nutu, omnia facillime peragant. Hinc quoque planete varietatem motuum sunt adepti; hinc Sol et Luna cursibus suis dies et menses metiuntur et annos, perque tempora hec metiuntur et secula.

What is marvelous is that the celestial spheres, the most insubstantial of all bodies and the most liquid so to speak, with a superlatively fast motion touch upon each other but without any [ensuing] collision or disruption—with heaven's ruler, that is, tempering the celestials in [their] turn and doing so out of His goodness. Hence in the *Hymn to Nature* Orpheus says nature enacts its circuit "providentially" and advances "without a din."[156] The celestial [spheres] are said to be liquid, because, being the furthest from earth, they have none of the hardness of earth. [Yet] they can be said too to be solid in a way, because with a wonderful power they preserve the everlasting determination of their substance, shape, and measure. 3

But why do such vehement motions, motions in frequent contact, not spark combustion there, since motion naturally is the author of heat? It is because the Good moistens (with a watery power so to speak) the extreme lips of the spheres and globes when they touch each other—something the astrologers of the Hebrews will not deny. For these watery powers perchance are the celestial waters in Moses and David.[157] 4

Finally, in Pythagorean reasoning the celestials can sing together and produce a melody that is imperceptible by earthly ears, but they cannot produce a din.[158] Thus in Orpheus the supercelestial Apollo felicitously tempers the strings of the celestial lyre and with joy tempers the tones of things mundane.[159] 5

Therefore, from the disposition itself of the Good, the stars of the firmament derive the fact that they are arranged in a certain order to shine as the most beautiful images and are steadfast on their throne; and that by the projection alone of their rays, as by a certain intuitive glance and command, they enact all things with greatest ease. Hence the planets too acquire a variety of motions, and hence the sun and moon in the course of their wanderings measure the days and months and years; and by way of these intervals they measure the centuries too. And the things that are 6

Et que sub tempore fiunt eadem mensura ducuntur, inde certis temporibus orta definitisque intervallis temporum restituta.

7 Probabile est sub providentia boni ut ab uno gradatim in multitudinem procedatur: empyreum celum uno tamen ab oriente ad occasum motu moveri; christallinum eodem quoque simulque opposito motu perferri; firmamentum vero preter geminos eiusmodi motus agit tertium, per accessum videlicet et recessum, septentrionem versus atque meridiem; planete deinceps, presertim propter epiciclos, pluribus etiam motibus agitantur, inter quos simplicissimus est solis tanquam domini motus.

: XCII :

Dionysius:
Ab ipso bono sunt dotes ordinesque celestes, et moderatio et decus et splendor.

1 Verum, quod in medio disputationis cursu nos effugerat, bonum ipsum causa est celestium principiorum atque definitionum, huius videlicet substantie que nec augeri, nec minui, nec omnino variari potest; causa rursum, ut celerrimus motus orbis immensi (ut ita dixerim) sine strepitu peragatur. Hinc preterea siderum ordines, decores, lumina, firmitates, hinc planetarum permutatio multiplex, hinc solis et lune, que magna lumina sacre littere nominant.

2 Circuitus ab eisdem ad eadem perpetuo restitutus, quibus sane restitutionibus apud nos dies et noctes mensesque et anni

subject to time are led by the same measure, having begun at certain instants and been restored in the fixed intervals of time and its durations.

Under the providence of the Good in all probability there is a procession from the One by degrees into the many. The empyrean is moved by one motion from the east to the west. The crystalline [sphere] is conveyed by the same but at the same time opposite motion. Besides such twin motions, the firmament enacts a third motion by way of access and recess, toward the north and toward the south. The planets finally, and notably on account of their epicycles, are impelled by even more motions, among which the simplest is that of the sun, being the motion of the ruler. 7

: XCII :

Dionysius:
From the Good come the celestial gifts and orders, moderation, glory, and splendor.

But what had escaped us in the middle section of the discourse is that the Good itself is the cause of the principles and definitions of things celestial, of the substance, that is, which can be neither increased nor diminished nor varied at all. Again, it is the cause that the fastest motion of the immense orb (as we might say) is enacted without an uproar. From it, moreover, come the orders of the constellations, and their glories, their lights, their steadfastness. From it too comes the manifold changing of the planets; and from it come the motions of the sun and moon, which the sacred Scriptures call the great lights.[160] 1

The circuit from the same to the same is perpetually renewed, and by these renewals days and nights and months and years are 2

definiuntur, que quidem definitiones reliquos orbiculares motus tam temporis quam temporalium determinant numerantque et ordinant atque continent.

: XCIII :

Marsilius: Lumen est imago boni, sol est celestium dominus et imago Dei.

1 Res nulla magis quam lumen refert naturam boni: primo quidem lumen in genere sensibili purissimum eminentissimumque apparet; secundo, facillime omnium et amplissime momentoque dilatatur; tertio, innoxium occurrit omnibus atque penetrat et lenissimum atque blandissimum; quarto, calorem secum fert almum omnia foventem et generantem atque moventem; quinto, dum adest inestque cunctis, a nullo inficitur, nulli miscetur.

2 Similiter ipsum bonum totum rerum ordinem supereminet, amplissime dilatatur, mulcet et allicit omnia, nihil cogit, amorem quasi calorem habet ubique comitem quo singula passim inescantur bonumque libenter asciscunt. Ubique rerum penetralibus presentissimum, commertium cum rebus nullum habet.

3 Denique sicut ipsum bonum inextimabile est atque ineffabile, ita ferme lumen; hoc enim nullus adhuc definit philosophorum, ut nihil lumine clarius sit alicubi, nihil rursus videatur obscurius, sicut et bonum et notissimum est omnium et pariter ignotissimum.

defined among us; and these definitions determine the rest of the orbital motions of time and of things temporal alike; and they number, order, and contain them.[161]

: XCIII :

Marsilio:
Light is the image of the Good. The sun is the lord of things celestial and the image of God.

No[162] existing thing relates to the nature of the Good more than light. First, in the class of sensibles, light appears as the purest and most eminent. Second, of all things it is most easily dilated and fully so in a moment. Third, it meets all things harmlessly and penetrates them, being the lightest and softest of all. Fourth, it carries heat with it, the kindly heat that nurtures all things and generates and moves them. Fifth, while it is present to, and present in, all things, it is neither tainted by anything nor mingled with anything. 1

Similarly, the Good itself is more eminent than the whole order of things. It is dilated to the full. It caresses and attracts all. It does not compel. It has love everywhere accompanying it like heat, the love by which single things are everywhere enticed to and gladly receive the Good. Though everywhere most present in the wombs of things, light has no commerce at all with them. 2

Finally, just as the Good is immeasurable and ineffable, so is light or almost so. For no one of the philosophers has defined it up till now, so that nothing seems clearer anywhere than light, and again nothing more unclear, just as the Good is both the most known of all, and equally the most unknown. 3

4 Quamobrem Iamblichus huc postremo confugit, ut lumen actum quendam et imaginem perspicuam divine intelligentie nominaret, quemadmodum emicans e visu radius est ipsius visus imago. Nos saltem lumen solemus dicere vestigium quoddam vite mundane quasi proportione quadam, ita seipsam oculis offerentis, vel quasi spiritum vitalem inter mundi animam atque corpus. Sed hoc in *Theologia* nostra satis diximus.

5 Sol, tanquam manifestus celi dominus, omnia prorsus celestia regit et moderatur; magnitudinem eius ingentem qua centies sexagiesque et sexies terram excedere iudicatur, in presentia pretermittam. Nam *De Sole et lumine* librum integrum[173] composuimus. Neque tamen pretermittere decet comparationem illam Platonicam alibi latius a me descriptam: quemadmodum sol et oculos generat et colores, oculisque vim prebet qua videant, coloribus qua videantur, et utrosque in unum lumine conciliante coniungit, ita Deus ad intellectus omnes resque intelligibiles se habere putatur, atque ita demum excedit hec omnia, quemadmodum sol oculos et colores.

6 Quoniam vero ab imagine ad exemplar partim adimendo quod deterius est,[174] partim addendo quod melius ascendere licet, deme si placet soli, cui materiam subtraxit Averrois, tu certam similiter quantitatem; sed interea cum luce relinque virtutem, ut supersit lumen ipsum mirifica virtute refertum, nec quantitate certa nec figura aliqua definitum, ideoque immensum imaginatione spatium sua circumferentia[175] tangens, ita tunc excedens[176] intelligentiam, sicut in se ipso nunc exsuperat aciem oculorum. Hac ferme ratione Deum, qui 'in sole posuit tabernaculum suum,' ex sole pro viribus invenisse videberis.

Therefore Iamblichus in the end takes refuge in calling light a certain act of the divine understanding and its perspicuous image,[163] just as a ray shining from the sight is an image of that sight. At all events, we usually say light is a certain trace of the world's life, life in a certain proportion as it were offering itself thus to the eyes; or it is like the vital spirit between the soul of the world and the body. But we have said enough about this in the *Platonic Theology*.[164] 4

The sun as the manifest lord of heaven rules and governs all celestial things absolutely. For the present I shall leave aside the sun's vast size in which it is judged to exceed the earth by a hundred and sixty-six times. For we have composed an entire book on the sun and on light.[165] Yet I must not pass over that Platonic comparison I described at length elsewhere.[166] Just as the sun generates both eyes and colors and gives force to the eyes by which they may see, and to colors that they may be seen, and joins both into one with light reconciling them,[167] so, we suppose, God relates to all intellects and intelligible things. And in that way He exceeds all these things, just as the sun exceeds eyes and colors. 5

But[168] since we must ascend from the image to the exemplar, partly by taking away what is worse, partly by adding what is better, remove if you will from the sun — from which Averroes abstracted matter[169] — a certain quantity likewise. Meanwhile, leave [its] power along with its light, so that the light itself may remain brimful with a marvelous power, light defined neither by a certain quantity nor by any shape, and thus touching with its circumference a space measureless by the imagination, and exceeding understanding. Similarly, in itself the sun now exceeds your eyes' gaze. For this reason, or almost so, you will appear to have found God, "who has placed his tabernacle in the sun,"[170] found Him as best you can from the sun. 6

7 Denique sicut nihil alienius est a luce divina quam materia prorsus informis, ita nihil a luce solis diversius[177] est quam terra; ideo corpora in quibus terrea conditio prevalet, tanquam ineptissima luci, lumen nullum intus accipiunt, non quod sit impotens lumen ad penetrandum. Hoc enim dum non illuminat intus lanam aut folium, interim penetrat momento christallum, alioquin difficilius admodum penetratu.[178] Ita divinum lumen etiam in tenebris anime lucet, sed 'tenebre non comprehendunt.'

8 Queritur inter hec quid potissimum primo Deus creaverit. Respondet Moses lucem. Merito enim ab ipsa divina luce plusquam intelligibili statim emanat lux omnium simillima Deo, lux quidem intelligibilis in mundo supra nos incorporeo, id est angelicus intellectus; lux autem sensibilis in mundo corporeo, id est lux ipsa solaris.

9 Sed hec primo quidem sui gradu, tanquam die primo, id ipsum simpliciter habet ut luceat intus illuminetque foris; secundo vero ut virtute calefactoria tum ipsa polleat, tum cetera vegetet; tertio rursum ut efficacia sua iussuque Dei seipsam propaget in molem; quarto denique nature ordinisque gradu, quasi die quarto, ut molem suam ita sortiatur in orbem, quemadmodum divine intelligentie lux unde manavit reflectitur in seipsam.

Finally, just as nothing is more alien from the light divine than utterly formless matter, so nothing is more different from the sun's light than earth. Therefore bodies, in which the earthy condition prevails, being most unsuited to light, do not admit any light within. But this is not because light is powerless to penetrate them; for while it does not shine out when it is inside wool or some trifle, yet it penetrates something crystal in a moment, crystal which is otherwise penetrated with extreme difficulty. Thus divine light shines even in the shadows of a soul, "but the darkness comprehended it not."[171] 7

In all this, the question is what did God create absolutely first. Moses replies "Light."[172] For fittingly from the divine light itself, light more than intelligible, emanated immediately the light of all things, the light most like God, the intelligible light in the incorporeal world above us, in other words, in the angelic intellect. The light in the corporeal world, however, is sensible, is, in other words, the sun's light. 8

But light in the first degree of itself (as on the first day) is simply the light that shines within and illuminates without. But in the second degree, with its heating power, it is potent in itself and enlivens other things. Again, in the third degree, as by its own effectiveness and at God's command, it extends itself into mass or magnitude. Finally, in the fourth degree of nature and order, as on the fourth day, light allots its magnitude to the [sun's] orb,[173] just as the light of divine understanding whence it has emanated[174] is reflected back to itself. 9

: XCIV :

Dionysius: Similitudo luminis atque solis[179] *ad Deum.*

1 Quid autem de ipsa dicam secundum se luce solari? Lumen sane ex ipso bono est atque bonitatis imago, quapropter ipsum bonum luminis cognomento laudatur, tanquam in imagine quadam exemplar expressum. Ipsa quidem transcendentis omnia deitatis bonitas a supremis antiquissimisque substantiis ad infimas usque pertingit atque interim extat super omnes, dum neque superiores essentie eminentiam eius supergrediuntur neque inferiores quin ab ipsa contineantur effugiunt. Sed et illuminat quecunque lumen admittere possunt et fabricat vivificatque atque continet et perficit omnia.

2 Rerum quoque omnium mensura est et evum et numerus atque ordo, custodia, causaque et finis; simili ferme ratione evidens divine bonitatis imago, magnus hic sol omnino semperque lucens, pro exigua boni similitudine quecunque lumen accipere possunt illuminat habetque lumen eminenter per omnia[180] explicatum[181] et per omnem hunc visibilem mundum supra pariter atque infra radiorum suorum splendores expandit.[182]

3 Siquid vero relinquitur lumine destitutum, id sane nec debilitati nec parvitati luminose distributionis est imputandum, sed his potius que inepta luci percipiende ad participationem luminis attollere se non valent. Iam vero radius, multa sic affecta pertransiens, que post ea sunt illuminat, nihilque visibile usquam est quod ob excellentem lucis proprie magnitudinem non attingat.

: XCIV :

Dionysius: The likeness of light and of the sun to God.

What shall I say about the solar light in and of itself? The light 1
from the Good itself is the image of goodness as it were. So the Good is lauded under the name of light just as an exemplar is expressed in its image. The goodness itself of the Deity transcending all extends from the highest and most revered substances down to the lowest ones, and yet it exists above all. The higher essences do not surpass its eminence, and the lower ones (in that they are contained by it) do not escape it. But it illuminates all that can admit light; and it makes and brings life to all things and contains and perfects them.

This goodness is also the measure of all things: it is eternity, 2
number, and order, is their care and cause and end. For a like reason, or almost so, the visible image of divine goodness is this great sun: it is always lighting in abundance; and, in proportion to its faint likeness to the Good, it illuminates all that can accept light. And preeminently it possesses the light which is unfolded through all things. It expands the splendors of its rays throughout this visible world, above and below equally.

But if anything is left destitute of this light, it must be imputed 3
neither to the weakness nor to the limited range of the light's distribution, but rather to the things themselves, which, ill-suited to perceiving the light, are unable to raise themselves to participate in it. But the ray, in traversing many things thus impaired, [still] illuminates those which come after; and nothing is visible anywhere which the ray does not attain to on account of the eminent magnitude of its own light.

4 Preterea ad ipsam quoque sensibilium corporum generationem confert eaque ad vitam movet nutritque et auget, perficit, purgat, renovat. Mensura quoque et numerus horarum atque dierum totiusque[183] nostri temporis est ipsum lumen: ipsum namque lumen est, etsi tunc adhuc erat infiguratum, quod divinus Moses ait primam illam dierum nostrorum trinitatem ab initio distinxisse.[184]

: XCV :

Marsilius: Similitudo rursum solis ad Deum.

1 Quando dicimus a Deo cuncta procedere, non intelligimus actum rerum se ipsas inde moventium, sed rerum quidem passionem, actionem vero Dei. Similiter ubi dicimus: 'omnia convertuntur in Deum,' non tam res movere se ipsas erga Deum quam ab ipso moveri, trahi, allici, cogitamus. Cum vero causa prima, non aliunde dependens, omnia sui gratia faciat, merito sicut principium universi est, ita et finis est universi; si principium est et finis, merito et conservatio est omnium atque perfectio.

2 Quatenus aliqua in uno quodam communi congruunt, eatenus et vicissim inter se conveniunt. Dum igitur cuncta ab eodem bono procedunt et appetendo convertuntur ad idem, nimirum et ab ipso bono videntur invicem congregari. Iam vero etsi[185] proprios queque fines appetunt, quia tamen finem unumquodque suum appetit ut bonum quiddam (boni videlicet summi portionem quandam

Moreover, light contributes to the generation itself of sensible bodies too, and these it enlivens, nourishes, grows, perfects, purges, and renews. Light itself is also the measure and number of hours, of days, and of the whole of our time. For this is the light, though it was then still without shape or form, which, so the divine Moses declares, distinguished from the beginning that opening trinity of our days.[175] 4

: XCV :

Marsilio: Again, the likeness of the sun to God.

When we say that all things proceed from God, we do not understand by this [procession] the act of things moving themselves, but rather the passivity of things and the action of God. Similarly, when we say that all things are converted to God, let us suppose, not so much that things move themselves toward God, as that they are moved, drawn, and attracted by Him. But since the first cause, which does not depend on anything else, does all things for its own sake, then fittingly, as He is the beginning of the universe, so is He the end of the universe. If He is the beginning and the end, then fittingly He is also the conservation and perfection of all. 1

To the extent that some things are in harmony with a one thing they have in common, they are in turn in accord with each other. So while all proceed from the same good and in desiring are converted to the same good, certainly they seem to be gathered together by the Good itself. Although they all desire their own ends, yet because each desires its own individual end as something good, that is, as a certain portion and likeness of the highest 2

atque similitudinem), consequenter ad idem ipsum bonum omnia confluunt, sed diversa ratione participant. Summus quidem gradus participationis eius habetur per intellectum; secundus per rationem; tertius per sensum; quartus per vitam; quintus per essentialem perfectionem atque formam.

3 Comparatione quadam simili sol effector est et conservator et finis optatus omnium mundanorum, ideoque omnium congregator. Hunc enim ἥλιον ab ipso conversionis et congregationis effectu, Plato noster[186] in *Cratylo* cognominat.[187] Summa participatio solis habetur in visu; secunda in virtute vitali; tertia in motu quodam ad solem converso qui in herbis lapillisque solisequiis evidenter apparet; quartus in fomento caloris; quintus in lumine.

4 Physici veteres nonnulli atque inde religiose gentes putaverunt ipsum Iovem summumque Deum esse mundum, animal eorum sententia beatissimum; mundi vero cor (ut diximus) esse solem, quod, sicut et in quolibet animali, primum maximeque vivat efficaciaque fecunda spheras omnes mundi globosque progeneret, quemadmodum et cor arterias et, ut plerique putant, venas atque nervos, et summatim omnia profert. Atque sicut hinc[188] per omnia membra spiritus diffunduntur, sic a sole radii per omnia mundana vibrantur. Ita sane solem opificem mundi putabant atque eadem ratione gubernatorem, nec solum calore vivifico omnia vegetantem, sed proiectis circum radiis singula contuentem et intima intelligentie luce omnia prorsus intelligentem.

5 Hinc Homerus harenarum quoque numerum marisque mensuras Apollinem non ignorare fatetur, Orpheusque similiter; theologi vero Pythagorici atque Platonici soli totique mundo sublimiorem Deum, veriore sententia, prefecerunt.[189]

Good, all flow in consequence toward the same Good itself; but they participate [in it] for a different reason. The highest level in the participation of it is achieved through intellect, the second through reason, the third through sense, the fourth through life, and the fifth through perfection of essence and form.

In a similar comparison, the sun is the maker, conserver, and 3
chosen end of all worldly things. So is he the gatherer of all; for our Plato in the *Cratylus* names him Helios from the effect itself of converting and gathering.[176] The highest participation of the sun is achieved in the sight, the second in the vital power, and the third in a certain motion of being returned to the sun (which obviously appears in heliotropic plants and tiny stones). The fourth participation is achieved in the fomenting of heat, and the fifth in light.

Several of the ancient natural philosophers and religious folk 4
after them believed that Jupiter himself, the highest god, is the world and is in their view the most blessed animate being. The world's heart (as we said) they believed is the sun,[177] which heart, as in any animal, is the first and greatest giver of life. By its fertile effectiveness the sun generates all the world's spheres and globes, just as the heart does the arteries, and, as many think, the veins and nerves.[178] In short it bestows all things. And just as the spirits are hence diffused through all the limbs, so the rays from the sun sparkle through all worldly things. Thus the philosophers deemed the sun the world's maker and for the same reason its governor: it not only enlivens all things with its life-giving heat, but, by casting its rays in all directions, it gazes upon individual objects, and with the inmost light of understanding absolutely understands all.

Hence Homer says that Apollo is not unacquainted with even 5
the number of the grains of sand and the measures of the sea;[179] and Orpheus says likewise.[180] But Pythagorean and Platonic theologians have bestowed the rule on God, He who is higher than the sun and the whole world—a view that is closer to the truth.

6 Si animus a mundo separatus esset, invisibilia Dei per proprios ipsorum radios primum intueretur, deinde per illa etiam mundana conspiceret. Cum vero sit creatura mundi—natus[190] videlicet in mundo et ex mundo—per mundana[191] instrumenta corporea nimirum que supra mundum sunt excogitat: per solem quidem Deum, per stellas vero fixas angelos, per erraticas autem animas, maxime vero per lunam.

: XCVI :

Dionysius: *Idem.*

1 Bonitas ad se convertit omnia primaque ipsa bonitas dispersa omnia congregat tanquam unitatis principium et unifica deitas, atque hanc omnia tanquam principium, tanquam continentiam, tanquam finem appetunt. Bonumque ipsum est, ut sacra tradunt eloquia, ex quo subsistunt omnia. Producta sunt inde velut a causa omnium perfectissima et in quo omnia constant, tanquam in omnipotente fundamento penitus conservata; ad quod omnia convertuntur, tanquam ad suum queque finem, quod videlicet cuncta desiderant: intellectualia quidem rationaliaque cognitrici[192] quadam conditione, sensualia vero sensuali, que autem sensu carent ingenito vitalis desiderii motu, que sunt expertia vite solaque sunt essentia predita sola quadam ad essentialem participantiam aptitudine.

If the rational soul were separated from the world, it would first see the invisible things of God through their own particular rays and then through those invisibles it would see worldly things too.[181] But since the soul is a creature of the world—has been born, that is, in the world and from the world—it thinks of course by way of this world's corporeal instruments about the [incorporeal] things which are above the world: it thinks about God through the sun, about angels through the fixed stars, and about souls through the wandering stars [the planets], but also, and mainly, through the moon. 6

: XCVI :

Dionysius: The same.

Goodness converts all things to itself. The first Goodness as the principle of unity and the unifying Deity gathers all dispersed things. And all desire this Goodness as the beginning, as the preserver, and as the end. And Goodness itself, as the sacred Scriptures tell us,[182] is that from which all things exist. They are produced from it as from the most perfect cause of all; and in its goodness all things stand firm as established securely on a steadfast foundation. All things are converted to it, as each to their end, namely to that which all desire: intellectual and rational things in a cognitive manner; sensual things in a sensual one; those that lack sense by way of an inborn motion of vital desire; and those that are without life and are endowed only with essence solely by way of a certain fitness for the participation of essence. 1

2 Eadem et evidentis imaginis ratione, lumen quoque congregat et convertit ad se ipsum omnia: que vident, que moventur, que illuminantur, que calefiunt, queve omnino ab eius radiis continentur. Quapropter sol Grece ἥλιος appellatur, quod congregabilia reddat omnia concilietque dispersa. Omnia solem sensibilia concupiscunt: videlicet videre aut moveri et illuminari atque calefieri, et omnino ab ipso lumine contineri desiderantia.

3 Neque vero hoc in presentia dico antiquorum sequens opinionem putantium solem esse Deum et opificem universi et idcirco patentem hunc oculis mundum ratione propria gubernare.[193] Verum hec ideo dixi, quoniam 'invisibilia Dei a creatura mundi per ea que facta sunt intellecta conspiciuntur, sempiterna quoque virtus eius atque divinitas.'

: XCVII :

Marsilius:
De quinque luminibus. Item quomodo divinum lumen agit in angelos atque animas.

1 Platonici quinque lumina ponunt: primum superintelligibile, secundum intelligibile, tertium cogitabile, quartum imaginabile, quintum visibile. Visibile hoc, cuius fons primus est sol, dependere putant ab imaginabili quod anime mundane imaginatio etiam excellentius isto apud se ipsam imaginatur; imaginabile quoque a lumine cogitabili quod rursum prestantius eiusdem anime ratio excellenter excogitat. Cogitabile hoc ab intelligibili similiter emicare

For the same reason as the visible image, light also gathers and converts to itself all things that see, that are moved, that are illuminated, that are heated, or those that are contained entirely by its rays. Wherefore the sun in Greek is called "Helios" because it restores all things that may be gathered together, and reconciles all that have been dispersed. All sensibles desire the sun, that is, to see or be moved or be illuminated or be heated, and they desire to be contained entirely by light itself. 2

I do not say at this present time that I am following the opinion of the ancients in thinking that the sun is God and the maker of the universe, and that therefore with his own reason he governs this world visible to our eyes. But I would agree that "the invisible things of God from the world's creation are clearly seen, being understood through the things that have been made, even His sempiternal power and divinity."[183] 3

: XCVII :

Marsilio: On the five lights and in what way the divine light acts upon angels and souls.

The Platonists postulate five lights: first the super-intelligible, second the intelligible, third the cogitable, fourth the imaginable, and fifth the visible.[184] They believe that this visible light, the first fountain of which is the sun, depends on the imaginable light which the imagination of the World Soul yonder imagines even more excellently in itself. The imaginable light too they think depends on the cogitable light, the light that in turn the reason of the same World Soul in its excellence cogitates in a more outstanding way. The cogitable light similarly shines forth from the 1

quod et per summam participationem existit in mundane huius anime intellectu, et per formam viget in intellectu supermundano, id est angelico.

2 Lumen autem ipsius boni proprium non appellatur intelligibile, quoniam nullam habet cum intellectu proportionem, sed plusquam intelligibile nominatur, et ab Apostolo Iacobo nuncupatur 'pater luminum,' scilicet quatuor reliquorum. Hoc ipsum lumen sic in fonte suo superat intellectum, quemadmodum lumen in ipso sole excedit noctue visum; temperat vero se ipsum benignitate sua graduque pleniore descendit in angelicos intellectus, in nostros vero parcius, excelsius videlicet lumen minime tolerantes.

3 Officium vero luminis est tenebras caliginesque discutere, item levitatem dare ac motum sursumque attollere. Hec igitur omnia facit divinum lumen in anima intellectuali quidem omni, etiam in tenebrosa per ignorantiam ac tenebrarum pondere pregravata per mundanos affectus precipitantes ad infima. Prima quidem portio luminis exhibetur intellectuali nature etiam non querenti; hinc e vestigio sequitur amor quidam, nimirum ex lumine calor. Amor vero ubi evadit ardentior, quia et purgat et transfert, uberiorem iure reportat luminis plenitudinem. Tot vero plenitudinis gradus anime conferuntur,[194] quot amor gradibus incalescit; fervet autem tum accensus afflante Deo, tum nostro arbitrio concitus.

intelligible light which by way of highest participation exists in the intellect of this World Soul. And by way of form it flourishes in the super-mundane intellect, that is, in the angelic intellect.

But the proper light of the Good itself is not called intelligible 2 light, because it has no proportion at all with the intellect, but rather is called more-than-intelligible. It is denominated by the Apostle James as "the Father of Lights,"[185] that is, as the Father of the four lower lights. This light itself in its source exceeds the intellect, just as the light in the sun dazzles the sight of an owl.[186] But in its kindness the light tempers itself: it descends in an abundant degree into the angelic intellects; but it descends into us more sparingly, we who do not tolerate the higher light.

But light's office is to dispel the shadows and darkness, and 3 likewise to endow with levity and to raise aloft. So the divine light does all these things in every intellectual soul, even in a soul made shadowy through ignorance and burdened with the weight of shadows, because worldly desires are precipitating it toward the lowest things. The first portion of light is manifested to the intellectual nature even when it is not seeking it out. Hence a certain love instantly follows—the heat indeed from the light. But love, when it becomes more ardent (in that it both purges and transforms), justly brings home a fullness of light that is the more abundant. But as many degrees of fullness are bestowed on the soul as are the degrees by which love grows hot. The soul bursts into flame, however, when inflamed by God inspiring it, and when fanned by our own choice.

: XCVIII :

Dionysius:
Idem.

Sed hec quidem ad theologiam symbolicam, id est significativam pertinent; in presentia vero[195] intelligibilem ipsius boni appellationem a lumine ductam celebrare debemus. Bonus quidem ipse lumen intelligibile nuncupatur quoniam intellectum omnem supercelestem lumine implet intelligibili; atque ex omnibus animabus, quibus se ipsum infuderit, ignorantiam omnem erroremque expellit easque sacri luminis participes efficit. Intellectuales harum oculos purgat obductamque ex ignorantia caliginem discutit atque profundo tenebrarum pondere obtusos suscitat explicatque in lucem. Primum quidem his mediocre lumen impertit; deinde, postquam anime gustantes lumen ardentius ipsum amare ceperunt, uberius affluit ideoque illuminat abundantius, quoniam plurimum dilexerunt; atque ita semper incendit ut gradatim ultra proficiant, quatenus sursum pro viribus se attollere valent.

: XCVIII :

Dionysius:
The same.

But these matters pertain to symbolic, that is, significative theology. For the present, however, we should celebrate the intelligible name of the Good itself, a name drawn from light. He who is the Good is called the intelligible light, because He fills every supercelestial intellect with intelligible light. And from all the souls into which He has poured Himself He expels all error and ignorance, and makes them participants of the sacred light. He purges their intellectual eyes and dispels the darkness derived from ignorance. He quickens those weighed down by the profound weight of darkness and enfolds them in light. First He imparts a moderate light to them. Then, after the souls enjoying this light have begun to love the light more ardently, He pours it in more abundantly, and so illuminates them more copiously, since they have loved it most. And He always sets them so on fire that by degrees they proceed to the furthest point of being capable, according to their powers, of raising themselves aloft.

: XCIX :

Marsilius:
Deus est lumen super lumen, illuminat mentes omnes, tum natura tum gratia, atque in unum illuminando conciliat.

1 Rerum principium non est formaliter lumen aliquod ab intellectu quovis excogitatum vel proportionem ullam habens ad intellectum; dicitur tamen intelligibile lumen, id est luminis intelligibilis auctor, atque deinceps luminis cogitabilis et imaginabilis visibilisque largitor.

2 Quemadmodum sol stellas fixas illustrat et planetas et elementa, ita ferme Deus angelos supermundanos (id est adsistentes Deo et dumtaxat contemplationi vacantes), item circamundanos (id est angelos in gubernatione mundi ministrantes Deo), rursum intramundanos (id est intellectus humanos).

3 Nec solum naturale lumen ab initio semel unicuique tribuit, sed etiam supernaturale multis novumque largitur, et quemadmodum sol distributa lumina penes se ipsum comprehendit in uno uberiusque possidet atque prius, ita multoque magis Deus intelligibiles et intellectuales rationalesque virtutes atque fulgores in uno penes se vigore comprehendit, qui sane et infinitis gradibus sequentes superat et naturali ordine vel temporali etiam antecedit.

4 Quoniam vero divinum lumen et simplicissimum est et ipsa unitas, ideo quoscunque intellectus ad se convertit in unam quasi formam et voluntatem et actionem mirifice congregat, ut non mirum sit, dum multe mentes eidem simul Deo sunt dedite

: XCIX :

Marsilio:

God is the light above light. He illuminates all minds by way of nature and of grace, and by illuminating them He reconciles them as one.

The principle of nature is not a light excogitated formally by some intellect, nor does it have any proportion to the intellect. Yet it is called the intelligible light, being the author, that is, of intelligible light; and subsequently it is called the giver of cogitable, imaginable, and visible light. 1

As the sun illuminates the fixed stars, the planets, and the elements, so in a way God illuminates both the super-mundane angels, that is, those assisting Him and devoting themselves solely to contemplation; and the circa-mundane angels, the angels ministering to Him, that is, by governing the world; and those [minds] that are intra-mundane, that is, human intellects. 2

God not only gives the natural light to each person from the beginning once and for all, He also bestows on many a new and supernatural light. And just as the sun takes the distributed lights and embraces them in one light in itself, and possesses this light more richly and prior, so does God embrace, and much more so, the intelligible, intellectual, and rational powers and splendors in one power within Himself, He who exceeds by infinite degrees all that follow Him, and who precedes the natural and even the temporal order. 3

Since the divine and absolutely simple light is unity itself, it therefore converts to itself as to one form all the many intellects, and it marvelously unites will and action. It is no wonder then, while many minds are dedicated to one and the same God, that 4

querendo, videlicet contemplando, amando, fruendo, ab alia vicissim in aliam cogitatus et affectus et motus aliquos redundare.

5 Mitto nunc quod circa idem una dumtaxat est vera sententia, esse vero false complurime possunt, unde confirmatur veritatis quidem lumen mentes invicem congregare, contra vero falsitatis tenebras disgregare. Animus denique, unifico Dei lumine plenus, unica virtute consequitur omnia que ceteri multis sensibus et imaginatione rationeque et intelligentia prosequuntur.

: C :

Dionysius: Idem.

1 Ipsum ergo bonum lumine quovis excelsius lumen intelligibile nuncupatur, tanquam fontana lux et exuberans profusio luminis intellectum omnem supermundanum, circamundanum, intramundanum sua illuminans plenitudine; totasque intellectuales horum vires renovans; et omnes denique intellectus comprehendens eo ipso quod se super eos expandit atque omnes excedens eo quod desuper exstat.

2 Et omnino, tanquam principium luminis super lumen, auctoritatem dominationemque omnem potestatis illuminantis in se complectens et excedens atque antecedens. Iam vero intellectualia rationaliaque omnia congregat atque conciliate. Nam quemadmodum ignorantia eos qui decepti sunt dividit, sic ipsa intelligibilis presentia luminis eos qui illuminantur congregat, unit, perficit; convertit quoque ad ipsum quod vere est ex opinionum diversitate.

in their seeking (that is, in their contemplating, loving, and enjoying), their discursive thoughts, desires, and various motions rebound in turn from one to another.[187]

I leave aside for the present that with regard to the same thing 5
there is only one true view, but that there can be countless false ones. This is confirmation that the light of truth gathers minds together, but contrariwise separates them from the shadows of error. Finally, the rational soul that is full of the unifying light of God pursues with its unifying power all the things which the remaining souls pursue with their several senses and with their imagination, reason, and understanding.

: C :

Dionysius:
The same.

The Good itself which is more excellent that any light is called the 1
intelligible light insofar as it is the fountain of light, light's overflowing profusion illuminating with its fullness every supermundane, circa-mundane, and intra-mundane intellect; renewing all their intellectual powers; and finally embracing all intellects by virtue of the fact that it unfolds itself above them, surpassing them all because it is above them.

As the principle of light above light, the Good wholly embraces 2
in itself and exceeds and precedes all the authority and sovereignty of the illuminating power [of light]. It gathers and unites all intellectual and rational things. For just as ignorance divides those who are deceived, so light's intelligible presence itself gathers those who are illuminated: it unites them, perfects them, and converts them from the diversity of their opinions to what truly is.

Variasque visiones sive, ut rectius loquamur, imaginationes in unam veram, puram, uniformem cognitionem cogit, ac uno tandem et unifico lumine complet.

: CI :

Marsilius: Ipsum bonum omnia reddit suo lumine pulchra.

1 Sol tribus potissimum gradibus per omnia diffundit intime lucis imaginem: primo quidem per celestia; secundo vero per[196] corpora penitus sub celo diaphana; tertio per superficiem corporum solidorum. Similiter ipsum bonum lucis proprie gratiam (que pulchritudo dicitur) per angelos, per animas, per corpora porrigit.

2 Pulchritudinem communiter circa corpora in duobus versari putamus: in proportione videlicet quadam membrorum atque linearum coloribusque perlucidis. In animis quoque pulchritudo tributa divinitus in proportione virium motuumque animi, item in cogitationis et intelligentie claritate consistit. In angelis etiam pulchritudo desuper emicans in proportione intelligentie voluntatisque et actionis, rursumque in veritatis lumine collocatur.

3 Summa tandem ipsius Dei simplicitas efficit ut propria pulchritudo Dei proportionem non habeat a luce distinctam, sicut neque sol calorem a lumine differentem. Efficit insuper ut pulchritudo et pulchrum, que duo quedam sunt in rebus, unum denique sint in ipso, sicut nec in ipsa luce simpliciter considerata aliud quidem lux est, aliud vero lucere.

It forces the various visions or, to speak more correctly, imaginations into one, true, pure, and uniform knowing; and it fills them at last with one unifying light.

: CI :

Marsilio:
The Good itself renders all things beautiful with its light.

1 The sun diffuses the image of its inner light through all things on three principal levels: first, through the celestials, second, [through] the subcelestial corporeal things that are nonetheless entirely transparent; and third, lighting the surface of solid bodies. Similarly, the Good itself extends the grace of its own light, which is called beauty, through angels, souls, and bodies.

2 We commonly suppose that beauty with regard to bodies depends on two factors: on a certain proportion of their parts and lines, and on bright colors. In souls too beauty, having been divinely bestowed in the proportion of the rational soul's powers and motions, consists likewise in clarity of reasoning and understanding. In angels also beauty shining from on high depends on the proportion of [their] understanding, will, and action, and again it is located in the light of truth.

3 Finally, the highest simplicity of God Himself ensures that His own beauty has no proportion separate from light, just as the sun has no heat distinct from light. God's simplicity ensures that beauty and what is beautiful (which in things are two distincts) are one at last in God, just as in light itself considered absolutely "light" is not one thing while "being light" is another.

4 Nec multa quidem hic de pulchritudine vel de amore dicam; plurima enim in libro *De amore* tractamus, *Convivium* Platonis interpretantes; quem sane librum placuisse Dionysio propterea coniectamus, quod Platonica verba in hoc precipue capite libenter imitatur et comprobat.

: CII :

Dionysius: *Idem.*

1 Hoc ipsum bonum a sanctis theologis ut pulchrum et pulchritudo, item ut dilectio diligendumque laudatur, et quecunque alie appellationes divine pulchritudinem illam decent gratiosissimam et omnis pulchritudinis auctorem. Pulchrum vero et pulchritudo in causa illa que in uno omnia colligit distinguenda non sunt; hec enim in rebus quidem post Deum omnibus, etiam intelligibilibus, in participationes participantiaque dividimus pulchrumque nominamus quod est particeps pulchritudinis, pulchritudinem vero participationem quandam cause prime pulchra omnia facientis.

2 Ipsum vero superessentiale pulchrum pulchritudo quidem dicitur propter illam quam rebus omnibus pro suo cuiusque modo pulchritudinem tradit, atque ut omnium concinnitatis nitorisque causa; luminis videlicet instar cunctis coruscans, fontani radii sui derivationes omnia passim pulchra reddentes, et tanquam ad se omnia vocans, unde et a vocando[197] pulchritudo Grece κάλλος cognominatur, ac denique tota in totis in unum colligens.

I will say no more here about beauty or love, for we have dealt with the topics at length in the book *On Love* when we interpreted Plato's *Symposium*. We assume moreover that this [Platonic] dialogue pleased Dionysius, because in this chapter especially he gladly imitated and approved of Plato's own words.[188] 4

: CII :

Dionysius: *The same.*

The Good itself is praised by the sacred theologians as the beautiful and as beauty;[189] likewise as loving[190] and as the beloved.[191] Moreover it is praised by way of all the other divine appellations that befit that most gracious beauty, the author of all beauty. But the beautiful and beauty must not be distinguished in that cause which gathers all things into one, for in all things subsequent to God, even in intelligible things, we divide into participations and participants. And we name the beautiful as that which participates in beauty, but beauty itself we call a sort of participation in the prime cause that makes all things beautiful. 1

But the super-essential beautiful is called beauty on account of the beauty it bestows on all things according to the mode of each thing, and as the cause of the harmony and brilliance of all. That is, like light, it shimmers over all; and the diffusions of its fountain-like ray everywhere render all things beautiful. It is as if it were summoning all things to itself; and from this calling to itself [*kaleô*], beauty in Greek is called *kallos*.[192] And finally it gathers all in all into one. 2

3 Appellatur et pulchrum tanquam universam comprehendens pulchritudinem atque superpulchrum, semperque et secundum eadem et eodem modo 'pulchrum, nec unquam ortum neque caducum, nec adauctum neque diminutioni subiectum, nec parte[198] quidem hac pulchrum, illa vero turpe, nec alias quidem pulchrum,[199] alias vero nequaquam, nec ad hoc pulchrum,[200] ad illud turpe, nec hic quidem ita, ibi vero aliter, nec his sane formosum, illis autem deforme, sed tanquam ipsum secundum se ipsum secum ipso uniforme semper existens pulchrum' atque ut universi pulchri fontanam pulchritudinem in se ipso eminenter anticipans. In ipsa enim simplici et excelsa pulchrorum universorum natura omnis pulchritudo et omne pulchrum uniformiter secundum causam preexistit.

: CIII :

Marsilius:
Pulchritudo prima est omnium principium et exemplar et finis, atque est ipsum bonum.

1 Omnia pulchra ad primam pulchritudinem referuntur, cuius participatione magis minusve pulchra fiunt. Est autem pulchritudo prima omnium causa efficiens finalisque et exemplar — efficiens, inquam, modo perfecto; nam non solum dat esse, sed et motum atque conservat.

2 Nemo dubitat rem quamlibet esse per formam; formositatem vero cuiusque, que et sua cuique pulchritudo est, esse integritatem forme nemo negabit. Ab eadem utique causa et formositas est atque forma; formositas autem, tanquam pulchritudo quedam, a pulchritudine prima dependet, que quidem cum tribuat unicuique formam, per quam est unumquodque, nimirum tanquam

It is also called the beautiful as comprehending the universal beauty, and the super-beautiful and what is always beautiful according to the same and in the same way—"something beautiful that is never born or dies, or is increased or subject to diminution, or is partly beautiful in this but partly ugly in that, or is beautiful in some ways, but not in others, or is beautiful to this thing but ugly to that, or is beautiful here but not beautiful there, or is beautifully formed for some people but deformed for others. But as itself and according to itself and with itself, it exists always uniformly as the beautiful."[193] And as the fountain of the beautiful universe, it anticipates beauty eminently in itself. For preexisting in this simple and lofty nature of all beautiful things is all beauty and all that is beautiful, and it preexists uniformly and as a cause. 3

: CIII :

Marsilio:
The prime beauty is the beginning, exemplar, and end of all, and is the Good itself.

All beautiful things are referred to the prime beauty by whose participation things are made more or less beautiful. But beauty is the prime cause of all, and the efficient, final, and exemplary cause. It is the efficient in a perfect manner, for it not only gives being but it preserves motion too. 1

Nobody doubts that a thing exists through form, but nobody will deny that each thing's formal beauty, which is also the beauty of each, is the integrity of the form. From the same cause comes formal beauty and form. But beauty as a particular beauty depends on the prime beauty, which, since it gives form to each single thing (through which form it exists as a single thing), it certainly gives 2

efficiens causa omnibus esse largitur. Preterea dum formam exhibet, que est principium motionis, adhibet interea motum—motum, inquam, certum forme proprie comitem. Illinc igitur habent singula ut ad salutem suam moveantur et in perfectore quiescant; hinc efficitur ut pulchritudo prima faciat et moveat omnia pariterque conservet.

3 Quoniam vero singula, quatenus pulchra sunt, amabilia sunt, merito pulchritudo prima maxime omnium est amabilis, tum sibi ipsi, tum ceteris. Sed quod sibi ipsi amanda est, ideo amore sui se ipsam propagat, tanquam in suas imagines, in omnia pulchra. Quia rursum omnibus est amanda, interim conciliat omnia; que, dum in singulis pulchris amandis pulchritudinem primam amant, et alia aliis amica fiunt et conveniunt in eodem. Quapropter per ipsam pulchritudinem societates omnes communionesque nascuntur, item intima unicuique rei in suis partibus congruentia: hec enim, tanquam proportio quedam, a pulchritudine prima proportionis omnis origine proficiscitur.

4 Hinc rursus efficitur ut pulchritudo prima sit finis omnium, quatenus omnia et ad hanc amandam confluunt et omnem conatum motumque suum huc dirigunt, ut integritatem forme formositatemque tum suam querant conserventque pro viribus in aliudque derivent, tum alienam comparent atque fruantur.

5 Denique pulchritudo prima est causa omnium exemplaris: singula enim sunt per formam; dispositio vero uniuscuiusque forme per dispositionem rationemque formalem prime forme peragitur. Cum vero dotes eiusmodi quas prime pulchritudini proprias attribuimus ipsi tantum bono sint proprie, concluditur primum pulchrum primumque bonum esse idem. Plotinus quinetiam, postquam pulchrum distinxit a bono tanquam emanantem foras

being to all as the efficient cause. Moreover, when it gives form which is the principle of motion, it also gives motion, motion being the sure companion of its own form. Thus on the one hand individuals find that they are moved for the sake of their own welfare and come to rest in a more perfect [condition]. On the other hand, it means that the prime beauty makes and moves all things, and preserves them alike.

However, since single things are lovable to the extent they are beautiful, fittingly the prime beauty is the most lovable of all, both to itself and to others. But because it must be loved in itself, by love of itself it propagates itself to all beautiful things as to its images. Again, because it needs must be loved by all, in the meanwhile it reconciles all. As long as, in loving individual beautiful things, all love the prime beauty, they all become friends with each other and agree on the same thing. Thus through beauty itself all societies and communities are born; and likewise the innermost parts of each single thing become congruent in their parts, and this as a kind of proportion proceeds from the prime beauty, the origin of all proportion. 3

Hence it happens again that the prime beauty is the end of all to the extent that all things unite to love this beauty and direct all their effort and motion toward it. The result is that they first seek and conserve as best they can their own integrity of form and their own formal beauty (and seek to impart it to something else), and then that they attain and enjoy that other beauty. 4

Finally, the prime beauty is the exemplary cause of all; for single things result from form, but the disposition of each single form is enacted through the disposition and formal reason of the prime form. But since these gifts which are proper to the prime beauty we have ourselves attributed, properly speaking, only to the Good, we must conclude that the first beautiful and the first good are the same. Plotinus indeed, having distinguished the beautiful from 5

splendorem ab intima luce, tandem ipsum bonum ratione quadam super pulchra pulchritudinem appellavit.

6 Materia prima, que non ens propter informitatem cognominatur, formam formositatemque, immo et omnes formas naturaliter appetit, atque ita appetit esse et pulchre pariter atque bene esse; ipsumque bonum pulchrumque primum in hoc saltem emulari videtur, quod quemadmodum illud ita et hec nullam habet formam, item quatenus illud omnes largitur formas, eatenus hec easdem et avide adsciscit et libenter amplectitur.

: CIV :

Dionysius:
Idem.

1 Ex hoc ipso pulchro omnibus que sunt inest ut pro modo suo sint pulchra, atque propter ipsum pulchrum omnium congruentie amicitieque et communiones unionesque proveniunt.

2 Idque omnium est principium ut causa efficiens et movens et continens universa, pulchritudinis videlicet sui ipsius amore. Est et finis omnium cunctisque amabile[201] tanquam finis; omnia enim pulchri gratia fiunt. Exemplaris quoque causa est; omnia enim per pulchrum definiuntur.

3 Quamobrem idem est pulchrum ipsum atque bonum, quoniam omnia pulchrum pariter atque bonum secundum omnem causam appetunt, nec quicquam est in rerum ordine quod non sit pulchri

the good [by calling it] a splendor emanating outward from the [good's] innermost light,[194] eventually called the Good itself beauty, for the reason it was above [all] beautiful things.[195]

Prime matter, which because of its formlessness is called non- 6
being, naturally desires form and formal beauty, or rather desires all forms,[196] and thus desires being and the beautiful alike and desires being well. Matter seems to copy the Good itself and the first beautiful in this respect at least that, like the Good itself, it too has no form at all. Again, insofar as the Good bestows all forms, so matter greedily appropriates these same forms and willingly embraces them.

: CIV :

Dionysius: The same.

From this beautiful itself in all existing things, it follows that all 1
are beautiful in their own way; and that the concords, friendships, communions, and unions of all proceed on account of the beautiful itself.

The beautiful is the principle of all as the cause effecting, mov- 2
ing, and keeping all things together, by the love, that is, of its own beauty. It is the end of all, and lovable to all as the end; for all things are made for the sake of the beautiful. It is also the exemplary cause, for all things are defined [or given limits] through the beautiful.

So the beautiful itself is the same as the Good, because all 3
things desire the beautiful and the good equally on account of every cause. Nor is there anything in the natural order that may not participate in the beautiful and the good. We will venture to say

bonique particeps. Audebimus quoque dicere ipsum etiam non ens pulchri bonique compos existere: tunc enim et ipsum est pulchrum atque bonum, quando in Deo, per omnium ablationem, supra modum essentie celebratur.

: CV :

Marsilius:
Idem est primum bonum atque pulchrum.
Item a pulchritudine prima sunt rerum essentie,
uniones, discretiones, communiones,
ordines, proportiones, status, motus.

1 Nemo argumentari debet primum principium, quia quam plurima facit, esse propterea multiplex vel in natura vel in actione, sed potius contra, quia videlicet est infinite simplex, ideo esse primum et idcirco illinc omnia proficisci; et quoniam propter miram simplicitatem est ipsa unitas, virtutem infinitam habere cuncta creantem, siquidem in singulis unaqueque virtus, quatenus unita magis est, eo potentior est efficitque plura. Ipsum ergo principium apud Dionysium, sicut summe unum est, sic unite, unice, unica virtute et actione dicitur omnia procreare.

2 Proinde si singula consideres nature opera, celum, elementa, plantas, animalia, videbis nature intentionem duo hec pariter ubique curare, commoditatem videlicet et ornatum, quod vel in[202] minimis quibusque est maxime manifestum, in herbarum foliis, in alis papilionum. Commoditas quidem et utilitas ad bonum

too that even non-being is composed of the beautiful and the good; for non-being is beautiful and good, when, following on the subtraction of all else, it is celebrated in God as above the mode of essence.

: CV :

Marsilio:
The prime Good and the beautiful are the same. From prime beauty issue the essences of things, their unions, differentiations, communions, orders, proportions, rests, and motions.

Nobody should argue that the first principle, because it makes so 1
many things, is on that account multiple in either its nature or its action. To the contrary, we should argue that because it is infinitely simple, it is the first, and all things accordingly proceed from it; and also because, since it is unity itself on account of its marvelous simplicity, that it has infinite power to create all, since in the case of every single power in individual things, the more the power is united, the more powerful it is and the more it effects. Therefore the principle itself in Dionysius, as it is one in the highest degree, so is it said to procreate all things with one power and one action in a united and unique way.

So if you ponder the individual works of nature, the sky, ele- 2
ments, plants, and animals, you will see that nature's intention everywhere takes care of two things equally: fitness of design and ornament. This is fully manifest even in the smallest objects: in the leaves of plants, in the wings of butterflies. Aptness and use-

pertinet; ornatus vero, modus, species, ordo, dispositio, proportio, concinnitas, consonantia, gratia, claritas, spectat ad pulchrum.

3 Ex his ergo colligitur in summo nature principio primam pulchritudinem cum prima bonitate concurrere, etsi Plotinus bonum anteponit pulchro tum rationibus aliis, tum etiam quia bonum usque ad materie prime centrum videt attingere, materia siquidem necessaria est et utilis et commoda mundo. Pulchrum vero non ad deformem materie sinum inspicit penetrare, sed circa superficiem eius in forma versari. Dicitur tamen primum principium, tam a Plotino quam a Dionysio, ipsum pulchrum et pulchritudo prima, non quia sit formalis aliqua pulchritudo, sed quoniam prima sit causa pulchritudinis.

4 Contemplatur preterea Dionysius noster in sole occultam solis naturam atque lucem, ubi natura quidem est lux ipsa se intus colligens in se ipsam, lux autem natura rursus existit se ipsam explicans in apertum. Similiter contemplatur in Deo efficacem nature fecunditatem et clarissime rursus intelligentie ordinem: illam quidem proprie nominat bonitatem, hanc vero nuncupat pulchritudinem, re quidem ipsa penitus unum, sed hanc ab illa quadam ratione distinctam.

5 Quemadmodum igitur quecunque fiunt a natura solis occulta, eadem proficiscuntur a luce atque vicissim, ita quecunque a bonitate nascuntur, eadem a pulchritudine disponuntur, sicut in artificio cuncta simul et virtus in artifice movens efficit, et ratio interim artificiosa dum fiunt ordine suo queque disponit.

6 Quecunque in ordine rerum ad gratiam, claritatem, proportionem, concinnitatem, consonantiam, ordinem attinent, tanquam propria pulchritudinis a pulchritudine prima perficiuntur. Hec igitur omnia Dionysius in presentia numerat. Essentiales quidem

fulness pertain to the good, whereas ornament, mode, species, order, disposition, proportion, harmony, consonance, grace, and clarity look to the beautiful.

Accordingly, we may gather from all this that in the highest principle of nature the first beauty coincides with the first goodness, though Plotinus puts the Good before the beautiful for other reasons, and also because he sees goodness extending down as far as the center of prime matter,[197] since matter is necessary for, useful to, and in harmony with the world. But the beautiful does not look to penetrate to the formless bosom of matter, but rather to haunt its surface in a form. Yet it is said by Plotinus and by Dionysius that the first principle is the beautiful itself, is the prime beauty, not because it is some formal beauty, but because it is the prime cause of beauty. 3

Moreover, our Dionysius contemplates in the sun the sun's hidden nature and light: its nature is its light folding itself into itself within; but its light is its nature unfolding itself without. Similarly, he contemplates in God both the effective fecundity of [His] nature and in turn the order of [His] clearest understanding. The former he properly calls [God's] goodness, but the latter he calls [His] beauty. In reality they are entirely one, but the latter is rationally distinguished as it were from the former. 4

Therefore, just as all the things that are made from the sun's hidden nature, the same proceed in turn from its light, so all that are born from goodness, the same are arranged in order by beauty. Likewise with craftsmanship, the power moving in the craftsman does everything simultaneously, as long as his craft-making reason disposes every thing, while they are being made, in their proper sequence. 5

All in the universal order which attain to grace, clarity, proportion, harmony, consonance, and order are perfected as beauty's own by the prime beauty. Therefore Dionysius enumerates all these in the present [instance]. The essential substances of things 6

subsistentie[203] rerum in claritate forme et eiusdem integritate consistunt; uniones quoque discretionesque rerum, sive in suis uniuscuiusque partibus insint, sive inter rem hanc et aliam considerentur, ad proportionem quandam spectare videntur. Similiter que per unionem discretionemque contingunt, scilicet identitates diversitatesque in natura. Item similitudines dissimilitudinesque in qualitate, ad proportionem aliquam mutuamque habitudinem referri putantur.[204]

7 In prima pulchritudine unitas cum multitudine ita semper est concors ut alterutrum non impediant; in unitate essentie Trinitas ineffabilis, et in Trinitate similiter unitas; in conceptu divino unica lux intelligentie simplicissime cum idealium radiorum mira multiplicitate[205] conspirat. Hinc efficitur ut in re qualibet et unitas sit essentie et partium seu virium multitudo, nec alterum impediat alterum; item ut in universo multe rerum species actionesque in una totius mundi forma ordineque conveniant. Per quam quidem convenientiam et superiora ad inferiora, et hec ad illa, et equalia invicem quodammodo se convertunt, mirabiliterque communicant; unumquodque tamen suam interim servat proprietatem.

8 Per eandem quoque convenientiam celestia sunt etiam in terrenis modo quodam prope terreno ac terrena sunt in celis sed ibi ratione celesti. Hinc utique totus sibimet mundus ceu vivens unum est connexus, totusque ubique respondet toti, ut si quis terrenum Mercurium exploraverit et opportune susceperit, sit quodammodo celestem ad se Mercurium attracturus; sed de his in libro *De vita* latius disputavimus.

9 Proinde proportio quevis harmonica vel exterior vel interior a prima pulchritudine omnibus est tributa, per proportionem[206] eiusmodi partium, virium, actionum, tum substantie stabiles

consist in the clarity of form and the integrity of the same. The unions and differentiations of things too — whether they are taken as present within the parts of each single thing or are considered as between this one thing and another — seem to look to a certain proportion. The like goes for all that happens through union and differentiation, that is, identities and differences in nature; and likenesses and un-likenesses in quality are thought to refer to some proportion, and to a shared habitual condition.

In prime beauty unity is always so concordant with multiplicity that they do not impede each other. In the unity of [its] essence the Trinity is ineffable and similarly in the Trinity the unity [is ineffable]. In divine conception the unique light of understanding in [its] utmost simplicity conspires with the marvelous multiplicity of the ideal rays. Hence it is that in any one thing there exists a unity of essence and a multiplicity of parts or powers, without the one impeding the other; and likewise that in the universe the many species and actions of things are in accord in the one form and order of the whole world. Through this accord superiors turn toward inferiors and the latter turn to them, and equals turn in a way to each other, and they share in a marvelous manner. Yet every single thing meanwhile preserves its own property. 7

Through this same accord celestials even exist in earthly things in an almost earthly manner; and earthly things are in the heavens though they are there for a celestial reason. Hence the whole world is connected to itself as one living being;[198] and the whole everywhere responds to the whole, just as someone who has looked for earthly mercury and acquired it at the opportune moment is in some manner about to draw the celestial Mercury down to himself. But we have discussed these matters at greater length in the *De Vita*.[199] 8

Consequently, each harmonic proportion, whether exterior or interior, is bestowed on all things by the prime beauty. Through the proportion of such parts, powers, and actions, the stable 9

permanent insolubiles, tum res fluxe perpetua quadam propagine speciem retinent sempiternam.

10 Denique series idearum divina mente concepta est proculdubio pulchritudo prima; ab hac igitur et in ipsa unumquodque est in certa specie rationeque propria constitutum, videlicet ut ignis necessario sit lucidus, calidus, siccus, levis. Per certam vero naturam inclinatio, motio, actio similiter est sua cuique destinata, illinc igitur et status et motus est omnibus assignatus.

11 Ipse vero Deus, ut Plato disputat in *Parmenide*, neque movetur, neque motus est ullus (alioquin imperfectus fore compelleretur), neque stat (esset enim ex statu quodam ac stante compositus), neque status est ullus quo scilicet formaliter aliquid stare dicatur. Primum namque principium est in nullo, neque est ipsa dumtaxat idea status (esset enim et certa specie definitus, et ad certum designatus effectum).

12 Sed ne pigeat mysterium hoc Dionysiacum memorie commendare: quemadmodum in principio numerorum summa unitas concurrit cum infinita numeralium virium multitudine, sic in principio rerum, penes ipsam nature unitatem inextimabilem, innumerabilis existit rationum idealium multitudo; nec eiusmodi multitudo summam impedit unitatem, sed necessario comitatur. Quamobrem divina unitas atque discretio usque adeo pariter ubique regnant, ut nulla vel tam inter se diversa esse possint quin in aliquo simul communi conveniant, vel tam exacte conflata ex pluribus quin plura hec suam adhuc aliquam servent proprietatem.

substances remain indestructible and things in flux retain the sempiternal species by [having] an endless offspring.

10 Finally, the series of ideas conceived in the divine mind is without a doubt the prime beauty. So from this beauty and in this beauty every single thing is constituted in a certain species and with its own rational principle, as, for instance, fire is necessarily bright, hot, dry, and weightless. But through this fixed nature, to each thing is appointed likewise its own inclination, motion, and action. Thence, accordingly, rest and motion are assigned to all things.

11 But God Himself, as Plato argues in the *Parmenides*,[200] is neither moved nor is He motion of any kind, otherwise He would be compelled to become imperfect. Nor does He rest, for He would be a compound then of a particular rest and of someone resting. Nor is He rest of any kind, in the way, that is, that something may be said to be at rest formally; for the first principle is not in anything at all. Nor is He only the idea of rest, for [then] He would be defined by way of a certain species and depicted as having a certain effect.

12 But do not shy away from entrusting this Dionysian mystery to memory. As in the beginning of numbers, the highest unity accords with the infinite multitude of numeral powers, so in the beginning of things, in the presence of nature's inestimable unity itself, a countless multitude of ideal rational principles exists. Such a multitude does not hinder the highest unity, but necessarily accompanies it. On this account, divine unity and differentiation reign everywhere so equally that things can neither be so diverse among themselves that they do not agree with one another in some commonality, nor so exactly compounded from many things that they do not preserve still some property of their own.

: CVI :

Dionysius:
Idem.

1 Hoc ipsum bonum unum atque pulchrum unice causa est multorum omnium pulchrorum atque bonorum: ex hoc omnes rerum essentiales subsistentie,[207] uniones, discretiones, identitates, alteritates, similitudines, dissimilitudines; preterea discretorum communiones, unitorum inconfuse proprietates, superiorum providentie, rerum eiusdem ordinis consortia mutua, conversiones inferiorum, omnium interea suimet conservatrices immutabilesque mansiones atque firmitates.

2 Rursus omnium in omnibus pro sua cuiusque proprietate communiones et congruentie inconfuseque amicitie consonantieque universi, atque omnes in universo, tum eorum que revera sunt contemperantie indissolubilesque connexus, tum eorum que fiunt perpetue successiones; denique status omnes motusque mentium, animarum, corporum. Status enim est omnibus atque motus quod omni statu motuque superius exstans rem quamlibet in ratione propria firmat et ad propriam dirigit motionem.

: CVI :

Dionysius: The same.

This Good, One, and Beautiful itself is uniquely the cause of all the many good and beautiful things. From this Good come all the essential substances of things, the unions, divisions, identities, differences, likenesses and un-likenesses; the communions of things separated, the unconfused properties of things united, the providences of those above, the mutual consorting of those of the same order, the conversions of those lower; and the self-preserving and unchangeable abodes and foundations of all. 1

From it again come the communions of all in all, according to the property of each; and the harmonious and untroubled friendships and consonances of the universe. And from it come all those existing in the universe, the tempered and indissoluble connections of those which truly are, and the perpetual successions of those that become. Finally, from the Good come all the rests and motions of minds, of souls, of bodies. For the Good is the rest and motion for all, because in existing far above and beyond every rest and motion, it firmly establishes each thing in its own rational principle and directs it to its own motion. 2

: CVII :

Marsilius: De motu angeli et anime triplici, id est circulari, recto, obliquo.

1 Inter virtutem naturalem atque cognitricem hoc interest potissimum, quod naturalis virtutis actio fertur foras ac desinit in subiectum; cognitricis vero virtutis actio permanet penes ipsam. Quapropter hec quidem circulare non nihil habet: quod enim in orbem movetur, versatur circa se ipsum reditque semper unde discessit; illa vero rectam videtur lineam imitari, ab altero videlicet puncto in alterum desinentem. Corpori quidem sola competit eiusmodi actio motioque consimilis; intellectui vero convenit actio circularis, cum enim cognitio quelibet in se videlicet quodammodo permanens circulare nonnihil habeat, et imaginatio quidem magis quam sensus, ratio quoque magis quam imaginatio, intellectus denique, tanquam cognitio summa, circularis est summopere.

2 Hinc fit ut anima, inter intellectum corpusque media, mediam habeat actionem motumque similiter tum orbis, tum recti participem. Una siquidem intellectus ipsius actio est intellectio, ex se exordiens et orbiculariter remeans in se ipsam, quatenus vero se suaque intelligit, eatenus intelligit, efficit, movet, regit alia; hic igitur recta quedam linea tendens in alia orbem intimum comitatur, videlicet inde profecta. Hec igitur actio circa alia intimam non distrahit actionem. Anima vero et animadversione sui facit circulum, et vegetatione corporis negocioque circa corpus rectam lineam imitatur. Sed quoniam hec non dependet ab illa, nimirum

: CVII :

Marsilio:
On the triple motion of the angel and the soul, that is, the circular, the straight, and the oblique.

As between natural power and cognitive power, the main difference is that the action of natural power is borne outside and ends up in an object; but the action of the cognitive power remains within itself. Because of this, the latter has something circular; for what is moved in a circle turns upon itself and always returns whence it [first] set out. But the former seems to imitate the straight line; [it goes] in other words from one point and ends in another. Such a [straight] action and motion likewise is alone suited to the body. But circular action accords with the intellect, since each act of cognition, in remaining in itself in a way, has something circular. The imagination is more so than the sense; the reason more so than the imagination; and finally the intellect as highest cognition is consummately circular. 1

Hence it is that the soul, the mean between intellect and body, has the intermediate action and motion alike as a participant both of a circle and of a straight line. The one action of the intellect itself is intellection, beginning from itself and returning in an orbital manner to itself. But to the extent it understands itself and its own, to that extent it understands, effects, moves, and rules other things. So here a sort of straight line extending toward others accompanies the inner circling—having proceeded, that is, from it. So this extending action with regard to others does not interrupt the inner [circular] action. The soul, however, in meditating on itself makes an orbit of itself; but in enlivening the body, and in its dealings with regard to the body, it imitates the straight line. But because the latter motion does not depend on the former, 2

anima sic agendo distracta videtur, et apud eam operatio altera vicissim impedit alteram.

3 Verum si ad mentem quidem circuitus attinet, ad animam vero motio quedam mixta, ad corpus denique recta, undenam celestis revolutio provenit? Non a corporea quidem celi natura, sed a motore celi, mente vel anima vel utraque ad circuitum interea conferente figura. Esse vero mundanum motum a mente simul et anima Platonicus quisque coniciet ex motibus mundi mixtis, orbicularibus videlicet atque rectis. Hactenus Platonice tantum locuti sumus; ad Dionysium revertamur, Platonica semper in melius reformantem.

4 Cum mens angelica per divinum lumen intelligens ipsum quoque lumen intelligat, idque uniformi perpetuoque actu semper efficiat, merito sic remeans unde cepit circulum quendam videtur efficere. Mox vero intelligens inferiora et intelligendo dispensans per rectam lineam ita procedere iudicatur, nec enim illuc spectat unde ceperat, nec que gubernantur inde similiter dispensantur.

5 Inter loquendum Dionysius, nostri Platonis amator, libenter verbis Platonicis utitur ubi inquit: 'recta quadam via omnia peragit,' quod quidem Platonis est in quarto *Legum* dicentis: 'Deum dum universa lustrat in orbem, omnia interim via recta peragere.' Ubi sane dicit: 'Deus secundum naturam circuitum agens via recta peragit,' id est: naturalis et prima Dei actio versatur circa se ipsum intellegendum atque amandum, ex hoc autem circulo linea recta suboritur dum videlicet se intelligens intelligit et efficit omnia. Animus vero noster contra, exordiens a linea recta qua versatur circa alia, desinit in circuitum quo seipsum animadvertit.

the soul, in acting in this way, certainly seems distracted, and the one operation in turn impedes the other.

If a circular motion pertains to mind, a mixed motion to soul, 3
and finally a straight motion to body, whence comes the celestial revolution? Not from the corporeal nature of the heavens, but from the mover of the heavens: that is, from mind or soul or both, conferring shape upon the circuit. However, from the mixed motions of the world, every Platonist will conjecture that the world motion comes from mind and soul together, that is, from orbicular motions and straight ones.[201] Thus far we have been speaking only Platonically. Let us return to Dionysius who always reforms Platonic matters for the better.

Since angelic mind, in understanding through the divine light, 4
also understands the light, and always does this in a uniform and perpetual act, fittingly in thus returning whence it began it seems to effect a circle. Next, in understanding inferiors and ruling them by understanding, it is therefore adjudged to proceed by way of a straight line. For the line does not look back to where it began; nor do those things which are being governed likewise [look back] to where they are being ruled.

In the course of speaking, Dionysius, who loves our Plato, 5
gladly uses Platonic words when he says that "God enacts all in a straight path." This is what Plato says in the fourth book of the *Laws* when he says that "God, while He considers all things in a circle, yet He enacts all things in a straight path."[202] He says there that God naturally acts Himself in a circle but acts on things in a straight line. In other words, he declares that the natural and prime act of God is concerned with understanding and loving Himself, but that from this circle is born the straight line, when, in understanding Himself, He understands and effects all things. But our rational soul to the contrary, beginning from a straight line, whereby it treats of other things, ends in the circle wherein it contemplates itself.

6 Proinde motus obliquus partem quidem habet recti, partem vero circuli. Angelus igitur, dum quasi recta quadam processione gubernans inferiora ab ipsa divinorum intelligentia non discedit, atque ita summum illum conservat circuitum, nimirum obliquum motum imitari videtur. Eatenus autem in eodem suo habitu perseverat, quatenus in Deo permanet velut centro.

7 Ipsa namque unitas status omnis principium est et ratio; stare enim censetur quod sui habitus retinet unitatem. Est et fundamentum motus; non enim motus est nisi continuus, neque continuatur actus nisi per unitatem vis ipsa movendi permanet.[208] Est et origo identitatis, equalitatis, similitudinis, siquidem per ipsam unitatem et que sunt eadem unum sunt in substantia, et que sunt equalia sunt unum in quantitate, et que similia unum in qualitate.

8 Quemadmodum vero a circulari celestium motu tum recti elementorum atque mixtorum, tum obliqui viventium motus proficiscuntur atque reguntur, ita et rectus obliquusque motus, id est actus angeli, ab intimo eius circa Deum circuitu vim omnem ordinemque sortitur.

9 Platonicus Timeus in celo circuitus precipue duos suspicit: erraticum scilicet planetarum atque non errantem, videlicet firmamenti. Circuitus ferme similes in anima contemplatur: erraticum quidem in ratione circa se et causam cognoscendam variis diversionibus aberrante, non errantem vero in intellectu se ipsum causamque suam per simplicem firmumque intuitum contuente.

10 Preterea quemadmodum sub luna motus recti sunt gemini, alter quidem ascendentium, alter vero descendentium, sic in anima motus quasi rectus est duplex: alter sentiendo corpora et imaginando imagines corporum ad externa descendit; alter ascendit aut ex

Consequently, oblique [or spiral] motion[203] has part of the straight line and part of the circle. So the angel, in governing lower things in a kind of straight procession, does not depart from the understanding itself of matters divine and so preserves that highest circuit that it surely seems to imitate spiral motion. It perseveres in its same habitual condition to the extent that it remains in God as in its center. 6

For unity itself is the principle and reason of all rest; for adjudged to be at rest is that which retains the unity of its habit.[204] Unity is also the foundation of motion. For it is not motion unless it is continuous, nor is the act continued unless, via unity, the power itself of moving perdures. Unity is also the origin of sameness, equality, and likeness, since through unity itself those which are the same are one in substance, those which are equal are one in quantity, and those which are alike are one in quality. 7

But just as from the circular motion of celestials proceed both the straight motions of elements and their mixtures and the spiral motions of living things (motions that are ruled by the circular motion of celestials), so from its inner circuit around God the angel's straight and spiral motions—that is, its act—receives all power and order. 8

Timaeus the Platonist acknowledged two principal circuits in the heavens, the erratic circuit of the planets and the non-erring circuit of the firmament.[205] He contemplates the two as being like or almost like the circuits in the soul: the wandering circuit in the reason wandering around itself and coming to know about [its] cause in various discursive ways; and the non-wandering circuit in the intellect gazing at itself and at its cause through a simple and steadfast gaze.[206] 9

Moreover, just as straight sublunar motions are twin, the one of things ascending, the other of things descending, so motion in the soul is straight as it were and [likewise] twin: by sensing bodies and imagining images of bodies one motion descends to externals; 10

multis sub specie singularibus speciem unam rationemque communem concipiens atque colligens, aut etiam ex natura corporea interdum excogitans incorpoream. In hoc autem officio refugiens multitudinem confugere videtur ad unitatem.

11 Inter hec vero memento quo superior virtus est, eo et minus multitudine indigere et magis in unitate multa complecti. Nempe visus unico intuitu figuram percipit circularem, quam actu multiplici digitorum tactus exhibet iudicandam. Imaginatio una conficit quotcumque multi sensus efficient. Ratio singula imaginationis spectacula summatim sub una specie contuetur. Intellectus uno sepius actu stabili conspicit quod ratio multis indagavit ambagibus. Appellatur tamen ratio etiam intellectus a Dionysio, sed inferior, et in utroque intellectu circulum Platonico more designat: circuitumque intellectus inferioris erraticum resolvit in orbem intellectus superioris non errantem, id est minime vagabundum, erroresque rationis emendantem atque firmantem.

12 Quemadmodum vero ex iactu lapilli in aquam circuli plures e vestigio subsequuntur, sic ex ingressu anime in se ipsam circuli deinceps multi nascuntur: Primo quod se ipsam animadvertit et ex propriis actionibus vires suas agnoscit atque naturam, atque ita nonnunquam ex rationali maxime intellectualis evadit unaque iam efficitur ex multiplici.

13 Secundo vero circuitu per intelligentiam suam animo participanti tributam angelicam excogitat intelligentiam, non in anima quidem ulla, sed in se ipsa constantem propriaque anime unitate longe simpliciorem. Tertio tandem circulo per intelligentiam angelicam contemplatur Deum omnis intelligentie lumen. Tres autem

but the other ascends either from the many individuals in the species to conceiving and collecting one species and a common reason; or it uses the corporeal nature meanwhile to think about the incorporeal. But in this office, in fleeing from multiplicity, it seems to flee to unity.

In these matters, bear in mind that the higher the power, the less it needs multiplicity and the more it embraces the many in unity. In one glance sight perceives a circular shape which the touch of fingers has to judge obviously in a multiple act. The imagination unites whatever the several senses will produce. Under one species the reason summarily gazes on the individual images of the imagination. The intellect more often sees in a stable act what the reason has tracked down by way of many meanderings. Yet the reason is also called the intellect by Dionysius, but a lower intellect; and in each intellect, in the Platonic manner, he depicts a circle. The erratic circuit of the lower intellect he resolves into the non-erring circuit of the higher intellect, that is, the circuit that does not wander away at all and that corrects and stabilizes the errors of the reason. 11

But just as from a stone's being cast into water many circles immediately radiate out, so from a soul's entering into itself many circles are successively born. First, it pays attention to itself, and from its own actions it recognizes its own powers and nature; and thus it emerges occasionally from being rational to being for the most part intellectual, and from being multiple it is now made one. 12

Second, from this circuit through its own understanding, an understanding granted to a participating rational soul, the soul ponders the angelic understanding which is not in any soul at all but is constant in itself and simpler by far than the unity proper to a soul. Third, finally, in the circle through the angelic understanding, the soul contemplates God, the light of all understanding. But 13

actus eiusmodi ideo circuitus appellantur, quoniam in suam originem se reflectunt.[209]

14 Nominatur autem motus obliquus in anima quando, luminibus infusis a Deo,[210] ipsummet Deum excogitare contendens, a divinitate procul aberrat: tunc enim, quia convertere se ipsam nititur illuc unde movetur, refert quodammodo circulum; quoniam vero non pervenit, non nihil adhuc recti retinens,[211] obliqua relinquitur.

15 Errat autem sic a Deo quotiens ratione utens potius quam intellectu notionem quandam sub divino lumine circa Deum concipit non simplicissimam quidem atque stabilissimam, qualem intellectus purus augurari solet, sed mobilem potius atque multiplicem, quam humana ratio confingere[212] consuevit, ideoque longissime a divina summitate distantem. Appellatur autem eiusmodi notio mixta, quoniam ibi rationis actio divinas intelligentie species cum imaginibus imaginationis humane commiscet.

: CVIII :

Dionysius: *Idem.*

1 Intellectus divini circulo quodam moveri dicuntur dum pulchri bonique splendoribus (principio et fine carentibus) coniunguntur; recta[213] vero linea quando ad inferiorum providentiam prodeunt recta omnia peragentes; oblique[214] vero quoniam, dum sequentibus

these three acts are called circuits because they bend themselves back toward their own origin.

14 But in the soul it is called spiral motion when, [though] inspired by light from God and in trying to think about God Himself, the souls wanders far away from the Divinity. Because the soul strives to return itself to its point of departure, it resembles in a way a circle. But because it does not arrive there, and retains something still of the straight line, its [motion] is consequently spiral.

15 The soul errs thus from God whenever, in using the reason rather than the intellect, it conceives under [the influence of] light divine of a certain notion regarding God, a notion that is not utterly simple and utterly unchanging (as the pure intellect customarily foresees), but that is mobile and multiple, the kind of notion that human reason usually devises and that is accordingly far distant from the summit divine. But such a notion is called a mixed notion, because the reason's action mingles the divine species of the understanding there with the images of the human imagination.

: CVIII :

Dionysius: The same.

1 Thus divine intellects are said to be moved in a circle as long as they are united with the splendors of the Beautiful and the Good, the splendors that have no beginning and no end. But they are moved in a straight line when they go forth to exercise care and forethought over their inferiors, driving all in a straight line. And they are said to be moved spirally in that, while they provide for

provident, nunquam a propria identitate discedunt, videlicet circa pulchrum atque bonum identitatis causam indeficientem choream agentes.

2 Anime vero motus circularis quidem est ingressus in se ipsam ab externis, atque intellectualium eius virium glomeratio uniformis, velut circulo quodam acta, munus non erraticum ei largiens, eamque a multis extrinsecus circumfusis divertens: atque colligens primo quidem in se ipsam; secundo, tanquam uniformem iam effectam, singulariter unitis potestatibus copulans; tertio hinc ad pulchrum bonumque perducens quod super omnia que sunt est unum atque idem, neque principium habens neque finem.

3 Oblique vero movetur anima quatenus divinis subrutilat notionibus, pro sua dumtaxat proprietate susceptis, non intellectuali quidem stabilique sorte, sed rationali discurrenteque conditione, transeuntibus scilicet actionibus atque permixtis. Linea vero recta movetur quando non ingreditur in se ipsam nec intellectuali uniformique proprietate movetur (hoc enim est, ut dixi, circuitum agere), sed ad externa procedens ab eis, velut a signis quibusdam variis multiplicibusque, ad simplices et unitas contemplationes erigitur.

subsequents, they never descend from their own identity; that is, they dance in chorus around the Beautiful and the Good, the never-ending cause of their identity.

The circular motion of soul, however, is the soul's entry into itself from externals, and the uniform rolling together of its intellectual powers, enacted as in a circle; and it is the bestowing on it of the gift of not wandering, and the turning away of the soul from the many surrounding externals. And it is the collecting first of itself into itself; second—have already been made uniform—it is the joining itself to its united powers individually; and third, it is the leading itself from here to the Beautiful and the Good, which is above all existing things and is one and the same, having neither beginning nor end. 2

The soul is moved spirally, however, insofar as it is somewhat aglow with divine notions but is only sustained according to its own property: not in an intellectual and unchanging condition but in a rational and discursive manner, that is, by way of transient and mixed actions. It is moved in a straight line, however, when it does not enter into itself and is not moved by an intellectual and uniform property (for this, as I said, is to enact a circle). Nonetheless, in proceeding to externals, it is lifted up from them, as from particular, various, and multiple signs to contemplations that are simple and united. 3

: CIX :

Marsilius:

Ipsum pulchrum bonumque est causa efficiens, exemplaris, finalis, conservatrix omnis status atque[215] *motus, et ordinis bonique totius rerum omnium.*

1 Primum rerum principium, quod ex ipsa quidem fecunditate nature dicitur ipsum bonum, ex ipsa vero intelligentie luce dicitur ipsum pulchrum, est causa motus omnis: recti, circularis, obliqui, tum in rebus incorporeis, tum corporeis. Multoque prius status omnis est causa, tum quia status perfectioni principii propinquior est, tum quia in unoquoque precedit ac regit uniuscuiusque motum, videlicet statum virtutis optantem.

2 Conclude: si status motusque omnis causa Deus est, ipsum omni statu motuque superiorem esse. Est autem causa utriusque modis quatuor: ex qua, per quam, ad quam sive cuius gratia, in qua: id est efficiens, exemplaris, finalis, conservans. Efficiens, inquam, quia dum unicuique dat essentiam essentialemque virtutem, interim et perseverantiam in essentia prestat et efficaciam ad motum[216] subito properantem. Exemplaris quoque quoniam species, modus et ordo utriusque designatur penes Deum. Finalis insuper ad quam utriusque et intentio spectat et cuius gratia editur actio. Conservans denique quoniam et ut principium ac exemplar servat ad destinatum tempus unicuique munera semel data, et ut finis quelibet ad se conversa pro modo cuiusque perficit atque reformat.

3 Omnis essentia vitaque mentis, anime, nature dependet ab ipso, quod quidem valde Platonicum est, naturam scilicet inter animam

: CIX :

Marsilio:
The Beautiful and the Good is the efficient, exemplary, final, and preserving cause of all rest and motion, and of the order and entire good of all things.

The first principle of things which is called the Good from the fecundity itself of [its] nature, but the Beautiful itself from the very light of [its] understanding, is the cause of all motion—straight, circular, and spiral—in both incorporeal and corporeal things. Long prior to this, it is the cause of all rest, both because rest is closer to the perfection of the principle, and because in every single thing rest precedes and rules over its every motion: it chooses, that is, the rest of potentiality. 1

Conclude: if the cause of all rest and motion is God, then He is superior to all rest and motion. But He is the cause of each in four ways: He is from which, through which, to which (or for the sake of which), and in which—He is, that is, the efficient, exemplary, final, and preserving cause. God is the efficient cause because, when He gives essence and essential power to each single thing, He is meanwhile giving both abiding essence and the ability to propel into sudden motion. He is the exemplary cause too, because the species, mode, and order of each is established with Him. He is also the final cause upon which the intentionality of each thing is focused and for whose sake action is produced. And lastly He is the preserving cause, because as principle and exemplar He preserves for the allotted time the gifts once bestowed on each thing, and as the end He perfects and reforms all that turn back to Him according to the mode of each. 2

All the essence and life of mind, of soul, and of nature depend on God and this is a central Platonic notion. Nature, in other 3

corpusque esse mediam vitamque habere; putant enim mentem quidem esse vitam a corporibus alienam, animam vero vitam ad corpus ex quadam sui parte vergentem, naturam denique vitam quandam esse ex accessu anime ad corpus e vestigio resultantem, sive natura sit universalis sub anima mundi corpori infusa mundano, sive particularis sub anima nostra nostro.

4 Post naturam Dionysius corpus Platonico more disponit et[217] narrat sane que pertinent ad quantitatem, vel continuam vel discretam,[218] et interim que spectant ad qualitatem, et que ad utranque, et que comitantur atque sequuntur; quales sunt mensure, modi, proportiones, harmonie, id est congruentie, mixtiones (servata tamen discretione, id est uniuscuiusque proprietate nature); item proprietates partium, perfectiones totius, concentus quibus partes partibus totique ligantur; preterea ordines comparationesque inter totum aliud atque totum atque summatim et cetera modis (ut dixi) quatuor ex bono pulchroque dependent.

5 Maxime vero sic[219] inde dotes anime, naturalis videlicet vel acquisitus habitus animi et sensus ratioque et intellectus; atqui in hoc ipso intellectu tum tactus (id est subitus principiorum universaliumve intuitus), tum scientia conclusionum argumentationibus comparata, tum unio in excelso mentis excessu cum Deo denique facta.

6 Principium ordinis uniuscuiusque proprium ex principio universi dependet; quicquid igitur in quovis ordine munus id obtinet, ut sit efficiens aut finis vel exemplar vel conservatio vel elementale fundamentum vel perfectio formalis, hoc sane totum primi

words, is the mean between soul and body and possesses life. For the Platonists suppose that mind is life separate from bodies; that soul is life inclining, in some part of it, toward body; and finally that nature is a certain life immediately resulting from the access of soul to body, whether that nature is universal under the World Soul and infused in the World Body, or particular under our soul [and infused in] our body.

After nature, Dionysius, in the Platonic manner, deals with body. He describes what pertains to quantity to be sure, whether continuous or discrete, and in the meantime what looks to quality, what to both, and what accompanies and follows them. Of such kind are measures, modes, proportions, harmonies, that is, congruencies, mixtures (yet preserving distinction, preserving the property, that is, of the nature of each single body); again the properties of parts, the perfections of the whole, the harmonies by which parts are bound to parts and to the whole, and the orders and comparisons between one whole and another. In sum, all the rest depend, in the four ways as I have said, on the Good and the Beautiful. 4

From it come in this way the most important gifts to the soul, namely the natural or acquired habit of the rational soul, and sense, reason, and intellect; and yet, in this very intellect, there are the [further] gifts (1) of the [intellectual] touch — that is, the immediate intuition of the principles or the universals; (2) of the knowledge of conclusions acquired from arguments; and (3) in the mind's lofty ecstasy [the gift of] the union which is achieved finally with God. 5

The principle proper to every single order depends on the universe's principle. Thus with any order, whatever gift this principle has to give — that it might be the efficient cause, or the end, or the exemplar, or the preservation, or the elemental foundation, or the formal perfection — all this it possesses as a benefit of the very first 6

principii beneficio possidet, id est ipsius boni pulchrique dono. Hoc enim tanquam primum et ultimum omnia petunt.

7 Denique et que sunt (id est sempiterna) et que non sunt (id est fluxa vel informia) dependent a principio rerum primo, modo quodam supra quam essentiali omnia continente, quod quidem et principium et finis est omnium supra principii finisque modum. Nullam enim propterea cum sequentibus proportionem habet qualem propria rerum principia propriique fines habere videntur. Quod autem dixit omnem infinitatem terminumque illinc existere, Platonici *Philebi* sensu intellige infinitatem capacitatis in materia atque anima, infinitatem propagationis in specie successionisque in tempore, terminum vero formas atque perfectiones.

: CX :

Dionysius: Idem.

1 Ipsum bonum atque pulchrum omni statu motuque superius auctor est et conservator et finis harum trium in mundo motionum atque etiam sensibilium, multoque prius uniuscuiusque mansionum et statuum atque firmitatum.[220] Per quod sane bonum atque pulchrum status omnis ac motus existit ex quo, et in quo, et ad quod, et cuius gratia hec omnia fiunt. Iam vero ex ipso atque

principle, that is, as the gift of the Good and the Beautiful. For all seek this as the first and the last [cause].

Finally, both those which are (that is, the sempiternals) and 7
those which are not (things, that is, in flux or unformed) depend on the first principle of things which contains all things in an utterly supra-essential way, because it is the beginning and end of all [and yet] above the mode of beginning and end. For it has no proportion at all with what follows it, such a proportion that the proper beginnings and ends of things seem to have. However, since Dionysius said that every infinity and every limit exist from that source, understand infinity in the [triple] sense of the Platonic *Philebus*, namely as the infinity of capacity in matter and in soul, as the infinity of propagation in the species, and as the infinity of succession in time. Understand limit, however, to mean forms and perfections.[207]

: CX :

Dionysius: The same.

The Good itself and the Beautiful is superior to all rest and mo- 1
tion; it is the author and preserver and end of these three motions in the world and even in sensibles. And in every single thing it is totally prior to that thing's remaining steadfast, its remaining at rest, and its foundations. By way of this Good and Beautiful all rest and motion exist; and from it and in it and to it and for its sake they all come about. But from it and through it the

per ipsum essentia vitaque omnis intellectus et anime natureque existit; preterea parvitates, equalitates, magnitudines, mensure omnes, proportiones rerum, congruentie, commixtiones, integritates, partes, quodlibet unum, quelibet multitudo, partium nexus, omnis multitudinis uniones, integritatum perfectiones, quale, quantum, quotum, cuiusmodi infinitum, coniunctiones, discretiones, omnium infinitudo, omnis terminus, fines omnes, ordines, excessus, elementa, species, quelibet essentia, quevis potentia, omnis actio, habitus omnis, sensus, ratio, intelligentia, tactus, scientia, unio.

2 Atque simpliciter quicquid est ex pulchro bonoque existit, et in pulchro bonoque consistit, et ad pulchrum bonumque convertitur. Nempe quecunque sunt et fiunt propter pulchrum bonumque sunt et fiunt. Ad ipsum omnia spectant ab eodem moventur atque continentur.

3 Preterea ipsius gratia et per ipsummet et in eodem est omne principium: exemplare, perficiens, efficiens, speciale, elementale, et simpliciter omne principium, quelibet conservatio, unusquisque terminus; sive, ut summatim dicam, quecunque sunt ex pulchro sunt atque bono. Immo et que non sunt, ratione quadam plusquam essentiali, in pulchro bonoque consistunt ipsumque est omnium principium atque finis super omnem principii finisque rationem, quoniam 'ex ipso atque per ipsum et in ipso atque ad ipsum omnia' pendent, quemadmodum sacrum testatur[221] eloquium.

essence and life of every intellect, soul, and nature exist along with the relationships of smallness, equality, and greatness, all measures, the proportions of things, the congruencies, mixtures, wholes and parts, whatever is one, whatsoever are many, the nexus of parts, the unions of every multitude, the perfections of wholes, quality, quantity, number, and the infinity of such, conjunctions, differentiations, the infinitude of all, all limit, all ends, orders, and departures [from order], all elements, species, every essence, every potency, all action, all habit, sense, reason, understanding, touch, knowledge, and union.

And in brief, whatever exists is from the Beautiful and the 2
Good and exists in the Beautiful and the Good and is turned back toward the Beautiful and the Good; and all that are and that become are so and become so on account of the Beautiful and the Good. All look to it and are moved by it and contained by it.

Moreover, for its sake and through it and in it every principle 3
exists: the exemplary, perfecting, effecting, special, and elemental—every principle in short, and all conservation and the limit of every single thing. In sum, all that exist are from the Beautiful and the Good. Nay, even those which do not exist, for a reason that goes beyond the essential, consist of this Beautiful and Good; and it is the principle and end of all and yet above every rational principle of beginning and end, because all things are derived "from it and through it and in it and to it," as sacred eloquence testifies.[208]

: CXI :

Marsilius:
Omnia pro modo suo appetunt ipsum bonum atque pulchrum; quo[222] *desiderio agunt quicquid agunt. Item ipsum bonum amore*[223] *sui omnia facit.*

1 Cum effectuum conditio sit ut quocunque possunt instinctu convertantur ad causam a qua processerunt, bonum vero pulchrumque sit omnium causa in omni genere causarum, merito ipsum appetunt omnia; que videlicet simpliciter sunt appetitu simpliciter naturali, que et sunt et sentiunt appetitu insuper sensuali, rationalia preterea rationali, intellectualia quinetiam intellectuali.

2 Quamvis autem ipsum appetant omnia, sola tamen rationalia intellectualiaque dicuntur amare, solus intellectus denique consequi. Amor quidem appetitus quidam est non qualiscunque, sed ardens, concitatus, anhelans; est igitur ardentissimus quidam motus. Et quemadomodum ardor in aere sequitur non lucem soli insitam proxime, sed splendorem illinc aeri prorsus infusum, sic amor erga bonum ardens non aliter ab ipso videtur accendi quam per intelligibile lumen intellectui rationique insertum, sive mox ex alto subrutilet mentibus scilicet segregatis, sive per sensibile lumen gradatim ascendatur ad ipsum.

3 Lumen vero intelligibile quidem pulchritudo prima est et prima bonitatis imago; sensibile vero pulchritudo secunda et imago secunda boni. Ipsum itaque bonum, alioquin mediocriter appetibile per pulchritudinem suam splendoremque, amore intus accenso ardenter appetitur et amanter. Quamobrem et qui novum

: CXI :

Marsilio:
All things desire the Good itself and the Beautiful in their own manner, and through this desire they do whatever they do; likewise the Good itself by love of itself creates all.[209]

Since the condition of things is such that with whatever instinct 1
they can they are converted to the cause from which they proceeded, but since the Good and the Beautiful is the cause of all in every class of causes, in justice all things desire it: those which simply exist with a simple natural desire; those which exist and also sense with a sensual desire as well; those who are rational with a rational desire too; and those who are intellectual with an intellectual desire in addition.

Although all desire [the Good], only rational and intellectual 2
beings are said to love it; and only the intellect at length attains it. Love is a certain desire, not just a desire of any kind but ardent desire, aroused, panting. It is then a motion hot in the extreme. And just as the heat in the air follows, not the light that is innermost in the sun, but rather the splendor radiated from the sun into the air, so burning love for the Good seems to be set on fire by it in no way other than through the intelligible splendor introduced into the intellect and reason; and this is whether it straightway glows from on high in separated minds, or whether one gradually ascends through the sensible light toward it.

But the intelligible light is the first beauty and the first image of 3
goodness, while the sensible light is the second beauty and the second image of the Good. Therefore the Good itself, otherwise desirable in moderation via its beauty and splendor, is ardently and lovingly desired by a love kindled within. Hence the person who

gratiosumque intelligentie lumen non est adeptus, ut Plotinus ait, nondum intus habet Deum, et qui non ardenter amat Deum, is[224] profecto nondum est lumen ipsum intelligibile consecutus.

4 Preterea solis radius plantarum motibus causam prebet efficientem atque finalem: nam et calor eius insitus efficit ut moveantur, et cum primum moventur ad lumen vergunt velut ad finem. Similiter ipsum bonum atque pulchrum et tanquam efficiens efficaciam prebet omnibus qua moveantur, atque ad id quod eis consentaneum est pro viribus annitantur. Et tanquam finis gratia quadam singula circunfundit per quam alliciant appetentia.

5 Iam vero quoniam ipsum est primum amans et amatum amorque primus, hinc habent omnia ut ament amenturque. Hinc omnes amores proficiscuntur—amores, inquam, genere quatuor: amor superiora provocans ut inferioribus benigne provideant; amor inferiora revocans ad superiorum virtutem vel similitudinem comparandam; amor eorum, que in eadem specie vel eodem genere vel ordine sunt, ad mutuam inter se communionem in conversando, dando, precipiendo; amor uniuscuiusque erga se ipsum pro viribus conservandum. Tum vero dum omnia gratia finis alicuius atque boni[225] agunt quicquid agunt, in singulis appetendis appetunt ipsum bonum. Sed quoniam non solum commoditatem verum etiam ornatum ubique spectant, quatenus bonum eatenus et pulchrum spectare videntur.

6 Denique si quatenus unumquodque est fitque bonum atque pulchrum, eatenus et sibi et aliis est evaditque amabile, merito coniicimus ipsum bonum pulchrumque primum a se ipso prorsus amari. Ex ipso autem sui ipsius amore immensam efficaciam possidente tum necessario inextimabile quiddam in semetipso prodit,

has not achieved the new and gracious light of understanding, as Plotinus says, does not yet have God within,[210] and he who does not love God ardently certainly has not yet acquired the intelligible light itself.

Moreover, the sun's ray is obviously the efficient and final cause of the motions of plants. For its innate heat ensures that they are moved, and as soon as they are moved, they turn toward the light as to their end. Similarly, the Good and the Beautiful, as the efficient cause, gives the capability to all of being moved and of striving with all their might toward that which is in harmony with them. And as the end cause, it envelops individual things with a certain grace and through this grace they may attract those desiring them. 4

But because it [the Good and the Beautiful] is the first lover and beloved, and the first love, all things derive from it the capacity to love and to be loved. All loves proceed from it, loves that are of four kinds: (1) the love that moves those higher to provide for things lower and to do so out of kindness; (2) the love recalling things lower so they may attain the power and likeness of things higher; (3) the love of those which are in the same species or the same class or order for mutual sharing among themselves by way of converting, giving, and teaching; and (4) the love of each single thing for preserving itself as best it can. Then indeed, while all things do whatever they do for the sake of some end and good, in desiring individual goods, they desire the Good itself. But because they everywhere look not only to what is apt or fit but also to adornment, they seem to look to the beautiful as much as they look to the good. 5

Finally, if, insofar as every single thing is and is made good and beautiful, it is and becomes lovable to itself and to others, then we may justly suppose that the prime Good and Beautiful itself is utterly loved by itself.[211] But from the love of itself, which has an infinite capability, it necessarily produces something of infinite 6

tum pro arbitrio multiformes extra resultant divinitatis imagines, id est rerum omnium species. Que quidem quo amore inde fiunt, eodem moventur perficiunturque et servantur atque convertuntur.

: CXII :

Dionysius: Idem.

1 Ipsum ergo pulchrum atque bonum est omnibus appetibile, amabile, diligendum. Rursus propter ipsum eiusque gratia inferiora quidem amant superiora, se ad illa videlicet convertendo; que vero in eodem ordine sunt communicando invicem consortia diligunt; sed prestantiora inferiora diligunt providendo, et singula semetipsa se videlicet continendo. Cuncta denique quicquid agunt atque volunt, boni pulchrique desiderio faciunt atque volunt.

2 Audebit et hoc vera ratio dicere: ipsam omnium causam propter bonitatis exuberantiam omnia amare, omnia facere, omnia perficere, continere, convertere. Est profecto divinus amor bonus boni propter bonum; ipse enim amor beneficus rerum auctor, cum antea in bono prorsus exuberaret, non permisit ipsum sine germine in se manere, sed ad agendum movit per excessum omnium genitorem.

worth within itself. Then by its free choice the multiform images of its divinity reverberate outside [itself], that is, the species of all things. The love that made them is the very same love by which they are moved, perfected, preserved, and converted.

: CXII :

Dionysius: The same.

Thus the Beautiful and Good is desirable to all, and is lovable and meet to be prized. Again, on account of it and for its sake lower things love higher, turning themselves back toward them. But those which are in the same order, sharing together, love things in accord with themselves. But more outstanding things love lower things by providing for them; and individual things love themselves by sustaining themselves. Finally, whatever they do and wish to do, all things do them and wish to do them out of desire for the Good and the Beautiful. 1

True reason will venture to say this: that the cause of all, on account of its abundance of goodness, loves all, fashions all, perfects all, contains them, and converts them. Certainly, the divine love of the Good is good on account of the Good. For love itself, the beneficent author of things, in that it was flowing over in abundance beforehand in the Good, did not permit itself to remain in itself without [producing] a seed; but it moved the Creator of all to create through [His] superabundance. 2

: CXIII :

Dionysius:[226]
De nomine amoris,
et quod intentionem loquentis
potius quam verba debemus perpendere.

Nemo vero nos arbitretur preter sacrarum litterarum auctoritatem amoris nomen colere. Est enim irrationabile, ut reor, atque absurdum non vim ipsam instituti spectare, sed dictionibus inherere. Neque vero hoc est hominum divina volentium intelligere, sed sonos dumtaxat nudos aucupantium, eosque tantum ad aures observantium, interiora nequaquam penetraturos,[227] neque nosse volentium quid potissimum talis significet dictio et quemadmodum deceat eam per alia tantundem valentia et apertiora verba nonnunquam exponere. Curiose namque versantur in elementis et lineis intellectu carentibus et syllabis dicitionibusque cognitionis expertibus, neque ad intellectualem vim anime penetrantibus, sed extrinsecus circum labia auresque sonantibus, perinde ac si non liceat quaternarium numerum exprimere per bis[228] duo, figuramque rectilineam per figuram[229] lineas directas habentem interpretari, sive matriam per patriam declarare, vel aliud quodvis[230] eorum que in pluribus orationis partibus tantundem significant.

: CXIII :

Dionysius:
On love's name;
and that we should weigh the intention
of the speaker rather than the words.

But nobody should think that we cultivate love's name over and beyond the authority of sacred Scripture. For I think it irrational and absurd not to look to the power itself of the intention but only to cling to the words. Such clinging is symptomatic not of men wanting to understand matters divine, but of men trying to catch only bare sounds; of men hearing only with their ears, not striving to penetrate to the meanings within, not wanting to know what such speech most signifies and how one ought to expound it at times by other words that are equally powerful and more revealing. For they are only concerned in their curiosity about the [superficial verbal] elements and features, those lacking intellectual meaning, and about syllables and words having no part in cognition, and about words never penetrating to the soul's intellectual power, but sounding externally on lips and ears. It is exactly as if one were not permitted to express the number four by two times two, or to interpret a rectilinear shape via a shape having straight lines, or to declare the motherland through the fatherland, or [to discuss] anything else you will of those factors in the many parts of [a] speech which are indeed of significance.

: CXIV :

Marsilius:
Quomodo imaginatio potest aliquid sine sensu,
ratio sine imaginatione,
intellectus absque ratione,
denique habitus animi Deo conformis potest,
vacante iam intelligentia, Deo frui.

1 Quemadmodum sensus interior, id est imaginatio, circa imaginanda se versat etiam ubi sensus exterior externum nihil in presentia sentit, sic et ratio circa excogitanda potest argumentari nonnunquam imaginatione vacante, multoque magis altior intellectus simpliciora quedam simpliciter intueri non argumentante ulterius ratione.

2 Similiter et unitas, apex anime prestantior intellectu cum Deo congruens intelligibile quodlibet excedente, frui Deo quandoque potest, intelligentia videlicet ad hoc interim non agente—frui, inquam, per actum quendam cognitione qualibet vel excelsa sublimiorem. Lumen namque divinum, re qualibet cognoscenda superius, attingi non potest nisi per actum cognitione quavis excelsiorem, ideoque oculos non habentem; oculus enim ad cognitionem necessario pertinet.

: CXIV :

Marsilio:
How the imagination can do something without the sense, the reason without the imagination, the intellect without the reason, and finally how the rational soul's habit in conforming to God can, with the understanding now empty, enjoy God.

Just as the inner sense, that is, the imagination, concerns itself with things to imagine, even when the external sense perceives nothing in the present, so the reason can sometimes argue about things we should think about when the imagination is empty. To a still greater degree is the higher intellect able to gaze in a simple way at simpler things when the reason is no longer arguing. 1

Similarly, the unity, the soul's crown, being more outstanding than the intellect and in harmony with God who exceeds anything intelligible, can some day enjoy God, when the understanding, that is, does not strive in the meantime for this intelligible — enjoy, I say, through an act more sublime than any cognition, however lofty.[212] For the divine light, higher than anything that can be known, cannot be attained except through an act higher than any knowing, an act therefore without eyes; for the eye necessarily pertains to knowing. 2

: CXV :

Dionysius:
Verbis utimur propter sensum.
Sensus cum sensibilibus superflui sunt,
quando intellectus intelligibilia penetravit;
superflua[231] *et intelligentia, quando animus*
cum Deo charitate coniungitur.

1 Decet autem recta ratione considerare nos elementis, syllabis, dictionibus, scripturis, sermonibus uti sensuum gratia. Quapropter ubi noster animus intellectualibus actionibus ad intelligibilia se iam confert, superflui sunt cum rebus sensibilibus sensus, quemadmodum et vires intellectuales supervacue sunt cum animus, divinam indutus speciem per ignotam unionem, luminis inaccessibilis radios iam[232] attingit perceptionibus quibusdam expertibus oculorum.

2 Quando vero mens per sensibilia studet ad contemplativas intelligentias provocari, illi pre ceteris sensuum usus eligendi sunt qui ad intelligenda planius introducunt apertioresque sermones et que inter visibilia videntur expressiora. Nisi enim expressa fuerint que sensibus occurrunt, ne ipsi quidem sensus sensibilia menti rite porrigere poterunt.

: CXV :

Dionysius: We use words because of our senses. [But] the senses along with sensibles are superfluous when intellect has penetrated intelligibles. And understanding is superfluous when the rational soul is joined with God in love.

It behooves us with right reason to consider that we use verbal elements,[213] syllables, speeches, and writings, for the sake of our senses. Therefore, when our rational soul betakes itself, by way now of intellectual actions, to the intelligibles, then the senses, along with the sensibles, are made superfluous. Similarly, the intellectual powers are rendered superfluous when the rational soul, having donned a divine species in an union beyond our knowing, now attains to the rays of inaccessible light by a kind of perception having nothing to do with eyes. 1

But when the mind studies through sensibles to be moved to feats of contemplative understanding, then those uses of the senses must be exclusively chosen which introduce us more explicitly to what must be understood, to more accessible discourses, and, among visible things, to those which are seen as more distinct. For unless the things which strike the senses have been made distinct, the senses themselves can not even offer sensibles correctly to the mind. 2

: CXVI :

Marsilius:[233]

1 Sicut pulchritudo ad humanam speciem pertinens nec in ullo hominum nec semel in cunctis integra reperitur, sed ex cunctis tandem per mentem nostram tota colligitur, sic generalis ipsa rerum omnium pulchritudo nec in aliqua formarum specie nec cunctis inest, sed in uno divine mentis sapientieque splendore (que prima pulchritudo est) velut fonte comprehenditur.

2 Primam enim pulchritudinem Plato Dionysiusque definiunt intelligentie prime lucem ideis formarum pulchritudinumque omnium coruscantem; ab hac intellectus quilibet procreatus est ad eam denique contuendam. Quisquis igitur ad hanc toto mentis ardore convertitur, unitum habet amorem; omnes enim formas amat consequiturque[234] in una. Qui vero extra illam ad pulchritudinem aliquam se divertit, amore statim in multa dividitur. Cum enim absolutam pulchritudinem naturaliter optet neque hanc inveniat usquam, vel in singulis vel in cunctis, merito passim sitibundus oberrat per varia solicitus, quotidie queritans quod in uno primoque semel fuerat perquirendum.

: CXVI :

Marsilio:

Just as beauty pertaining to the human species is not wholly found in any one human being, nor at once in all of them, but via our mind is garnered at length as a whole from all mankind, so the general beauty itself of all things is present neither in any one species of forms nor in all of the species, but is embraced in the one splendor of the divine mind and wisdom, which is the prime beauty, as in a fountain. 1

For Plato and Dionysius define prime beauty as the light of the prime understanding sparkling in the Ideas of all the forms and beauties. From this beauty each intellect is created for contemplating it at last. So whoever is converted to this beauty with his mind's whole ardor has a unified love; for he loves and pursues all the forms in the one beauty.[214] But he who turns himself away toward some individual beauty outside that prime beauty, is immediately divided by that [new] love into many. For, since he naturally chooses absolute beauty and never finds it anywhere, either in individuals or in all things, he wanders everywhere, and justly so, thirsting and anxiously searching through different things, and daily bemoaning what he should have sought for, once and for all, in the One and the First. 2

: CXVII :

Dionysius:
Nomine amoris utimur in divinis tum quia efficacius illa significat, tum etiam ut vulgarem huius nominis abusum auferamus.

1 Ceterum ne hec dicere videamur sacra eloquia pervertentes, audiant illa qui in appellationem amoris calumniantur: 'Ama illam,' inquit, 'et servabit te.' 'Valla te illa atque extollet te. Honora illam ut te complectatur,' et quotcumque alia a theologis ratione quadam amatoria celebrantur.

2 Iam vero quibusdam ex nostris sacrorum tractatoribus visum est amoris nomen dilectionis charitatisve nomine divinius esse: scribit enim et divinus Ignatius: 'Meus amor crucifixus est,' atque in ipsis instructionibus ad sacra ducentibus quendam (id est Philonem) de divina sapientia dicentem audies: 'Amator equidem forme illius sum effectus.'

3 Quamobrem nomen hoc amoris minime formidemus neque nos ulla perturbet oratio ab hac appellatione deterrens. Mihi sane videntur theologi commune quidem arbitrari dilectionis amorisque nomen, sed propterea divinis amorem ipsum verum potius assignare ut istiusmodi hominum absurdam presumptionem feriant.[235]

4 Cum enim verus amor non solum a nobis, sed etiam a divinis eloquiis quemadmodum divinitatem decet celebretur, vulgus tamen uniforme illud appellationis amatorie capere minime potens suo quodam more[236] ad particularem corporeumque atque divisum

: CXVII :

Dionysius:
We use love's name in matters divine both because it signifies these matters more effectively, and also that we might do away with the vulgar abuse of love's name.

But lest we seem to say things perverting sacred Scripture, may 1
those who bear false witness against the name of love give ear to the following: "Love her [Wisdom]," Scripture says, "and she will minister to you,"[215] "Fortify yourself with her and she will raise you. Honor her so that she might embrace you."[216] And one could adduce many other celebrated quotations by the theologians that have an amatory principle in them.

But with certain of our writers about things sacred it seems 2
that the designation "love" is more divine even than "dilection"[217] or "charity." For the divine Ignatius writes: "My love has been crucified."[218] And in the instructions themselves that guide us to things sacred, you will hear a certain man, that is, Philo, speaking about the divine wisdom: "I was made a lover of her form."[219]

Wherefore we should not dread at all this designation "love." 3
Nor should any discourse perturb us and frighten us away from using that appellation. Theologians seem to me to think that "dilection" and "love" designate the same thing. Therefore, in order to strike down the absurd presumption of its detractors, they would rather assign true love itself to things divine.

But true love is celebrated not only by us but also by the divine 4
Scriptures as befits the Divinity, and yet the crowd, being unable to grasp the uniform meaning behind love's naming, has fallen in its own manner into the particular, corporeal, and divided love,

amorem est prolapsum, qui profecto non est verus amor, sed imago quedam vel potius ab amore vero ruina — unitas enim ipsa divini uniusque amoris a vulgari multitudine comprehendi non potest — quamobrem quod multis nomen videtur ingratius, in divina sapientia ponitur ad illos erigendos atque provehendos in amoris ipsius veri notitiam, atque ut inde minus amoris appellationi suscenseant.

5 Inter nos autem, ubi abiectiores ingenio non nihil obscenum suspicari nonnunquam possint, vocabulo quod videatur honestius scriptura utens inquit: 'cecidit dilectio tua super me sicut dilectio mulierum.'

: CXVIII :

Marsilius:
Virtus amoris est unire duo in uno quodam tertio, copulare invicem, commiscere ad novum aliquid inde conflandum.

1 Tria consideravimus[237] in sole: primo quidem naturam; secundo lucem naturalem; tertio in luce naturali virtutem calefactoriam. Tria ferme similiter cogitamus in Deo: nam in bonitate divina (id est potestate fecunda) intelligentie lucem tanquam pulchritudinem eius; in hac rursus amorem, quasi calorem. Hic igitur amor in bono pulchroque consistens diligit omnia non aliunde pendens, sed boni pulchrique sui propagandi, communicandi, imitandi gratia. Hinc quoque rebus inde creatis accensus est amor bonum pulchrumque desiderans, sed bonum quidem suaviter, pulchrum vero admodum vehementer.

which is certainly not true love, but a certain image [of it], or rather a precipitous fall from true love (since the unity itself of the one divine love cannot be comprehended by the vulgar many). Since this is so, that name, which seems unpalatable to the many, is used in divine wisdom for lifting and conveying men to the knowledge of true love itself, and to ensure they are less incensed at the name of love.

But among us, when those who have a more contemptible intel- 5
ligence are able to suspect at times something obscene, Scripture says, using the word [*dilectio*] which seems more honorable: "Your loving favor (*dilectio*) has fallen upon me as the love (*dilectio*) of women."[220]

: CXVIII :

Marsilio:
Love's power is to unite two things into a unitary third, to join together, and to mingle in order to make some new thing from the mingling.

In the sun we considered three aspects: first its nature, second its 1
natural light, third the power in this natural light to heat. In much the same way we think about three aspects in God. For in the divine goodness, that is, in His abundant power, is the light of understanding as His beauty; and in His beauty again is His love as the [divine] heat. So this love existing in Him, the Good and the Beautiful, loves all: the love does not depend on anything else but is there for the sake of propagating, sharing, and imitating the good and the beautiful in Him. Hence in things created from this love is ignited a love desiring the good and the beautiful, but the good more gently, the beautiful much more vehemently.

2 Dicitur autem amor unire, connectere, commiscere: unire quidem duo quedam in uno quodam tertio utriusque communi; quatenus enim animi duo amant[238] idem ipsum divinum bonum pulchrumque, quod est ipsa unitas, in hoc ipso sunt unum. Rursus quantum alter diligit alterum invicem connectuntur, id est voluntate et actione mutua copulantur; denique mirifice commiscentur.

3 Neque nunc quidem de coitu venereo loquimur, sed de naturali quodam et occulto mirabilique effectu, qui ex mutuo amantium affectu sepius frequentato quandoque contingit. Sepe enim hinc mores, ingenia, nature miscentur, ut et alter in his tribus alterum imitetur et ex propinquo utriusque congressu novus et inopinatus confletur effectus, ad hunc ipsum clam eorum spiritu conferente, quemadmodum fieri solet ex coitu planetarum. Amor tandem est vinculum universi, siquidem inferiora convertit ad superiora atque vicissim et equalia invicem.

: CXIX :

Dionysius:
Idem.

Apud illos autem qui divina recte audiunt nomen dilectionis amorisque a sacris theologis in eadem potentia ponitur ubi exprimere divina conantur. Est autem hec ipsa virtus quedam unifica et connectens mirificeque commiscens, in ipso quidem pulchro bonoque propter pulchrum bonumque primo consistens, deinde vero ex pulchro bonoque propter pulchrum atque bonum foras

But love is said to unite, to join, to mingle: [first] to unite two things into some one third thing common to both of them; for insofar as two rational souls love the same divine good and beautiful thing, which is unity itself, [then] in this they are united. Again, insofar as the one rational soul cherishes the other, they are joined together, that is, they are joined by mutual will and action. Finally, they are mingled in a wonderful way. 2

We speak now not about sexual coitus but about the natural, hidden, and marvelous effect which derives at some point from the mutual feeling of lovers who meet very often. For our customary behavior, our native wits, and our natures are often commingled, so that one person imitates the other with regard to these three; and from the close association of each, a new and unexpected effect is produced with the spirit of them both secretly contributing to this, just as it customarily happens with the conjunctions of the planets. Finally, love is the bond of the universe, since it returns lower things to higher and the reverse, and brings equals together. 3

: CXIX :

Dionysius: The same.

But with those who rightly pay heed to matters divine, the designations "dilection" and "love" are located in the same power by the sacred theologians, when they strive to talk about such matters. But this power is itself a unifying, joining, and wondrously mingling power, existing first within the Beautiful and the Good, and existing on account of the Beautiful and the Good; but then shining out from the Beautiful and the Good on account of the Beautiful and the Good. There indeed it contains the things which are

emicans, ubi sane que sunt eiusdem ordinis alterna continet communione, priora vero ad inferiorum providentiam movet, inferiora denique conversione quadam superioribus alligat.

: CXX :

Marsilius:
Amor impellit amantem in amatum se transferre. Motionumque et actionum omnium est principium.

1 Cognitio et amor hoc inter se maxime differunt, quod rem quidem externam cognoscimus pro ratione forme imaginisque rei quam intus ipsi iam habemus, atque ad hanc in aciem mentis intendimus. Amamus autem quod bonum iam iudicavimus pro natura ipsius boni eaque, qualis in se ipsa est frui prorsus appetimus. Quamobrem amor dicitur in amante extasim facere, id est excessum quendam quo quasi extra se traducitur in amatum. Cum igitur cognoscendo quidem quasi rem cognitam ad nos trahamus, amando vero vicissim trahamur[239] videlicet nos ad ipsam, nimirum inferiora quidem satius est cognoscere quam amare, superiora vero prestat amare quam nosse.

2 Quod igitur physici tradunt motus actionesque omnes ab inclinatione sive naturaliter insita, sive[240] quomodovis infusa procedere, qua cessante desinit statim motus simul et actio, possumus amori prorsus accommodare; inclinatio enim eiusmodi nihil aliud est

of the same order [i.e., are equal in metaphysical rank] in alternate communion; but it moves those that are prior to provide for those that come later; and finally it unites things lower in a kind of conversion to things higher.

: CXX :

Marsilio:
Love impels the lover to transfer himself into the beloved. It is the principle of all motions and actions.

Knowledge and love differ most among themselves in that we know an external thing by reason of the thing's form and image that we already have within. And we first concentrate our attention on this [form]. But we love what we have already judged to be good by virtue of the nature of the Good itself, and we desire utterly to enjoy that nature as it is in itself. Wherefore love is said to cause ecstasy in the lover, that is, a certain excess by which he is led out of himself as it were into the beloved. Since in understanding we attract to ourselves as it were the thing known, but in loving we ourselves are drawn in turn toward it, certainly it is more satisfactory to become acquainted with lower things than to love them, but it is better to love higher things than to know them.[221] 1

Therefore, because the natural philosophers say that all motions and actions proceed by an inclination (whether naturally instilled or infused in some way or other), and that when this inclination ceases, the motion along too with the action immediately ceases, we can wholly accommodate [this inclination] to love. For such an 2

quam amor. Amor igitur actionum omnium est principium, ut et superiora inferioribus abunde provideant, et inferiora superioribus se tota devoveant, et equalia affectu quodam atque commertio se invicem complectantur.

: CXXI :

Dionysius:
Idem.

1 Preterea divinus amor excessum efficit dum amantes sui iuris esse non sinit, sed amatorum iubet existere. Idque declarant omnia: nempe superiora inferiorum providentie sese dedunt; equalia vero conservationi mutue mancipare se solent; inferiora denique divine cuidam ad suprema conversioni se ipsa devovent.

2 Quapropter et Paulus ille magnus divino amore iam occupatus traductoriaque amoris huius virtute comprehensus, ore divinitus afflato proclamat: 'Vivo iam non ego, vivit autem in me Christus,' tanquam verus[241] amator atque in Deo, ut inquit, extra se positus vivensque iam vitam non suam sed amatoriam, tanquam prorsus amabilem.

inclination is nothing other than love. Love therefore is the principle of all actions, so that higher things may abundantly provide for lower things and lower things totally dedicate themselves to higher, and equals, with a certain feeling and a mutual sharing of emotion, in turn embrace each other.

: CXXI :

Dionysius:
The same.

Moreover, divine love causes ecstasy when it does not permit lov- 1
ers to be under their own rule, but orders them to exist for their beloveds. And all things declare this. Higher things devote themselves to the providence of lower things. Equal things customarily deliver themselves over to mutual preservation. Lower things, lastly, devote themselves to a divine conversion toward things higher.

Wherefore Paul, that great man, already possessed by divine 2
love and seized by the transformative power of this love, with a mouth divinely inspired, proclaims, "I no longer live, but Christ lives in me"[222] as a true lover existing in God, as he says, and being placed outside himself and living now, not his own life, but the life of love, as someone who is totally lovable.

: CXXII :

Marsilius: Deus amore facit omnia, adest omnibus ac providet.

1 Sol, visibilis imago Dei, neque per occultam naturam neque per manifestam lucem naturalia generat, nisi accesserit calefactoria virtus et motio calorem proferens. Similiter Deus neque nature neque intelligentie necessitate res procreat, sed potius voluntatis actu et amante propriam bonitatem et sic eligente communicationem eius in procreando. Amor ergo divinus rerum omnium est principium. Quoniam vero hic amor a bonitate pulchritudineque prima sumens exordium revertitur in eandem, merito semper amor omnis ad bonum pulchrumque dirigitur.

2 Etsi ad summam Dei simplicitatem pertinet ut in se ipso consistens sit ab omnibus mirabiliter segregatus, tamen, propter beneficum amorem bonitatis proprie diffundende, quasi procedit ex se in omnia, adest omnibus presentissimus, diligentissime providet. Quoniam vero sua quisque amat, ac maxime Dei sunt omnia, nimirum amans omnia plurimum providet omnibus.

3 Videtur quoque zelotes: nam more zelotum non leviter diligit, sed vehementer amat et explorat accuratissime singula; vult etiam quasi zelotes ita singulariter amare atque redamari, ut solus ipse sua re vera amare putandus sit, solus re vera sit amandus, zeloque pre ceteris observandus.

: CXXII :

Marsilio: God makes all things with love. He is present to and provides for all.

The sun, the visible image of God, either through its hidden nature or through its manifest light, does not generate natural things until [its] heating power and heat-carrying motion have been brought to bear. Similarly, God procreates things by the necessity neither of [His] nature nor of [His] understanding, but rather by the act of [His] will and by loving His own goodness; and thus by choosing to communicate it in procreating. Hence divine love is the principle of all things. But since this love, in taking its beginning from the first goodness and beauty, is brought back to the same, then justly all love is always directed to the Good and the Beautiful. 1

Although it pertains to God's highest simplicity that in consisting in Himself He is marvelously separate from all things, yet, on account of the beneficent love that moves Him to pour forth His own goodness (proceeding out of Himself as it were into all things), He is most present to all; and with greatest diligence He provides for all. Since each person loves his own, however, but all things are totally God's own, certainly in loving all things God most provides for all. 2

God seems also a zealot.[223] For in the manner of zealots He does not cherish mildly: rather He loves with vehemence and puts individuals to the test with exacting care. Also like a zealous lover, He wants in a singular manner so to love and to be loved again that He alone should be thought to truly love His own, alone should truly be loved and cared for with preemptory zeal. 3

4 Deus denique non, sicut nos, que vult ideo vult quoniam ipsa in se sint bona, sed contra, quia vult ipse sunt bona; quoniam amat sunt amanda. Item quasi[242] zelotes observanter amat, ne quando deficiant. Preterea quoniam ita curat hec (ut ita dixerim) sunt zelanda, id est cura quadam studioque sunt digna. Inter hec amorem esse magico cuidam illicio ductuique vel raptui similem ex Dionysii verbis percipere licet, quod in *Symposio* disputamus.

: CXXIII :

Dionysius:
Beneficus[243] *amor quasi Deum allicit*
ut extra se per omnia diffundatur,
et zelo quodam omnia curet.

1 Audendum quoque id insuper pro veritate loqui: ipsum etiam omnium auctorem pulchro bonoque amore omnium propter bonitatis amatorie vehementiam extra se prodire, dum providet omnibus; atque bonitate et dilectione et amore quasi mulcetur, atque ex illo statu, quo super omnia exstat ab omnibus segregatus, ad id profecto ut in omnibus sit deducitur, per supersubstantialem[244] videlicet virtutem illam, que traducit quidem ipsum interim a se ipso nusquam digredientem.

Finally, God does not, like us, will the things that He wills because the things in themselves are good, but to the contrary, because He wills, the things themselves are good. Because He loves them, things should be loved. Again, like a zealot, He loves [things] by caring for their needs, lest they ever want. Moreover, because He so cares for them, these things must become (so to speak) the object of zeal, become worthy, that is, of a particular care and study. In these matters we are allowed to perceive from Dionysius' words that love is like some magical enticement, inducement, or rapture. We discuss this in the *Symposium* commentary.[224] 4

: CXXIII :

Dionysius:
God is so moved by beneficent love as it were that He diffuses Himself outside Himself through all things and cares for all with a kind of zeal.

One must venture to speak this, moreover, for the truth's sake [that] the Author Himself of all, out of a good and beautiful love of all [and] on account of the vehemence of His amatory goodness, proceeds out of Himself when He provides for all. And He is delighted as it were by goodness, dilection, and love; and from that state in which He exists above and apart from all, He is led to the condition of being in all, by way, that is, of that supersubstantial power which transports Him even as He nowhere departs from Himself. 1

2 Quamobrem divinarum rerum periti zelotem illum appellaverunt, ut amore benigno erga omnia prorsus exuberantem excitantemque[245] ad amatorii desiderii sui zelum, desideriumque ipsum declarantem zelo dignum, quo etiam que desiderabilia ipsi sunt promerentur et zelum, atque ipse ad illa que providet zelo quodam videtur affectus.

3 Denique ipsum quod est amabile ipseque amor pulchri bonique est, et in pulchro bonoque priorem habet sedem et existit efficiturque propter pulchrum atque bonum.

: CXXIV :

Marsilius:

Qua ratione Deus appelletur amor, qua rursus amabilis, et quomodo amor tum in Deo, tum extra sit motus aliquis circularis.

1 Principium universi appellatur diligibile quidem quia bonum, amabile vero quia pulchrum; pulchritudo enim acrius quam bonitas concitat appetitum. Quamobrem ad bonitatem spectat temperata dilectio, ad pulchritudinem pertinet amor nesciens tenere modum. Preterea Deus appellatur amor tum quoniam amorem in omnibus procreat, sicut a Peripateticis nominatur in sole calor quoniam caloris est causa; tum etiam quia se ipsum amat. Est

Wherefore those who are experts in matters divine have called Him a zealous God[225] in that He flows over absolutely with benign love toward all things, rousing them to the zeal of amatory desire [for Him] and declaring that desire itself deserving of zeal, to the point that even the [lower] things which are desirable to Him merit His zeal too; and He Himself seems moved by a certain zeal for the things which He provides for. 2

Finally, what is lovable, along with love itself, belongs to the Beautiful and the Good, and has its first seat in the Beautiful and the Good, and exists and is made on account of the Beautiful and the Good. 3

: CXXIV :

Marsilio:
The reason why God can be called love, and why lovable. And in what way love, whether it is within God or without, is a circular motion.

The universe's principle is called deserving of love (*diligibile*) because good, but lovable (*amabile*) because beautiful. For beauty more keenly than goodness awakens desire. Wherefore tempered dilection (*dilectio*) looks to goodness, love (*amor*) in its ardor pertains to beauty and does not know how to hold to the mean. Moreover, God is called love, both because He creates love in all things (just as heat is said by the Aristotelians to be in the sun because it is the cause of heat), and because He loves Himself. 1

igitur penes Deum amans, amor, amatum. Qua quidem ratione amabile movet, qua vero amans quasi movetur, qua denique se ipsum amans quodammodo a se ipso movetur, qua rursum amor est existit et motus — motus, inquam, quo Deus se amando quasi circulo revolvitur in se ipsum.

2 Profecto nisi consideraremus in Deo distinctionem[246] eiusmodi qua se contemplatur et amat interim contemplando, ultra unitatem nature divine nullam ibi distinctionem inveniremus. Amor igitur ille contemplativus et expressio sui dicitur, et videtur in multitudinem quandam ab eximia unitate procedere, simplicitatem tamen interea conservare: permanet enim semper in eadem unitate nature. Appellatur et actio per se mobilis, per se operans: non enim aliunde dependet quam ab intima sui forma.

3 Primus amor penes primum bonum ex ipso in ipsum[247] circulariter se revolvens, hoc suo quasi motu calorem accendit omnibus amatorium in orbem similiter revolutum. Amor enim ubique a primo bono tanquam principio prodit, item in bono unicuique proprio sedem habet, rursus ad bonum uniuscuiusque suum tanquam ad finem propinquiorem aspicit, denique ad primum omnibus commune bonum tanquam ad ultimum finem prospicit cunctis communiter expetendum. Motus igitur amatorius propter actum[248] orbicularem principio fineque carentem infiniti meruit cognomentum.

Therefore, with God there is loving, love itself, and the beloved. This is the reason why what is lovable moves [another], and why the lover as it were is moved, and why loving oneself is being moved in a way by oneself; and why again that love exists and motion exists, the motion, I say, by which God, in loving Himself, is returned as it were in a circle back to Himself.

Certainly, unless we were to consider in God the distinction 2 wherein He contemplates Himself and yet loves in that contemplation, we would find no distinction there beyond the unity of the divine nature. Therefore love—that contemplative love—is called the unfolding or expression of Himself; and from sublime unity it seems to proceed into a many, and yet to preserve its simplicity meanwhile; for it remains always in the same unity of [its] nature. It is also called the action which is mobile of itself and operates through itself; for it depends on nothing else than on the inner form of itself.

The first love in the first Good comes from itself and in the 3 manner of a circle returns to itself. With this its motion as it were, love ignites an amatory heat in all, a heat that has similarly turned in a circle. For love proceeds everywhere from the first Good as from its principle; next it has its seat in the good proper to each single thing; again, it looks to the good of each single thing as to its nearer end; and finally it looks to the first Good common to all as to its ultimate end—the Good that must be commonly sought by all. Therefore amatory motion, by way of its circular act, an act lacking beginning and end, deserves the name "the infinite."

: CXXV :

Dionysius:
Idem.

1 Quid vero theologi sibi volunt cum aliquando quidem Deum amorem dilectionemque vocant, aliquando vero amabilem atque diligibilem nominant? Sane alterius quidem causa est ac veluti productor et genitor, alterum vero ipse Deus existit; rursus altero quidem movetur, altero vero movet, quippe cum ipse sui sibique[249] sit provector et motor. Hac utique ratione diligibilem ipsum nominant et amabilem tanquam pulchrum atque bonum. Amorem rursus dilectionemque cognominant propter virtutem eius moventem provehentemque ad se ipsum, quippe cum solum id sit per se ipsum pulchrum atque bonum. Item propter quandam sui ipsius per se ipsum expressionem eminentissimeque unitatis benignam processionem motumque amatorium simplicem, se moventem, per se operantem, precedentem quidem in ipso bono atque ex ipso per omnia procedentem, rursumque ad bonum se reflectentem.

2 In quo sane munus suum fine principioque carens precipue divinus amor ostendit tanquam circulus aliquis sempiternus propter ipsum bonum, ex bono, in bono, ad bonum revolutione quadam nequaquam errante se glomerans, et in eodem atque secundum idem progrediens semper et manens et denique restitutus. Hec inclitus quoque noster in sacris litteris institutor divine admodum in amatoriis hymnis exposuit; quos profecto commemorare fas est et tanquam sacrum quoddam caput apponere nostro de amore sermoni.

: CXXV :

Dionysius:
The same.

But what do the theologians mean when sometimes they call God "love" (*amor*) or "dilection" (*dilectio*),[226] but at other times "lovable" (*amabilis*) or "deserving of love" (*diligibilis*). Indeed God is the cause of the one as author and father, but He exists Himself as the other. Again, in the one He is moved, in the other He moves, since He Himself is the bearer and mover of Himself and for Himself. For this reason they say He is deserving of love, and is lovable being both beautiful and good. Again, they call Him both love and dilection on account of His power to move and to draw to Himself, since only this is beautiful and good in itself. It is also on account of a sort of expression of Himself through Himself, namely, the benign procession of His highest unity, and the simple loving motion that moves itself, operating through itself, advancing in the good, proceeding from the good through all things, and then turning itself back toward the good. 1

It is in the good indeed that divine love especially reveals its gift as a gift without end or beginning; as a sempiternal circle on account of the good, from the good, into the good, and toward the good; as forming itself into a sphere in a never-erring revolution; as always advancing in the same and according to the same, and [yet] remaining at rest; and finally as having been restored. [Hierotheus] our illustrious instructor in sacred letters also expounded these matters most divinely in amatory hymns—hymns it is lawful to recall here and to place as a sacred crown upon our speech on love. 2

: CXXVI :

Marsilius:
Amores quinque:
primus in Deo, secundus in angelo,
tertius in intellectu anime, quartus in parte
anime inferiore, quintus in natura.

1 Ubi Dionysius una cum Hierotheo preceptore amorem vim appellat, intellige motum intimum efficacemque ad uniendum et commiscendum. Quid autem sit unire, connectere, commiscere, in superioribus exposuimus. Amores vero quinque in presentia numerat: primum quidem divinum, quo se ipsum Deus amat amatque alia se amando: ex hoc primo amore, ex quo accenduntur omnes, factum est ut unumquodque quodammodo prius se ipsum quam cetera diligat; secundum amorem in angelo se amante Deumque et reliqua; tertium in parte anime nostre intellectuali intelligibilia divinaque venerante; quartum in parte animali ad discursionem et imaginationem sensumque pertinente, quo vel sensibilia simpliciter affectantur vel intelligibilia sensibiliter diliguntur.

2 Quintum in natura, id est vel in potentia uniuscuiusque anime vegetali, vel in certa quadam cuiuslibet corporis qualitate ubique consentanea quedam pro viribus asciscente. Hinc ortus est et famelicus amor ad solidum et sitibundus ad liquidum; amor in foliis et floribus ad calorem, in radicibus ad humorem, in levibus ad circumferentiam, in gravibus ad mundi centrum, in paleis ad succinum, in magnete ad ferrum, in igne ad humorem aerium atque

: CCXVI :

Marsilio: The five loves: the first is in God, the second in the angel, the third in the soul's intellect, the fourth in the soul's lower part, and the fifth in nature.

1 When Dionysius, in following his teacher Hierotheus, refers to "power," understand him to mean the inner effective motion for uniting and mingling. Earlier we explained what it is to unite, to join, to mingle.[227] But in the present [chapter] Dionysius numbers five loves. The first is the divine love by which God loves Himself and loves others in loving Himself.[228] From this first love, from which all [loves] are ignited, it follows that every single thing in a way delights in itself before delighting in others. The second love is in the angel loving itself and God and the rest of creation. The third is in our soul's intellectual part venerating matters intelligible and divine. The fourth is in the animate part, the part pertaining to discursiveness, imagination, and sense, the love through which sensibles are simply desired or intelligibles are enjoyed in a sensuous way.

2 The fifth love is in nature, that is, either in the vegetal power of each single soul, or in a particular fixed quality of any body, a quality everywhere admitting things suitable to itself as best it can. Hence arose the hungry love for solid food and the thirsty love for liquid; and in leaves and flowers the love for heat, and in roots for sap; in things weightless the love for the [world's outer] circumference, and in things heavy the love for the world's center; in chaff [or straws] the love for amber, in the magnet for iron, and in the

pinguem; in qua quidem observatione Platonici magorum[250] machinas existimant adinventas. Mittamus magiam.

3 Denique, si amorem universo sustuleris, neque superiora inferioribus providebunt, neque inferiora se superioribus commendabunt, neque que eiusdem ordinis sunt communionem mutuam exercebunt.

: CXXVII :

Dionysius:
Hierothei sanctissimi ex amatoriis hymnis.

Amorem sive divinum sive angelicum sive intellectualem sive animalem sive naturalem dixerimus, vim quandam intelligamus[251] unificam atque commiscentem, superiora quidem moventem ad inferiorum providentiam, rursum que sunt eiusdem ordinis ad communionem mutuam adhortantem, inferiora tandem revocantem ut ad sublimia convertantur.

: CXXVIII :

Marsilius:
Amores omnes referuntur ad duos, duo ad unum.

Antequam amatorias vires que sunt complurime ad unum primumque amorem referat, omnes in capita duo, ritu Pythagoreo, colligit. Alie namque[252] amatorie vires sunt mundane, alie vero mundo superiores; mundane rursus gemine sunt: alie animales,

fire for airy and fatty greasiness, by observing which indeed the Platonists think that the magicians devised their contrivances. But let us leave aside magic.

Finally, if you subtract love from the universe, the higher will not provide for the lower, inferiors will not commend themselves to superiors, and those of the same order will not give themselves over to sharing with one another. 3

: CXXVII :

Dionysius:
From the amatory hymns of the most holy Hierotheus.

When we have said love is divine or angelic or intellectual or animate or natural, let us understand a certain power that is unifying and commingling; and that moves superiors to provide for inferiors; urges those that are of the same order to a mutual communion; and recalls inferiors so that they may return toward matters sublime.

: CXXVIII :

Marsilio:
All loves are referred to two loves; the two to one.

Before he refers the amatory powers which are many to one prime love, he collects all, in the Pythagorean manner, under two heads; for some of the amatory powers are worldly, but some are superior to the world. Again, the worldly powers are twin: some are

alie naturales. Superiores item mundo sunt gemine: alie quidem intellectuales humaneque, alie autem angelice sunt atque divine. Mundanis intellectuales presunt, intellectualibus autem angelice, angelicis tandem amor ipse divinus. Hic autem, in ipsa primi boni luce penes se micante mirabiliter intus accensus, mox quasi foras emicat variosque per varia spirat amores. Omnia denique passim amantia, in forma quavis amanda, primam consequenter amant formarum amorumque omnium principium atque finem.

: CXXIX :

Dionysius et Hierotheus: Eiusdem ex eisdem hymnis.

1 Hactenus multos amores ex uno pendentes disposuimus diximusque deinceps quales sint notiones viresque amorum tum mundanorum, tum mundo superiorum; quibus sane mundanis secundum designatam orationis intentionem presunt ordines ornatusque intellectualium intelligibiliumque amorum. Super eos autem exstant ipsi per se intelligibiles atque divini amorum ibi re vera pulchrorum, a nobisque pro viribus proprie sunt celebrati.

2 Nunc iterum resumentes omnes in unum et conglobatum amorem amorum omnium patrem, colligamus simul atque congregemus primo quidem ex multis in duas cogentes amatorias vires universales, quas quidem omnes continet regitque absoluta totius amoris causa penes principium omnia supereminens, ad quam contendit pro cuiusque natura universus rerum omnium amor.

animate, others natural. Likewise the powers higher than the world are twin: some are intellectual and human, others are angelic and divine. The intellectual powers are in charge of the mundane, the angelic in charge of the intellectual, and divine love itself is in charge finally of the angelic. But in the light of the first Good which shines throughout itself, this love, having been marvelously ignited within, straightway blazes without as it were and inspires various loves in various things. Finally, all things loving everywhere, whenever they love any form, they love in consequence the first form, the principle and end of all forms and all loves.

: CXXIX :

Dionysius and Hierotheus: On the same [subject] from the same hymns.

Thus far we have arranged many loves as dependent on one love; and we have then talked about the various notions and powers of loves, of mundane loves and super-mundane. Ruling over the mundane, indeed, according to the symbolic meaning of [Hierotheus'] speech, are the orders and ornaments of intellectual and intelligible loves. Above them in the beyond exist the intelligibles in themselves along with the divine [orders] of truly beautiful loves, those duly celebrated by us as best we can. 1

Now resuming all loves again into one encompassing love, the father of all loves, first let us gather and join together the many loves into two compelling amatory powers, into twin universal powers, that is, which the absolute cause of all love contains and rules over in its super-eminence and as sovereign over all in its possession as the principle. The universal love of all things, according to the nature of each, strives for this cause. 2

: CXXX :

Marsilius:
Vis amatoria ex primo bono,
luminis instar, per omnia profluit refluitque
circulariter in ipsum bonum.

1 Eadem videtur esse lux qua sol et lucet intus et foras emicat, emicansque illuminat omnia; eadem rursus qua omnia hec illuminata tum in se ipsis nitent, tum transverso radiorum iactu refulgent in alia, tum etiam recto quodam proiectu remicant erga solem. Ubi sane Plotinus excogitat ipsummet solis lumen ex sole perpetue dependere comitarique solem ubique ac versus solem undique se reflectere.

2 Similiter quoniam Deus est ubique, amor quoque quo Deus se ipsum aliaque diligit est ubique; dum vero se ipsum aliaque amat, amorem cunctis accendit quo se ipsa, Deum et alia diligent. Accendit autem amorem hunc omnibus vel extremis gradibus universi, quandoquidem ipse pariter est ubique et omnia diligit.

3 Uniuscuiusque vero amor ratione tam necessaria pendet ex primo — quatenus illinc oritur et conservatur atque movetur — ut unica quedam vis amatoria vigere videatur uique: ex primo quidem bono suspensa et in se ipsa residens sicut lumen in sua passim puritate consistit nullis immixtum. Reflexa denique in primum bonum luminis instar, quatenus omnia, in bono quovis amando, primum consequenter optant[253] bonorum omnium bonum.

: CXXX :

Marsilio: The amatory power flows forth from the prime Good like light through all things; and it flows back in a circular manner to the Good itself.

The light with which the sun lights itself within and shines without, and, in shining without, illuminates all, is seen to be the same light. Again, the light with which all these illuminated things shine in themselves — with the transverse striking of their rays reflecting light on others, and with a straight reflection shining back toward the sun — this light is seen to be the same light. Here Plotinus thinks that the sun's light itself perpetually depends on the sun, and everywhere accompanies the sun, and from all sides reflects itself back toward the sun.[229] 1

Similarly, because God is everywhere,[230] the love whereby God loves Himself and other things is also everywhere. But in loving Himself and other things, He ignites the love in all wherein they love themselves, love God, and love other things. And He ignites this love in all things even at the outermost levels of the universe, since He Himself is equally everywhere and loves all. 2

But the love of each single thing, as by a necessary reason, depends on the first [love] inasmuch as it arises from it, preserves itself, and is moved, so that there seems to be one unique amatory force flourishing everywhere, a force dependent on the prime Good indeed and residing in itself, just as light exists everywhere in its unmingled purity. And like light this force is turned back finally to the first Good, inasmuch as all things, in loving a particular good, choose as a consequence the Good of all goods. 3

4 Sicut autem solaris radius, ubique virtute vigens, non tam efficit ut omnia ubique luceant quam ut omnia quodammodo caleant vivantque multa calendo potius quam lucendo, sic ad bonum ubique presens non consequitur ut singula cognitionis eius sint capacia, sed amoris. Omnia enim semperque bonum ipsum amant, cognoscunt vero vix tandem quam paucissima. Amor igitur ad consequendum bonum hauriendamque inde vitam magis admodum[254] est necessarius quam cognitio. Quamobrem radiorum illa catena in superioribus introducta, que apprehensa supplicantem trahit ad bonum, est amor potius quam investigatio divinorum.

: CXXXI :

Dionysius atque Hierotheus:
Eiusdem ex eisdem hymnis.
Idem.

Age iam has iterum colligentes in unum dicamus unam quandam esse simplicemque virtutem se ipsa moventem ad unificam quandam commixtionem ex ipso bono usque ad extremum universi, ab eoque rursum deinceps per omnia ad ipsum bonum ex se ipsa, et per se, et in se ipsa semet in circulum reflectentem atque in se ipsam semper eodem modo se glomerantem.

But just as the sun's ray, with its power waxing everywhere, does not shine in order that all things may shine everywhere, but rather that all things may heat up so to speak, and that the many may live by being heated rather than by being lit, so it does not follow with regard to the good present everywhere that single things are capable of knowing, but rather that they are capable of loving. For all things always love the Good itself; yet they barely know in the end even the lowliest things. So loving to have the Good and to imbibe life from that Good is far more necessary than having knowledge of it. Hence that "chain" of rays introduced earlier,[231] which, being once grasped, draws the supplicant toward the Good, and is the love rather than the investigation of matters divine. 4

: CXXXI :

Dionysius and Hierotheus: Of the same from the same hymns. The same.

Well then, assembling these [powers] into one, let us say that there is one simple power which, in moving itself toward a unified mingling as it were, moves from the Good itself out to the furthest limit of the universe, and thence turns to traverse again through all things and to return to the Good itself. This power is from itself, through itself, and in itself, and it turns itself in a circle, always gathering itself into itself in the same way.

: CXXXII :

Marsilius:
Materia est inferior ente, Deus ente superior. Cum materia bonum appetat, multo magis reliqua bonum optant. Item de malo demonum.

1 Quemadmodum alibi diximus, res unaqueque esse possidet in hac specie aut illa per hanc formam aut illam; ipsum ergo simpliciter esse simpliciter est per formam. Quapropter materia, cum per se careat omni forma, merito nec proprium habet esse, sed mutuari videtur a formis nec ipsum sibi aliquando vendicare; semper enim sub speciei alicuius esse latet hoc iterum amissura. Dicitur ergo non ens, sed ente deterior; Deus quoque non ens, quia videlicet nulla definitus est forma, sed ente superior quoniam auctor est formarum.

2 Etsi naturales inclinationes ad certos quosdam terminos contendentes in ipsis rerum formis sedem habent, ceu inclinatio quidem ad centrum in gravitate, sed ad circunferentiam in levitate, inclinatio tamen ad omnem terminum pariter atque formam non potest in aliquo formali sed potius informi formabilique consistere. Inclinatio igitur ad formas quaslibet in materia est ipsa materie formabilitas proclivior ad formam quamlibet quam sulphur ad ignem. Materie igitur expositio tam prompta vel agilis ad subeundas formas, imagines primi boni, est naturalis quedam appetitio boni. Cum igitur non ens eiusmodi, quod fingitur umbra quedam confusa boni, necessario bonum appetat, multo magis ens quodlibet, quod per formam est imago quedam boni, bonum appetit.

: CXXXII :

Marsilio:
Matter is lower than being, God is higher than being. Since matter desires the Good, so much the more do all others yearn for the Good. Again, on the evil of demons.

As we declared elsewhere, each thing has being in this or that species and through this or that form. Therefore, what is simply being itself is simply through form. Wherefore matter, since in itself it lacks all form, fittingly has no being of its own, but seems to be borrowed by [various] forms, and lays no claim to itself at any time; for it always hides under the species of some other being which species in turn it is about to lose. Thus matter is called non-being, but it is worse than being. God is also called non-being, because He is limited by no form at all, and He is higher than being, since He is the author of forms. 1

Although the natural inclinations which strive for particular fixed limits have their seat in things' forms themselves — for example, the inclination in heaviness strives toward the center, but in lightness, toward the circumference — yet the inclination for all limit and form alike cannot exist in anything formal, but rather in something unformed and [yet] formable. So the inclination in matter for all forms whatsoever is the formability itself of matter which is more open to any form than sulfur is to fire. For matter, therefore, the explanation for its being so prompt or agile to submit to forms, the images of the prime Good, is a certain natural appetite for good. Since, therefore, such non-being, which is imagined to be just a disordered [or formless] shadow of the Good, necessarily desires the Good, then much more so does some being desire the Good, since through [its] form it is an image of the Good. 2

3 Inter hec ambigitur utrum demones a Deo rebelles bonum diligant necne, et qua ratione sint mali, quidve malum sit, et in quo, et unde, et quomodo providentia Dei malum permittat alicubi. Appellat Dionysius malorum demonum turbam *πρόσυλον*, id est proclivem ad materiam addictamve materie, sive aeria quedam mixtaque corpora post peccatum demones sint induti, quod Platonici comprobant et Greci theologi non negabunt, sive ad materialem ut ita dixerim cultum afficiantur animosque alliciant ad materiam, quod etiam Platonici confitentur. Putat vero Dionysius, sicut omnia bona ex primo bono proficiscuntur, sic omnia mala scilicet nostra ex primo malo demonum dependere.

4 Plotinus una cum Platone ipsam simpliciter malorum originem esse vult materiam, malorum vero nostrorum inclinationem anime ad materiam, sive ex ipsa, sive incitamento demonum pronior ad hanc evadat. Sit[255] igitur vel materia vel mutatio quedam in demonibus aut animis accidens origo malorum, dummodo non sit principium malorum efficiens, sed deficiens. Ipsa vero materia proprie neque bonum est neque malum. Non quidem revera bonum: ratio namque boni est cuius gratia sit aliquid aut fiat; nihil[256] autem materie gratia (est enim infimum). Item neque revera malum, cum sit ex bono boni avida; sed necessarium proprie nominatur, cum sit tantum gratia ceterorum, sitque inchoatio necessaria. Videtur igitur[257] eiusmodi necessarium inter[258] bonum malumque medium obtinere.

All this raises the questions whether the demons who were the rebels against God loved the good or not, and why they were bad; and what is evil, and in what, and whence, and in what way does God's providence permit evil anywhere. Dionysius calls the host of evil demons *prosulon,* that is, prone to matter or addicted to matter, whether the demons, having sinned, are clothed in airy and mixed bodies — a view the Platonists hold to and the Greek theologians will not deny — or whether they are drawn to material worship as it were, and attract souls into matter — a view Platonists also profess.[232] But Dionysius thinks that just as all good things proceed from the prime Good, so all bad things, our evils that is, depend on the first of the bad demons. 3

Along with Plato,[233] Plotinus wants matter itself to be the origin itself of evils absolutely, but the origin of our particular ills to be the soul's inclination toward such matter,[234] whether this inclination comes from itself or we become more prone to it by the demons' prompting. Therefore, let the origin of ills be either matter, or some change in the demons, or an accident in souls, provided it is not the efficient but the deficient principle of evils. But matter itself is properly neither a good thing nor a bad. Truly it is not a good. For the rational principle of good is that something is or becomes for the sake of it; but nothing is for matter's sake (being the lowest). Again, it is not truly a bad thing, since it is from the good and is eager for the good. But matter is named appropriately the "necessary," since it is only for the sake of all the rest: it is a necessary inchoation. Such a "necessary" is seen, therefore, to occupy the mean position between the good and the bad. 4

: CXXXIII :

Dionysius:
Cum omnia bonum appetant, cur demones non diligunt ipsum bonum? Item, unde demon malus, quidve malum sit et unde?

1 Dixerit forte quispiam: si pulchrum bonumque omnibus est amabile, desiderabile, diligendum (appetit enim ipsum id quoque quod non ens appellari solet, ut est dictum) contenditque quodammodo in ipso esse, ipsumque[259] bonum est quod etiam informibus formam facit, atque in ipso non ens ratione quadam superessentiali dicitur et existit, quonam pacto turba demonum pulchrum bonumque non desiderat.

2 Sed materie dedita et ab angelica circa boni ipsius desiderium identitate delapsa, malorum omnium causa et sibi ipsi et aliis, quecunque depravata sunt, dicitur extitisse. Quo rursus modo demonica gens, ex bono profecta, speciem boni nequaquam prefert? Aut quomodo bona ex bono facta mutari potuit? Et quidnam ipsam reddidit[260] malam? Et omnino quid est malum, et ex quo initio substitit, et in qua rerum est? Item quomodo Deus ipse bonus malum facere voluit, aut volens potuit? Atqui si ex alia causa malum trahitur, quenam alia rebus causa est preter ipsum bonum? Denique cum sit providentia, quonam modo malum est, aut omnino fit, aut certe non tollitur, et quo pacto aliquid ipsum dimisso bono desiderat?

: CXXXIII :

Dionysius: Since all things desire what is good, why do the demons not love the good? Whence the bad demon? What is evil and where does it come from?

Perhaps someone will have argued: If the Beautiful and the Good is lovable, desirable, and meet to be the object of love for all—for even that which is usually called non-being (as it is said) desires it, and strives in a way to be in it—and [if] the Good itself is that which creates form even for things formless, and non-being is said to exist in it for a super-essential reason, then why does the host of demons not desire the Beautiful and the Good? 1

Rather, dedicated to matter and having fallen away from the angelic nature in its desiring the Good itself, [why] is this host—all those that are corrupted—said to have existed as the cause of all evils both for itself and for others? Again, in what way does the race of demons, having originated from the Good, not prefer the form of the Good? Or in what way could a good breed that is generated from the Good be altered? And what has made the demonic breed bad? And in general what is the bad? And from where does it take its beginning? And in what kind of thing does it exist? Again, how did God Himself, the Good, wish to make the bad, or was able to wish to? And if the bad is derived from another cause, what other cause in things is there except the Good? Finally, since Providence exists, in what way does the bad exist, or in general become, or at least is not done away with? And how can something, having put the good aside, desire the bad? 2

: CXXXIV :

Marsilius:
Malum nec habet efficientem causam, nec ipsum est causa efficiens, nec est aliquid ipsa essentia malum. Item quomodo non ens dicatur de malo, quomodo de primo bono.

1 Cum naturalis intentio agentis cuiusque sit aliquid simile sit pro viribus generare, et quo queque causa magis est particeps bonitatis, eo magis possit sibi similia procreare, consequens est ut ipsum bonum facillime similia sibi et valeat et velit efficere. Malum vero bono dissimillimum est atque repugnans. Malum igitur non fit ex bono.

2 Sed neque malum efficit et generat aliquid: efficere enim atque servare propria est ipsius boni ratio. Nequit autem esse et ratio mali repugnantis bono, immo ratio mali contraria est rationi boni, scilicet perdere. Malum igitur nullius rei causa est efficiens.

3 Hinc sequitur ut malum nec ex malo sit tanquam ab efficiente causa, nec etiam ex ipso primo bono, immo neque ex quovis bono: unaqueque enim res tunc maxime generat, quando maxime in natura sua bene se habet; ratio igitur generandi efficiendique bonitas ipsa est. Cum itaque unumquodque qua ratione bonum est eadem et naturaliter agat, sequitur ut bonum faciat. Malum igitur non fit ex bono qua bonum; quamobrem cum malum nec ex bono nec ex

: CXXXIV :

Marsilio:
The bad does not have an efficient cause, nor is it itself an efficient cause; nor is something bad in essence. Again, in what way may non-being be predicated of the bad, in what way of the prime Good.

Since each agent's natural intent is to generate as best it can something similar to itself, and to the extent each cause participates more in goodness, the more it can procreate things similar to itself—it follows that the Good with consummate ease can fashion things like itself, and that it wishes to do so. But the bad is opposite to and assaults the Good; so the bad does not emerge from the Good. 1

The bad neither makes nor generates anything; for to make and to preserve pertains to the rational principle of the Good, and this cannot also be the rational principle of the bad opposing the Good. Rather, the rational principle of the bad, namely to destroy, is contrary to that of the Good. So the bad is not the efficient cause of anything at all. 2

Hence it follows that the bad does not derive from the bad as from an efficient cause, or derive from the prime Good, or indeed from any good. For each single thing generates most when it best finds itself, to the highest degree, in its own nature. Therefore, the rational principle of generating and of making is goodness itself. So, since every single thing, by reason it is good, naturally does what it does for the same reason, it follows that it produces good. So the bad does not come from the Good qua good. Thus, since it 3

malo tanquam ab efficiente causa fiat, nec ipsum insuper tanquam efficiens agat aliquid, merito nec efficiens causa est nec efficientis effectus.

4 Preterea quicquid est ipsa sua essentia tale est etiam tale totum atque converso, sicut quod per essentiam calidum est calet utique totum. Si quid ergo fingatur se ipso, id est secundum essentiam malum, omnino malum est futurum atque vicissim. Non potest autem esse per essentiam malum, quoniam esse tanquam bonum naturaliter omnibus est optabile. Igitur non omnino malum, atque contra nulla res potest penitus[261] esse mala. Cum enim malum significet defectum atque perniciem, nihil erit essentie reliquum ubi malum integrum confingetur. Non est igitur malum aliquid per essentiam. Itaque quod malum dicitur (si quid modo est) ipso quidem suo esse bonum est, malum vero per accidens, scilicet per defectum quo videlicet a bono quodam deficit, quod quidem expediret adesse.

5 Proinde naturalis entium omnium et agentium appetitio contendit ad bonum, et tanquam ad principium quod appetitum movet, et tanquam ad finem in quo appetitus denique conquiescit. Ad malum igitur qua ratione malum nullus intenditur appetitus. Malum ergo vicissim qua malum affectare non potest bonum.

6 Itaque si quid fingatur ipsa sua essentia malum, id, tanquam boni omnino contrarium, non desideraret bonum, sicut nec ipsa siccitas humorem expetit[262] peremptorem, quamvis subiectum olim humidum humore iam exhausto pristinum affectet humorem. Eadem ferme ratione res aliqua per naturam quidem bona, per defectum vero aliquem mala, bonum optat. Non licet[263] ergo fingere quicquam ipsa essentia malum, siquidem quicquid in essentie ordine computatur bonum expetit. Fictum vero illud nequit desiderare bonum.

comes neither from the Good nor from the bad as efficient cause, nor does it do anything itself, moreover, as efficient cause, it follows that it is neither the efficient cause nor the effect of the efficient cause.

Moreover, whatever is such in its own essence is totally such and the reverse, just as what is hot through its essence is totally hot. Hence whatever we might imagine as bad in itself, that is, as essentially bad, will be totally bad and the reverse. But it cannot be essentially bad, because to be is what is naturally desirable to all as a good. So it is not entirely bad. To the contrary, no existing thing can be utterly bad. Since badness signifies defect and ruin, wherever badness is deemed wholly bad, nothing will remain there of its essence. So no essentially bad thing exists. So what is said to be bad (in whatever way) is good in its being, but accidentlly bad through some defect, insofar as the defect lacks, in other words, a particular good which might help it to be. 4

Hence the natural appetite of all entities and agents strives for the Good, both as the principle which moves the appetite and as the end in which the appetite finally comes to rest. Therefore no appetite strives for the bad for the reason it is bad. So in turn the bad as bad cannot aspire to good. 5

Therefore, if something is imagined as bad in its essence, being entirely contrary to goodness, it will not desire goodness, just as dryness itself does not seek out wetness (which is its destroyer), whereas a subject originally wet, if the wetness has now evaporated, aspires to its original wetness. For much the same reason, some one thing that is naturally good, but through some defect becomes bad, [still] chooses good. It is impermissible, therefore, to imagine anything as essentially bad, for whatever is numbered in the order of essence seeks out its own good. To imagine what cannot desire goodness is just a fantasy. 6

7 Proinde, quod omnia per appetitum convertantur ad bonum argumento nobis est ex bono entia omnia processisse, ideoque bonum esse universo ente superius, presertim cum esse non simpliciter appetatur, sed ratione boni. Quemadmodum vero quod est super entia corporea non est corpus sed toto genere corporeo melius, ita quod est super entia non est ens, sed ente toto prestantius.

8 Iam vero ubi de hoc dicimus non ens hoc ipsum ibi est ens, id est negationem illam in affirmationem quandam mente resolvimus dicendo non ens videlicet superius quiddam ente principiumque entis totius atque finem.

9 Contra vero quando de malo non ens predicamus, in negationem id resolvimus, id est in quendam essendi defectum. Atqui malum non est appellandum ens, adeo scilicet ut qua ratione est ens, eadem sit et malum; si ita est, non omnino malum esse potest. Neque rursus cognominandum non ens scilicet simpliciter extra omnem entis conditionem: sic enim nulli noxium foret, nulli malum.

10 Preterea nusquam ponere possumus omnino non ens nisi ponamus in ipso bono, quatenus nullum Deus ens est, sed totius entis causa totoque superius. Denique bonum ipsum non solum est altius ente quantumlibet excelso, sed etiam est sublimius quolibet non ente, si forte non ens fingatur quomodolibet ente superius.

11 Malum vero, sicut diximus, neque est in ente ullo qua ratione est ens; hac enim ratione bonum est et optandum. Neque pro fundamento potest habere quod nihilum simpliciter nominatur; nihilum enim non potest fingi malum, id est adversum alicui, aut

Therefore, because all things are turned through their appetite back toward the Good, it serves as an argument for us that all entities have proceeded from this Good, and thus that it is superior to universal being—especially since such being does not desire simply to be unless the reason is to be good. Just as what surpasses corporeal entities is not body but something better than the whole corporeal class, so what surpasses [incorporeal] beings is not being, but is more outstanding than the whole of being. 7

Now when we predicate non-being of this [Good], this predicating itself implies being. That is, we have turned the negation round into a certain mental affirmation by saying, in effect, that this non-being [is] something higher than being, and [is] the principle and end of the whole of being. 8

Contrariwise, when we predicate non-being of the bad, we have turned it into a negation, that is, predicated a certain defect of being. The bad should not be called being, in other words. For the reason it has being will then be the same reason it is bad; and if this is so, it cannot be wholly bad. Nor again should the bad be called non-being, that is, completely outside every condition of being; for as non-being it would be harmful to none and bad for none. 9

Furthermore, we cannot locate non-being anywhere at all unless we locate it in the Good itself, insofar as God is not any being but the cause of the whole of being and is higher than the whole of being. Finally, the Good itself is not only higher than being, however lofty, but also more sublime than any non-being, if non-being perforce can be imagined in some way as higher than being. 10

But the bad (as we said) is not in any being for the reason it is being; for by this reasoning it would be good and fit to be chosen. Nor can it have as a foundation what is called simply nothing; for this nothing can be imagined neither as bad (meaning counter to 11

mancum, sed fundamentum habet ens aliquod atque bonum, in quo videlicet est aliquis bene se habendi defectus. Defectus autem eiusmodi longius discrepare videtur a nihilo quam a bono: in bono enim tanquam substentaculo quodam iacet, non in[264] nihilo; et quoniam malum semper alteri cuidam inherere putatur, quod autem nihil cogitatur non ita fingitur; inherere vero a substantia est alienum, ideo malum fertur habere conditionem quandam a substantia diversam, potius quam quod nihilum appellatur.

12 Est et alius textus significans malum magis discrepare a bono quam nihilum ac similiter ab essentia. Id ergo sic expones:[265] malum ledere bonum essentiamque posse; quod vero fingitur nihilum omnino ledere nihil posse. Cum eiusmodi textu consentit Proculus in libro *De malo*.

: CXXXV :

Dionysius: Idem.

1 Hec forsan dicat eiusmodi disputatio dubitans; nos autem admonebimus dubitantem ut rerum aspiciat veritatem. Atqui hoc primum audebimus dicere: malum ex ipso bono nequaquam existere, ac si ex bono sit, non esse malum: non enim ignis est frigefacere, nec boni facere non bona.

2 Preterea si que sunt omnia ex bono procedunt (natura enim boni est producere atque servare, mali vero perdere atque dissolvere), profecto nullum existentium est ex malo. Atqui nec ipsum

something) nor as [itself] crippled. But the bad has as a foundation some good entity wherein there is some failure in well-being. But such a defect seems to be as far distant from nothing as it is from the Good; for it is located in the Good, as in a sort of foundation, not in nothing. And because the bad is always deemed to inhere in something else, but what is thought to be nothing is not imaginable as inhering, and because to inhere [in another] is alien to being a substance, so the bad, rather than being denominated nothing, is said to have a sort of condition different from that of being a substance.

There is another text [or reading] which signifies that the bad is more different from the Good than nothing is, and different similarly from essence. And you may take this to mean that the bad can harm the good and can harm essence, whereas what we imagine as simply nothing cannot harm anything at all. Proclus agrees with such a reading in his book *On Evil*.[235] 12

: CXXXV :

Dionysius: The same.

You may say perhaps that such a dispute generates doubts: but we will admonish the doubter that he look to the truth of things. And first we shall venture to say this. Bad does not come from good in any way. And if it does come from good, it is not bad; for it is not for fire to freeze or for good to do things that are not good. 1

Moreover, if all things which exist proceed from good—for the nature of good is to produce and to preserve, but of bad to destroy and to dissolve—certainly no existing thing is from the bad. Nor 2

malum erit, siquidem se ipso sit malum, atque nisi ita fit non omnino malum erit malum, sed boni portionem quandam, per quam sit, habebit.

3 Item, si quecunque sunt pulchrum bonumque petunt et quicquid agunt propter id quod videtur bonum faciunt, omnisque rerum intentio bonum spectat ut principium atque finem (nihil enim mali naturam[266] spectans facit que aggreditur facienda), quonam modo in ordine rerum erit malum, aut quo pacto in rebus omnino est aliquid, cum huiusmodi bono appetitu sit destitutum?

4 Rursus quecunque sunt ex ipso bono dependent ipsumque bonum entibus est superius, siquidem in bono etiam quod non ens dicitur ens existit; malum vero neque ens est (propterea nec est omnino malum), neque rursus omnino non ens; nihil enim erit ipsum quod dicitur omnino non ens, nisi per rationem quandam ente superiorem in ipso bono dicatur.

5 Bonum itaque et ipso simpliciter ente et ipso non ente multo prius in se ipso consistit; malum vero neque in his que sunt neque in his que non sunt existit, sed etiam[267] ab ipso non ente alienius est et distantius quam a bono minusque habet substantie rationem. Legitur aliter: sed magis quam non ens a bono et essentia dissidet.

will the bad itself exist, since it is the absolute bad [and so nonexistent]; and unless this were so, the bad would not be entirely bad, but would have a portion of the good through which to exist.

Again, if all that exist seek the beautiful and good and whatever 3
they do they do for what appears to be good, and every intention of things looks to good as the beginning and end—for nothing looks to the nature of the bad to do what it has to do—in what way is evil in the order of things? Or how in things generally is evil something, since it is destitute of such a desire for good?

Again, all existing things depend on the Good itself and the 4
Good is superior to beings, since in the Good even what is said to be a non-being exists as a being. But the bad is neither a being (hence it is not entirely bad), nor again is it a non-being at all; for nothing which is said to be a total non-being will exist, unless such non-being may be said to be in the Good itself by way of a sort of reason superior to being.

So the Good exists in itself far prior to its existence both in 5
being in its simplicity and in non-being. But the bad exists neither in those things which exist, nor in those which do not exist. However, it is more alien and more distant from non-being itself than from the Good; and it does not have the rational principle of a substance. An alternative reading might be: But the bad is more at variance with the Good and with essence than non-being is.

APPENDIX

1 Marsilius Ficinus Florentinus reverendissimo in Christo patri Domino Iohanni Cardinali Sancte Marie in Domnica suppliciter se commendat.

2 Cum et me genius meus semel interpretandis Platonicis destinaverit, et ego magnis Medicibus patronis meis Platonica ferme omnia dedicaverim, cetera quidem maiorum tuorum fuerint sintque fratrum, que vero inter hec in primis ad theologiam pertinent et idcirco sacra censentur, ipse sacer antistes iure optimo tibi vendicare videris. Itaque Platonicum Iamblichum sacerdotem iampridem ad te misi sacra Egyptiorum mysteria pertractantem, post hec autem ad Dionysium Areopagitam Platonicum Christianumque theologum interpretandum tibi me contuli, precipuum Atheniensium antistitem summo Florentinorum antistiti dicaturus.

3 Cum vero superioribus diebus me ad calcem operis properantem morbus iliacus impediret, imminentem Dionysii ad te remoraturus accessum, tu interim Dionysio (ut reor) afflatus, exquisitissimo quodam Liberi patris munere et me liberasti languore et Dionysium Dionyso suscitasti iam torpentem. Heri tandem extremam huic operi manum impositurus nescio quo instinctu

APPENDIX

*The Longer Versions of the Letter of Dedication to Giovanni Cardinal de' Medici**

1 Marsilio Ficino the Florentine commends himself in supplication to the Reverend Father in Christ, the Lord Giovanni de' Medici, Cardinal of Santa Maria in Domnica,[1] 1492.

2 Since my genius has destined me ever to interpret the Platonists, and I have dedicated to my patrons, the great Medici, all the works of the Platonists up to now, and since the others have gone to and are going to your elders and brothers, those that especially pertain to theology and are therefore deemed sacred, the sacred high priest himself in truth and justice seems to have claimed for you. Accordingly I sent you a while ago the Platonic Iamblichus, a priest treating of the sacred mysteries of the Egyptians.[2] After these I betook myself to interpreting for you Dionysius the Areopagite, the Platonic and Christian theologian. It was my intention to dedicate this most eminent priest of the Athenians to you, the highest priest of the Florentines.

3 But since in earlier days a stomach illness prevented me from hastening to conclude the work, and Dionysius' imminent arrival to you was delayed, in the meantime, inspired as I think by Dionysius, you gave me a most exquisite gift of your Father Liber.[3] This liberated me from my languor and reawoke [my] drowsing Dionysius with [your] rousing Dionysus. Yesterday at last, and as I was about to put the final touches to this work, by some instinct

* This longer "A" version is found only in the two manuscripts, *B* and *P*; the briefer "B" version (= chapter 1, above) is found only in the 1496 incunable *I*. (For the manuscripts, see the Note on the Texts, below.)

sum compulsus in ipsis tuarum edium penetralibus in cubiculo tuo tuum hoc opus absolvere: ita semper nescio quod te mihi meque tibi temperat astrum. Illic igitur ante cenam, dum solus extremam commentarii clausulam hoc fine concluderem, scilicet 'Deus menti Deum ardenter amanti miro quodam splendore coruscat,' tu nobis protinus ingressus cubiculum coruscasti, ut felicibus auspiciis tuis tuum opus prorsus absolveretur. Tibi quoque plurimum, venerande pater, divus ille Dionysius ex alto tam clara luce refulsit, ut mysterium illud totum alioquin arduum atque reconditum lynceis statim oculis penetrares. Perge feliciter, obsecro, optime mi patrone, in dies magis ac magis sub ipsa Dionysii luce frequenter inspecta et intimum intelligentie lumen et externum glorie splendorem consecuturus.

(I know not what) I was drawn into the innermost recesses of your home and led to finish this work of yours in your bedroom.[4] Thus I never know when you are tempering the [reigning] star for me and I for you. So there before dinner, while still alone, and concluding the last clause of my commentary with this ending: "God blazes out in a wonderful splendor to the mind that ardently loves Him,"[5] you suddenly entered the bedroom and blazed upon me, so that this your very own work could be wholly finished under your own happy auspices. Down on you especially, venerable father, that divine Dionysius has radiated from on high with such a clear light that with a lynx's eyes[6] you might instantly gaze upon that otherwise most difficult and hidden mystery. Set forth in happiness, I beseech you, my best patron, proceed daily and ever more under the light of Dionysius. Having often gazed upon him, you will achieve both the inner light of understanding and the outer splendor of glory.

Note on the Texts

We now have authoritative editions of the Greek texts of the (Pseudo-) Areopagite. For the *Mystical Theology*, see *Corpus Dionysiacum*, vol. 2: *Pseudo-Dionysius Areopagita: De coelesti hierarchia, De ecclesiastica hierarchia, De mystica theologia, Epistulae*, edited by Günther Heil and Adolf Martin Ritter, Patristische Texte und Studien, vol. 67, 2nd ed. (Berlin: Walter De Gruyter, 2012); the text is on pp. 141–50.[1] For the *Divine Names*, see *Corpus Dionysiacum*, vol. 1: *Pseudo-Dionysius Areopagita: De divinis nominibus*, edited by Beate Regina Suchla, Patristische Texte und Studien, vol. 33 (Berlin: Walter De Gruyter, 1990), where the text itself is on 107–231. It is accompanied by an extensive apparatus criticus and German notes and commentary. This edition of the *Corpus Dionysiacum* is also available online through the De Gruyter website.

The dating and textual history of Ficino's Latin translations with introductory comments (*argumenta*) were established by Paul Oskar Kristeller in his *Supplementum*, 1:xxxvii, lxviii–lxvix, cxv–cxvi.[2] His conclusions have been accepted by Pietro Podolak, who produced a critical edition of the two Latin texts in 2011 and addressed in a long introduction many of the difficulties. Kristeller pointed to the authority of the *editio princeps*, datable to 1496 or early 1497: *Dionysii Areopagitae: De mystica theologia et De divinis nominibus* (Kristeller's siglum *m 1;* Podolak's *I* = *ISTC* no. id00241000).[3] He also identified the two authoritative manuscripts.

The first and most important of these is the late fifteenth- century manuscript Par. lat. 2613 in the Bibliothèque Nationale de France (Kristeller's siglum *P2;* Podolak's *P*). This contains Ficino's Latin translation of both the *MT* (fols. 1r–17v) and the *DN* (fols. 18r–166v), along with the *argumenta* for both works and a proem for the *MT*.[4] Gentile has proved that this was the manuscript Ficino sent to Germain de Ganay in Paris in 1494, two years before the *editio princeps*. In the light of the variants/errors they do not share, it is clear that it was not the archetype of the text in that *editio*.[5] This means that *I* and *P* constitute, in Podolak's

formulation, "due portatori di tradizione indipendenti l'uno dall'altro" (p. xli).

The other manuscript, Par. lat. 2614 (Kristeller's siglum *P3*; Podolak's *B*), is copied in the hand of Ficino's amanuensis Luca Fabiani and contains only Ficino's translation of the *MT* (fols. 1r–35r) along with the dedication, proem, and *argumentum*. It has a handful of variants (including three lacunae) but enough to demonstrate its independence of both *P* and *I*.[6]

Both the manuscripts and the *editio princeps* include versions of a 1492 dedicatory epistle to Cardinal Giovanni de' Medici (the version in the *princeps* being the shorter; see my Appendix).

Ficino's Dionysian translations and introductory comments were later included in the defective but still standard second edition of Ficino's *Opera Omnia*, printed in Basel in 1576 (with modern photo-reprints). The *MT*'s dedicatory epistle and proem appear on page 1013, while the translation and introductory comments appear on pages 1013–24. The *DN* occupies pages 1025–1128.

We should note that in both works each introductory comment or argument *precedes* the translation chapter it is interpreting, rather than following it, as is usual in modern running commentaries. In the *MT* and in the earlier chapters of the *DN*, each chapter, whether of commentary or of translation, has its own title. In the later chapters of the *DN*, however, beginning with chapter 44, the commentary chapter with increasing regularity provides a title for the two-chapter unit; the translation chapter then follows under the title *Idem* (The same).[7] In general, the introductory comments vary in nature: some are mere synopses or paraphrases, while others are semi-independent speculative excursus. Oddly, in seven chapters of the *DN* Ficino provides a chapter title but no accompanying comment. Another anomaly is that the *MT* contains fourteen chapters of comments and twelve chapters of Dionysius' text (in Latin) as established by Ficino; that is, there are two more commentary chapters than translation chapters. There are comparable discrepancies in the *DN*, where there are four more translation than commentary chapters. (Cases where it may not be obvious which comments go with which portion of Dionysian text are clarified in the Notes to the Translation.) The disor-

derly and inconsistent presentation of chapter headings seems to indicate that Ficino allowed the text to be published in an unfinished or unpolished state.

My apparatus includes all significant *I*, *P*, and *B* readings (and very occasionally an interesting reading from *Op.*). For the two manuscripts' readings, I rely throughout on Podolak's collation, though, on some occasions, my choice of a variant differs from his. However, I was able to check his collation of the *editio princeps* (*I*), since for several years I had been using that text for my translation, before I learned of his dissertation and before we were able to make contact. It should be noted that in the final stages of editing these volumes all the variants of *I* and *P* recorded in the textual apparatus were verified against digital reproductions, which accounts for some additional discrepancies between Podolak's text and my own. I have established my own punctuation. As for spelling, given the great inconsistencies within and among the various witnesses, I have followed Podolak's practice (see his p. l) of regularizing the spelling in accordance with Ficino's known orthographic preferences.

In *P*, the indication of author or commentator in each chapter (*Dionysius* or *Marsilius*) generally precedes the title, whereas in *I* it usually follows the title. This edition follows the practice of *P*.

Note that the Vatican's manuscript Borgianus Graecus 22 (in the hand of Scutariotes) contains the Greek text of the *DN* that Ficino worked from and annotated. While Pio Franchi de' Cavalieri first identified this manuscript as being in Ficino's library, and Kristeller signaled it was the one Ficino used,[8] we are indebted to Podolak, li–lxii, for providing us with detailed proof both of Ficino's reliance on it and of his willingness to emend it by way of collation with other texts (some of which Podolak lists on lxii–lxiv).

As to the vexed question of references, for the Dionysian text I have not reproduced the cornucopia of citations adduced by Suchla, Ritter, and their predecessors. Over the centuries many scholars have contributed to this abundance to the point that the critical apparatus of the De Gruyter editions have become monuments both of determination and of suggestion. I have merely tried to identify references in the Dionysian texts that Ficino would (or could) have recognized immediately, given his

knowledge of the Bible. Dionysius' debts to Proclus and the other Neoplatonists remain a separate and long-standing issue.[9]

The references in Ficino's commentary pose other problems, alluding as they do to Ficino's own *Platonic Theology* and Plotinus commentary, to Plato's *Parmenides* and *Second Letter*, to Iamblichus and Proclus, to Exodus and the Apocalypse, and so on. That Ficino's *Platonic Theology*, his work on Plotinus and Iamblichus, and his *Parmenides* commentary dominate is not surprising, since in these major exegetical works, he had already elaborated the Neoplatonic metaphysics he saw embedded in the Dionysian texts. As to identifying Ficino's sources, we are indebted to Podolak's pioneering work. However, he supplies an array of comparative references to Plotinus and other Neoplatonists, many of which by his own admission are merely parallel passages[10] that Ficino might never have known about or recalled, or at least recalled at the time of writing. This especially goes, I would argue, for Moerbeke's *ad litteram* translations, despite Carlos Steel's recent advocacy of Ficino's debts to Moerbeke in his *Parmenides* commentary.[11] We must constantly bear in mind that, in the eyes of Ficino and of the vast majority of his contemporaries, Plotinus and his successors were successors of Dionysius, were in effect his disciples (whether acknowledged or not). Consequently, Ficino's own references to the *Enneads*, to Iamblichus' *De mysteriis*, to Proclus, and so on, are not references to sources, but to what he sees as derivative appropriations or, at the best, analogues.

In short, the scope for speculation in this area is well-nigh endless. By design, therefore, my *apparatus fontium* is slimmer than Podolak's, even as I have kept an appreciative eye on his suggestions while adducing others of my own. The ultimate desideratum is a comprehensive index of parallel passages in Ficino's own works, particularly in light of his exploratory repetitiveness. But this is still out of our scholarly reach, given our inadequate knowledge of his immense achievement.

REFERENCE SYSTEM AND CONCORDANCES

Podolak rightly insists on the importance of retaining Ficino's "chapter" divisions of Dionysius' text (which he refers to on pages liii and lviii not

as *capita* but as *paragrafi*), and the present text also preserves them. In addition, I have adhered to the *editio princeps'* establishment of paragraphs within its chapters of translation and commentary, and I have added numbers for each paragraph in the margin, in accordance with the practice of this ITRL series. Instead of this internal paragraphing, Podolak's edition introduces line numbering for each chapter.

For Ficino's two works, I have introduced through-numbering in Roman numerals of Ficino's textual units — indicated in the original only by unnumbered chapter headings — without differentiating between dedication, proem, argument, or translation. Hence, in the *MT* the numbering begins with Ficino's dedication to Cardinal de' Medici as chapter I and ends with chapter XXIX; and in the *DN* it begins with Ficino's *argumentum* as I and ends with Dionysius' summary as CCCLI. Cross-references are to chapter and paragraph numbers, e.g., *DN*, CCXVIII.6 signifies the sixth paragraph of *DN*'s 218th chapter.

Concordance A allows the reader to locate in the present edition references to two earlier editions: to that found in volume two of the standard 1576 *Opera omnia* of Ficino and that of Podolak (2011). Concordance B helps readers find their way from the present edition of Ficino's Latin translation of Dionysius' *MT* and *DN* to the relevant Greek text in Migne's *Patrologia Graeca* and to the modern editions in Patristische Texte und Studien (mentioned above) by Heil/Ritter and Suchla, respectively. Migne simply reprinted the seventeenth-century text of Balthasar Cordier, who introduced his own book and chapter numberings. Since these are frequently referred to in the later literature, and were retained by Podolak as the basis for his chapter numberings, his reference system is also included in Concordance B.

GENERAL ABBREVIATIONS

MT Dionysius' *Mystical Theology*
DN Dionysius' *On the Divine Names*
B MS Parisinus lat. 2614 for *MT* only
I *editio princeps* for *MT* and *DN*, printed in 1496 in Florence by Lorenzo de Alopa

Op.	*Ficini Opera Omnia*, Basel 1576, for *MT* and *DN*
P	MS Parisinus lat. 2613 for *MT* and *DN*

ABBREVIATIONS USED IN THE NOTES TO THE TEXTS

add.	added
ante corr.	before correction
cont.	continued
corr.	corrected
post corr.	after correction
del.	deleted
om.	omitted
sec.	according to (*secundum*)
perperam	mistakenly
transp.	transposed

The occasional references to Dionysius' Greek text in the textual apparatus for the *DN* are accompanied by the Suchla edition's page and line numbering.

NOTES

1. An edition of John of Scythopolis' prologue and scholia for the *DN*, along with additions by others, was published by Beate Regina Suchla in vol. 4.1 of the same series, Patristische Texte und Studien (vol. 62) in 2011. See also *Pseudo-Dionysius Areopagita: Über die mystische Theologie und Briefe*, ed. with notes by Adolf Martin Ritter (Stuttgart: Hiersemann, 1994).

2. See Bibliography for the full reference; and for full descriptions of the manuscripts and their fates, see also Gentile's entry in *Marsilio Ficino e il ritorno di Platone: Mostra*, 157; idem, "Giano Lascaris, Germain de Ganay et la 'Prisca Theologia' in Francia," at 73ff.; also Raymond Marcel, *Marsile Ficin (1433–1499)* (Paris: Les Belles Lettres, 1958), 517–21. *Dionysius Areopagita*, ed. Podolak, xxxi–xxxviii, has a full description of the principal

manuscripts, secondary (derivative) manuscripts, and printed editions of the sixteenth century.

3. The description in the online *Incunabula Short-Title Catalog (ISTC)* may be accessed via the British Library website. The edition itself is viewable online via the website of the Bayerische Staatsbibliothek, Munich. Note that this exemplar (4to Inc. 900), formerly owned by the German humanist Hartmann Schedel (1440–1514), contains a few handwritten textual corrections at the beginning of the *MT*, some of which I have noted in the apparatus. The relationship of these corrections to Ficino's exemplar has not been studied, but they were possibly entered by Hartmann Schedel himself, who compiled in his own hand a table of contents on the flyleaf.

4. See also Paul Oskar Kristeller, *Iter Italicum*, 7 vols. (London: E. J. Brill, 1963–1997), 3:216, and idem, *Marsilio Ficino and His Work after Five Hundred Years* (Florence: Olschki, 1986), 98.

5. Gentile, "Giano Lascaris," 51–76 at 74ff.; *Dionysius Areopagita*, ed. Podolak, xl–xli. For the 1494 date, see Ficino's letters to de Ganay in *Op.* 957.2, 960.2 (the last being dated October 16).

6. *Dionysius Areopagita*, ed. Podolak, xli–xlii. For full descriptions of both these manuscripts and for the secondary witnesses, see ibid., xxxi–xxxviii, and for the problem of determining the archetype and a stemma, ibid, xlii–l.

7. The recurring word *Idem* in the chapter titles of *DN* is silently omitted in Podolak's edition.

8. Pio Franchi de' Cavalieri, *Codices graeci Chisiani et Borgiani* (Rome: Biblioteca Apostolica Vaticana, 1927), 137ff.; and Kristeller, *Marsilio Ficino and His Work*, 141.

9. See, for example, the well-known studies of Hermann Friedrich Müller, *Dionysius, Proklos, Plotinus: Ein historischer Beitrag zur neoplatonischen Philosophie*, 2 vols. (Münster: Aschendorff, 1926), and Roques, *L'univers dionysien*, with references to the earlier literature; and, more recently, those of Perl, *Theophany*; and Wear and Dillon, *Dionysius the Areopagite and the Neoplatonist Tradition*.

10. *Dionysius Areopagita,* ed. Podolak, l: "L'apparato delle fonti cerca di rendere ragione di tutti i passi non solo esplicitamente citati . . . ma anche allusi da Ficino, per quanto l'esaustività fosse in questo senso impossibile."

11. Steel, "Ficino and Proclus."

Notes to the Texts

MYSTICA THEOLOGIA

1. reverendissimo *B (recte)*
2. Florentini *om. I*
3. Dionysi *B I*
4. ratione *P*
5. eiusdem *P*
6. hec *P*
7. ad *om. P*
8. ad *P*
9. extat *P*
10. passionibus corporis *B ante corr.*
11. diversa est: est diversa *B*
12. De firmitate . . . Parmenide *om. B*
13. nature *I P B Podolak;* natura *Op.*
14. *emendavi*: nature *I P B Op. Podolak*
15. Differat *P*
16. patria *B ante corr.*
17. iterum *P*
18. privationem *I*
19. singu⟨la⟩rem *I*
20. forme *B ante corr.*
21. esse *I (sed corr. manu alt. in exemplari Monacensi)*
22. vitam *B ante corr.*
23. vero *B*

24. in *I (sed corr. manu alt. in exemplari Monacensi)*
25. impartit] quam parit *I* (impartit *post corr. in exemplari Monacensi)*
26. proprius *I (P ante corr.)*
27. exultat *P*
28. substantia *B*
29. qui] qui in *B post corr.*
30. aliquid *P*
31. ita *om. P*
32. nullus] intellectus *B ante corr.*
33. revera *P*
34. singularium *P*
35. imaginem *P*
36. infinita *P (B ante corr.)*
37. infinitum *B ante corr.*
38. fuerit *I*
39. est *om. B ante corr.*
40. significas *sc.* significativas
41. demonstratur *om. I*
42. intelligibiliaque *P ante corr.*
43. cognoscendo *B ante corr.*
44. id est *om. B*
45. omnes motusque] omnesque motus *I*
46. dempseris *B*
47. terrenumque *B ante corr.*
48. beneficium *I*
49. et *B ante corr.*
50. qua *I*
51. circum apposita] circum opposita *P*

52. adhibeamus *I* (*P ante corr.*)
53. cognoscibilibus *P Podolak*
54. altitudinem *I*
55. profundo *I*
56. cum *om. B ante corr.*
57. celebrabimus *B ante corr.*
58. pauciora *I*
59. res *om. B ante corr.*
60. gestu *I*
61. conscendes *P*
62. evadat *I*
63. in primis] infimis *I*
64. atque *I*
65. possint *I P*
66. amantem *P*
67. consequentem *B*
68. experti: ex parti *I*
69. *add. Podolak*
70. fiunt *I*
71. De his . . . disputamus *om. B*
72. essentiali intellectualique: intellectuali essentialique *B ante corr.*
73. intelligibilique *P ante corr.*
74. verisimile *I*
75. essentia *I*
76. videtur *B ante corr.*
77. esse *om. B ante corr.*
78. quin *B ante corr.*
79. neque sapientia, nec unum *om. B*

80. sit *I*

81. totusque *P*

DE DIVINIS NOMINIBUS

PART I, CHAPTERS I–CXXXV

1. infundit *P*

2. theologicis *P*

3. copulantur *P*

4. *post* accommodat *I et hinc inde (vid. Note on the Texts)*

5. pertingere *I*

6. preterea *P*

7. docet *P*

8. possit *I*

9. si *I*

10. neque visus] in visu *P*

11. intellectus *P*

12. infinitas superessentialis *P ante corr.*

13. intellectus *I*

14. vocatio *I*

15. apprehendere *om. P*

16. divino *P*

17. ininvestigabilem *P*: investigabilemque *I*

18. vero] demum *P ante corr.*

19. labentur *I*

20. insolenterque *P ante corr.*

21. quam si] quasi *I*

22. seculo *I*

23. fontem] facti fontem *I;* sacrum fontem *Op.*

24. divinus *I*

25. agat *om. I*

26. delectum *I*

27. intera *Podolak sed perperam*

28. Iupiter] supra *P*

29. Deum *P*

30. singularis *I*

31. eternam *P*

32. ex Deo] ex Deo ex *sic I*

33. forme *I*

34. theologia *P ante corr.*

35. solis *P*

36. eterno *Op.*

37. Deo *om. P*

38. suos *om. P*

39. particeps *I*

40. cognitionem *P*

41. per anticipat *I* (peranticipat *sec. Podolak*)

42. fingant *I*

43. cognitione *I*

44. essentiam *I*

45. superessentialia *P*

46. anima *P*

47. quantumlicet *I*

48. iustum *I*

49. contra] quod contra *I*

50. super *I*

51. ibi *om. I*

52. nihili *I*

53. ad *P*

54. inde creata] incerta *P*

55. cognitione *P*

56. ex *correxit Podolak*: est *I P*

57. per vitalem] parvitatem *I*

58. calores *I*

59. increpasse] more passe *I*

60. est *om. P*

61. et *post* comprehendens *P*

62. incircumscripte (*ἀπεριορίστως 120.5–6*): in circumscripte *I*; circumscripte *P*

63. liberante *P*

64. Hierarchia *Op.*

65. et *Podolak seclusit*

66. perfectior est] perfectionem *I*

67. litteris *om. I*

68. supremum *P ante corr.*

69. Haec (*τάδε 123.3*): Hic *Op.*; *cf. Revelation 1:4, 1:8*

70. Colocenses *P*

71. attribuuntur *I*

72. fontanam *emendavi*; fontiam *I P Podolak Op.*

73. Dionysius: *add. Podolak recte; om. I P*

74. illic *P*

75. essentia *P*

76. et *post* bonum *I*

77. eademque *I*

78. dicimus *P*

79. cuncta *I*

80. veritatem *P*

81. apponas *P*

82. convincta *I*

83. et *P*

84. essentia *P*

85. anime ipsius] ipsius anime *transp. I*

86. discretioneque *I*

87. aere *I Podolak*

88. redit *I*

89. duo *I*

90. Celestinus atque Valerianus *I P, sed minime congruenter; vid. Notes to the Translations (n. 102) ad loc.*

91. et *om. I*

92. ut *post* aut *I*

93. at *I*

94. supereminent *I*

95. appellemus *P*

96. velut *I*

97. divinos *I*

98. ad centrum *P*

99. proficiuntur *I*

100. representant *P ante corr.*

101. intellectuali *P*

102. nec *P*

103. quoddam *P*

104. oblectemus *P*

105. ignis *Podolak correxit (τὸ πῦρ 132.19)*: in his *I P Op.*

106. struthus *sc.* struthio; *vid. Notes to the Translations (n. 108) ad loc.*

107. ovium *I*

108. uniente *P ut vid.*

109. auxisse *I*

110. Iesum *I*

111. possunt *P*

112. eruditis *I*

113. humanam *I*

114. consequatur *P*

115. et *om. P*

116. dicens *I*

117. consentiuntur *I*

118. neque *I*

119. quodam admodum] quodammodo *I*

120. totaliter *I*

121. vero *P*

122. reperata (*sc.* reparata?) *I*

123. in immensum *I*

124. minus *I*

125. eo *I P*: ego *Op. Podolak*

126. Dionysius . . . loquitur *post* Christi *I*: verbis Hierothei *transp. I*

127. etiam *om. P*

128. communicabit *I*

129. supra *P*

130. et *om. P*

131. natura *I*

132. -que *om. P*

133. descriptione *I*

134. deficientia *I*

135. munere *I*

136. unus *I*

137. declaramus *I*

138. sui *I*

139. processione *I*

140. bona *P*

141. non *om. I*

142. orationibus] omnibus *I*

143. est *I*

144. *om. P*

145. promovemus *I*

146. concludit *I*

147. Hierotheus *I*

148. mirabitur *correxit Podolak (post Op.)*: mirabiliter *I P*

149. ceterisve *P*

150. radium *I*

151. Hierotheus *P*

152. delibatis *I*

153. Deum *I*

154. ipsum *I*

155. per] et per *I*

156. est *om. P*

157. enim *om. P*

158. lumen *om. P*

159. bonorum *P (δώρων 144.17).*

160. perfectiones *P post corr.*

161. consummationis *P ante corr.*

162. Necnon . . . nanciscantur *post* pertinet ut rectorem [85.6] *transposuit P*

163. principem *I*

164. boni forme *P*

165. reportabit *I*

166. et *P*

167. tandem *I*

168. *emendavi*: forma *I P*

169. materiam *I*

170. sortitur *P* (*cf. Wisdom 8:1*)

171. perfudit *I*

172. Moisem *I*

173. integrum] vite gravi *I*

174. est *om. P*

175. circum presentia *I*

176. cedens *P*

177. diversis *I*

178. penetratum *I*

179. atque solis *om. P*

180. per omnia eminenter *transposuit I*

181. explicitum *I*

182. sex pandit *I*

183. -que *om. P*

184. ab initio distinxisse *om. P*

185. etsi: si *I*

186. Plato noster: Platonici *I*

187. cognominant *I*

188. hic *P*

189. preferunt *P*

190. nactus *P*

191. per mundana *transposui;* instrumenta corporea . . . excogitat per mundana *I P*

192. cognitrice *P*

193. gubernari *P*

194. conferunt *P*

195. vero] vero ad *P*

196. *om. I*

197. a vocando: advocando *I*

198. partim *I*

199. illa vero turpe nec alias quidem pulchrum *post* nec ad hoc pulchrum *transposuit* P

200. alias vero nequaquam nec ad hoc pulchrum *bis P*

201. amabilis *P*

202. in *om. I*

203. substantie *P (vid. n. 207 infra)*

204. putentur *I*

205. multiplicate *I*

206. per proportionem] perportionem *I*

207. substantie *P ante corr.*

208. permaneat *P*

209. reflectuntur *I*

210. a Deo] adeo *I*

211. recinens *I*

212. conficere *P*

213. recte *I*

214. obliqui *P*

215. atque *om. P*

216. ad motum: admodum *I*

217. et *om. I*

218. disertam *I*

219. si *I*

220. firmatum *I*

221. textarum *I*

222. que *I*

223. amor *I*

224. his *I*

225. bonum *I*

226. Dionysius *post titulum insolenter P*

227. penetrature *I*

228. per bis: prebis *I*

229. figuras *P*

230. quodvis *om. P*

231. superfrua *sic I*

232. radios iam] radiosam *P*

233. *titulus capituli deest in I P*

234. consequenterque *I*

235. feriantur *I*

236. amore *P*

237. consideramus *P*

238. ament *I*

239. trahamus *I*

240. seu *I*

241. verus *Op. Podolak* (ὡς ἀληθὴς ἐραστὴς *159.6*): velut *I P*

242. quoque *I*

243. beneficius *I*

244. substantialem *P ante corr.*

245. exciantemque *I*

246. rationem *I*

247. ipso *P*

248. perractum *sic I*

249. -que *om.* *P*

250. magnorum *I*

251. intelligimus *P*

252. alie namque] alienamque *I*

253. optat *I*

254. amandum *I*

255. Sit] Si *P Podolak*

256. nullius *I*

257. ergo *I*

258. item *I*

259. -que *om.* *P*

260. reddit *P*

261. penitus potest *transp.* *P*

262. expedit *I*

263. licet *om.* *P*

264. in *om.* *P*

265. exponens *P ante corr.*

266. natura *P*

267. et *I*

Notes to the Translations

MYSTICAL THEOLOGY

1. The work lacks a title in the earliest manuscripts (*B P*) and in the *editio princeps* (*I*).

2. This shorter version of the dedication is found in the *editio princeps* of 1496. For the longer version, found only in the manuscripts, see the Appendix, above. The longer version of the dedication makes clear that Ficino was presenting to Cardinal Giovanni both the *Mystical Theology* and *On Divine Names* (see p. 485, n. 5, below).

3. The reference is to his own Latin rendering or version of Iamblichus' *De mysteriis Aegyptorum*, composed 1488/90 and printed by Aldus in 1497; among the seven later editions, the most accessible one now is *Op.* 1873–1908.

4. Cf. Ficino's *In Phaedrum*, summae 7 and 10 (ed. Allen, 107–8 and 111).

5. Romans 11:33–34; Plato, *Parmenides* 142A ff.

6. *De adoratione* (*Op.* 915.2), originally in Ficino's tenth book of letters and dated September 20, 1490.

7. Cf. Plato, *Timaeus* 29C–30A; Plotinus, *Enneads* 2.9.3.4–11; and Proclus, *Elements of Theology*, props. 25 and 27.

8. Psalm 139:12 [138:12]: "[Quia tenebrae non obscurabuntur a te,] et nox sicut dies illuminabitur: sicut tenebrae eius, ita et lumen eius." Notice the variations in Ficino's rendering: "nec tenebrae habent tenebras apud te, et nox quasi dies lucet; similes sunt tenebrae et lux."

9. *Enneads* 6.9 passim, and notably 6.9.8–11.

10. I.e., the first-century Pythagorean ascetic Apollonius of Tyana.

11. Plato, *Letters* 7.341CD; cf. 7.344B and 2.314BC. Cf. Ficino, *Platonic Theology* 8.3.5.

12. Both §§8 and 9 comment on the Dionysian text in §11.

13. Plato, *Letters* 2.314A, 7.341C–E. See n. 11 above.

14. Ficino, *Platonic Theology* 2.1.1–4, 12.3.5–8.

15. *In Plotinum* passim, but again especially his commentary on 6.9 (*Op.* 1798–1800).

16. I.e., in Ficino's *In Parmenidem* passim.

17. Cf. Ficino's argument at §15.6 below: "I shall also leave aside the three substances in Proclus, and the three principles under the First, that is, essence, life and understanding. With Plotinus it is more probable that, in the case of the gods, these latter three differ among themselves in terms of their definition rather than of their substance; yet he asserts that the one which is under the First [One], being constituted from the three principles, is the [one] principle of the universe, since it is born from the First."

18. 1 Corinthians 13:8.

19. Psalm 18:11 [17:12]: "posuit tenebras latibulum suum in circuitu eius tabernaculum eius, tenebrosa aqua in nubibus aeris."

20. *Parmenides* 137C–155E (i.e., the first two hypotheses of the dialogue's second part).

21. A reference to the events on Mount Sinai as described in Exodus 19:16–19. Cf. nn. 25, 26, and 35 below.

22. Bartholomew the apostle? Or is this a reference to the apocryphal and fragmentary Gospel of *Bartholomew* or to the "Questions of Bartholomew," which survives in a number of Greek and Roman manuscripts? For God's "short work," cf. Romans 9:28.

23. Exodus 20:21.

24. Both §§15 and 16 comment on the Dionysian text in §17.

25. Exodus 19:9, 16; 24:16, 18.

26. Exodus 19:16–19, 20:18, 24:16–18, as becomes clear in §6 below. Cf. James 1:17; Revelation 4:5, 8:5, 11:19, 16:18.

27. Plotinus, *Enneads* 5.9.8.10ff.; Iamblichus apud Proclum, *In Timaeum* 1 (ed. Diehl 1:308); idem, *De mysteriis* 1.19; Proclus, *Elements of Theology*, prop. 101; idem, *In Parmenidem* (ed. Cousin, 1:617).

28. In Proclus' *Theologia Platonica*, the third book is devoted to the intelligible gods, the fourth to the intelligible-intellectual, and the fifth to the intellectual.

29. Proclus had argued that the three principles as henads were separate substances.

30. *Enneads* 3.6.6.15ff., 5.6.6.20ff., 5.9.8–9. Plotinus' hierarchical metaphysical system is difficult to interpret in terms of the Christian Trinity since it subordinates Mind to the One and Soul to Mind. Hence, the importance of the Areopagite for Ficino, and indirectly the importance of Proclus' arguments if not of Proclus himself.

31. Cf. *Phaedrus* 247C ff.

32. *Republic* 6.508B ff. paraphrased.

33. *Enneads* 6.9.9–11; Podolak by contrast suggests 5.3.17.35ff.

34. Revelation 3:18; cf. Ficino's *Platonic Theology* 18.8.17, with same argument.

35. Cf. Exodus 19:16–20, 20:21, 33:20–23, 34:5.

36. Genesis 1:26–27; cf. Plotinus, *Enneads* 1.6.9.8–16. Michelangelo has popularized this notion of the sculptor as liberator of the forms within the stone; see, for instance, his famous poem to Vittoria Colonna, "Non ha l'ottimo artista alcun concetto" (*Rime* 151). For Ficino and statues, see my "To gaze upon the face of God again: Philosophic Statuary, Pygmalion, and Marsilio Ficino," *Rinascimento*, ser. 2, 48 (2008): 123–36.

37. Notably in the *Compendium Platonicae Theologiae* (ed. Gentile, *Lettere* 2:44–61), and in the *Argumentum in Platonicam Theologiam*, which both dwell on the three steps of Platonic contemplation (ed. Gentile, 2:85–110; ed. and trans. Allen and Hankins, 6:220–71, in the appendix to the sixth volume of Ficino's *Platonic Theology*).

38. *Platonic Theology* 8.1.1–6, 10.8.3–10, 12.2–3, 15.16.10; etc.

39. This is in the second book of Ficino's *Letters*, also between the *Compendium* and the *Argumentum*; cf. n. 37 above (ed. Gentile, 2:62–84).

40. Plato, *Letters* 7.341CD; cf. *Protagoras* 334E ff., 336B ff.; Plotinus, *Enneads* 6.9.10.5ff.

41. Podolak cites *In Plotinum* (*Op.* 1793, 1799–1800).

42. Alluding to the three treatises entitled respectively, *On the Principles of Theology, On Divine Names,* and *Symbolic Theology*. See §21 above.

43. *Enneads* 2.9 (the great treatise *Against the Gnostics*).

44. *Platonic Theology* 2.2, and esp. 2.2.9–10 (an attack on the notion of two equally supreme gods, where the Manicheans are specifically named at 2.2.10).

45. Genesis 1:10, 12, 18, 21, 25, 31—"and God saw that it was good."

46. *Platonic Theology* 2.7 (esp. 2.7.6–9), 2.11.10–11; *In Plotinum* 2.9.1, 3.2.19–20 (*Op.* 1663.3–1666, 1669.2–1700).

47. *Platonic Theology* 1.3–4. Podolak refers us to 2.9 and 2.11.

48. *Parmenides* 137C4–142A8 (the first hypothesis of the dialogue's second part).

49. *In Parmenidem* 53–79 (ed. Vanhaelen, 2:20–167).

50. The *logos* (the reason, or rational principle, or word) is the first "name" in John 1:1: "In the beginning was the Word." It was taken to refer to the second Person of the Trinity. Ficino does not mean to say, surely, that "knowledge is the rational principle."

51. *Parmenides* 137C4–142A8.

THE DIVINE NAMES

PART I, CHAPTERS I–CXXXV

1. Cf. Ficino's reference to Dionysius as *Platonicorum culmen* in his letter to Germanus Ganaiensis (Germain de Ganay) dated October 16, 1494, in his twelfth and last book of *Letters* (*Op.* 960.2).

2. Here Ficino gives what is in effect a second title, this time for the translation only, as distinct from the "Introductory Comments" (*Argumenta*), which began in §1. Only here in the internal title does he claim responsibility for the translation.

3. Referred to elsewhere as the *Symbolic Theology*; e.g., at §29.1 infra. This has not survived.

4. 1 Corinthians 2:4.

5. *Timaeus* 40E.

6. *Laws* 5.738BC.

7. Cf. §78.4, below, and §199, in vol. 2.

8. *Enneads* 5.3.13.10–end.

9. As in Aristotle's *Metaphysics* Λ 6.1071b ff.

10. Cf. Plato, *Republic* 4.509B; Plotinus, *Enneads* 1.7.1, 3.7.2, 5.3.13–17 et passim; also Iamblichus, *De mysteriis* 8.2, with its great "mystery" of the god who is the father and son of himself (see Ficino's *Op.* 1903).

11. *Platonic Theology* 1.6.4–5.

12. *Enneads* 1.6.6.18–20, 1.6.9.32–end.

13. 2 Corinthians 12:2–5; cf. 1 Corinthians 2:9.

14. *Seventh Letter* 341CD; cf. 344B and *Timaeus* 28C.

15. *Republic* 6.508A–511A. Cf. Plotinus, *Enneads* 6.7.16.24–end.

16. "Hymn to Love" 58.2 (ed. Quandt); cf. *Phaedrus* 252B.

17. *Phaedrus* 246A–E; 251A–252B.

18. Exodus 20:7; Ephesians 1:21; Philippians 2:9; *Oracula Chaldaica*, frag. 87 (Des Places); Iamblichus, *De mysteriis* 1.12.42.15ff. Cf. Ficino's *In Philebum* 1.11–12 (ed. Allen, 140–45). Note this is a highly unusual reference in Ficino to the mysteries of Kabbalah.

19. *Statesman* 269CD, 271D–272C (and indeed the entire myth 269A–274D); *Protagoras* 322A; *Critias* 109B ff., 110CD, 120D ff.

20. E.g., Plotinus, *Enneads* 6.7.35.20ff.; Iamblichus, *De mysteriis* 1.12.41.12ff. (cf. n. 18 above).

21. "Hymn to Helios" 8.13–16 = Orphic frag. 21a (Kern) as cited in the pseudo-Aristotle, *De mundo* 7.401a28–b7, and again in Eusebius' *Praeparatio evangelica* 3.9. Cf. Ficino's *Lettere* 1.6 (ed. Gentile, 1:27).

22. *Platonic Theology* 4.1.2–8, 11.4.10–11.

23. *Platonic Theology* 18.1.6, citing Proclus.

24. *Sixth Letter* 323D.

25. *De mysteriis* 8.2; see n. 10 above.

26. *Enneads* 6.8.13–15, esp. 6.8.14.40ff.

27. *Timaeus* 29E–30B.

28. Amelius' enthusiasm for the prologue of St. John's Gospel is noted by Eusebius, *Praeparatio evangelica* 11.19.1ff. (ed. Mras, 45); cf. Augustine, *City of God* 10.29.

29. *Laws* 4.716C; cf. *Cratylus* 386A and *Theaetetus* 152A, which cite the famous trope by Protagoras.

30. *De Christiana religione* 16 (*Op.* 20–21).

31. Ephesians 3:15.

32. Aristotle, *Metaphysics* Δ 2.1003b22–25, 11.3.1061a15–18. "Equal" in the metaphysical sense of having the same extension.

33. E.g., *Republic* 6.509D ff. (the divided line); *Timaeus* 34C ff., 43D ff., 53C ff.; *Phaedo* 72B; and *Phaedrus* 246A–257A.

34. *Republic* 6.508A–509C, 7.517BC.

35. Isaiah 6:1–3.

36. Ezekiel 1:4–26.

37. *Statesman* 270B–274A; *Chaldaean Oracles*, frag. 158 (Des Places), with Psellus' commentary, the latter in Migne's *Patrologia graeca* 122: 1125a11 ff. Cf. Ficino's *Platonic Theology* 13.4.15–16, 18.4.3–4, and 18.9.2–3.

38. *Chaldaean Oracles*, frag. 104 (Des Places), with Psellus' commentary as above, 1137c8 ff.; see also frag. 158. Again cf. Ficino's *Platonic Theology* 13.4.15–16, 18.4.3–4, and 18.9.2–3.

39. Again, *Chaldaean Oracles*, frag. 158 (Des Places). Cf. nn. 37 and 38 above.

40. Philippians 3:21.

41. Luke 20:36.

42. See 2 Corinthians 12:2–4. Ficino commented on this passage in a letter-treatise to Giovanni Cavalcanti entitled *On the Rapture of Paul to the Third Heaven* (2.6, ed. Gentile 2:62–84).

43. *Phaedrus* 247C8, 248A3. Cf. Ficino's *In Phaedrum* 2.7.1–2 (ed. Allen, 66–69).

44. Professor Hankins suggests this may be an allusion to the Avicennian concept of God as *dator formarum*.

45. 1 Thessalonians 4:17.

46. Matthew 17:1–8; Mark 9:2–8; Luke 9:28–36.

47. Luke 20:36.

48. *Republic* 7.514A–516B, esp. 516AB.

49. E.g., *Enneads* 1.7.1.23 (on radii); 2.2.3.5ff.; 5.1.9.18–23 (on heavenly spheres); 6.8.18.8ff. (on radii again).

50. An explicit witness that Ficino regards Plotinus as Dionysius' successor; cf. §23.5 below.

51. For this supra- or pre-intellectual vision of intellect, see, for example, *Enneads* 3.8.9.29–32, 5.3.11.4–12, 5.4.2.4–7, and 6.7.35.20–25.

52. Following Plato, *Timaeus* 45B–46C; Plotinus, *Enneads* 4.5.2.8ff. and 4.5.4. Note that the Greek *bolê* means a "throw" or "stroke"; hence *epibolê*, *parabolê*, *probolê*, *prosbolê*, etc. Cf. *Enneads* 3.8.10.32–35, where *prosbolê* means intuition.

53. Following Aristotle, *De anima* 2.7.418a26 ff. and 3.12.435a5–10.

54. I.e., Ficino is combining the Neoplatonic triad of essence-life-intellect both with the five categories of being explored in Plato's *Sophist* (summarized at 254DE) and with the dyad of the limit and the infinite from the *Philebus* 23C.

55. *Second Letter* 312DE. For Ficino this is the first of Plato's letters, since he attributed what we now call the *First Letter* to Dion.

56. Cf. §19.4 above — on Dionysius' primacy as the first Neoplatonist, the first to interpret Plato in the way we now associate with Plotinus.

57. Dionysius is echoing Plato's wording in the *Second Letter* 312DE: "'Around (*peri*) the king of all are all: all things are for his sake (*heneka*): he is the cause of all good things.'"

58. *Corpus Hermeticum* 5.10.

59. I.e., in Pythagorean reasoning the point proceeds to the line, thence to the two-dimensional plane, and thence to the three-dimensional solid. See Aristotle, *Topics* 4.141b5–22, and *Metaphysics* Γ 5.1001b26–1002b11. Ficino frequently cites this trope.

60. *Parmenides* 137C–155E, i.e., the first two hypotheses of the dialogue's second part. Ficino habitually refers to Parmenides himself and his followers in the Eleatic school as Pythagoreans.

61. Genesis 32:29; Judges 13:18.

62. Genesis 32:29.

63. Judges 13:18; Isaiah 9:6.

64. Ephesians 1:21; Philippians 2:9.

65. Exodus 3:14.

66. Respectively, John 11:25, 14.6, 8:12; Genesis 28:13; and John 14:6.

67. "good": Luke 18:19; "beautiful": Song of Songs 1:16; "wise": Job 9:4; "meet to be loved": Song of Songs 5:2; "God of gods": Psalm 50(49):1; "Lord of lords": 1 Timothy 6:15, Revelation 17:14 and 19:16; "Holy of holies": Daniel 9:24; "eternal": Baruch 4:10; "existent": Job 14.4; "the cause of the ages, the author of life": Acts 17:25; "He who anticipates all the treasures of all knowledge": Colossians 2:3; "power": 1 Corinthians 1:24; "the King of kings": 1 Timothy 6:15, Revelation 17:14 and 19:16; "the ancient of days": Daniel 7:9, 13; "He who can never age," "the immutable": James 1:17; [found] "in the lightest breeze": 1 Kings 19:11–12.

68. *Second Letter* 312E.

69. *Laws* 4.715E ff.

70. *Timaeus* 28C ff., *Parmenides* 142B–155E.

71. Again, Dionysius is calling on the language of the passage at 312E ff. in the *Second Letter*.

72. 1 Corinthians 15:28.

73. Unknown to Ficino and to us. Ficino is simply reproducing the reference in Dionysius' text.

74. *Second Letter* 314A; cf. *Seventh Letter* 341C.

75. *De mysteriis* 2.3–9.

76. Or electrum, the gold and silver alloy taken to resemble amber.

77. Notice the progression: *facere-efficere-perficere.*

78. Matthew 19:17; Mark 10:18; Luke 18:19.

79. Matthew 20:15; cf. John 10:11.

80. Psalm 143:10.

81. Exodus 3:14.

82. Revelation 1:8; cf. 1:4.

83. Psalm 102:27.

84. John 15:26.

85. John 5:21.

86. John 6:63.

87. 2 Corinthians 3:17.

88. Colossians 1:15–20.

89. Ibid. Cf. Romans 11:36 and 1 Corinthians 8:6. Ficino read these Pauline texts in the light of Plato's *Second Letter* 312E and *Sixth Letter* 323D (see Allen, "Ficino on Plato"). Note the addition of the "conserving" fourth cause keyed to Colossians 1:17, "and by him all things consist" (*omnia in ipso constant*).

90. Psalm 104:30; cf. 33:6.

91. John 17:10; cf. 16:15.

92. 1 Corinthians 11:12.

93. Ibid.

94. Colossians 1:16; cf. John 1:3.

95. Colossians 1:17.

96. Psalm 104:30.

97. John 10:30.

98. John 16:15.

99. John 17:10.

100. *Enneads* 1.7.1.24ff.

101. I.e., the same title as in the preceding chapter. "The same" (*Idem*) indicates that the title of Ficino's introductory comment in the preceding chapter is meant to apply as well to the present chapter containing Dionysius' text. See the Note on the Texts.

102. Celestinus and Valerianus: thus Ficino. Podolak omits Celestinus and corrects "Valerianus" to Valentinus, citing Augustine, *De haeresibus* 11 (CCSL, ed. R. Vander Plaetse and C. Beukers, p. 295.12); see also n. 105 below. Valentinus (second century CE) was an important Gnostic who held views similar to the ones described here. By "Celestinus" Ficino possibly meant Caelestius, the fifth-century CE heretic condemned by Augustine, but he is linked with the Pelagian heresy, not a Gnostic one.

103. Augustine, *De haeresibus* 49 (320.9ff.). Arius denied the godhead of Christ.

104. Augustine, *De haeresibus* 55 (325.1ff.). Apollinaris argued that Christ possessed a human body and soul, but that He had the divine Logos instead of the human spirit. He did not possess therefore our whole nature.

105. Augustine, *De haeresibus* 46 (318.155ff.). For all these heretical views, see also Thomas Aquinas, *In librum beati Dionysii De divinis nominibus expositio* 1.2.60 and 2.3.168 (ed. Ceslai Pera, O. P. [Turin: Marietti, 1950], 19, 53) — hereafter Aquinas, *In librum Dionysii*.

106. *Second Letter* 312E4–313A2, paraphrased.

107. *Simpliciter* in the technical scholastic sense of "without qualification or remainder."

108. Cf. *Platonic Theology* 13.4.9. Ficino must be thinking of an ostrich (Latin, *struthio* or *struthiocamelus*; Greek, *strouthokamêlos*) rather than a sparrow (Greek, *strouthos*), since, according to the medieval *Physiologus*, "The ostrich lays eggs but does not brood them in the usual way: it sits facing them and stares at them intensely. They grow warm in the heat of its gaze, and the young are hatched." Of course, he may have thought that sparrows' eggs were hatched in the same way!

109. Aristotle, *De anima* 2.1.412a20–2.1.413a9.

110. E.g., Plotinus, *Enneads* 1.1.4 passim, 2.1.5.18ff., 5.1.10.11ff. I.e., is the Platonic thesis of the plurality of souls in the human subject somehow akin to the dual nature of Christ?

111. Averroes, *In Aristotelis de anima* 3.5 (ed. Crawford, 401–13). Cf. Ficino's *Platonic Theology* Book 15 for an extensive analysis of this; see also, briefly, Letter 39 in his first book of *Letters* (ed. Gentile, 1:77–78), a letter addressed to Cavalcanti.

112. Ficino treats this very delicate and once-controversial theological question carefully, via interrogatives. Since in Aristotle the form of a living thing is called its Φύσις, generally translated as *natura*, the difficulty of reconciling Aristotle with Chalcedonian [Roman Catholic] orthodoxy—that Christ subsisted as one person of the Trinity with two natures—is gently implied without further comment. The question of a Platonic solution is left open, though a hostile reader could construe it as Apollinarism, a form of the Monophysite heresy. Finally, Ficino raises the possibility, only to dismiss it, that in an Averroistic account of human intellect, Christ's cogitative faculty would be subject to a separable Mind, or even to a separate divine Mind.

113. *Apud* Eusebius, *Praeparatio evangelica* 11.19.1 (ed. Mras, 45).

114. *Seventh Letter* 341C ff. Cf. *Second Letter* 314A–C.

115. Philippians 2:6; John 5:18, 10:30, 16:15, 17:10.

116. Ficino regarded the *Epinomis*, not *Laws* 12, as the last book of the *Laws*, as his epitome makes clear, *Op.* 1525–30. For the harmonic proportions, see *Epinomis* 990A–991B, with Ficino's commentary, *Op.* 1529–30.

117. *Timaeus* 31C ff., with extensive commentary in Ficino's *In Timaeum* (*Op.* 1438–84).

118. See *Timaeus* 37D–39E.

119. *Phaedrus* 248A3.

120. Pletho, *Contra obiectiones* 23 (ed. Maltese, 22.30–34) is Podolak's suggestion.

121. *Republic* 6.508B and the Cave myth passim.

122. Ficino, *De vita* 3.4 (ed. Kaske and Clark, 258–63).

123. *Phaedrus* 246E ff. Cf. Ficino's *In Phaedrum* 10 (ed. Allen, 80–93).

124. Cf. Matthew 5:14; John 8:12.

125. 1 Corinthians 8:5–6.

126. *Chaldaean Oracles* frag. 128 (ed. Des Places), with Psellus' commentary 1140b1 ff. The oracle refers to the "watery" or "melting" body (*rheuston*) not the "fallen" one; cf. Ficino, *Platonic Theology* 13.4.10.

127. *Republic* 10.616BC.

128. *Iliad* 8.15–28. Cf. Plato's *Theaetetus* 153CD; Macrobius, *In Somnium Scipionis* 1.14.15; and Ficino's *Platonic Theology* 13.4.15.

129. See in particular Plotinus' *Enneads* 3.2–3 (the long treatise "On Providence") and Proclus' treatise *De providentia et fato* (ed. H. Boese [Berlin: De Gruyter, 1960], 109–71).

130. A reference to the cabalists? Cf. §91.4 below.

131. *Enneads* 3.2.9, and again in general 3.2 and 3.3.

132. Deuteronomy 6:4–5; 2 Kings 23:25.

133. *De mysteriis*, 5.26; cf. 1.12, 1.15.

134. *Eighth Letter* 352E–353A.

135. *Timaeus* 27C.

136. *Protagoras* 342E–343C.

137. This Hierothean work has already been referred to as the *Principles of Theology*. It is not to be confused with either of Dionysius' two books: *Symbolic Theology* and *Principles of Theology*. None of these works has of course survived.

138. Hebrews 5:14.

139. If this chapter heading is by Ficino, then it and the Areopagite's accompanying §76, which it glosses, demonstrate Ficino's acceptance of one of the most striking features of the Dionysius legend. Whereas others had interpreted "the body which sustained the prince of life" as being a reference to Christ's own body — see, for instance, Aquinas, *In librum Dio-*

nysii 3.1.255 (ed. Pera, 78)—Ficino, by contrast, adopts the story that Dionysius, after his conversion by St. Paul, had traveled to Jerusalem to visit Mary as the *theotokos* (the god-bearer). Struck with amazement at the glory surrounding her, Dionysius subsequently became a witness of her death (referred to as her "dormition") and assumption, along with the apostles James and Peter and other "saintly brothers," including Hierotheus, "a man possessed by God." Afterward, Dionysius went to Rome and witnessed St. Paul's martyrdom.

140. Porphyry, *Life of Plotinus* 23.

141. The meaning of *theologi* here and the reference to coming "after" the theologians two sentences below has been disputed. See Roques, *L'univers dionysien,* 181–83. Ficino simply translates without glossing.

142. Cf. Augustine, *Confessions* 13.11.12; *City of God* 11.26; *De Trinitate* 9.4–5.

143. *Timaeus* 29E–30D, 41AB.

144. *Republic* 6.508A–C.

145. Julian, "Hymn to Helios" 6, 44.

146. Iamblichus *apud* Proclus, *In Timaeum* 1.308.17ff. (ed. Diehl); Proclus, *Theologia platonica,* 3.24, 4.27ff., 5.37ff. (ed. Saffrey and Westerink).

147. Plotinus, *Enneads* 5.5.1.35ff. Note that the metaphysical distinction between intelligible and intellectual became dogmatic only with Iamblichus. Ficino of course read it back into Plotinus.

148. Otherwise unknown. Unless this is a reference to the *Celestial Hierarchy*.

149. The subtitle of Ficino's great work is "on the immortality of soul," echoing the titles of treatises by Plotinus (*Enneads* 4.7) and Augustine.

150. *De mysteriis* 2.6.83, 2.9.87–89.

151. Otherwise unknown.

152. *Enneads* 3.6.7.24ff., 41ff.; 3.6.13.34ff., 43–50; etc. This is an oft-repeated trope in Ficino's work.

153. §17.3 above.

154. E.g., *Enneads* 1.8.2.5.ff., 5.3.13, 6.8.16.

155. Wisdom 8:1; quoted in one of the Great Antiphons of Advent, "O Sapientia."

156. "Hymn to Nature" 10.16, 10.7; cf. "Hymn to Earth" 26.2–6, 9.

157. Genesis 1:6–7; Psalm 148:4.

158. Porphyry, *Life of Pythagoras* 31; Macrobius, *In somnium Scipionis* 6.18.18.

159. "Hymn to Apollo" 34.16–23.

160. Genesis 1:16; Psalm 136:7.

161. Cf. Genesis 1:14.

162. Paragraphs 1 to 4 correspond to the first two-thirds of Ficino's *De Sole* chapter 2, while the opening sentence of paragraph 5 (*Sol . . . praetermittam*) corresponds to the opening sentence of the *De Sole's* chapter 3 (*Op.* 966.1 and 2). See n. 165 below.

163. *De mysteriis* 1.9.30.17–32.9, esp. 32.8.

164. E.g., 6.2.18–20, 8.13.1, and 9.3.3–4.

165. Ficino is alluding to two separate treatises he first wrote in briefer versions and later amplified: the *De sole,* completed in the autumn of 1492 (*Op.* 965–75); and the *De lumine,* dating from November 1476 but enlarged before January 1493 (*Op.* 976–86); see Kristeller, *Supplementum,* 1:cxi–cxiii. The *De sole* 3 (*Op.* 966.2) also notes that the sun's size is 166 times that of the earth's. See n. 162 above.

166. Notably in his *De amore* 2.2 (ed. Laurens, 24–25), his *Philebus* Commentary 1.5 (ed. Allen, 108–11), his *Platonic Theology* 12.1.11, and his *De sole* 9 (*Op.* 971; see n. 168 below).

167. Plato, *Republic* 6.507D–509B.

168. Paragraphs 6 and 7 correspond to a passage in the *De sole* 9, and paragraphs 8 and 9, to the beginning of *De sole* 10 (*Op.* 971–72).

169. See Averroes' gloss on Aristotle's *Metaphysics* H 4.1044b7–8 in his commentary (Venice, 1562), 8:220.

170. Psalm 19:4/5.

171. John 1:5.

172. Genesis 1:3.

173. Only with the fourth day, that is, does Genesis 1.14–19 introduce the sun and the moon, the first three days being distinguished by absolute, pre-solar light.

174. Again, note that these two paragraphs 8 and 9 correspond to the *De sole* 10. See n. 168 above.

175. Genesis 1:3–4.

176. *Cratylus* 408E–409A: *Helios*, says Socrates, is derived from *halizoi* (he gathers) or *aei eilein iôn* (always rolling in his course [about the earth]) or *aiolein* (to variegate).

177. Cf. Macrobius, *In Somnium Scipionis* 1.20.6.

178. Cf. *Timaeus* 70A6 ff.

179. Cf. Herodotus, *Histories* 1.47, which cites a hexametral oracle given by the Pythia at Delphi to a Lydian embassy from Croesus: the saw was falsely attributed to Homer. Podolak also refers us to Maximus of Tyre's *Philosophical Orations* (*Philosophumena*) 3.1b (ed. H. Hobein [Leipzig: Teubner, 1910]).

180. "Hymn to Apollo" 34.11–15 — a general reference to Apollo's universal sway but with no mention of sands or the measures of the sea.

181. Cf. Romans 1:19–20.

182. Romans 11:36; 1 Corinthians 8:6; Colossians 1:16.

183. Romans 1:20.

184. Again compare *De sole* 10 (*Op.* 971–72).

185. James 1:17. Cf. Ficino, *Argumentum in Platonicam Theologiam* 13 (included as an appendix in the Allen and Hankins edition of the *Platonic Theology* 6:236–37).

186. Aristotle, *Metaphysics* B 1.993b9–11, makes the same point but refers to the eyes of bats rather than those of owls.

187. See James Hankins, "Ficino, Avicenna and the Occult Powers of the Rational Soul," in *La magia nell'Europa moderna: Tra antica sapienza e filosofia naturale*, ed. Fabrizio Meroi and Elisabetta Scapparone, Atti del con-

vegno Istituto nazionale di studi sul Rinascimento 23 (Florence: Leo S. Olschki, 2003), 1:35–52.

188. Specifically, *Symposium* 211AB. See the Dionysian quotation below in §102.3.

189. Song of Songs 1:15–16; Psalm 45:2.

190. 1 John 4:8, 16.

191. Matthew 3:17, 17:5; Mark 1:11; Luke 3:22; 2 Peter 1:17.

192. *Cratylus* 416B–C. For *kaleô* (to call or summon), cf. 1 Thessalonians 2:12; 1 Peter 2:9.

193. Extrapolating from and paraphrasing Plato's *Symposium* 211A1–B2.

194. *Enneads* 1.6.9.35–end.

195. *Enneads* 6.7.22, 6.7.32—and, indeed, 6.7 passim, one of Plotinus' greatest treatises.

196. *Enneads* 2.4.11.42ff., 3.6.7, 3.6.11.16–end, 3.6.12.1–28, 3.6.19.

197. Again see *Enneads* 1.6.9.35–end; also 5.5.12.

198. Cf. Plato, *Timaeus* 30A–31B; Plotinus, *Enneads* 3.2.3.19ff.; cf. Ficino, *Platonic Theology* 13.2.16.

199. *De vita* 3.2, and, indeed, Book 3 passim.

200. *Parmenides* 139BC.

201. Cf. Plotinus, *Enneads* 2.2.1 passim.

202. *Laws* 4.716A.

203. Aristotle discusses this spiral or "mixed" motion in the *Physics* 8.8.261b28 ff., and *De caelo* 1.2.268b17–18. In the creation story of the *Timaeus*, the planetary motions of the Same and the Different combined generate spiral motion; see the commentary of Calcidius, well-known to Ficino (ed. Waszink, 162, 165).

204. Habit: i.e., acquired disposition or state, the Aristotelian *hexis*, *habitus*, in Latin; in this case the acquired disposition of rest.

205. *Timaeus* 36B–D.

206. *Timaeus* 37A–C.

207. *Philebus* 23C, 24A, 25D, 26C, 30A–C; cf. Plotinus, *Enneads* 2.4.15 passim. See Ficino's *In Philebum* 2.1–4 (ed. Allen, 384–425).

208. Romans 11:36. This famous dictum has been variously Latinized. The Vulgate reading, adopted for instance by Augustine and Aquinas, is "quoniam ex ipso et per ipsum et in ipso sunt omnia." But in his commentary on Romans ad loc., for "in ipso," Ficino adopted St. Ambrose's reading, "in ipsum," and saw Paul as signifying God as the exemplary, efficient, and final cause (*Op.* 437). Here he has compounded a quadruple rendering: "ex ipso atque per ipsum et in ipso atque ad ipsum omnia" — "ad ipsum" being the same as "in ipsum" — in order to accommodate the notion of a conserving cause. See E. Wind, *Pagan Mysteries in the Renaissance*, rev. ed. (Oxford: Oxford University Press, 1980), 243–44.

209. §111 comments on the two chapters of Dionysian text that follow, 112 and 113.

210. *Enneads* 6.7.22. Here Plotinus is deploying the imagery of the *Phaedrus* 246A ff., and notably of 251B, as Ficino must have recognized, given his lifelong obsession with the dialogue's mythical hymn and its imagery.

211. Cf. Plotinus, *Enneads* 6.8.15.1 ff.

212. Again a reference to the soul's head or unity in the *Phaedrus* 248A3; cf. Ficino, *In Phaedrum* 7 (ed. Allen, 66–67), and Ficino, *Platonic Theology* 13.5.3.

213. Or "the letters of the alphabet."

214. *Symposium* 210A–212A — Diotima's ladder.

215. Proverbs 4:6.

216. Proverbs 4:8.

217. I have retained the obsolete word "dilection" in order to preserve the Areopagite's and Ficino's careful distinctions between *amor, dilectio,* and *caritas. Dilectio* and its cognate verb *diligere* is a constant, for instance, in the Vulgate's rendering of St. John's Gospel (in 8:42, 10:17, 11:5, etc.).

218. Ignatius of Antioch, *Letters to the Romans* 7:2. These words by Ignatius are cited by Origen, *Commentary on the Song of Songs*, 71, lines 25–26 (ed. Baehrens, vol. 8 of *Origines Werke*, in the series Griechischen christlichen Schriftsteller der ersten drei Jahrhunderte [Leipzig: J. C. Hinrichs,

1899–1955], vol. 33) and again by Aquinas, *In librum Dionysii* 4.9.419 (ed. Pera, 136).

219. Wisdom 8:2. For the reference to Philo, see Origen, *Commentary* (ed. Baehrens, 69.1), and Aquinas, *In librum Dionysii* 4.9.419 (ed. Pera, 136). It is not in the Dionysian text.

220. 2 Samuel 1:26.

221. Cf. Ficino, *In Convivium* 4.6 (ed. Laurens, 80–83), and *Platonic Theology* 14.3.4–7.

222. Galatians 2:20.

223. Cf. Aquinas, *In librum Dionysii* 4.10.438–39 (ed. Pera, 143–44).

224. I.e., *In Convivium* 6.10 (ed. Laurens, 164–69), where Ficino glosses the lemmata in the *Symposium* 203D. Cf. Plotinus, *Enneads* 4.4.40.

225. Exodus 20:5, 34:14; Deuteronomy 5:9, 6:15; Nahum 1:2.

226. See n. 217 above.

227. §118.2 above.

228. Cf. Plotinus, *Enneads* 6.8.15.1ff.

229. *Enneads* 1.7.1.25–29.

230. Cf. *Enneads* 3.9.4.

231. §69.1–4 above.

232. For Ficino's Neoplatonic demonology, see his *Platonic Theology* 16.7.14, 17–18, 18.10.3, 18.10.13–14. On the one hand he could turn to such non-Christian texts as Plotinus' *Enneads* 3.4.6.10–18 and 4.8.5.10–24, Hermias' *In Phaedrum*, 163.24–27 (ed. Couvreur), and Proclus' *In Timaeum* 4.9 (ed. Diehl 3:157.26–158.23) and *De malorum subsistentia* 16 (ed. Boese). On the other hand, he could turn to such Christian texts as Origen's *De principiis* 3.2, and Augustine's *De civitate dei* 9.3.12–13 and Book 9 passim. While acknowledging the debt to Proclus' *De malorum subsistentia*, Podolak refers us by contrast to Iamblichus' *De mysteriis* 3.31, 5.12; to Athenagoras' *Legatio pro Christianis* 25.1 (ed. Marcovich, 82); to Origen's *Contra Celsum* 4.92 (ed. Marcovich, 309); and to Athanasius' *Vita Antonii* 32.1 (ed. Bartelink, 220).

233. E.g., *Theaetetus* 176A; *Statesman* 273B–D.

234. See Plotinus, *Enneads* 1.8 and 2.4 passim, which recall such texts as *Timaeus* 47E–48A and 41B. In 2.4 he mainly deals with the notion of two matters and with the views of the Aristotelians and the Stoics.

235. *De malorum subsistentia* 3.7ff. and 9.10ff. This is not a source for Ficino but a derivative meditation. But what does "the other text" refer to at the start of the paragraph?

APPENDIX

1. Giovanni de' Medici's titular church in Rome as Cardinal-Deacon. This ancient church on the Caelian Hill has the rank of a minor basilica and was refounded in the early ninth century. It is otherwise known as Santa Maria alla Navicella. As Pope Leo X, Giovanni had Sansovino add a Renaissance portico and a carved ceiling.

2. *Op.* 1873–1908.

3. Presumbly, Giovanni had sent Ficino a gift of wine; "Father Liber" was identified in later Roman cult with the Greek god Dionysus and with Bacchus, the god of wine. In 1 Timothy 5:23, the apostle Paul advises Timothy to "stop drinking only water, and take a little wine for your stomach's sake."

4. This whole intimate, not to say liberal, story is omitted in the incunable's briefer version of the dedication. Critics have argued that this briefer version reflects the changing Savonarolan situation in Florence: see S. Toussaint, "L'influence de Ficin à Paris," at 413; also Gentile's entry in *Marsilio Ficino e il ritorno di Platone: Mostra*, 157; and *Dionysius Areopagita*, ed. Podolak, p. xlix.

5. These are the last words of Ficino's commentary itself *On the Divine Names* §349.4 (though there are two more chapters of translation).

6. According to medieval bestiaries, the lynx had such sharp vision that it could see through walls. The lynx was also an animal associated with Bacchus and wine; see Ovid, *Metamorphoses* 15.413: "Vanquished India gave lynxes to Bacchus of the branching vine."

CONCORDANCE A

Editions of Ficino's Translation and Commentary

MYSTICAL THEOLOGY

Allen	*Opera* (1576)	Podolak
I	1013	—
II	1013	1
III	1013	1.2
IV	1014	1.3
V	1014	1.4
VI	1015	1.5
VII	1015	1.6
VIII	1015	1.7
IX	1016	1.8
X	1017	1.9
XI	1017	1.10
XII	1018	1.11
XIII	1018	1.12
XIV	1018	1.13
XV	1018	1.14
XVI	1019	1.15
XVII	1019	1.16
XVIII	1020	2.1
XIX	1020	2.2
XX	1021	3.1
XXI	1021	3.2
XXII	1021	3.3
XXIII	1021	3.4
XXIV	1022	3.5
XXV	1022	3.6
XXVI	1022	4.1

Allen	*Opera* (1576)	Podolak
XXVII	1023	4.2
XXVIII	1023	5.1
XXIX	1023	5.2

THE DIVINE NAMES

PART I, CHAPTERS I–CXXXV

Allen	*Opera* (1576)	Podolak
I	1024	1.1
II	1025	1.2
III	1025	1.3
IV	1026	1.4
V	1026	1.5
VI	1026	1.6
VII	1026	1.7
VIII	1027	1.8
IX	1027	1.9
X	1027	1.10
XI	1027	1.11
XII	1028	1.12
XIII	1028	1.13
XIV	1028	1.14
XV	1029	1.15
XVI	1030	1.16
XVII	1030	1.17
XVIII	1031	1.18
XIX	1031	1.19
XX	1032	1.20
XXI	1032	1.21
XXII	1033	1.22
XXIII	1033	1.23
XXIV	1034	1.24
XXV	1034	1.25
XXVI	1034	1.26

Allen	*Opera* (1576)	Podolak
XXVII	1035	1.27
XXVIII	1036	1.28
XXIX	1036	1.29
XXX	1036	1.30
XXXI	1037	2.1
XXXII	1037	2.2
XXXIII	1038	2.3
XXXIV	1038	2.4
XXXV	1039	2.5
XXXVI	1039	2.6
XXXVII	1039	2.7
XXXVIII	1039	2.8
XXXIX	1039	2.9
XL	1040	2.10
XLI	1040	2.11
XLII	1040	2.12
XLIII	1041	2.13
XLIV	1041	2.14
XLV	1041	2.15
XLVI	1041	2.16
XLVII	1041	2.17
XLVIII	1042	2.18
XLIX	1042	2.19
L	1042	2.20
LI	1042	2.21
LII	1043	2.22
LIII	1043	2.23
LIV	1043	2.24
LV	1043	2.25
LVI	1044	2.26
LVII	1044	2.27
LVIII	1044	2.28
LIX	1045	2.29
LX	1045	2.30

Allen	*Opera* (1576)	Podolak
LXI	1045	2.31
LXII	1046	2.32
LXIII	1047	2.33
LXIV	1047	2.34
LXV	1047	2.35
LXVI	1048	2.36
LXVII	1048	3.1
LXVIII	1048	3.2
LXIX	1049	3.3
LXX	1049	3.4
LXXI	1049	3.5
LXXII	1050	3.6
LXXIII	1050	3.7
LXXIV	1050	3.8
LXXV	1050	3.9
LXXVI	1050	3.10
LXXVII	1051	3.11
LXXVIII	1051	3.12
LXXIX	1051	4.1
LXXX	1052	4.2
LXXXI	1052	4.3
LXXXII	1053	4.4
LXXXIII	1053	4.5
LXXXIV	1053	4.6
LXXXV	1054	4.7
LXXXVI	1054	4.8
LXXXVII	1054	4.9
LXXXVIII	1054	4.10
LXXXIX	1054	4.11
XC	1055	4.12
XCI	1055	4.13
XCII	1056	4.14
XCIII	1056	4.15
XCIV	1057	4.16

Allen	*Opera* (1576)	Podolak
XCV	1057	4.17
XCVI	1058	4.18
XCVII	1058	4.19
XCVIII	1058	4.20
XCIX	1059	4.21
C	1059	4.22
CI	1059	4.23
CII	1060	4.24
CIII	1060	4.25
CIV	1061	4.26
CV	1061	4.27
CVI	1062	4.28
CVII	1062	4.29
CVIII	1063	4.30
CIX	1064	4.31
CX	1065	4.32
CXI	1065	4.33
CXII	1066	4.34
CXIII	1066	4.35
CXIV	1066	4.36
CXV	1066	4.37
CXVI	1067	4.38
CXVII	1067	4.39
CXVIII	1067	4.40
CXIX	1068	4.41
CXX	1068	4.42
CXXI	1068	4.43
CXXII	1068	4.44
CXXIII	1069	4.45
CXXIV	1069	4.46
CXXV	1069	4.47
CXXVI	1070	4.48
CXXVII	1070	4.49
CXXVIII	1070	4.50

Allen	*Opera* (1576)	Podolak
CXXIX	1070	4.51
CXXX	1071	4.52
CXXXI	1071	4.53
CXXXII	1071	4.54
CXXXIII	1072	4.55
CXXXIV	1072	4.56
CXXXV	1073	4.57

CONCORDANCE B

Editions of Dionysius Areopagita

MYSTICAL THEOLOGY

Allen	Migne	Cordier	Heil/Ritter
V	997A	I.1	141.1
VII	997B	I.1	142.5
X	1000A	I.2	142.12
XII	1000B	I.2	143.3
XIV	1000B	I.3	143.8
XVII	1000C	I.3	143.17
XIX	1025A	II	145.1
XXI	1032D	III	146.1
XXIII	1033B	III	147.4
XXV	1033C	III	147.15
XXVII	1040D	IV	148.1
XXIX	1045D	V	149.1

THE DIVINE NAMES

PART I, CHAPTERS I–CXXXV

Allen	Migne	Cordier	Suchla
II	585B	I.1	107.1
IV	588A	I.1	108.6
VI	588B	I.1	109.7
VIII	588C	I.2	110.4
X	588C	I.2	110.11
XII	589A	I.3	111.3
XIV	589B	I.3	111.12
XVI	589D	I.4	112.7
XVIII	592B	I.4	114.1

Allen	Migne	Cordier	Suchla
XX	592D	I.4	115.6
XXII	593A	I.5	115.19
XXIV	593C	I.5	117.5
XXVI	596A	I.6	118.2
XXVIII	596C	I.7	119.10
XXX	597A	I.8	120.9
XXXII	636C	II.1	122.1
XXXIV	637B	II.1	123.15
XXXVI	637D	II.2	124.16
XXXVIII	640B	II.3	125.13
XL	640C	II.4	126.3
XLII	641B	II.4	127.8
XLIV	641D	II.5	128.8
XLVI	641D	II.5	128.15
XLVIII	644B	II.6	129.12
L	644C	II.6	130.5
LII	644D	II.7	130.14
LIV	645B	II.7	132.1
LVI	645C	II.8	132.14
LVIII	648A	II.9	133.5
LX	648A	II.9	133.13
LXII	648C	II.10	134.7
LXIV	648D	II.11	135.13
LXVI	649C	II.11	136.13
LXVIII	652A	II.11	138.1
LXX	680C	III.1	139.1
LXXII	681A	III.2	139.17
LXXIV	681B	III.2	140.17
LXXVI	681C	III.2	141.4
LXXVIII	684A	III.3	142.1
LXXX	693B	IV.1	143.9
LXXXII	693B	IV.1	144.6
LXXXIV	696B	IV.2	144.18
LXXXVI	696C	IV.2	145.10

Allen	Migne	Cordier	Suchla
LXXXVIII	696C	IV.2	145.18
XC	697A	IV.3	146.6
XCII	697B	IV.4	146.13
XCIV	697B	IV.4	147.2
XCVI	700A	IV.4	148.8
XCVIII	700C	IV.5	149.9
C	701A	IV.6	150.1
CII	701C	IV.7	150.15
CIV	704A	IV.7	151.19
CVI	704B	IV.7	152.12
CVIII	704D	IV.8	153.4
CX	705B	IV.10	154.7
CXII	708A	IV.10	155.8
CXIII	708B	IV.11	156.1
CXV	708D	IV.11	156.13
CXVII	709A	IV.11	157.4
CXIX	709C	IV.12	158.9
CXXI	712A	IV.13	158.19
CXXIII	712A	IV.13	159.9
CXXV	712C	IV.14	160.1
CXXVII	713A	IV.15	161.1
CXXIX	713B	IV.16	161.6
CXXXI	713D	IV.17	162.1
CXXXIII	713D	IV.18	162.6
CXXXV	716B	IV.19	163.7

Bibliography

❧

EDITIONS AND TRANSLATIONS

Dionysius the Areopagite [pseudo-]. *Opera omnia quae extant, una cum eiusdem vitae scriptoribus nunc primum Graece et Latine coniunctim edita* [. . .]. Edited by Petrus Lansselius, S. J. Paris: Michael Sonnius, 1615.

——. *Opera . . . cum scholiis S. Maximi et paraphrasi Pachymerae.* Latin translation with notes by Balthasar Cordier, S. J. 2 vols. Antwerp: Plantin, 1634. With the Greek text of Pierre Lansselius in parallel columns. The *MT* and *DN* are in vol. 1.

——. *Operum omnium quae extant, et commentariorum quibus illustrantur, tomus primus [secundus].* Latin translation with notes by Balthasar Cordier, S. J. 2 vols. Paris: Antonius Stephanus, 1644. A new edition of the volumes printed by Plantin, 1634, with the Greek text of Lansselius. The *MT* and *DN* are in vol. 1.

——. *Opera omnia quae extant et commentarii quibus illustrantur.* Latin translation by Balthasar Cordier. 2 vols. Venice: Antonio Zatta, 1755–56. With the Greek text of Lansselius, revised by Bernardo Maria de Rubeis [or Rossi], O. P. The *MT* and *DN* are in vol. 1.

——. *Opera omnia quae extant et commentarii quibus illustrantur.* 2 vols. Edited by Balthasar Cordier and J.-P. Migne. In Migne's *Patrologiae cursus completus . . . series graeca*, vols. 3 and 4 (Paris: Migne, 1857–89). The *MT* and *DT* are in vol. 3.

——. *Dionysiaca. Recueil donnant l'ensemble des traductions latines des ouvrages attribués au Denise de l'Aréopage.* Edited by Phillipe Chevallier et al. 2 vols. Paris-Bruges: Desclée, 1937–49. Available online through Brepols' Library of Latin Texts.

——. *Corpus Dionysiacum.* Edited by Beate Regina Suchla. Vol. 1: *De divinis nominibus*, edited by Beate Regina Suchla. Patristische Texte und Studien 33. Berlin: Walter De Gruyter, 1990.

——. *Corpus Dionysiacum.* Edited by Beate Regina Suchla. Vol. 2: *De coelesti hierarchia, De ecclesiastica hierarchia, De mystica theologia, Epistulae,*

edited by Günthur Heil and Adolf Martin Ritter. Patristiche Texte und Studien 36. Berlin: Walter De Gruyter, 1991. 2nd ed., 2012, Patristische Texte und Studien 67.

——. *The Complete Works*. Translated by Colm Luibheid. New York: Paulist Press, 1987.

——. *The* Divine Names *and the* Mystical Theology. Translated by John D. Jones. Milwaukee, WI: Marquette University Press, 1980.

Ficino, Marsilio. [Latin translation of and commentary on Dionysius Areopagita, *De mystica theologia* and *De divinis nominibus*]. Florence: Lorenzo de Alopa, [after December 2, 1496]. See Note on the Texts.

——. *Dionysii Areopagitae De mystica theologia, De divinis nominibus, interprete Marsilio Ficino*. Edited by Pietro Podolak. Naples: M. D'Auria, 2011.

——. *Commentaries on Plato, Volume 1: Phaedrus* and *Ion*. Edited and translated by Michael J. B. Allen. Cambridge, MA: Harvard University Press, 2008.

——. *Commentaries on Plato, Volume 2: Parmenides*. Edited and translated by Maude Vanhaelen. 2 vols. Cambridge, MA: Harvard University Pess, 2012.

——. *The Philebus Commentary*. Edited by Michael J. B. Allen. Berkeley: University of California Press, 1975.

——. *Lettere*. Edited by Sebastiano Gentile. 2 vols. to date. Florence: Olschki, 1990–2010.

——. *Platonic Theology*. Edited and translated by Michael J. B. Allen and James Hankins. 6 vols. Cambridge, MA: Harvard University Press, 2001–6.

Migne, Jacques-Paul, ed. *Patrologiae cursus completus, series latina*. 221 vols. Paris: Migne, 1844–91.

Plato. *Opera*. Edited by John Burnet. 5 vols. Oxford: Clarendon Press, 1958.

Plotinus. *Opera*. Edited by Paul Henry and Hans-Rudolf Schwyzer. 3 vols. Paris: Desclée de Brouwer, and Brussels: Edition Universelle, 1951–73.

Proclus. *Commentaire sur le Parménide de Platon, traduction de Guillaume de Moerbeke*. Edited by Carlos Steel. 2 vols. Louvain: Presses universitaires, and Leiden: E. J. Brill, 1982–85.

——. *In Platonis Parmenidem Commentaria,* ed. Carlos Steel. 3 vols. Oxford: Clarendon Press, 2007–9.

——. *The Elements of Theology.* Edited and translated by E. R Dodds. 2nd ed.. Oxford: Clarendon Press, 1963.

——. *Théologie platonicienne.* Edited and translated by Henri Dominique Saffrey and Leendert Gerrit Westerink. 6 vols. Paris: Les Belles Lettres, 1968–97.

——. *In Platonis Timaeum commentaria.* Edited by Ernst Diehl. 3 vols. Leipzig: Teubner, 1903–6.

——. *Tria opuscula: De providentia, libertate, malo, latine Guillelmo de Moerbeka vertente et Graece ex Isaacii Sebastocratoris aliorumque scriptis collecta.* Edited by Helmut Boese. Berlin: De Gruyter, 1960.

Thomas Aquinas. *In librum beati Dionysii De divinis nominibus expositio.* Edited by Ceslai Pera. Turin: Marietti, 1950.

——. *In Librum de Causis expositio.* Edited by Ceslai Pera. Turin: Marietti, 1955.

——. *Summa theologiae cum textu ex recensione Leonina.* 8 vols. Edited by Pietro Caramello. Rome: Ex Typographia Polyglotta, 1948–52.

MODERN STUDIES

Allen, Michael J. B. *Icastes: Marsilo Ficino's Interpretation of Plato's Sophist.* Berkeley: University of California Press, 1989.

——. "*In principio:* Marsilio Ficino on the Life of Text." In *Res et Verba in der Renaissance,* edited by Eckhard Kessler and Ian Maclean (Wolfenbütteler Abhandlungen zur Renaissance-forschung 21), 11–28. Wiesbaden: Harrassowitz Verlag, 2002.

——. "Marsilio Ficino on Plato, the Neoplatonists, and the Christian Doctrine of the Trinity." *Renaissance Quarterly* 27.4 (1984): 555–84.

——. "Sending Archedemus: Ficino, Plato's Second Letter, and Its Four Epistolary Mysteries." In *Sol et Homo: Mensch und Natur in der Renaissance: Festschrift zum 70. Geburtstag für Eckhard Kessler,* edited by Sabrina Ebbersmeyer, Helga Pirner-Pareschi, and Thomas Ricklin, 405–20. Munich: Fink, 2008.

——. *Synoptic Art: Marsilio Ficino on the History of Platonic Interpretation.* Florence: Olschki, 1998.

Corrigan, Kevin, and L. Michael Harrington. "Pseudo-Dionysius the Areopagite." In *The Stanford Encyclopedia of Philosophy* (Spring 2014 edition), edited by Edward N. Zalta. URL = <http://plato.stanford.edu/archives/spr2014/entries/pseudo-dionysius-areopagite/>. With ample bibliographies.

Dillon, John M. "Dionysius the Areopagite." In *Interpreting Proclus: From Antiquity to the Renaissance,* edited by Stephen Gersh, 111–24. Cambridge: Cambridge University Press, 2014.

Gentile, Sebastiano. "Giano Lascaris, Germain de Ganay et la *Prisca Theologia* in Francia." *Rinascimento* n.s. 26 (1986): 51–76.

Gersh, Stephen. *From Iamblichus to Eriugena: An Investigation of the Prehistory and Evolution of the Pseudo-Dionysian Tradition.* Leiden: E. J. Brill, 1978.

Hankins, James. *Humanism and Platonism in the Italian Renaissance.* 2 vols. Rome: Edizioni di Storia e Letteratura, 2004–5.

——. *Plato in the Italian Renaissance.* 2 vols. Leiden: E. J. Brill, 1990.

Kristeller, Paul Oskar. *The Philosophy of Marsilio Ficino.* New York: Columbia University Press, 1943. Reprint, Gloucester, MA: Peter Smith, 1964. First Italian version, *Il pensiero filosofico di Marsilio Ficino.* Florence: Sansoni, 1953. Revised ed., Florence: Le Lettere, 1988.

——. "Proclus as a Reader of Plato and Plotinus, and His Influence in the Middle Ages and in the Renaissance." In *Proclus, lecteur et interprète des anciens: Actes du colloque international du CNRS, Paris, 2–4 octobre 1986,* edited by Jean Pépin and Henri Dominique Saffrey, 191–211. Paris: Editions du CNRS, 1987.

——. *Supplementum Ficinianum: Marsilii Ficini Florentini philosophi platonici opuscula inedita et dispersa.* 2 vols. Florence: Olschki, 1937.

Le Pseudo-Denys à la Renaissance. Edited by Stéphane Toussaint and Christian Trottmann. Paris: Champion, 2014.

Leinkauf, Thomas. *Cusanus, Ficino, Patrizi: Formen platonischen Denkens in der Renaissance.* Berlin: Trafo, 2014.

——. "Marsilio Ficino e lo Pseudo-Dionigi: ricezione e trasformazione." In *Le Pseudo-Denys à la Renaissance,* edited by Stéphane Toussaint and Christian Trottmann, 127–42. Paris: Champion, 2014.

——. "Philologie, Mystik, Metaphysik. Aspekte der Rezeption des Dionysius Areopagita in der Renaissance." In *Denys l'Aréopagite et sa postérité en Orient et En Occident*, edited by Ysabel de Andia, 583–609. Paris: Institut d'études augustiniennes, 1997.

Louth, Andrew. *Dionysius the Areopagite*. London: Geoffrey Chapman, 1989.

Luscombe, David. "Denis the Pseudo-Areopagite in the Writings of Nicholas of Cusa, Marsilio Ficino and Pico della Mirandola." In *Néoplatonisme et philosophie médiévale: Actes du colloque international Corfou, 6–8 octobre 1995*, edited by Linos G. Benakis, 93–108. Turnhout: Brepols, 1997.

Marsilio Ficino e il ritorno di Platone: Mostra di manoscritti, stampe e documenti, 17 maggio — 16 giugno 1984. Edited by Sebastiano Gentile, Sandra Niccoli, and Paolo Viti. Florence: Le Lettere, 1984.

Marsilio Ficino: His Theology, His Philosophy, His Legacy. Edited by Michael J. B. Allen and Valery Rees. Leiden: E. J. Brill, 2002.

Monfasani, John. "Pseudo-Dionysius the Areopagite in Mid-Quattrocento Rome." In *Supplementum Festivum: Studies in Honor of Paul Oskar Kristeller*, edited by James Hankins, John Monfasani, and Frederick Purnell, Jr., 189–214. Binghamton, NY: Center for Medieval and Renaissance Studies, 1987. Reprinted in Monfasani's collection *Language and Learning in Renaissance Italy* (Aldershot: Variorum, 1994), article 9.

Perl, Eric David. *Theophany: The Neoplatonic Philosophy of Dionysius the Areopagite*. Albany: State University of New York Press, 2007.

Podolak, Pietro. "Le commentaire de Marsile Ficin au ps. Denys l'Aréopagite entre Renaissance et philosophie médiévale." In *Le Pseudo-Denys*, edited by Toussaint and Trottmann, 143–57.

Re-thinking Dionysius the Areopagite. Edited by Sarah Coakley, Sarah and Charles M. Stang. Chichester, UK: Wiley-Blackwell, 2009.

Roques, René. *L'univers dionysien: Structure hiérarchique du monde selon le Pseudo-Denys*. Paris: Aubier, 1954. Repr., Paris: Editions du Cerf, 1983.

Rorem, Paul. *Pseudo-Dionysius: A Commentary on the Texts and an Introduction to their Influence*. New York: Oxford University Press, 1993. Part 4 focuses on *DN*, Part 5 on *MT*.

Schäfer, Christian. *The Philosophy of Dionysius the Areopagite: An Introduction to the Structure and the Content of the Treatise "On the Divine Names."* Leiden: E. J. Brill, 2006.

Steel, Carlos. "Ficino and Proclus: Arguments for the Platonic Doctrine of the Ideas." In *The Rebirth of Platonic Theology*, edited by James Hankins and Fabrizio Meroi, 63–118. Florence: Olschki, 2013.

Toussaint, Stéphane. "L'influence de Ficin à Paris et le pseudo-Denys des Humanistes: Traversari, Cusain, Lefèvre D'Etaples." *Bruniana & Campanelliana* 5/2 (1999): 381–414.

Vasoli, Cesare. "L'Un-Bien dans le commentaire de Ficin à la *Mystica Theologia* du Pseudo-Denys." In *Marsile Ficin: Les Platonismes à la Renaissance*, edited by Pierre Magnard, 181–93. Paris: J. Vrin, 2001.

——. *Quasi sit Deus: Studi sul Marsilio Ficino*. Lecce: Conte, 1999.

Wear, Sarah Klitenic, and John Dillon. *Dionysius the Areopagite and the Neoplatonist Tradition: Despoiling the Hellenes*. Aldershot: Ashgate, 2007.

Index

Publication of this volume has been made possible by

The Myron and Sheila Gilmore Publication Fund at I Tatti
The Robert Lehman Endowment Fund
The Jean-François Malle Scholarly Programs and Publications Fund
The Andrew W. Mellon Scholarly Publications Fund
The Craig and Barbara Smyth Fund
for Scholarly Programs and Publications
The Lila Wallace–Reader's Digest Endowment Fund
The Malcolm Wiener Fund for Scholarly Programs and Publications